@@@@@@@@@@@@@@@@@@@@@@@@@

PROFILE
OF
THE
SCHOOL
DROPOUT

Random House   New York

PROFILE OF THE SCHOOL
DR O POUT

EDITED BY
Daniel Schreiber

A READER ON AMERICA'S
MAJOR EDUCATIONAL PROBLEM

THE EDITOR WISHES TO THANK the following for permission to reprint: The National Education Association for "Realities of the Job Market for the High School Dropout" by Herbert Bienstock; "Early Social Environment: Its Influence on School Adaptation" by Martin Deutsch; "An Ideology of School Withdrawal" by Edgar Z. Friedenberg; "The Universal Trap" by Paul Goodman; "Social Status Differences: Counseling and Guidance for Disadvantaged Youth" by Edmund W. Gordon; "No Hiding Place: The Negro Search" by Herman H. Long; "Dropouts—A Political Problem" by S. M. Miller; "Home-School Interaction" by John H. Niemeyer; and "The Dropout and the School Counselor" by C. Gilbert Wrenn, © Copyright 1964 by the National Education Association; The National Society for the Study of Education for "A School Curriculum for Prevention and Remediation of Deviancy" by Carl L. Byerly; and "Work-Experience Programs" by Daniel Schreiber, from *1966 Yearbook, Part I, Social Deviancy Among Youth* edited by William W. Wattenberg, © Copyright 1966 by Herman C. Richey, Secretary of the National Society for the Study of Education; The *New York Review* and Bruno Bettelheim for "How Much Can Man Change?", © Copyright 1964 by Bruno Bettelheim; Arthur Pearl for "Slim and None —The Poor's Two Chances"; Frank Riessman for "It's Time for a Moonshot in Education"; Syracuse University Press for "The Search for an Educational Revolution" by S. M. Miller, and "Deprivation and Alienation: A Compounded Situation" by Charles V. Willie, from *Urban Education and Cultural Deprivation*, edited by C. W. Hunnicutt, © Copyright 1964 by the Syracuse University School of Education; the Washington Center for Metropolitan Studies for "In Search of a Future" by Eunice S. Grier, © Copyright 1963 by the Washington Center for Metropolitan Studies; The National Education Association and Robert D. Hess for "Maternal Teaching Styles and Educational Retardation"; and Eli Ginzberg for "Jobs, Dropouts, and Automation," reprinted from *The Consultants' Papers*, The White House Conference on Education, July 20–21, 1965.

The editor wishes to acknowledge the source of two chapters and to express his appreciation to the authors of "Children of the Poor" by Mollie Orshansky, reprinted from the *Social Security Bulletin* (U. S. Department of Health, Education and Welfare, Social Security Administration, July 1963), and "Out-of-School Youth" by Thomas E. Swanstrom, reprinted from the *Monthly Labor Review* (U. S. Department of Labor, Bureau of Labor Statistics, December 1964).

ACKNOWLEDGMENTS

I wish to thank the contributors who wrote especially for this volume and those who gave permission to use their articles. This book could not have been written and collated without the aid of Marcellus B. Winston, and I acknowledge my debt to him.

D. S.

To BERNICE

CONTRIBUTORS

BRUNO BETTELHEIM
The Rowley Professor of Education
University of Chicago

HERBERT BIENSTOCK
Regional Director,
Middle Atlantic Region
U. S. Department of Labor
Bureau of Labor Statistics

CARL L. BYERLY
Assistant Superintendent
Detroit Public Schools

MARTIN DEUTSCH
Professor of Education and
Director of the Institute for Developmental Studies
New York University

EDGAR Z. FRIEDENBERG
Professor of Sociology
University of California at Davis

ELI GINZBERG
Professor of Economics and
Director, Conservation of Human Resources
Columbia University

PAUL GOODMAN
Author and Critic

EDMUND W. GORDON
Chairman, Department of Educational Psychology and Guidance
Yeshiva University

EUNICE S. GRIER
Director of Research Division
U. S. Commission of Civil Rights

ROBERT D. HESS
Director, Committee on Human Development
University of Chicago

HERMAN H. LONG
President
Talledega College

S. M. MILLER
Professor of Education and Sociology
New York University

JOHN H. NIEMEYER
President
Bank Street College

MOLLIE ORSHANSKY
Division of Research and Statistics
Social Security Administration
U. S. Department of Health, Education and Welfare

ARTHUR PEARL
Professor of Education
University of Oregon

FRANK RIESSMAN
Professor of Educational Sociology
New York University

DANIEL SCHREIBER
Assistant Superintendent
Board of Education, New York City
(Formerly Director, Project: School Dropouts, National Education Association)

THOMAS E. SWANSTROM
Division of Population and Labor Force Studies
Bureau of Labor Statistics
U. S. Department of Labor

CHARLES V. WILLIE
  Associate Professor of Sociology and Research Associate
    Youth Development Center
  Syracuse University

C. GILBERT WRENN
  Professor of Educational Psychology and Guidance
  Arizona State University at Tempe

CONTENTS

Introduction

THE
ISSUES
AT
STAKE

The school dropout for all the authentic concern the public has recently shown is not a new phenomenon, but the *problem* of the school dropout is. A little more than fifteen years ago, when more students dropped out of school than graduated, there was no noticeable public concern. A boy could leave school, find a job, and become an adult; today, he quickly finds out that he is not wanted by industry. Instead of a job, he has a promise of long periods of unemployment interspersed with short periods of working at dead-end unskilled jobs for low wages. President John F. Kennedy was sufficiently concerned about the problem to bring it to the attention of Congress and the American people in his 1963 State of the Union message, relating it to the economic well-being of our country: "The loss of only one year's income due to unemployment is more than the total cost of twelve years of education through high school. Failure to improve educational performance is thus not only poor social policy, it is poor economics."

Less than two years later President Lyndon B. Johnson, after extolling the development of America's free educational system through college, told Congress of "the darker side to education." One student in three drops out before finishing high school—a total of almost one million every year. And to some extent, President Johnson predicted the violent disturbances that have occurred and continue to occur in the slum areas of the northern cities when he said: "In our fifteen largest cities, 60 percent of the tenth grade students from poverty neighborhoods drop out before finishing high school." He did not mention that at least another 10 percent never reach the tenth grade.

Undoubtedly, the dropout problem has been brought into being by a multiplicity of factors, largely extrinsic to the school, and peculiar to our times. Some of them are:

* the high and almost constant rate of unemployment. (Negro unemployment is twice that of white unemployment.)
* large-scale migration from rural and farm areas to urban centers.
* the population explosion—a million more youths reached age eighteen in 1965 than did in 1964.
* the continual rise in delinquency and crime among youths, although large sums of money are being spent to counteract this development.
* the increase in the number of welfare families, especially in the large cities, further heightened by a marked increase in the total cost of public assistance.
* the increased use of technology in farming,
* the elimination of unskilled jobs through automation, and
* the racial riots in northern cities, in which the participants are overwhelmingly the unemployed, out-of-school youths of the area.

Today, it is impossible not to see the problem of the school dropout as the keystone of a conglomeration of problems which threatens to overwhelm the stability of America's existence.

In this book, I have attempted to present the school dropout as a national problem and to indicate its relation to the continuing crises in American education. My purpose is to offer the reader a sufficiently wide-ranging selection of articles to provide the bases for intelligent discussion, decision-making, and action.

One of the inherent dangers well-meaning people face in dealing with the dropout problem is the tendency to stereotype dropout youths—a school failure, a nonacademic-oriented youth, a discipline case, a delinquent, a future welfare recipient who comes from a welfare family, and, if a girl, a breeder of illegitimate children. Another pitfall is the apparent desire to oversimplify this complex problem in order to propose solutions for its resolution—solutions that are only palliatives and do not deal with the underlying causes. Devices are sought and strategies developed to compel or entice youths to remain in or return to school, but this remedy only presages failure and doom. One example is a solution usually proposed by well-meaning, well-intentioned legislators. It is simple and direct! Raise the compulsory school attendance age to eighteen or nineteen so that youths will be compelled to remain in school through graduation. Another example is the drive to get dropouts to return to school. Here, too, the assumption is that once a youth returns to school, he will remain and graduate. (Studies show that from 50 to 75 percent drop out again.) In neither case are efforts made to change or suggestions given for changing the social institutions, specifically the schools, to better accommodate these children. The child must conform and the school remains inviolate—a bastion of rigidity.

Industry too is guilty of a persistent propensity to oversimplify qualifications, and the school dropout is suspect. The high school diploma has become the credential for employment, and personnel officers are using it as a screening device even where the job does not require it. The tendency of industry to escalate its entrance requirements as the educational level of the new workers rises (from a little more than ten years of schooling in 1952 to twelve years of schooling in 1962 with the prediction that two years of college will be needed by 1975), plus the real need for better-educated workers will increase the already desperate plight of the school dropout.

The correlation between the number of years of schooling and employment also holds true between the number of years of schooling and lifetime income. The difference of approximately $65,000 between the lifetime earnings of graduates and dropouts represents the difference between owning one's home, or renting a good apartment—or living in squalor. It represents the difference between being able to feed, clothe, and educate one's children properly or having them live on starches, wear second-hand clothing and possibly become dropouts too. More important, it may determine whether an individual feels that he is a participating, contributing member of society rather than alienated from it.

Let me sketch briefly for you a profile of the average dropout. The dropout is a child just past his sixteenth birthday who has average or slightly below average intelligence, and is more likely to be a boy than a girl. He is not achieving according to his potential; he is not reading at grade level; and academically he is in the lowest quarter of his class. He is slightly overage for his grade placement, having been held back once in the elementary or junior high school grades. He has not been in trouble with the law although he does take up an inordinate amount of the school administrator's time because of discipline problems. He seldom participates in extracurricular activities, feels rejected by the school and his fellow classmates, and in turn rejects them as well as himself. He is insecure in his school status, hostile toward others, and is less respected by his teachers because of his academic inadequacies. His parents were school dropouts as were his older brothers and sisters. His friends are persons outside the school, usually older dropouts. He says he is quitting school because of lack of interest but that he intends to get a high school diploma in some manner because without it he can't get a job. He strongly resents being called a dropout, knows the pitfalls that await him in the outside world, yet believes that they can't be worse than those that await him were he to remain in school. To a great extent he is a fugitive from failure, fleeing Kafka-like into more failure.

In the past, a youth had alternative paths for growing up. A young person could quit school, find a job, discover what he was good at, and eventually become a successful participating adult; or, he could reach adulthood by remaining in school and graduating. Today there seems to be only one way—the school way. The dropout, never really learning in school what he is good at, leaps into adulthood confused, bewildered, insecure and unsure of himself, wondering whether he is good at, or for that matter, good for anything. For the overriding fact is that there are fewer and fewer places in our society for the dropout, and it becomes increasingly clear that he has no future.

The United States, no matter how productive and affluent it is, cannot afford to have almost one million youths drop out each year only to become unwanted and unemployed. The accumulation of the millions of excluded and alienated youths and young adults, unceremoniously relegated to the ever increasing slag heap, cannot and will not remain there without causing serious dislocation in our society. If we cannot reconstruct our educational system to provide meaningful, successful experiences for all of our children so that they will become an integral part of our society, then the possibilities for growth and stability in America may be lost.

Part
One

IDEOLOGICAL
STATEMENTS

@@@@@@@@@@@@@@@@@@@@@@@@@@@@@@@@@

INTRODUCTION

@@@@@@@@@@@@@@@@@@@@@@@@@@@@@@@@@

The school dropout problem is no new phenomenon on the American educational scene. Indeed, for much the greater part of public education history, the dropout has been as much a part of the fabric of national life as the high school graduate. The original democratic urge to extend education to all was not primarily a commitment to any particular qualitative notion of education but, more simply and fundamentally, to make available to every man the means of accommodating to and advancing the circumstances of his and the general life. Until fairly recently the relationship of education to the occupations people settled in was important perhaps in some cases but often was not crucial. People learned most of what they had to do on the job. One can imagine nostalgically with Paul Goodman that there was a certain richness in the general texture of life during periods when, at least in some respects, many alternative modes of growing up were available, and not all of them were dependent upon formal education.

Paradoxically, the dropout problem surfaces at a time when the proportion of youngsters who quit school before graduating is lower than ever. What has happened is that the general national rise in affluence has enabled increasing numbers of people to afford the luxury of extended formal education for their children. At the same time, jobs have become increasingly specialized and technical, requiring greater amounts of formal education. The dropout has suddenly become a problem because, among other reasons, the range and number of jobs requiring little formal education has drastically diminished. And his predicament has become all the more visible, as more and more people accommodate themselves to the nearly complete dominance of formal education as the major path to fulfillment.

The papers in this section—especially those of Edgar Friedenberg and Paul Goodman—are highly critical of present-day American schools. They find the schools grievously at fault in their inability to educate the potential dropout and the culturally disadvantaged child. More fundamentally, Friedenberg and Goodman find the roots of the educational problems of the dropout and disadvantaged youngster in their outraged sense of what the schools have made of themselves in order to serve the purposes of our developing national life. Hence, in the end, their criticisms of American schools evolve into criticisms of American culture. But their (implicitly) hopeful diagnosis is that, in becoming what they have to be to serve the poor and disadvantaged, the schools in fact will better serve all their clients.

S. M. Miller's call for reform in school administration and organization presents a narrower focus than do the articles by Friedenberg and Goodman. But on closer examination, Miller too, proves to be mistrustful of proposed technical solutions to educational problems. His suggestions for administrative reorganization are highly value-oriented, even ideological, and aimed at liberating schools from those "old ways" which impede the success of innovation and flexibility.

AN IDEOLOGY OF
SCHOOL WITHDRAWAL

EDGAR Z. FRIEDENBERG

Compulsory school attendance in the United States has been justified from the beginning as essential to democratic polity. Everyone knows Madison's statement to the effect that popular government without popular education is the prelude to a tragedy, or a farce, or both. We have had both continuously ever since. I have just finished Theodore H. White's *The Making of the President, 1960*,[1] and I think this book is the strongest indictment of American public education that I have ever seen—though Mr. White does not discuss the issue directly. Still, the laws are on the books. Within a century, with the Kalamazoo decision, the legal basis has been laid for what Madison thought so necessary.

And, be it noted, for the reasons he gave. So far as I know, public support of education in this country has never been justified on the grounds that education was beneficial to the individual student, except insofar as this pertained to equality of opportunity. It is logical to argue that the individuals who share the responsibilities of citizenship must learn what they have to do in order to discharge them. I wouldn't say the logic was watertight. In Louisiana, where I was raised, we have never regarded either ignorance or lunacy a bar to high public

---

[1] Theodore H. White, *The Making of the President, 1960* (New York: Atheneum Publishers, 1961).

office; and this liberalism has permitted us to enjoy unusually creative leadership. But, on the whole, the point is well taken. If public education can be justified on the grounds that it is essential to citizenship, it can also claim, for that reason, to be good for the future citizens themselves.

COMPULSORY SCHOOL ATTENDANCE

School attendance laws, however, are a very distorted reflection of the purpose implicit in Madison's phrase. They are not *licensing* laws. They do not require attendance until a specified minimum level of competence deemed essential to the conduct of adult life has been attained; this would mean a life sentence for some. Nor are they *contractual;* they do not guarantee the student any outcome or even any minimum standard of educational service or decent treatment in return for his obligation to attend. Other laws, to be sure, do set up such standards; but the student has no remedy against their breach. Even if he can establish that the school is substandard and that he is personally mistreated there, he cannot legally withdraw; he can only try to force the school authorities to make improvements which, usually, they would already have made long ago if they possibly could.

From this point of view, compulsory school attendance appears as a gross violation of civil liberty: a bill of attainder against a specific age group that guarantees no compensation in return. The school may, indeed, benefit the child; but it doesn't have to in order to earn the right to retain him. I am not, therefore, going to start with the assumption that the youngsters who drop out ought to be retained. My hunch is that a large proportion of the dropouts may be doing what is best for themselves under the atrocious circumstances that exist. But I do want to analyze those circumstances and see why the schools have so little to offer these youngsters and why they are miserable there.

SCHOOL CURRICULUM FUNCTIONS

In the small Southern Methodist college I attended, we had chapel services twice a week. After the opening hymn there was a responsive reading. The Dean—it was a poor school and could only afford one—would read a portion of Scripture aloud, and the students, assembled as a congregation, would read the following portion—his in light-faced type, ours in bold. There was one of these that I liked especially well, and I remember fragments of it distinctly—not accurately, but distinctly. It began:

Dean: Whereof from a young man's fancy shall he wend his way?

Students: By taking heed unto the Lord, and the firmament thereof.

This responsive reading, in the version in which I recall it, is admirably suited to its purpose. The first line shows real evidence of poetic influence. It ties in with the culture and shows that we share in its heritage. It alludes to the necessity for progress and achievement while the second line asserts the necessity of basing these on a sound moral imperative. By saying it over together we experienced a feeling of mutuality and belonging, of being the same kind. Yet we ran no risk of binding ourselves to too literal an interpretation of its mandate, because it doesn't actually make sense.

For the kinds of students it is designed for, the public high school and junior high school curriculum serves, I believe, exactly the same purpose as this responsive reading. Its function is liturgical. This is not as true of elementary school, because the basic skills really work. If you read as you are taught there, you will understand at least the words; if you write, your words will be understood; if you follow the rules of arithmetic, your calculations will check out and your books will balance, though you may never have the remotest conception of mathematics.

The High School

This is not true of high school. What would happen to the businessman, or just citizen, who attempted to apply what he has been taught in civics to the actual power structure of his community or his country? Who learns to love reading or to find the kind of reading he can love among the classics and the bitty anthologies of the high school English course? High school history, by and large, is not even propaganda, because nobody is expected to believe it or to be moved by it; it is received as official myth. We tell youngsters that the Pilgrims came to New England searching for religious freedom, not in order to give them an understanding of the actual root values of Colonial New England but in order to provide them with the relevant cliché about the relation of church and state in America—so that they will know that a good middle-class American thinks of "my religious affiliation" or "the faith of my choice." This keeps him from getting hung up on religion, like an Italian peasant or rural Southerner.

High school science, since Sputnik, has increased its workload enormously and often tries to duplicate the content of college science courses. But essentially, it serves not as an introduction to science but to legitimate the American middle-class epistemology; science proves that Truth is an aggregate of general principles induced from empirical data that observers can agree on. The function of science is to protect people from oddballs by setting up the rules so that subjective feeling is discounted. The scientific method, then, becomes a way of separating ends and means. When we want to win an election, or spy on the Soviet Union, or redevelop a slum, we go about it scientifically; i.e., by defining what we are trying to do as a technical problem. Naturally, we care about the feelings of the people affected; people's emotions are a very important factor. That's why we have psychologists on our team.

It is even truer than the progressives have maintained that there is no valid distinction between the curriculum and the extracurriculum. It is the total experience of the student that counts; and what he learns in both is a posture—a pattern of anxieties and a pattern of responses for dealing with it. There is seldom any pleasure in scholarship or ideas as such; both the classroom and the playing field are places where you try to make it and learn the techniques for making it that alienate you least from your peers. The overall rules are the same in both: learn the ropes; don't get hung up; always be friendly, sincere, and creative. And win!

I have sketched in this familiar picture again because I need it here for reference. I propose to draw some implications from it that I hope will be less familiar. The important thing about it is that it is a picture of a totally instrumental institution. Nothing about it is meant to be valuable, there and now, for its own sake. I don't mean that high school students don't have any fun. Of course they do; in the suburbs, at least, the high school is a fun place. But this sort of fun is a part of the social pattern to be learned; being fun helps you to make it as well or better than anything, and it takes a great deal of social skill which American adolescents, notably, do learn.

SCHOOL VALUES

We have never had much interest in what education means and feels like to the youngsters who are subjected to it; only in what it might help them to make of themselves. Even the Supreme Court, in its decision against segregation, could not rest on the moral obloquy and insult that segregation imposes on Negro children; that was not enough. It had to support its position further by pointing out that a major reason why separate schools could not be equal even if they were identical was that the Negro students couldn't make the same contacts in their schools that white students could in theirs—that this was what people really go to school for.

So it is; the Court has done our motives no discredit. It has merely reaffirmed our tradition. The public school gives poor boys a chance to develop their potentialities, both by formal education and by providing an opportunity to mingle with and learn from their social superordinates. The commonwealth is then the richer for the skills they later contribute, which would otherwise have been forever lost. This is exactly the opportunity our dropouts need, and which they ought presumably to welcome. So what has gone wrong?

The Past

What has gone wrong is pretty complicated; but basically I think one might locate it in the school's assumptions about the nature of what it had to offer the children of the poor. These assumptions were probably never valid; but both the school and the poor believed them. Now, only the school continues to assert them, though no longer with much conviction.

The schools assumed that in order to get ahead in America the student had to learn not only a body of skills, but also a set of social conventions, increasingly subtle and refined, as he climbed the ladder. In school he learned techniques for handling things and manners for getting along with people. The teachers were the transmitters of an alien culture—alien to them, too. Social mobility was a process like preparing to get a job as a rice farmer in China or a coffee grower in Brazil. There was a strange language to be learned—from instructors who didn't speak it too well themselves; a strange body of techniques to be mastered—from teachers who had never practiced them firsthand. It would all have to be learned over again when he got there; but at the time it seemed relevant and made the student feel that he was on his way.

Three Differences Today

Now, there are three important ways in which this situation is different from the condition in the high school today. In the first place, the very problem we are discussing did not then exist. Most of the students who now drop out would never have been in high school fifty years ago; the school-leaving age has risen irregularly over the past decades, and a more rigid and self-confident school policy would not have hesitated to keep students in grade school until they reached it—whatever it was —if they did not pass. A good many of these dropped out and took unskilled jobs, which existed; and that was the last anyone thought of them till election day six or seven years later. They weren't a dropout problem; they were the working class.

But those who didn't drop out, even though they came from a working-class background, did not feel at the time that they were losing their identity. This happened later; after they had made it, in the classical discovery of the loneliness of the long-distance runner. In school, you were still you; *striving* didn't separate you from other poor, immigrant boys; it was exactly what poor, immigrant boys were supposed to do. There was no intimation at the time that you were leaving yourself behind; you had no way of knowing even that the teacher, as he repeated "the rain in Spain . . . ," had an accent almost as thick as your own, and that this kept it from sounding too foreign. You weren't becoming a different person; the old YOU was learning new tricks. Education was instrumental, all right—it has always been that in America—but the instruments were thought to be in the curriculum. The student didn't have to learn to think of *himself* as one.

And finally, nobody doubted what the norms were. It seemed very clear that the people in the next stratum up were the ones who knew what he had to learn; he had to be able to do what they did. This wouldn't make them accept him willingly; but it would allow him to work his way in even if they didn't.

I don't mean to imply that the school actually delivered the social mobility it promised; sometimes it did, more often it didn't. But this was the way it was supposed to work and why there was so little controversy over whether compulsory school attendance was good for the individual as well as for the commonwealth. As long as the students who stayed in school believed in education naïvely, it served much better than religion could have in this heterogeneous country as the opiate of the people. And opium vendors, usually, don't have dropout problems.

But, apparently they can; the American poor are getting over their addiction. It takes more and more education every year to invoke the same dream; and reality breaks through too often, leaving them sick, mean, and edgy. One thing that makes me a bit nervous about this new concern is that I'm afraid it may be the opening battle in a new "Opium War" conducted on behalf of an educational establishment fearful of losing popular support and more interested in keeping the youngsters on an education kick than in giving them any real help. But our purpose here is to explore the possibilities of *rapprochement* and continued educational relations; and this is eminently worth trying.

FACING THE DROPOUT PROBLEM

Two basic *rapprochements* have already been tried; and I am rather skeptical of both of them, though for quite different reasons.

Two Attempts at Solution

The simplest of these is an effort to beef up the traditional, but paradoxically faltering, economic appeal of education. Students are reminded over and over that today, more than ever, you need a high school diploma to get any sort of job—and a college degree to get a good one. They are given the statistics on the fabulous return that education, as an investment, brings in, over a lifetime, in increments of annual income. The unemployment data on adolescents and unskilled labor are stressed so that they will understand how hopeless they will be if they drop out of school. If they and their teachers are sophisticated enough, the demographic shift in job type may be explained— how unskilled and blue-collar work has fallen off while service and white-collar jobs, demanding a higher level of school achievement, have enormously increased in proportion.

All this is true enough; but the implication is false. It does not follow that most of the students now dropping out would have a better chance—even economically—if they stayed in school. As S. M. Miller and Frank Riessman have pointed out in a recent WBAI broadcast, the illusory success of some of these school-retention efforts in leading students to better jobs is based on the fact that they made hardly a dent in the number of school dropouts. If the programs had been successful in reaching the students, they would inevitably have failed in delivering the jobs. In our economy, the demonstrable economic value of an education is partly a consequence of its scarcity. The blue-collar, white-collar figures are relative; and one loses sight of how much smaller the white-collar one was to begin with. The absolute increase in white-collar opportunity does not compensate for the absolute loss in blue-collar jobs—a discrepancy which is rapidly increasing in magnitude as automation proceeds. Today's dropouts are, perhaps fortunately, pretty skeptical kids; if they all believed that the school could deliver them to a brighter economic future, we would soon have unemployed IBM operators and technicians hanging around, the way India and Africa have lawyers.

The other and more sophisticated *rapprochement* is represented by the Higher Horizons Program itself; and I am sorry, indeed, to have to be so reserved in my reception of a program that seems to me characterized by so much intelligence, ingenuity, enthusiasm, and sheer good will. It has all those, and its appeal is not purely economic. I understand it to be an attempt to convey to students that middle-class culture, *in toto,* is not beyond their grasp. It can be theirs, if they do their work and save their boxtops. As the title implies, the Higher Horizons approach seeks to make education seem more worthwhile to the student and encourages him to remain in school to develop his potentialities by raising his level of aspiration not just economically but culturally. As the boy lifts himself hopefully to gaze beyond the slum there comes into view the beautiful Museum of Modern Art.

Rejection of Middle-Class Culture

It is heartening to find the middle class so generously willing to share its resources, and for once, apparently confident of their value. It is also obvious that if the middle class cannot somehow make public education acceptable to the poor on its terms rather than theirs, middle-class dominance of public education—a long-established fact of American life—is doomed. But if the effort is successful, it will remind me of a story that a very intelligent, very British, very working-class hospital orderly used to tell, in a sensitive effort to ease his middle-class patients' embarrassment at the services he was obliged to perform for them. This story concerned a small pharmaceutical firm that was facing bankruptcy. It had an established reputation as Britain's most reputable manufacturer of suppositories. But respect for craftsmanship, as is well known, was declinning; their customers, apparently, were turning to other sources for satisfaction. Things looked black. Then the firm consulted one of Madison Avenue's most resourceful advertising agencies. And the agency, after much brainstorming, came up with a slogan that at once opened vast markets to the company by motivating the very segment of the population which had hitherto most successfully resisted its appeal. The slogan was, very simply, very succinctly, "If you don't like our suppositories, you know what you can do with them!"

The dropouts, by and large, don't like middle-class culture; and they know quite well what we can do with it. Dropping out is one way of telling us, and it is about time we turned our attention to the things about the school that are bugging them. The school is the arena in which these youngsters encounter middle-class life; this is where the dropouts fight the ten-year ideological war that ends in their defeat and rout. In this warfare, core values of both their culture and that which the school represents are at issue; any one that we start by considering will lead to the others. I think that the most fruitful might be the familiar question of deferred gratification, or impulse control, which is the source of so much conflict with the school authorities.

Impulse Control

We all know the school's side of the question; and we all know that lower-class youngsters act out their conflicts. Retention programs try to face up to this by helping the youngsters learn more self-control and by giving them some valid experience of being rewarded for it—so that they will learn for themselves that there are some very desirable goals that can only be achieved by people who plan, save, and give a soft answer to wrath-provoking circumstances. In this way one learns that there may be more desirable rewards than the immediate pleasure of blowing up and shooting your bolt. "Now, Dionysus, let's think about what we're really trying to get done here," friendly Apollo is always urging; and we all know he is right. The trouble is, how do you get Dionysus to listen?

Current Moral Attitudes

Are we so sure? Let me return for a moment to Mr. White's account of the 1960 election, and the Apollonian behavior it elicited from the Republican candidate.

And this, finally, was the only summary one could make of the campaign that Richard M. Nixon had so valiantly waged, under such personal suffering: that there was neither philosophy nor structure to it, no whole picture either of the man or of the future he offered. One could perceive neither in this last climactic proposal nor in his prepared speeches nor in his personal discourses any shape of history, any sense of the stream of time or flow of forces by which America had come to this point in history and might move on. Nixon's skills in politics were enormous, his courage unquestioned, his endurance substantial. But they were the skills, courage, and endurance of the sailor who knows the winds and can brave the storm and recognizes the tide. There was missing in him always the direction of the navigator. . . .

Thus it is impossible to distinguish, from his campaign performance, what Nixon's personal political attitude was to the arrest of Martin Luther King when that hero figure of American Negroes was arrested in the last days of the campaign. . . . On the afternoon of the sentencing of Martin Luther King to four months of hard labor in Georgia, the Department of Justice—at the suggestion of a wise yet shrewd Republican Deputy Attorney-General

. . . composed a draft statement to support the application for release of the imprisoned Negro minister. Two copies of the draft were sent out immediately for approval—one to the White House, one to Mr. Nixon's traveling headquarters. . . . No one has yet revealed who killed this draft statement that was so critically important in the tense politics of civil rights. Either President Eisenhower or Vice-President Nixon could have acted—yet neither did. However obscure Eisenhower's motivations were, Nixon's are more perplexing, for he was the candidate. He had made the political decision at Chicago . . . to court the Negro vote in the North; only now, apparently, he felt it quite possible that Texas, South Carolina and Louisiana might all be won to him by the white vote and he did not wish to offend that vote. So he did not act—there was no whole philosophy of politics to instruct him.

There could never be any doubt of the Vice-President's pugnacity or innate courage; yet it was a pugnacity and courage committed without a framing strategy to make them effective.[2]

The terms of Mr. White's criticism are as interesting as the incident itself. No philosophy of politics? No framing strategy? On the contrary, he was all strategy. What he lacked was heart and a sense of outrage, the capacity to make moral judgments. Yet Mr. White cannot say this because his whole book, though very sensitive to moral factors in the contest, shares the assumption that a candidate's first duty is to get elected. Nixon lost, and the way the figures broke down later does indeed show that his expediency on this issue may have cost him the election. But to infer from this fact that the worst thing about Mr. Nixon's behavior was that it didn't work is to share his posture.

Earlier on, Mr. White describes the situations in the campaign that found Mr. Nixon at his best.

One had to see Nixon entering a small Iowa village—the streets lined with school children, all waving American flags until it seemed as if the cavalcade were entering a defile lined by fluttering, peppermint-striped little banners—then see him stop at a Harvest Festival (in Red Oaks)—where on the festival tables lay the ripened ears of field corn—to see him at his best. For in such small towns he found an echo. . . . These people were his natural constituency, his idiom their idiom. . . . He woke in Marietta, Ohio, on Monday, October 25th, to begin his last "peak" effort, and it was clear from his first speech of the day that he was at one with his audience as he had not been since he had passed

---

[2] *Ibid.*, pp. 314-316.

through the cornfields of Iowa in the first week of the campaign. A sign outside the courthouse of Marietta, Ohio, read: HIGH SCHOOL DEBATERS GREET WORLD DEBATER—the sign was apropos and of the essence of this last trip as he revived. For he *was* a high school debater, the boy who had, some thirty years before, won a Los Angeles *Times* prize for his high school oration on the Constitution. He was seeking not so much to score home a message as to win the hearts of his little audiences; his style was home-style and during the next two weeks told much about him.[3]

In Red Oaks and Marietta they don't have much of a dropout problem. Good, solid communities, with woodsheds ample to the needs of youth, they turn out clean-cut boys and girls among whom Mr. Nixon is right at home. It was the urban proletariat, and overwhelmingly the Negroes, who refused to take part in his Harvest Festival—though the corn be ripe and the harvests long overdue.

To carry this illustration further would not make my point any clearer; in any case, it is simple enough. I think the youngsters who drop out are probably, in many ways, a more promising moral resource than those who stay in; and I think they are driven out in part by moral revulsion from the middle-class life of the school. They could never, themselves, identify their feelings as moral repugnance because they think morality is on the side of the enemy and therefore square. They think they dislike morality and have never been allowed to realize that they have morals of their own. They don't have a complete moral *system* because they are not systematic; they are unprincipled in their behavior because principles are too abstract for them to handle. But in a concrete situation they can be trusted more safely than their middle-class peers who are trying to make it.

Mr. Nixon and his silent superior are symbols too; and I am not naïve enough to attribute the lower-class response to them solely to the revulsion they arouse in the breast of the noble savage. The opposition was well organized and well manipulated. But there are natural affinities and polarities in politics that set limits to what manipulation can achieve; and these, among other things, are reflected in the class structure of American society. Officially, American society is, however, middle-class and opportunistic; in the Land of Opportunity, these are the values that receive official support and that, in fact, prevail. It is surely fair enough to take Mr. Eisenhower, and Mr. Nixon

---

[3] *Ibid.*, pp. 277, 300.

at the zenith of his presidential aspirations, as representative of what is most American. But one need not be wholly partisan. The late President Kennedy has also stated emphatically that we need technical rather than ideological or philosophical approaches to the problems that confront us.[4]

This moral attitude dominates our life. We are caught in this position in crisis after crisis: in the U-2 incident; the Cuban invasion; the presence of our observers in Vietnam—organizing the forced evacuation of peasants so that their farms can be burned and helping the government see to it that the Viet Cong guerrillas don't get any antibiotics. Time after time the world finds a nice, friendly American standing in the middle of somebody else's ruins with no more to say for himself than a rueful, "It shoulda worked, but somebody musta goofed!"

The Dropout Described

I have a name for this boy; I call him Edsel; and I think it is time we withdrew him from production and got out a more responsive and less hazardous model. Even the practical-minded may not have much use for him any more; the locals seem to be getting pretty tired of Edsel and are about ready to get him out of there, with a hammer and sickle if necessary. But if we are to grow anything better, the dropouts are the kids to start with, for they have come part way on their own, against heavy opposition, already. They are ill-disciplined. They have no basic skills. They are so sore that any place you touch them hurts; and when they are hurt, they hurt back. They are extremely parochial, limited in their experience of the world to a few city blocks of desolate slum, and therefore, both gullible and suspicious about anything beyond it. They are sometimes homeless; they never have any quiet place to study and think. They are inconveniently aware of their own sexuality and inconveniently skilled at bringing it to the attention of others. They live, their teachers sometimes say, like animals; and as they say it, a ghost sobs, harshly. But if these youngsters are trapped, it is not in their apprehensions of pseudo events. They are not alienated. They still have access to their sense-data, and on their own terms, are accustomed to fidelity.

---

[4] Commencement address at Yale University. *Cf.* William Lee Miller, "Some Academic Questions About a New Yale Man," *Reporter* Vol. 27 (July 5, 1962), pp. 22-23.

These are the qualities that I believe we hoped to preserve and continually renew by building an open society in which a sensitive, compulsively masculine boy could become an Ernest Hemingway and a poor but beautiful waif, a Marilyn Monroe. At this juncture, less fatal alternatives to mediocrity are needed. Can a school geared to success and social mobility help formulate them? Its traditions are against it, its staff are against it; its relationship to the community power structure is against it.

REACHING THE DROPOUT

To reach the dropouts and give them a reason for staying, the school would have to start by accepting their *raison d'être.* It would have to take lower-class life seriously as a condition and a pattern of experience, not just as a contemptible and humiliating set of circumstances that every decent boy or girl is anxious to escape from. It would have to accept their language, their dress, and their values as a point of departure for disciplined exploration, to be understood not as a trick for luring them into the middle class but as a way of helping them to explore the meaning of their own lives. This is the way to encourage and nurture potentialities from *whatever* social class. Talent, and genius, when real, are expressions of individual experience and the inner life. But success and higher status are not the first goal to which talent or genius is devoted; though they are sometimes the last.

I do not mean to imply that I accept Sitwell's Fallacy: that the poor are happier in their station in life and should be left to enjoy it. Most lower-class people of whatever age hate lower-class life, I am sure: the noise, and the filth, and the crowding; and the vulnerability to the police, and illness; never feeling quite well or quite rested. Worst of all, perhaps, is the constant din of the mass media—including the school—telling them that if they were any good at all they would be middle class like everybody else and live in loveliness in Larchmont. But the fact that they have reason to hate their life of fear and deprivation does not give us the right to force ours on them as the only acceptable alternative to it. This is something they must work out for themselves; the school's job is to help them understand most fully the meaning and nature of what they have to work with. Basically, the problem of reaching the dropout is analogous to that faced by the Peace Corps in reaching the peoples of underdeveloped countries. Can we—do we even really wish to—help them deal with their situation on their terms with our resources, while leaving our way of life aside till somebody asks for it?

Frankly, I doubt it. This isn't the way the teachers I know approach lower-status youngsters. They are afraid of them, for one thing. The principal is afraid of disorder, which looks bad in his record and theirs; and they have their careers to think of too. So they learn early to keep the kids in line; this comes first. Order *is* helpful to learning, but it doesn't come first; it grows out of the common task. And teachers who put it first are not enthusiastic allies in keeping disorderly youngsters in school till a basis for order can be created. Order is not, to be sure, the central issue; but it will serve to symbolize the sharpness of the issue between those whose security depends on the suppression of impulse and those who depend on its expression.

In the urban public school today, these teachers predominate. I don't think they can be easily changed within the limits of personality and bureaucracy that characterize the school. If they can be, there is no fundamental reason why the kinds of youngsters who now drop out may not be well served. But this is a big IF; for the public school, as it is, is profoundly expressive of our culture; and the fate of the "dropouts" is just one more expression of their actual status in our democracy.

The answer, then, may be: "No; this plant makes only Edsels." But if it is, I see no dropout problem. Let them go, let them go, God bless them. They may pop up again. St. James is not merely more merciful than the school system; he is far more flexible and versatile. He can accommodate a wider range of talent; he has a great Court, as well as an Infirmary, and though no familiar avenue bears his name, he has, like James Madison, been thus honored by the inhabitants of certain cities. The nearest, unfortunately, in Cuba.

@@@@@@@@@@@@@@@@@@@@@@@@@@@@@@@@@@@@

THE UNIVERSAL TRAP

@@@@@@@@@@@@@@@@@@@@@@@@@@@@@@@@@@@@

PAUL GOODMAN

The dropouts are importantly victims of poverty, cultural deprivation, race prejudice, family and emotional troubles, and
neighborhood uprooting. This book will surely thoroughly explore these background conditions, will suggest ingenious ex-
pedients to counteract them, and will—I guess much less thoroughly and ingeniously—look to remedying them. There are,
however, other questions: Where are the dropouts *from?* Is the
schooling good for them or much good for anybody? Since
there are difficulties with the present arrangements for growing
up, might not some better arrangements be found? Unless we
lay stress on these other questions, our inquiry can well be an
evil one—at best a smoke screen for the real troubles of youth,
at worst social engineering for the crew that have power in the
world. Certainly in the discussions of this subject which I have
read, there has been an appalling lack of the philosophical and
Enlightenment ideas that *cannot* be omitted from education,
for youth *are* the future.

ASSESSING THE SCHOOL SYSTEM

Education is a natural community function and goes on anyway, since the young grow up on the old, toward their activities, and into their institutions; and the old foster, train, exploit,
and abuse the young. Formal schooling is a reasonable auxiliary of the inevitable process. Nevertheless it by no means follows that the complicated artifact of our school system has
much to do with education, and certainly not with good education. If it presumes to be compulsory, then it must prove that it

does not do more harm than good—both to persons and society as a whole.

Let us keep in mind the ways in which big school systems have nothing to do with education at all. The New York system turns over $1 billion annually. It is a vast vested interest, and it is very probable that—like much of our economy and almost all of our political structure (of which the public schools are a part)—it goes on for its own sake. In doing so, it keeps thousands busy, wastes wealth, crushes life, and pre-empts the space in which something interesting could go on. Notoriously, the school system is a gigantic market for textbook manufacturers and building contractors. Further, its fundamental design is ancient, yet has not been altered although its present operation is altogether different in scale and must be in meaning. For example, in 1900, high school graduates were 6 percent of the 17-year-olds, and 4 percent went to college. In 1961, nearly 61 percent are graduates; and of these, nearly 60 percent are bound for something called college. Likewise, there is a difference between a few hours' attendance in school intermitted in life on a farm or in a city with plenty of small jobs and schooling that is a child's only adult contact. Thus, a perhaps outmoded institution has become almost the only available way of growing up. And this pre-empting has occurred not only in extent but also in meaning. Just as our American society as a whole is more and more tightly organized, so its school system is more and more regimented as a part of that organization, with little leeway of its own. Unfortunately, that organization of society is mindlessly drifting toward catastrophe. In the organizational plan, the schools play a noneducational and an educational role. The noneducational role is very important: in the tender grades, the schools are a baby-sitting service during a period of collapse of the old type of family and of great neighborhood mobility; in the junior high and high school grades, they are an arm of the police, providing cops and concentration camps paid for in the budget under the heading "Board of Education." The educational role is, increasingly, to provide apprentice training for corporations and the War Department and to train the young—as New York's Commissioner of Education, James Allen, said (in the Worley case)—"to handle constructively their problems of adjustment to authority."

There is no doubt that the school system has been, and continues to be, a powerful force for the democratizing of our great and mixed population. But we must be careful to keep reassessing it when it becomes a universal trap and democracy begins to look like regimentation.

COMPULSORY NATURE OF EDUCATION

Let us spend a page on the history of the compulsory nature of the system. When, in *The Child, the Parent, and the State,* James Conant[1] refers to the possible incompatibility between "individual development" and "national needs," it is a watershed in American philosophy of education and puts us back to the ideology of Imperial Germany, or on a par with contemporary Russia. When Jefferson and Madison conceived of compulsory schooling, such an incompatibility would have been unthinkable. They were in the climate of the Enlightenment, were strongly influenced by Congregational (town-meeting) ideas, and were of course makers of a revolution. To them "citizen" meant society maker, not one adjusted to society; and it is clear that they regarded themselves and their friends as citizens existentially, so to speak. To make society was their breath of life. (In my opinion, the majority of Americans at that time were less citizens in this sense, and nearer to small-community anarchists and guerrillas.) Obviously such conceptions are worlds removed from, and diametrically opposed to, our present political reality, where the ground rules, and indeed the game, are predetermined. For Jefferson, *people had to be taught in order to multiply the sources of initiative.* And the curriculum that those of good parts were to learn was corresponding: a technological natural philosophy, in order to make inventions and produce useful goods; and the social study of history, in order to make constitutional innovations and be fired to defend freedom. What are the compelling reasons compelling everybody to know how to know what goes on? To keep the economy expanding, to choose between indistinguishable Democrats and Republicans, and to understand the official press and TV. Planning and decision making are lodged in the top managers; rarely, and at most, the electorate serves as a pressure group.

Scientifically, the urban mass exists only as consumers. (As serious education, let us note, under these circumstances of

---

[1] James B. Conant, *The Child, the Parent, and the State.* (Cambridge, Mass.: Harvard University Press, 1959).

powerlessness and noninvolvement, there is not much way to learn anything, and not much is learned.)

Another great impulse for compulsory education came from the new industrialism and urbanism, especially during the three or four decades after the Civil War, a time also of great immigration. Here the curricular demands were most modest: in the grades, literacy and arithmetic; in the colleges, professional skills to man the expanding economy. But again, no one would have spoken of an incompatibility between "individual development" and "national needs," for it was considered to be an open society, abounding in opportunity. And indeed there was an endless proliferation of economic and technical small enterprises—plus westward emigration and considerable imperialism in Latin America and the Far East. Typically, the novels of Horatio Alger, Jr., treat education as morally excellent as well as essential for getting ahead; and there is no doubt that the immigrants saw education-for-success as also a human value for their children. Also, the system was not an academic trap. The 94 percent who in 1900 did not finish high school had other life opportunities, including often the possibility of making a lot of money or/and of rising in politics—though not in high policy, an area which belonged to the schooled.

But again, by and large, this is not our present situation. There is plenty of social mobility; there are plenty of opportunities to rise—except for the ethnic minorities who are precisely our main concern as dropouts. But how to rise and what to rise to are increasingly rigidified, stratified, cut and dried. Most enterprise is parceled out by the feudal corporations, or by the state; and these determine the requirements and assign the statuses and salaries. Ambition with average talent meets their rules, or fails; and those without relevant talent, or with unfortunate backgrounds, cannot even survive in decent poverty. And the requirements of survival are importantly academic, or at least have come to be attained in public schools and in universities. We do not have an open economy. Jobs are scarce, and the corporations and state can dictate the terms. Thus, IBM, Westinghouse, etc., swoop down on the colleges and skim off the youth who have been given what amounts to an apprenticeship at public and private expense (the private expense running upwards of $10,000). Even a department store requires a diploma or diplomas for its salespeople, not so much because of the skills they have learned but because it sets a guarantee of the character useful for sales help: punctual, obedient, and with a smooth record. And more generally, since our powers-that-be have opted for an expanding economy with a galloping "high standard of living" and since all the powers of the world are in an arms and space race, there *is* a national need for many academic graduates specifically trained. Such a need is irrelevant to citizenly initiative, the progress of an open society, or personal happiness.

Thus, education becomes equivalent to regimentation. The schools become a universal trap. Those not in the schools fall outside of society altogether.

REACTIONS TO THE SCHOOL TRAP

These schools are *not* geared to "middle-class values," a misleading use of words which has become common. The schools less and less represent *any* human values, but simply adjustment to a mechanism.

Varying Philosophies

In the face of the increasing failure of the schools with the poor urban mass, there has developed a line of criticism—e.g., Oscar Lewis, Patricia Sexton, Frank Riessman, and even Edgar Friedenberg (who should know better)—asserting that there is a "culture of poverty" that the "middle-class" schools do not fit, but which has its own virtues of spontaneity, sociality, animality, etc. The implication is that the "middle class," for all its virtues, is obsessional, prejudiced, prudish. Pedagogically, this insight is indispensable: we must try to reach a child in terms of his background, his habits, and the language he understands. But if taken to be more than technical, it is disastrous. For our philosophic aim must be to get each one out of his isolated class and into the one humanity. Prudence and responsibility are not middle-class virtues but human virtues; and spontaneity and sexuality are not powers of the simple but of human health. (One has the impression that our critics are looking not to a human community but to a future in which the obsessionals will take care of the impulsives.)

In fact, some of the most important strengths that have historically belonged to the middle class are flouted by the schools: independence, initiative, scrupulous honesty, earnest-

ness, utility, thoroughness, respect for disinterested scholarship
and science. Rather than bourgeois, our schools are petty bourgeois, bureaucratic, gradgrind-practical, and *nouveau riche*
climbing; and added to these, last but not least, they exude a
cynicism, in the upper grades and colleges, that belongs to rotten aristocrats and racketeers.

The Poor and Middle-Class Dropouts

Naturally, however, the youth of the poor and the middle
class respond differently to the school trap. Many poor youth,
herded into a situation that does not fit their disposition, for
which they are unprepared by their background, and which
does not interest them, simply develop a reactive stupidity very
different from their behavior on the street or ball field. They
drop behind, play truant, and as soon as possible drop out. If
the school situation is immediately useless and damaging to
them, their response must be said to be life preservative. They
thereby somewhat diminish their chances of a decent living
and of being effective citizens. We must remember that the
usual propaganda—that schooling is a road to high salaries—is,
for most of these poor youth, a lie; and the increase in security
is arguably not worth the torture involved, for we allow almost
nobody actually to starve.

Certainly the reasonable social policy would be not to have
these youth in school, but to educate them otherwise and provide opportunity for a decent future in some other way. It
would be wise to have a conference on *this* issue, omitting the
notion of dropout altogether. At present, our society does not
know how to cope with these youth, and really isn't interested.
I fear that most of the concern for the dropouts is because
they are a nuisance and a threat and can't be socialized by the
existing machinery. Ethically, therefore, I am dubious about
the attempts of James Coleman, or even Dan Schreiber, to use
methods and bait which are not beautiful in themselves and
which sometimes come to conning and cajoling these young
people by adolescent tricks and prizes rather than treating
them earnestly as persons. Very different is the aspect of the
Higher Horizons Program as reopening hope for a future that
is really worthwhile and desirable. This is to take the young
seriously and to be their champion.

"Stay-in-School" Dropouts

But numerically far more important than these overt drop-outs at 16 are the children who conform to schooling between the ages of 6 to 16 or 20, but who drop out internally through daydreaming—their days wasted, their liberty caged and scheduled, their desires inhibited, their imagination and aspiration lost. There are many such in the middle class, from backgrounds that have not been so horrendous as to foment overt rebellion—where there is some interest in books and arts; where the youth is seduced by the prospect of money and status, but even more where he is terrified to jeopardize the only pattern of life he knows.

It is in the schools and from the mass media, rather than at home or from their friends, that the mass of our citizens in all classes learn that life is inevitably routine and phony, depersonalized, venally graded, and bureaucratized; that it is best to toe the mark and shut up; that there is no place for spontaneity, open sexuality, free spirit. Trained in the schools, they go on to the same quality of jobs, culture, politics. This *is* education, bad education—socializing to the national norm, regimenting to the national needs.

The educational psychology of it is elementary. Our society and its school trap first deprive the young of objective human opportunities, including virtues that belonged to the middle class. As I put it in *Growing Up Absurd*—

> With all the tidying up of background conditions that you please our abundant society is at present simply deficient in many of the most elementary objective opportunities that could make growing up possible. It is lacking in enough man's work. It is lacking in honest public speech and people are not taken seriously. It is lacking in the opportunity to be useful. It thwarts aptitude and creates stupidity. It corrupts ingenuous patriotism. It corrupts the fine arts. It shackles science. It dampens animal ardor. It discourages the religious convictions of Justification and Vocation and it dims the sense that there is a Creation. It has no honor. It has no community.[2]

----

[2] Paul Goodman, *Growing Up Absurd* (New York: Random House, 1961), p. 12.

But once frustrated in these things, and sometimes punished for dumbly trying for them, it is a short step to resignation. And since the resigned must have something, it is another short step to narcissism and cynicism or spite.

ANALYZING THE SCHOOL

Let us examine realistically three or four aspects of the school that is dropped out *from.*

The Emphasis on Literacy

There is a widespread anxiety about teaching reading. And indeed, reading deficiency is an accumulating disadvantage that results in painful inferiority, truancy, and dropout. Reading is crucial—by the standards of the school and because of the kinds of success that schooling leads to. Yet there is something phony here. What does "reading" mean today? We cannot say that, as humanities or science, the reading matter of the great majority is in any way superior to the movies or TV that the illiterate can share. Certainly many people would be better off without most of this mass culture, including the reading matter. And why should most people *bother* to learn to read seriously? In the decision making of our society, serious literacy is of no practical importance whatever. It is as powerless as it is rare. Anyway, those who achieve it do not do so by the route of "Run, Spot, Run" to *Silas Marner,* but by their own explorations.

It is claimed that without universal literacy our economy and technology could not operate. I doubt that this is true for many unskilled and many craft and mechanical jobs. Unlike the expanding industrialism mentioned above—or the present situation in the underdeveloped regions of Africa, Asia, and Latin America—the automated future that we face in the United States will have no need for workers. In my opinion, it is rather the kind of urbanism, politics, and buying and selling that we have that has put a premium on literacy; and, in my opinion, these are of dubious human value. Since I do not think that an indefinitely expanding economy is the right use of modern technology, I am unimpressed by the need for artificial demand fomented by advertising. Also, I am hostile to the common denominator produced by the mass media.

In the present dispensation, we would be as well off if it were socially acceptable for large numbers not to read. It would be harder to regiment people. There would be more folk culture. Serious letters would benefit if society were less swamped by trash, lies, and bland verbiage. Much suffering of inferiority would be obviated. And conceivably, *more people might become genuinely literate if it were understood that reading is a useful art with a proper subject matter, imagination and truth—not "communication" of top down decisions and bad norms.*

Restrictions on the Child

The young rightly resist animal constraint. But, at least in New York, most teachers—and many principals who visit their classes—operate as if Progressive Education had not proved the case for noise and freedom of bodily motion. Of course, the classes are too large to cope with without "discipline." Then make them smaller; or don't wonder if children escape out of the cage, either into truancy or baffled daydream. Here is a case: an architect replacing a Harlem school is forbidden by the Board to spend money on soundproofing the classrooms even though the wise principal has declared it to be a must for the therapy of the pent-up and resentful children. Resentment —pent-up hostility—is a major cause of reactive stupidity; yet there is usually an absolute discouragement of any overt expression of resentment, or even of normal anger or aggression.

Again, one has to be blind not to see that the dissidence from school is importantly sexual, especially from the onset of puberty. Theoretically, the junior high school was introduced precisely to fit this change of life, yet astoundingly it is sexless. My own view, for what it's worth, is that sexuality is lovely, that there cannot be too much of it, that it is self-limiting if it is satisfactory, and that satisfaction diminishes tension and clears the mind for attention and learning. Therefore sexual expression should be approved in and out of season, also in school, and where necessary made the subject of instruction. But whether or not this view is ideal, it is at present the only practical one. Our society has so developed that sexual drives cannot be kept out of consciousness (in repression). Then there is no alternative, to avoid distortion and preoccupation, except to raise the discharge to the level of the tension. When, on so crucial an issue, the schools act 100 years out of date, they are crucially irrelevant.

But let me mention a further aspect of inhibition of the motoric, the sexual, and the angry. There is now public alarm about children's physical unfitness. The President's Committee ludicrously proposes a standard of three chin-ups, etc.; schools institute some calisthenics and proudly record the improvement in meeting the standard. But no program is instituted to unblock the muscles tensed by inhibition—the fear of expression, the fear of body contact, and the fear of nakedness. Physical training teachers do not try to free the bodies of the children to weep, shout, reach in love, strive with determination, strike in anger, and dance in rhythm. The children are supposed, somehow, to manifest grace, agility, and strength as if they were not unitary organisms. Is this realistic? Of course, if a teacher used eurythmics and physical therapy to unblock feeling, there would be an outcry from the churches, some parents, and the yellow press that fattens on pornography and murder. The officials would cower, the teacher would be fired. Instead, the children are sacrificed—or drop out.

Lack of Education for Leisure

The schools are supposed to educate for the satisfaction of life and for leisure. Again, let us try to be realistic. For most people, I think that a candid self-examination will show that their most absorbing, long, and satisfactory hours are spent in things like friendly competitive sports, friendly gambling, love making and sex, earnest or argumentative conversation, dedicated political activity, solitary study and reading, contemplation of nature and the cosmos, art-working, music, and religion. Now none of these requires the use of many commodities. Indeed, elaborate arrangements and equipment take the life out of them. Friends use one another as resources; and God, nature, and creativity are free. The media of fine arts are cheap stuff. Health, luck, and a simple heart are the only requirements for good sex. Good food requires taking pains more than spending money.

On the other hand, it is the necessity of a profitable economy, with high employment and expanding by reinvestment, to *in-*

crease the number of commodities consumed, and therefore to
prevent, curtail, or debauch the profound satisfactions of life;
that is, to see to it that a "high standard of living" is a bad,
wasteful, and unsatisfactory, but titillating, standard of living.
In our present political and economic dispensation, an advanced technology *cannot* be humane.

What is the moral for our purposes? Can it be denied that in
some respects the dropouts make a wiser choice than many
who go to school, not to get real goods, but to get money?
Their choice of the "immediate" is not altogether impulsive and
neurotic. The bother is that in our present culture they are so
nagged by inferiority, exclusion, and despair of the future that
they cannot much enjoy their leisure. Because they know little,
they are deprived of many profound satisfactions; being afraid
of exposing themselves, they just hang around. And our urban
social arrangements—for example, rent—have made it impossible for anybody to be decently poor on a "low" standard.

School Size and Standardization

Untold damage is done to children simply by the size and
standardization of the big system. Suppose a class size of 20 is
good for some purpose: it does not follow that 35 is better than
nothing. Rather, it is likely to be positively harmful for the children who have ceased to be persons, and it destroys the
teacher. A teacher with a 10-year-old class reading at 7-year
level will have to use the content as well as the vocabulary of
Dick and Jane since that is the textbook bought by the hundred
thousand. The experience of a wise principal is that the most
essential part of his job is to know every child's name and be an
available godfather. Yet the city will build the school for 2,000.
The chief part of learning is in the community of scholars,
where classwork and social life cohere; yet social engineers like
Dr. Conant will, for putative efficiencies, centralize the high
schools.

A program—for example, to prevent dropout—will be, by
an attentive teacher, exquisitely tailored to the children he
works with; he will have a success. Therefore his program must
be standardized (watered down) in 75 schools—otherwise it
cannot be financed. But here is an unbeatable anecdote: An
architect is employed to replace a dilapidated school but is forbidden to consult the principal and teachers of the school as to

their needs, since his building must conform to uniform plans at headquarters (the plans are a generation out of date). Being a functionalist, the architect demurs, and it requires an *ad hoc* assembly of all the superintendents to write a special contract!

Presumably all the standardization, etc., is administratively necessary, but then it is also necessary for bruised children to quit. Our society makes a persistent error in metaphysics. Production techniques which apply to commodities, to administrative and logistics techniques, to armies and banks have *no relevance whatever* to the personal relations of teaching and learning and to the community relations of educating the young. When they are applied, what the young learn is not the lesson but a reaction to the Procrustean bed. (Theseus did the crook in.)

Academic Standardization

As a loyal academic, I must make a further observation. Mainly to provide apprentices, as I have said, there is at present a strong pressure to gear the "better" elementary schools to the colleges and universities. This is the great current reform, genre of Rickover. But what if the top of the ladder is corrupt and corrupts the lower grades? On visits to 50 colleges everywhere in the country, I have been appalled at how rarely the subjects are studied in a right academic spirit, for their truth and beauty and as part of humane international culture. Rather, the students are given, and seek, a narrow expertise aimed at licenses and salary. They are indoctrinated with a national thoughtlessness that is not even chauvinistic. Administrators sacrifice the community of scholars to aggrandizement and subsidized research.

Conversely, there is almost never conveyed the sense in which learning is a truly practical, enlightening experience, initiating and giving courage for change, reforming the state, deepening personal and social peace. On the contrary, there is a professional cynicism and the resigned conviction that Nothing Can Be Done. This is Yale. If this is the University, how can we hope for aspiring scholarship in the elementary schools? On the contrary, everything will be grading, conformist "citizenship," and getting ahead—not in the subject, but up the ladder. Students will "do" Bronx Science in order to "make" MIT, and they will "do" MIT in order to "make" Westinghouse, and they will "do" Westinghouse in order to "make" jail. The improvement of "academic" standards is a sell, and the bright boys and girls are being had. Some of them know it and balk.

ALLEVIATION FROM THE TRAP

The compulsory system has become a universal trap, and it is no good. Very many, and perhaps most, of the youth—both underprivileged and middle-class—might be better off if the system did not exist, even if they then had no formal schooling at all. But what would become of them? For very many—both underprivileged and middle-class—their homes are worse than the schools, and the streets are worse in another way. Our urban and suburban environments are precisely not cities or communities where adults attend to the young and educate to a viable life. Also, perhaps especially in the case of the overt dropouts, the state of their body and soul is such that we must give them some refuge and remedy—whether it be called school, youth work, work camp, or settlement house.

This is not the place for a long list of practical proposals to make the schools worth attending. However, it is relevant to offer a few ideas toward the main subject we have been discussing—the system as a compulsory trap. In principle, when a law begins to do more harm than good, the best policy is to alleviate it. I would suggest the following experiments:

1. Have "no school at all" for a few classes. These children should be selected from tolerable, though not necessarily cultured, homes. They should be numerous enough and neighborly enough to be a society for one another. Will they learn the rudiments anyway? The experiment could not harm them, since there is evidence (Sloan Wayland) that normal children can make up the first six or seven school years with a few months of good teaching.

2. Largely dispense with the school building for a few classes, and use the city itself as a school—the streets, cafeterias, stores, movies, museums, parks, and factories. Such a class should probably not exceed 10 children for 1 pedagogue. The idea (an Athenian one) is not dissimilar to Youth gang work, though not employing delinquents nor playing to the gang ideology.

3. Along the same lines, but both outside and inside the

school, use appropriate adults of the community—such as the druggist, the storekeeper, the mechanic—as the proper educators of the young into the grown-up world. By this means, it would be possible to overcome the separation of the young from the grown-up world in our urban life and to diminish the omnivorous authority of the school. This experience would be useful and animating for the adults. (We have begun a volunteer program along these lines in New York City.)

4. Make class attendance not compulsory (A. S. Neill). If the teachers are good, absence should soon be eliminated. The reason for the compulsory law is to get the children from the parents, but it must not be a trap for the children. A modification might be permission to spend a week or a month in any worthwhile enterprise or environment (Frank Brown).

5. Decentralize the school into small units of perhaps 100—in clubhouses—combining play, social activity, discussion, and formal teaching. Special events could bring together the many small units to a common auditorium or gymnasium so as to give the sense of the greater community.

6. For a couple of months of the school year, send children to farms to take part in the farm life, perhaps two or three children to a farmer. This would serve to give the farmer cash, as part of a generally desirable program to redress the urban-rural ratio to something nearer to 70-30.

Above all, apply these or any other proposals to particular individuals or small groups, without the obligation of uniformity. There is a case for uniform standards of achievement, but they *cannot* be reached by uniform techniques. The claim that standardization of procedure is more efficient, less costly, or alone administratively practical is usually false. Particular inventiveness requires thought, but thought does not cost money. And the more the authority to initiate is delegated to many, the wiser and freer we will be.

THE SEARCH FOR AN

EDUCATIONAL REVOLUTION

S. M. MILLER

BREAKTHROUGHS AND BREAKDOWNS

A revolutionary vision has emerged in American education. This vision is to educate the disadvantaged, for education today is central to security and status. The issue today is how to promote this vision into deep-seated change and effective practice. We need to move from an image of what we wish to its realization in practice.

Each year, for the last five years or so, a new major educational breakthrough has been heralded. One year it is programed instruction. Another year it is team teaching. This year it is obviously pre-kindergartens for "the culturally deprived." We hunger for a one-shot, magic potion.

I vacillate between two reactions to these claims and efforts. On one hand, I feel that we know very little about how to do an effective job of educating the disadvantaged. On the other hand, I feel that if we implemented what we know we would be much further along the line. We really cannot talk about programs unless we have assurance that we have an educational structure and citizen and professional pressure to implement programs. We are not utilizing what we know, as Alvin Eurich has contended, about the neglect of educational television. Demonstration and pilot projects often do not grow into modal practice, even when they prove out.

Despite the "breakthroughs," the vaunted "educational revolutions," I am disturbed about what is going on. I feel that we are not advancing very rapidly toward the goal of effective education for low-income groups in the United States.

Recently, I wrote an article for an English periodical on current programs for school dropouts in the United States. It was not until after I had finished the article that I realized I had misinterpreted the request from the editor. He had asked for a piece to fit into an issue on breakthroughs in the United States. Somehow, I misinterpreted the request and wrote of breakdowns in the United States, for my sorrowful feeling is that a good deal of what is taking place in educational circles really is a breakdown. A friend of mine who is very active in this field wrote me a letter to say that he detected a note of pessimism in this article, citing six or seven paragraphs. My reply was, "Man, that was no note, that was a chorus." My impression is that we are making a lot of sound and fury, but the actual net produce is of very limited value so far. Despite all the hoopla about higher horizons, educational saturations, change agents, we are not really achieving much. The breakthroughs rapidly break down. True, there is considerable change in some schools and some of the disadvantaged have been benefited, but the change is not very great nor does it tend to be continuing.

Unfortunately, the failure to achieve great educational advance in the face of the new vision of the mission of the schools is leading to scapegoating of low-income children. Frequently, the struggle to aid children who do not easily fit into the school situation is given up. I think, for example, that the concept of "cultural deprivation" is not a useful one. I think it leads people into confusing ways of beginning to analyze the problem. True, people are different—but the *obligation* of the school system is to learn how to deal with people who are quite different in terms of their ways of dealing with the learning situation.

The emphasis should not be upon a standard approach to which people measure up and then we deal effectively with them, but rather that we learn how to deal effectively with people who are quite different in outlooks, experiences and capacities.

The obligation is not in the people who are different, but is rather in the professional, to learn to deal with a wide variety of students. If a physician's patient is not successfully treated with penicillin, he moves to sulpha or to another form of treatment. The medical model is that the obligation is the physician's to do something about the problem. I submit that this obligation attaches to all professionals who have to avoid the stance that problems rest fundamentally with clientele. *Patients or clientele do not fail; only practitioners do.* The use of a term like "cultural deprivation" leads us away from looking at ourselves as practitioners. We begin to scapegoat those with whom we are having difficulty.

I fear that we are beginning to move toward the possibility of a do-nothing policy in regard to making sweeping changes in the school. For example, the present emphasis upon pre-kindergarten education as basically necessary for the advance of low-income kids is terribly exaggerated. Obviously, there is an important role for it, but we should not act as though it is a panacea that obviates other changes.[1] Martin Mayer has stated the issue with his usual eloquence: "The argument for greatly enriched preschool experience is certainly strong enough without an insistence on eternal damnation for those not lucky enough to enjoy it." Increasingly, the notion is being spread that if kids cannot make school by grade one or by grade three, they can have no educational future. The school does not really have to bother to try to do something in the later years, because the essential emphasis is upon the child's ability to succeed early. Further, he has to have a particular kind of personal experience in order to learn.

I do not think that this view is valid. This ideology bars schools from moving in more flexible, adaptive directions. The escape from failure, the fear of defeat, is leading to a search for gimmicks, for movement without change. We are trying to avoid upsetting the old ways as we paste on some new ways. At its worst, we are subjected to a series of public relations maneuvers masquerading as educational programs. I sometimes think that no one believes in the power of the printed word as much as some patrons of the public relations office. In their minds, if you write that something is occurring, it is actually taking place. In my most bitter moments, I conclude that there is nothing as aged as yesterday's educational publicity release, nor as fraudulent as tomorrow's. We need less public relations announcements and more internal reorganization of the schools.

We are basically looking for a technology to solve our problems with the disadvantaged. Technological changes in the way of pre-kindergarten programs, team teaching or reading machines and the like will be an important part of any educational revolution. But I doubt very much that they will be the

---

[1] I am not discussing Martin Deutsch's useful programs, but the way in which an *ideology* is being built around a useful idea. See Alvin W. Gouldner's discussion of this process in "The Metaphysical Pathos of Bureaucracy," *American Political Science Review* (1953).

most important part of the revolution *today*. And I emphasize *today*: Different times, different problems, different procedures. Today, something else is needed in addition to new technologies. Just as we may have false gods, so may we have false revolutions.

Though I think many issues spur an educational revolution, I shall emphasize the neglected role of administration: The need for adaptability and flexibility and for an effective school climate.

THE NATURE OF THE
EDUCATIONAL REVOLUTION

When I was a graduate student in economics I read a book, *The Fall of Rome* by Vladimir Simkhovitch, an economic historian at Columbia, that strongly influenced me. Everybody knows why Rome fell—the Goths came down from the North and took over the city. Many explanations stress the external forces that subjugated the mighty Roman Empire. Simkhovitch had another approach: Rome fell because of the declining marginal productivity of the land. Rome was no longer able to support itself agriculturally; this weakened the population. The tensions which existed within Rome emerged out of the economic plights. The important element in the failure of Rome was not the coming of the Goths, but the internal stress and strain; that was the core thing to be analyzed in the demise of Rome's imperial grandeur. The questions were: What was happening within Rome to weaken it? What were the kinds of tensions, the schisms, that were taking place, making it possible for an outside group to be victorious?

I think this mode of analysis is appropriate to education. What are the problems *within* educational institutions today? We have to look increasingly toward the internal structure and operation of education. This is particularly important now, for many of the new technologies and new programs require a new kind of administrative structure which will permit and facilitate these programs.

It is my belief—and I am sure that everyone who has had close contact with schools has a similar feeling—that the administration of a school impregnates every nook and cranny of the school. Frequently, after a half-hour stay in a school, one can describe what the chief administrator is like without ever meeting him. You can walk along the halls, look into class-rooms, and you really know the institution. It has an atmosphere and climate, a way of operating, which affects everything that takes place.

Many programs of innovation succeed because they really are changes in school administration, and sometimes school administrators, rather than because of the specific content of the program. For example, I suspect that a core element of the positive phase of progressive education was that its supporters devotedly provided an effective climate for the teachers, and found school administrators who made it possible for teachers to be flexible and imaginative. To some extent, at its beginning, progressive education was a revolution in educational administration, permitting teachers to be experimental and adaptive. In the absence of an appropriate organizational base, innovational programs fail.

In the summer of 1963, President Kennedy provided funds for the U. S. Office of Education to encourage school dropouts to return to school. In the month of August, counselors went out into some communities to talk to dropouts; and a sizeable number of youth did return to school. From what one can learn, many, if not most of those who returned to school, dropped out shortly afterwards. This gung-ho campaign did not accompany any change in schools. Dropouts went back to the same kind of situation they were in before. They were returning exiles. Shortly, they again became expellees and refugees from the school, the displaced persons of the affluent society.

Many innovations require an atmosphere, an organization, a structure, which permits them to take root. For example, many schools in low-income areas are now emphasizing school-community relations, getting parents more involved in the educational outlook of their children and closer to their schools. In one school, this increased contact has backfired. The low-income parents are more alienated from the school than ever before. Through greater intimacy with the school, they have learned how the school operates and how their children are treated by teachers and administrators. And they do not like what they think are the punitive behaviors of school personnel. Increased parent contact with the schools, if it is to be effective, may be more important in changing the attitude and behavior of school personnel than of parents!

New technology and procedures are needed, but they will

tend to have limited effects without organizational change. New technologies will rapidly become arid unless there is organizational change. Fortunately, the new technology can be a leverage for organizational change. For example, pre-kindergarten programs may lead to widespread modifications. Once we strive to improve the preschool years, we have to plan to make it possible for the later school years to latch on to the gains of the early school experience. A successful preschool program demands changes in the second grade or the fifth grade.

ADMINISTRATIVE IMPERATIVES

Let me turn now to the ingredients of this revolution in educational administration:

First, I think we need today an authentic commitment to low-income youth. The commitment has to be clear, honest, dedicated and implemented. Increasingly, it will have to include a commitment to school integration. As David Hunter has pointed out, it has to include money for schools, especially those in low-income areas. Thus, a commitment toward low-income youth includes a commitment toward integration and a commitment for funds. These are basic. Against these fundamentals, I want to make more specific comments about school outlook, organization and climate.

First, the schools have to adapt to the variations in the students. There is no one method which works with everybody. Variability and flexibility of programs and approaches are central.

Secondly, school has to provide satisfactions to students. If school operates as, or is perceived as, a prisoner-of-war camp, then I think Edgar Friedenberg and Paul Goodman are correct in their defense of the dropout. The only honorable course for a prisoner of war is to break out of the camp. School climate and effective school programs are obviously crucial here in building satisfactions in the school.

Third, more effective teachers are needed. We have routinized and overorganized schools, making it very difficult for teachers to be effective. I sometimes think that our basic perspective in administering schools is that we believe the task is to make it possible for morons to teach idiots. This view can be a self-fulfilling prophecy. The teacher's role has been overly circumscribed and overly determined from on top. Standardization, routinization and accountability have been positive steps in the development of schools, as they have been in industrial practice. But I think the present situation calls increasingly for flexibility and individualization within the school. This is a general problem of large-scale organization.

FLEXIBILITY AND ADAPTABILITY

What is involved in moving towards more organizational flexibility and adaptability?

Assumption A: Education today is not a continuous process but a discontinuous one. I think this is increasingly going to be true. People will be dropping out of public schools and returning; college students will drop out and return—this is already exceedingly common. With changing occupational demands, people are going to have to be retrained—"redeveloped," in a sense—at different points of their lives. Education and training are not one-time, one-shot activities. Leaving and returning to education and training at different points of one's life will be the modal practice. The principle which I think is involved here is that we need many entry and re-entry points to the school system and training. This is especially true of those who have difficulty in making the educational grade. We need programs which fit the unique development and experience of individuals at the time they re-enter school. The tenth grader who has dropped out and worked for a couple of years and returned to school, differs from the tenth grader who never did. We need new bridges and linkages between school and the outside. It is not enough to open a few re-entry doors; the returning student has to be provided an experience which is individually useful.

Assumption B: People vary. There is tremendous difference among youth today, whatever the social class level. In any given socio-economic level, there are many different kinds of youths. Upper middle-class progeny are both beatniks and Goldwaterites. Some school dropouts are able to get decent jobs, while others are candidates for permanent economic dependence. Variations in experience and outlook mean that different people need different things at various points in their lives. *No one method works equally effectively with everybody.* I think this is our experience with teaching reading. Adherents of some educational practices are members of religious cults, vying in protestations about which cult has the revealed truth. I think the unfortunate truth is that everyone has the revealed truth, but only a small part of it. From what I have been able to learn, it appears that certain methods work very well with certain groups, but they do not work very effectively with others.

We cannot be bound to method. To some extent, arguments about methods are controversies about different ends. Obviously, different ends may require different means. The more frequent situation is that we do not recognize that there may be many different routes to the same end. We have become bound up in the means. The teaching of reading, for example, should be based on a set of empirically based generalizations. What procedures work with whom? If a procedure does not work with some—then we have to learn ways that are more effective with them.

One of the central issues in achieving effective differentiation is how to avoid stigma. The less "normal," less "typical" tracks tend to become stigmatized. In turn, stigma leads to degradation and low-quality education. Those recruited to do the low-prestige teaching jobs tend to be of lower quality; they frequently do not have much esteem for what they are doing. Many youth who are receiving special attention in school or out are stigmatized because of this attention. Consequently, the help they receive from the new programs is very slight indeed.

The need in our society is for differentiation without stigma. Historically, though, perceived differences are attached to a scale of values, and honor and stigma are parcelled out accordingly. We need differentiation in society—I certainly would not want everyone to be like me—but the criteria of the present distribution of honor-stigma are certainly questionable. Perhaps, too, the intensity of feeling about honor or stigma might well be reduced.

These are large issues. For the school administrator, their immediate mandate is to treat as a major task the achievement of individualization and differentiation without producing stigma.

Assumption C: Good teachers emerge when they have enough independence and scope to permit personal style to flourish. There is no one best type of teacher, nor one all-purpose teaching approach. Teachers have to be permitted more independence, more scope and more initiative. A perplexing difficulty here is how to build teachers' accountability for performance at the same time that individual teacher variations are encouraged. In order to attain teacher accountability, school systems have determined what the teacher puts into the system: the boundaries of the syllabus, the class plan, and so on. The end product, the output in terms of students' achievements, is often given less attention than the inputs. If outputs are emphasized as the mark of success, then teachers can have wider latitude and still be held accountable for their behavior. When, for example, class plans are stressed, then inputs are central and individual initiative curbed. New administrative outlooks are necessary.

Assumption D: No permanent solutions exist. We have had too much of the feeling that if we followed a particular policy or procedure, our problems would be solved for all time. Different times, different places, different issues, require different policies. Change and adaptability, assessment and appropriateness, are the continuing imperatives. No one-time change will safeguard us forevermore. We constantly have to adapt to new circumstances. As our political climate changes, as our economy moves in new directions, as education becomes the prime route to social mobility in America, as we develop a new poor, we have new demands upon education. Educational systems have to move. All organizations, including educational systems, have to adapt or become anachronistic. There is no necessarily enduring value in any particular strategy or procedure.

The orientation to change runs the danger of falling into novelty and fadism for change's sake. The question is, can we become adaptive and flexible without becoming fadists and novelty hunters, thrill-seekers of the new?

ORGANIZATIONAL CLIMATE

The climate of the school is of great importance. It affects—as well as is a product of—the behavior of students *and* teachers. In consequence, it is paramountly the administrators' responsibility to improve it.

In analyzing the important ingredients of a "positive" school climate, we are caught up in personal biases since our values determine our definition of what is positive. We need a pluralism in our quest of desirable ends. What is the best way depends upon particular circumstances. What is positive in some group or situation may not be positive for others. Nor do we know enough to be definitive about what builds the different types of effective climates. It is important to recognize that there are many different kinds of positive school climates and that there may be diverse roads to each.

It seems to me one of the basic ingredients in a positive school climate is *respect*. Students have to be respected. Teachers have to be respected, particularly by school administrators who frequently implicitly denigrate their staff by such devices as time clocks.

My impression of many programs aimed at low-income youth is that the school personnel not only have meager understanding of these youth, but that they really do not like them. I doubt that you can go very far with a youth whom you do not like. Thus, the attitude of the school towards disadvantaged youth—who are disturbing to the more affluent in part because they are disadvantaged—is essential to effective programs.

Learning and knowledge have to be respected, which is not always true in our schools. We are sometimes more respectful of particular teaching methods than we are of knowledge itself. There are many different kinds of positive school climates, many different ways of achieving this condition. Respect has many different doors.

A second important theme of a positive school climate is authenticity. The faculty and administration have to stand on what they say. Edgar Z. Friedenberg in his *The Vanishing Adolescent* and elsewhere has been trying to show us the inauthenticity in the relationship between schools, school personnel and students. Frequently, school administrators are phonies. Youth recognize that they do not say what they mean. Little is going to work as long as inauthentic relationships prevail. If a school system changes, it has to believe in what it is doing. The changes cannot be for public relations effectiveness alone. There has to be a real commitment, and this includes an authentic commitment to integration.

The third theme of a positive school climate is the fostering of *competence*. The school has to be able to do the job it sets out to do. Youth generally, and low-income youth particularly, do not respect authority figures who are incompetent, who make promises which they cannot achieve, who have goals which have little relationship to the outside world. The school situation has to be built on competence.

The fourth need is for *consistency* and *predictability* in a school. I think many schools do not have predictability. The prison experience is interesting. Prison riots occur when the practiced, predictable rules, the formal and informal procedures, are broken by the warden. In most prisons, the inmates have taken over a good deal of the functioning of the prison. This is known by the warden and it is permitted. It is an easier way to run a prison. In fact, it is difficult to run it any other way. When the warden is forced to change procedures because of a break or the insistence of the board of overseers, he begins to get tough, to put the screws on, to break up the informal groups; the informal loci of power are prevented from operating as they did before. Then a food riot or strike may occur. The predictable modes of behavior have been supplanted and prevented from operating in their usual way.

I do not want to liken schools to prisons, although highly controlled institutions have many similar characteristics. This is reflected in René Clair's great movie, *A Nous La Liberté*, the predecessor of Charlie Chaplin's *Modern Times*, which has a fascinating sequence where the camera moves between a factory's mass production line and a prison, showing the similarity between the pace and control of the prison and the pace and control of the production line.

Predictability and consistency are essential to any positive school climate. I have observed that consistency is perhaps the most important element in the personality or outlook of those who are effective with low-income youth. A wide diversity of personality types—not just the hearty athlete or the "one of the boys" types can do well. I think of a dandified, pedantic, little Frenchman whom few would predict could be effective with tough New York City boys. Yet he was; he showed respect for them even when he forced them to take off their hats; his behavior was always predictable and consistent.

Fifth, the school has to have *purpose* and *direction*. It has to believe in something. It has to have a mission. A school is unlikely to have a positive climate without a mission. If the theme is just that everyone love everyone else and there is no tie beyond that, the love won't last very long. A good deal of the positive impact of programs aimed at low-income youth depends on the Hawthorne effect on school personnel. They believe in what they are doing; they are consulted and involved in the new programs. Morale is high in the pursuit of a common goal.

Finally, I think school programs have to be relevant to low-income youth. They have to see that what the school is doing has some relationship to their own lives.

Important developments are occurring in the United States. We are learning important things. But we are not sufficiently implementing them. We are moving toward a more positive school situation for center-city youth, despite hesitations and obstacles. The greatest lag is in the area of internal school organization.

IMPLEMENTATION

New technology may produce revolutionary changes. When technology has wide impact, it is usually because changes occur in the relationships among those who are involved through the technology. I think this is the crucial point to see. What are the needed new changes in the relationships between the administrators, the teachers and the students? New technology is necessary to work more adequately with low-income youth, but this technology will be inadequate unless facilitating administrative change occurs.

How is the kind of educational revolution that we need going to be produced? Pressure from within the educational establishment and from without are both necessary. I think that we are getting more of the necessary externally important pressure than we are of the internal drive for change. The Negro Revolution and the beginning war on poverty, are focusing attention on schools, asking how well they are doing the job of educating low-income students. Many recent changes have resulted from these pressure thrusts. I expect them to continue.

The recent availability of funds for education of the "culturally deprived" are leading many who have had no interest in disadvantaged youth to begin to manifest a concern so that they can drink at the new financial trough. With the smell of poverty money, many will be running to the youth they have long neglected. My initial response to this phenomenon, I must confess, is a moralistic one: Repugnance at the new-found "mission" that money can now buy, but social responsibility did not. But my more reflective friends have convinced me that if you want change, you have to give people a reward, a material interest, in moving in new directions; altruism cannot be depended on. Poverty money is providing school systems, schools of education and affluent professors, with a stake in doing new things about the poor. Sometimes, the interest in low-income youth comes out of unloving things like developing good public relations, or obtaining money to do other things under the guise of helping the poor, or striving to reduce politically important pressures. But the most important result is that more attention is being given to low-income youth. Nevertheless, these activities have to be policed—held accountable—to see that they actually benefit those to whom we dedicate ourselves in the preambles to our projects.

External pressure is thus leading to increased attention to low-income youth, though not without difficulties. But have teachers done all they could to bring about change? Teacher organizations—both the unions and the professional organizations—have paid inadequate attention to the reorganization and rededication of schools so that they can deal more effectively with low-income pupils. It is important that teachers and their organizations take the responsibility of initiating and demanding action for the improvement of schools, especially those in low-income areas.

Until broader changes are made, teachers' initiative in securing modifications in the schools are of grave importance. One of the frequent complaints of fledgling teachers is that they cannot implement their good ideas because the school authorities resist them. Schools of education are caught in the bind of preparing students for what is desirable practice, which may lead to strain in the actual teaching situation, or to reduce their goals to what is acceptable practice to many school officials. This is a widespread problem in American life, having many different faces.

I am beginning to believe that the encrustations of professionalization and the rigidities of bureaucratic organizations require each of us, as professionals, to be in tension with the organizations in which we work. We have to subvert as well as live with our bureaucracies. Every large organization has a bureaucratic underground, a group resistant to the existing practices of the organization. Much of what we learn about American foreign policy is leaked out by dissident groups within the State Department. Some of us will have to be provocative, raising questions and following policies which are not fully acceptable to the organizations in which we work if we are to fulfill our responsibilities to our students and to our society. We need courageous, creative discontent.

Increasingly, as we live in bureaucracies, we shall have to face the Eichmann question: What is our individual responsibility for what our organization does? To what extent does organizational loyalty supersede personal morality and require us to ignore or protect incompetence and irresponsibility? Should not teachers, singly and in association, publicly and privately, criticize what their schools are doing when youth are victimized?

Obviously, such pressure is insufficient to swing the battle to the improvement of conditions for low-income youth. But it is one of the things that can be done.

I have stressed that respect for students and competence are important elements in successful teaching of low-income youth. Does this imply that teachers must have "mature" personalities or exceptional intellect; that we can only succeed if we have more restricted criteria of admission to teaching, thereby aggravating the teacher shortage? No one, of course, can argue against the desirability of getting more feeling teachers into the system; this may happen as salaries and the status of the profession increase. But this is unlikely in the short-run. Nor will we be getting the intellectual giants who made lycées and gymnasiums the superior schools they have been; the special factors leading learned persons into lower levels of education do not exist in our society. What are our possibilities of getting better teachers in the immediate situation?

Few of us can consistently rise above our surroundings. In a fascinating study of physicians, it has been shown that those with the best training—attendance at elite medical schools—do not do well in poor medical settings. More important than the training of a physician is whether or not he is in a hospital situation which permits and pushes him into the high-level practice of medicine. Similarly, for teachers, the community and organizational setting of a school affect whether or not teachers can have authentic relationships with their students. If a community does not have commitment to low-income youth, few authentic responses can occur. Authenticity occurs not only because of personality and value characteristics of the teachers, but from the situation as well. Some people can triumph over adverse conditions and demonstrate devotion and respect. But for most of us, if the situation indicts authenticity or does not encourage it, then authenticity will be a rarity.

Nonetheless, I think that we can do more than we have to promote teachers' positive feelings about low-income youth.

The emphasis, I have asserted, is that teacher training should lead to the development of each individual's style rather than to the emulation of one grand style of teaching. People have different ways of developing and of expressing their style. Many teachers have to become more aware of how they can more effectively use themselves in the teaching situation. I do not mean that they need psychotherapy, but that they lack adequate mirrors in their training so that they can learn their strengths and weaknesses. They are not aided in discovering useful leads to develop teaching approaches with which they are creative. I think much of this can be learned. And I think that, as Frank Riessman has contended, we can give teachers and prospective teachers experiences and knowledge about low-income youth that will build positive feelings and respect.

Schools of education will have to change. There is much to criticize here, but I think too that there has been terrible scapegoating. I have endured department meetings in the social sciences where almost every time some inkling of criticism of the department appeared, within ten minutes an indictment of the school of education would emerge as the central theme of what had started as self-examination. The education school was causing the problem, no matter what it was.

We have to shed the strait jacket of thought about the process of teaching and the overemphasis on formal credentials, a mark of our uncertainty about what is effective performance. Research has to be conducted in a serious way. Reading studies of school dropouts fills me with oceanic despair; many are criminally incompetent.

The cookbook approach to pedagogy, research and administration prevents teachers and administrators from learning how to think imaginatively about their problems. Underlying much of the teaching in schools of education is an absence of respect for the students and their potential. Lacking, frequently, is a sense of vitality and enthusiasm about teaching itself.

Schools of education—like medical schools—have a tremendous impact on practice. A mission to work with the disadvantaged is needed—and a willingness to forego comforting clichés, to face the anxiety and adventure of discovering how to deal effectively with low-income youth and to build school institutions which attract rather than repel.

CONCLUSION

If we agree that "Loyalty to petrified opinion never yet broke a chain or freed a human soul," then we must beware of the persistent danger of traveling on old roads and triumphing on old fields, lacking the courage to take off from where we are. We hope for great breakthroughs in pedagogy. Perhaps they will soon come; probably even not. In either case, the educational revolution largely depends on the outlook and behavior of the educational establishment.

Part
Two

STATISTICS

INTRODUCTION

High among the sources of awakened concern over the plight of the dropout and the disadvantaged youngster—as high during the late 1950's as the incipient civil rights movement and the frantic review of American education occasioned by the success of Sputnik—were (a) the expansion of automation technology, which threatened to annihilate the market of low-skill jobs; (b) the beginning of a prolonged period of high unemployment, which particularly afflicted young workers; and (c) the prospect of an enormous increase in the number of young people who, during the 1960's, would pass through—and a goodly proportion of them drop out from—the schools. There would, it was thought, be more less-qualified workers applying for the kinds of jobs that were going out of existence.

Most of these problems, if not completely solved, have been dealt with and modified in the intervening course of time. Automation appears to be not so imminently the ogre it threatened to be; the national economy rose from its doldrums, providing nearly full employment for young and old workers alike (though unemployment is still twice as high among young workers); and various programs of the Great Society have been mobilized to alleviate the needs of the poor and the disadvantaged. But however much these problem areas have been redefined, they have stimulated large amounts of important research into the identity and status of the poor and the disadvantaged and into the reality of the occupational world they must confront.

If dropping out of school is most frequent and most drastic in its consequences among the children of the poor, and if as

Mollie Orshansky concludes, it is poverty itself more than any other factor which breeds poverty, then there can well be serious question (which Bruno Bettelheim and others raise, in other contexts) as to how much the schools and education can realistically be expected to accomplish. Thomas E. Swanstrom's study indicates the great difficulty dropouts, in comparison with graduates, are likely to experience in the job market, but leaves open the question of whether the diploma actually makes the crucial difference. Herbert Bienstock describes the actuality of the job market which is providing diminishing place for the uneducated. Finally, Eli Ginzberg, in synthesizing most of the considerations presented in the previous papers, discusses their specific implications for and challenges to our educational resources.

❀❀❀❀❀❀❀❀❀❀❀❀❀❀❀❀❀❀❀❀❀❀❀❀❀❀❀❀❀

CHILDREN OF THE POOR

❀❀❀❀❀❀❀❀❀❀❀❀❀❀❀❀❀❀❀❀❀❀❀❀❀❀❀❀❀

MOLLIE ORSHANSKY

We live in a time of rapid change. The wonders of science and technology applied to a generous endowment of natural resources have wrought a way of life our grandfathers never knew. Creature comforts once the hallmark of luxury have descended to the realm of the commonplace, and the marvels of modern industry find their way into the home of the American worker as well as that of his boss. Yet there is an underlying disquietude reflected in our current social literature, an uncomfortable realization that an expanding economy has not brought gains to all in equal measure. It is reflected in the preoccupation with counting the poor—do they number 30 million, 40 million, or 50 million? Is it still, as in the 1930's, one-third of a nation that is ill-fed, ill-clothed, and ill-housed, or is it now only a fourth or fifth? Shall one point with pride or view with alarm?

There is, of course, no single, simple, answer. The mere fact of income inequality alone need not disturb us, but how to distinguish between the absolute deprivation of poverty and mere lower-than-average income status is still a matter of controversy if not a matter of taste. As the general level of living moves upward and expands beyond necessities, the standards of what constitutes an irreducible minimum also change. Furthermore, with the great revolution in expectations and our historic heritage of equal opportunity as a goal, there is concern that the boons of prosperity are withheld from some.

It would be one thing if poverty hit at random, and no one group were singled out. It is another thing to realize that some seem destined to poverty almost from birth—by their color or by the economic status or occupation of their parents. It has become a truism that, in good times and in bad, certain groups lag behind in the long-term upswing of our economy. Prominent among these are the aged, the families headed by a woman, and minority groups—particularly the Negro.

Year after year the same kinds of people continually appear at the bottom of the income pyramid. In 1961, for example, of the families in the lowest income group (the lowest 20 percent) almost a third were aged families, a fourth were broken families (usually headed by a woman) and a fifth were non-white—proportions identical with those in 1951.

When yet another measure is used, the perennial plight of the disadvantaged is seen as even more severe. It has always been true in our society that economic well-being rests on earning power. Public support programs are generally for those unable to work or deprived of the earnings of the relative on whom they could expect to rely. But opportunities for work are no longer what they were. In yesterday's world, jobs paid better if one was trained, but even an untrained worker could find a place and expect that in time his earnings would improve along with his skill. The highly educated man did better, but his numbers were few and even for him the starting salary was often low.

Today in large measure an automated economy demands an increasingly productive and skilled labor force. Jobs ask more and pay more from the outset, and the unskilled worker cannot hope to better himself much: He will remain, as he started, in a low-paid job, if indeed he has a job at all. As a result, the composition of the group we call our poor is changing too. Once it included not only those able to earn little or nothing but a fair number who would eventually improve their lot. As the higher education and the increased skills called for in many modern-day jobs upgrade our labor force more and more, the ranks of the poor seem to be reserved for those families with heads not able or not permitted to qualify for the better-paying jobs—the retired, the women, and the nonwhites.

More and more, such families will see themselves and their counterparts comprising the dwindling number with low dollar income while the general average climbs farther out of their reach. This segregation of the pocketbook can be illustrated by comparing families having less than $3,000 today and those of a decade ago, bearing in mind that this amount now is about half the average for all families but in 1951 represented four-fifths of average income. Only 1 out of every 5 families now has income this low, compared with 1 in every 3 then. Yet today more of these families are headed by a nonwhite or an aged person or by a woman, as the following figures show.

| | Families with less than $3,000 | | | |
| Type of head | Number (in millions) | | Percent | |
	1961	1951	1961	1951
Total	9.9	14.5	100	100
Aged head	3.3	3.3	33	23
Female head	2.3	2.5	23	17
Nonwhite head	2.1	2.5	21	17

Some families, of course, bear more than one of these stigmas. The low incomes of the aged are receiving much attention in existing and proposed programs. The broken families and nonwhite poor harbor a disadvantaged group from the other end of the age spectrum—children under age 18. By almost any standard of adequacy the number of children underprivileged by too low income is as large as or larger than the total aged population. And many of the children are not subject to help from existing programs to combat poverty.

Our population today includes about 66 million children

under age 18, distributed among some 27.5 million families. In 1961 the median income for these families ranged from $5,905 for those with one child to $4,745 among the million or so with six or more children.[1]

TABLE 1 / MEDIAN MONEY INCOME IN 1961 OF FAMILIES WITH OWN CHILDREN UNDER AGE 18 AND FAMILIES WITH RELATED CHILDREN UNDER AGE 18

| | Families with 1 or more— | | | |
| Number of children | Own children* | | Related children* | |
	Number (in thousands)	Median income	Number (in thousands)	Median income
Families, total ...	26,224	$6,010	27,600	$5,950
1 child	8,321	6,000	8,896	5,905
2 children	8,010	6,235	8,353	6,185
3 children	5,049	6,260	5,227	6,235
4 children	2,679	5,835	2,775	5,760
5 children	1,072	5,195	1,149	5,240
6 or more	1,093	4,855	1,200	4,745
Children, total ...	62,655	..	65,805	..

* Own children under age 18 include never-married sons, daughters, stepchildren, or adopted children of the family head; related children include these and any other never-married family members under age 18 and related to the head by blood, marriage, or adoption.

SOURCE: Data for families with own children derived from tabulations from the *Current Population Survey* (March 1962), made by the Bureau of the Census for the Social Security Administration; for families with related children, from *Current Population Reports: Consumer Income,* P-60, No. 39 (February 1963). The figures in this and the following tables are estimated from a sample survey and therefore are subject to sampling variability. For discussion of nature and extent of variability, see the publication cited.

Some of these families, and significantly more of the larger ones, live on farms; their housing and a considerable portion of their food are thus obtained as part of an ongoing business operation and need not be met out of net money income. Farm families, however, like those in cities, purchase much of their family living. In both places the wherewithal to do so decreases

---

[1] Bureau of the Census, *Current Population Reports,* Series P-60, No. 39 (February 1963).

rather than increases with additional family members to support.

The Bureau of the Census data on income by number of children customarily refer to all children who are related to the family head—that is, all "related" children under age 18, regardless of their relationship to the head. Much of the discussion in this article centers on "own" children only—that is, never-married sons, daughters, adopted children, or stepchildren of the family head. Table 1 compares the incomes of the families of the "own" children with those of all families with "related" children. For most purposes, the two sets of figures are interchangeable.

Today's average incomes represent one more step in the continuing uptrend in real income of the American population since the end of World War II. But even in the midst of plenty many children are growing up in families with incomes too low to provide for them properly. The estimated number of such families can be varied almost at will, but if there is no consensus on the standard, there can be no doubt that, whatever the definition of income inadequacy, a large number of families will be below it. We can also predict with high degree of certainty what kinds of families they will be. Current Census data suggest, for example, that low-income status is unduly concentrated among the relatively small number of families with a mother and children but no father in the home. These families are seldom found on farms where they would benefit from home-produced food and farm-furnished housing (tables 2 and 3).

The children in nonwhite families are also overrepresented in the roster of the poor, and, as would be expected, children in a family whose head is not employed the year round must get along on far lower incomes than children in other families.

THE CHILD POPULATION

In 1962, if the same relationship held as at the time of the Decennial Census 2 years earlier, 87 percent of the 66 million children under age 18 were living with both their parents, about 10 percent with only one parent, usually the mother, and the remaining few with other relatives, in institutions, or in foster homes. Nonwhite children were much less likely to have the benefit—both economic and otherwise—of a normal parental

Total money income	Families with specified number of own children						
	Any	1	2	3	4	5	6 or more
	All families						
Total number (in thousands)	.23,748	7,313	7,362	4,637	2,478	975	983
Percent	100.0	100.0	100.0	100.0	100.0	100.0	100.0
Under $1,000 . . .	2.5	2.5	2.1	2.4	2.5	4.6	5.4
$1,000-$1,999 . . .	3.5	3.5	2.7	2.8	3.8	5.8	8.4
$2,000-$2,999 . . .	6.1	6.7	4.9	5.0	6.6	9.7	10.8
$3,000-$3,999 . . .	8.5	8.5	8.1	7.7	10.1	9.8	10.3
$4,000-$4,999 . . .	11.1	10.7	11.1	10.9	10.9	13.5	12.1
$5,000-$5,999 . . .	14.4	13.4	14.7	14.5	15.2	14.5	17.4
$6,000-$6,999 . . .	12.3	11.3	13.5	12.7	11.5	12.3	10.0
$7,000-$7,999 . . .	11.2	11.2	10.8	12.0	13.8	6.2	8.0
$8,000-$9,999 . . .	13.5	14.1	15.0	12.5	11.9	11.2	8.0
$10,000 and over	17.0	18.2	16.9	19.4	13.6	12.5	9.5
Median income . .	$6,315	$6,415	$6,475	$6,530	$6,080	$5,455	$5,170
Families with head year-round full-time worker:							
Percent of total	75.5	73.9	77.6	77.3	75.3	69.2	70.6
Median income	$6,890	$7,115	$6,925	$6,985	$6,785	$6,035	$5,620
	Rural-farm families						
Total number (in thousands)	1,795	479	482	329	201	129	175
Percent	100.0	100.0	100.0	100.0	100.0	100.0	100.0
Under $1,000 . . .	13.4	12.6	13.6	11.4	11.7	17.6	17.4
$1,000-$1,999 . . .	13.1	13.1	10.6	11.5	20.0	13.9	15.9
$2,000-$2,999 . . .	15.1	18.3	12.8	14.5	13.7	15.8	15.2
$3,000-$3,999 . . .	14.4	16.0	13.6	12.2	18.6	9.3	15.9
$4,000-$4,999 . . .	10.0	7.1	12.6	12.2	7.5	6.5	12.9
$5,000-$5,999 . . .	11.4	10.7	12.5	9.5	9.0	20.4	9.1
$6,000-$6,999 . . .	6.8	6.8	7.2	9.2	4.8	5.6	3.8
$7,000-$7,999 . . .	5.2	5.8	5.6	6.9	2.1	2.8	4.5
$8,000-$9,999 . . .	4.3	3.1	6.1	5.0	6.9	2.8	. .
$10,000 and over	6.2	6.5	5.3	7.6	5.5	6.5	5.3
Median income . .	$3,550	$3,395	$3,940	$4,050	$3,300	$3,285	$3,110

SOURCE: Tabulations from the *Current Population Survey* (March 1962), made by the Bureau of the Census for the Social Security Administration.

TABLE 3 / INCOME IN 1961 OF ALL FAMILIES WITH FEMALE
HEAD WITH OWN CHILDREN UNDER AGE 18

Total money income	Families with specified number of own children				
	Any	1	2	3	4 or more
Total number (in thousands) ..	2,225	871	577	386	391
Percent	100.0	100.0	100.0	100.0	100.0
Under $1,000	22.2	18.7	23.1	22.7	28.4
$1,000-$1,999	21.7	20.7	21.1	22.1	24.8
$2,000-$2,999	18.1	19.0	15.3	20.2	17.7
$3,000-$3,999	12.3	11.0	10.2	17.3	13.7
$4,000-$4,999	10.6	11.9	11.1	9.0	8.3
$5,000-$5,999	5.5	7.1	7.0	1.8	3.2
$6,000-$6,999	3.2	3.2	5.1	1.8	1.8
$7,000-$7,999	2.3	2.8	1.9	2.2	1.8
$8,000-$9,999	1.9	1.8	3.2	1.4	.4
$10,000 and over ...	2.2	3.7	1.9	1.4	..
Median income	$2,320	$2,535	$2,385	$2,255	$1,860
Families with head year-round full-time worker:					
Percent of total ...	25.8	33.7	25.8	18.7	14.3
Median income ...	$3,875	$3,970	$4,385	(°)	(°)

° Median not shown where base is less than 100,000.

SOURCE: Tabulations from the *Current Population Survey* (March 1962), made by the Bureau of the Census for the Social Security Administration.

home, with 1 in every 3 living with only one parent, in contrast to only 1 in 10 of the white children. Nonwhite women are more than three times as likely to have their marriages disrupted as white women, and more often by separation than by divorce.[2]

The divorced or widowed mother is more likely to have formal financial support arrangements for herself and the children than the mother in a family that breaks up for other reasons. In

---

[2] Paul C. Glick, *Marriage Patterns by Size of Place* (presented at the annual meeting of the Population Association of America, May 1962).

TABLE 4 / INCOME IN 1961 OF HUSBAND-WIFE FAMILIES WITH OWN CHILDREN UNDER AGE 18, BY RACE

Total money income	Families with specified number of own children				
	Any	1	2	3	4 or more
	White families				
Total number (in thousands) ..	21,815	6,792	6,925	4,310	3,788
Percent	100.0	100.0	100.0	100.0	100.0
Under $1,000	2.1	2.1	1.7	2.2	2.7
$1,000-$1,999	2.7	3.0	2.3	2.2	3.8
$2,000-$2,999	5.0	6.0	4.0	4.0	6.0
$3,000-$3,999	7.9	7.9	8.0	6.7	9.2
$4,000-$4,999	10.9	10.6	11.2	10.6	11.2
$5,000-$5,999	14.8	13.9	14.8	15.1	16.4
$6,000-$6,999	12.9	11.7	13.9	13.2	12.6
$7,000-$7,999	11.6	11.4	11.2	12.4	11.7
$8,000-$9,999	14.1	14.5	15.3	13.2	12.3
$10,000 and over ...	17.9	18.9	17.5	20.3	14.0
Median income	$6,510	$6,555	$6,575	$6,695	$6,055
Families with head year-round full-time worker:					
Percent of total ...	77.1	75.1	78.7	78.5	76.3
Median income ...	$7,000	$7,190	$6,995	$7,100	$6,600
	Nonwhite families				
Total number (in thousands) ..	1,933	521	437	327	648
Percent	100.0	100.0	100.0	100.0	100.0
Under $1,000	6.8	7.0	6.6	4.4	8.3
$1,000-$1,999	11.2	9.9	9.6	10.4	13.8
$2,000-$2,999	18.4	15.9	17.7	17.8	21.2
$3,000-$3,999	15.1	15.0	11.4	21.1	14.8
$4,000-$4,999	13.2	12.9	8.4	16.6	15.1
$5,000-$5,999	9.9	7.5	14.3	5.6	10.9
$6,000-$6,999	5.9	5.4	8.1	6.7	4.3
$7,000-$7,999	6.2	8.0	4.8	6.3	5.6
$8,000-$9,999	6.4	9.1	10.7	3.2	2.9
$10,000 and over ...	6.9	9.4	8.7	7.9	3.3
Median income	$3,895	$4,140	$4,560	$3,670	$3,540

TABLE 4 / (*Cont.*)

Total money income	Families with specified number of own children				
	Any	1	2	3	4 or more
Families with head year-round full-time worker:					
Percent of total ...	58.4	58.0	60.7	62.7	54.9
Median income ...	$4,610	$5,200	$5,485	$4,250	$4,195

SOURCE: Tabulations from the *Current Population Survey* (March 1962), made by the Bureau of the Census for the Social Security Administration.

TABLE 5 / INCOME IN 1961 OF FAMILIES WITH FEMALE HEAD WITH OWN CHILDREN UNDER AGE 18, BY RACE

Total money income	Families with specified number of own children				
	Any	1	2	3	4 or more
	White families				
Total number (in thousands) ..	1,654	704	443	282	225
Percent	100.0	100.0	100.0	100.0	100.0
Under $1,000	22.2	16.1	22.9	23.5	39.1
$1,000-$1,999	16.3	16.7	17.1	14.9	14.9
$2,000-$2,999	17.5	19.6	13.3	21.5	14.3
$3,000-$3,999	12.8	11.8	12.1	17.4	11.8
$4,000-$4,999	14.3	14.5	13.9	11.8	9.9
$5,000-$5,999	7.1	8.7	8.6	2.6	4.3
$6,000-$6,999	3.5	3.5	5.1	2.6	1.9
$7,000-$7,999	2.9	3.5	2.5	1.5	3.1
$8,000-$9,999	2.2	2.3	2.9	2.1	.6
$10,000 and over ...	2.3	3.5	1.6	2.1	..
Median income	$2,675	$2,875	$2,815	$2,580	$1,750
Families with head year-round full-time worker:					
Percent of total ...	27.5	35.4	26.9	20.1	12.4
Median income ...	$4,285	$4,310	$4,590	(*)	(*)

TABLE 5 / (*Cont.*)

Total money income	Families with specified number of own children				
	Any	1	2	3	4 or more
	Nonwhite families				
Total number (in thousands) ..	571	167	134	104	166
Percent	100.0	100.0	100.0	100.0	100.0
Under $1,000	22.2	28.7	23.5	22.2	13.8
$1,000-$1,999	37.1	36.0	34.7	39.5	38.8
$2,000-$2,999	19.5	17.6	21.4	17.3	21.6
$3,000-$3,999	11.4	8.0	5.1	17.2	16.3
$4,000-$4,999	3.0	2.2	2.0	1.2	6.0
$5,000-$5,999	.9	.7	1.0	..	1.7
$6,000-$6,999	2.3	2.2	5.1	..	1.7
$7,000-$7,999	.5	..	..	2.5	..
$8,000-$9,999	.9	..	4.1	..	..
$10,000 and over ...	2.1	4.4	3.1	..	..
Median income	$1,665	$1,465	$1,730	$1,470	$1,920
Families with head year-round full-time worker:					
Percent of total ...	22.1	27.6	..	..	17.9
Median income° .	$2,338	..	..	.:	..

° Median not shown where base is less than 100,000.

Source: Tabulations from the *Current Population Survey* (March 1962), by the Bureau of the Census for the Social Security Administration.

the 1960 Census, three-fifths of the white mothers with children under age 18 and no father in the home were divorced or widowed; only 2 percent said they had never been married. By contrast, only one-third of the nonwhite mothers without a husband claimed that they were divorced or widowed, and 1 in 8 said they were never married to the father of their children.

These figures include the large number of mother-child groups counted in the Census as subfamilies (rather than families) because they lived in the home of a related family rather than in their own household. More than 1 in 5 of all mother-child units in 1960 lived as a subfamily.[3]

A rise in the marriage disruption rate could signify a breakdown in family stability or an increase in the emancipation of women. In any case it is likely to be accompanied by lower family income. Despite the resulting economic disadvantage, among both white and nonwhite families there is a growing number headed only by a mother. By 1960 the total was 7½ percent of all families with own children rather than the 6 percent of ten years earlier. By March 1962 the mother-child families represented 8½ percent of all families with own children.

Judged by the 1960 Census, young mothers who are themselves family heads may have more children than young women living with a husband. Nearly one-third of all nonwhite women under age 35 who were family heads had four or more children, compared with a fourth of the wives of men under age 35. For white women in this age group, 1 in 7 of the family heads had at least four children but only 1 in 9 of the women married to a family head under age 35.[4] Until additional information is available, one can only speculate on the possible relationship between too many children, too little family income, and marriage disruption. Among broken families as among two-parent families, the larger ones are more often found among those with lower incomes.

INCOME OF FAMILIES WITH CHILDREN

On the average, in 1962 the mother raising her children alone had the same number to look after as the mother sharing family responsibility with a husband, although she usually had about 40 percent as much income to do it on. The nonwhite family, though larger, had lower income than the white, as the figures on page 71 (from tables 4 and 5) show:

---

[3] *U. S. Census of Population: 1960, Final Report,* PC(1)-1D, table 185.

[4] In a paper entitled "Characteristics of Other Families," given at the Population Association of America meeting in April 1963, John C. Beresford and Alice Rivlin reported a cumulative fertility rate one-fourth greater among women who were mothers in 1960 but no longer living with a husband than among those still living with a husband.

Family status	Median income, 1961	Children per family
White:		
Husband-wife	$6,510	2.4
Mother only	2,675	2.1
Nonwhite:		
Husband-wife	3,895	3.0
Mother only	1,665	2.8

Only 1 in 13 of the husband-wife families with children, and even fewer of the broken families (3 percent) had the advantage, in terms of income, of living on a farm. The 2.2 million nonfarm families composed of a mother and her children under age 18 included 5 million "own" children in 1961. Half of these units had less than $2,340 to live on for the year. Four out of every 10 had less than $2,000. What is even more significant is the consistent drop in income as the number of children increased:

Number of own children	Mother-child families	Husband-wife families
1	$2,550	$6,625
2	2,390	6,615
3	2,345	6,680
4	} 1,860	6,305
5		5,740
6+		5,515

Families headed by a woman include on the average one more person in addition to the mother and her own children (0.8 adult and 0.2 child), and it is likely that the relatively few units with incomes of $5,000 or more include other adults who contribute their income to swell the family exchequer. By contrast, husband-wife families include on the average only 0.04 related children in addition to their own, and only 0.2 additional adults.[5]

---

[5] Unpublished tabulations purchased by the Social Security Administration from the Bureau of the Census show that 3 in every 10 mother-child families in 1956 had relatives in the home, ranging from 32 percent

There is no information on the income of the more than one-half million mother-child units living as a subfamily in a household headed by a relative. Judged by the data for 1956, these family units have even less money of their own than the mother-child groups who do not share a relative's home. At that time the subfamilies of mothers and children reported median income of $995 for the year, less than three-fifths the median ($1,770) for the other mother-child groups. The subfamilies average only one-half child less per unit, hardly enough to make up for the difference in income. In some cases, to be sure, the subfamily may share in the income of the family with whom it makes its home, and in others it is the subfamily income that helps out the family.

The difference in income between husband-wife families with children and similar subfamilies is also great (medians for 1956 of $5,025 and $3,650, respectively), but the number of such subfamilies is small. The chances are 16 times as high for a mother-child unit as for a unit including a mother and father to live as a subfamily in the home of relatives; this fact in itself denotes the disadvantages faced by a mother raising her children alone.[6]

Of the nearly 1 million subfamilies with own children in 1960, more than half were headed by a mother. All told, 1.7 percent of all family groups consisting of both parents and their children under age 18 were subfamilies, compared with 27.2 percent of the units consisting of a mother and her children under age 18.

Estimated Incidence of Poverty

A crude criterion of income adequacy—that the low-cost food plan priced by the Department of Agriculture in January 1962 represents no more than one-third of total income—consigns about 71 percent of the mother-child families to low-income status. Even the use of the Department's economy plan, estimated to cost about 20 percent less than the low-cost plan, leaves at 61 percent the proportion of the mother-child families

---

when there was only one child to 21 percent when there were five or more children. Among families with both father and mother present, only 2 in every 10 included relatives.

[6] *U. S. Census of Population: 1960, Final Report,* PC(1)-1D, table 185.

TABLE 6 / NUMBER OF FAMILIES WITH OWN CHILDREN UNDER AGE 18 IN LOW-INCOME STATUS AND NUMBER OF CHILDREN IN THESE FAMILIES, BY POVERTY STATUS°

[In thousands]

Residence and presence of parents	Families with own children°			Own children in families †		
	Total	Poor by low-cost diet	Poor by economy diet	Total	Poor by low-cost diet	Poor by economy diet
Total number ..	26,227	6,936	4,805	62,655	21,996	15,859
Mother and father ..	23,748	5,256	3,375	57,109	17,481	11,725
Mother only	2,225	1,578	1,355	5,108	4,333	4,012
Father only	254	102	75	438	182	122
Nonfarm, number	24,349	6,237	4,239	57,425	19,634	13,932
Mother and father ..	21,953	4,610	2,854	52,072	15,202	9,866
Mother only	2,163	1,536	1,320	4,951	4,268	3,962
Father only	233	91	65	402	164	104
Farm, number ...	1,878	699	566	5,230	2,362	1,927

° Families designated poor if total money income in 1961 was less than three times the cost of an adequate diet in terms of (1) a low-cost food plan and (2) an economy plan. For the low-cost criterion, cost of an adequate diet was estimated for each family size on the basis of food quantities for adults and children at January 1962 prices as suggested by the Department of Agriculture for obtaining an adequate diet at low cost. A dollar total of four-fifths of this low-cost estimate was taken as the cost of the more restricted but still adequate diet suggested in the economy plan to estimate the number of families for whom the purchase of even the less expensive economy diet would require over one-third of money income.

For farm families, who raise some of their own food, the purchased portion of an adequate diet was assumed to be 60 percent of that of a nonfarm family of similar composition. See Department of Agriculture, Agricultural Research Service, *Family Food Plans, and Food Costs,* Home Economics Research Report No. 20 (November 1962), and Household Food Consumption Service, *Food Consumption and Dietary Levels of Households in the U.S.,* Spring 1955, ARS 62-6 (August 1957).

† Sons, daughters, stepchildren or adopted children of the family head only; excludes children otherwise related to family head and all children living in subfamilies.

SOURCE: Estimates derived from special tabulations of the *Current Population Survey* (March 1962), made by the Bureau of the Census for the Social Security Administration, and from food plans and food costs published by the Agricultural Research Service of the Department of Agriculture.

who must devote to food more than $1 out of $3 to get a nutritious diet.

The proportion of income that must be used for food has long been regarded as an indicator of the standard of living. Commonly, high-income families spend more dollars for their food than low-income families but nevertheless use up a smaller share of total income in doing so; they thus have relatively more money free for other things. Recent studies of food consumed by families in the United States showed that, on an average, the expenditures for food came to one-third of family money income (after taxes) for both farm and nonfarm families. Poorer families generally devoted more than one-third of income to food, and those better off used less of their income in this way.[7]

The food plans of the Department of Agriculture suggest quantities and types of food that meet desirable nutritional goals and at the same time conform to the common food preferences of American families. Their low-cost food plan has long been used as a guide for families who must watch food expenses because of low income or who choose to do so for other reasons. The economy plan at even lower cost, recently issued by the Department, still will provide adequate nutrition. Though not every family spending as much as these plans will automatically choose the foods that make up an adequate diet, a family spending less is not likely to end up with food meeting recommended nutritional goals. The economy and low-cost food plans are by no means subsistence diets, but they do assume that the housewife will be a careful shopper, a skillful cook, and a good manager who will prepare all the family's meals at home. There is no additional allowance for snacks or the higher cost of meals away from home or meals served to guests. Nor is there extra allowance for the ice-cream vendor or the soda pop so often a part of our children's daily diet. According to recent surveys, the average family, unless restricted by lack of income, is likely to spend considerably more than the low-cost plan or the economy plan suggests.

Having a father in the home by no means guarantees income adequacy. Among nonfarm husband-wife families the proportion bringing up their children on income too low to permit

---

[7] The Census distributions relate to income before rather than after taxes. This timing should not affect the relationship for low-income families, many of whom are not subject to tax.

adequate living ranges from 13 percent to 21 percent—3-5 million families in all. The exact number depends on whether one chooses the low-cost or the economy food plan as the frame of reference.

There are few farm families composed of a mother and her children under age 18. But of the 1¾ million farm families in which young children live with both parents, a food-income relationship similar to that for the nonfarm families[8] designates 29-36 percent as being in low-income status. In sum, for all families with one or more own children under age 18, irrespective of where they lived, it is estimated that at least 4¾ million, and perhaps as many as 7 million—18-26 percent—had incomes so low in 1961 that to buy the food needed for an inexpensive but adequate diet might well mean doing without other necessities (table 6).

Because larger families tend to have incomes less nearly adequate for their needs than other families, the proportion of children in poverty status is even higher than the proportion of families. It ranges from 25 percent to 35 percent, depending on whether one uses the economy diet or the low-cost food plan as the criterion. As of March 1962, if allowance is made not only for own children but for related children, most of whom are in subfamilies,[9] it is found that 17-23 million children are subject to the hazards of insufficient family funds. Even with the minimum estimate of 17 million, there would be 1 poor child under age 18 for nearly every person aged 65 or older.

The criteria used for classification are admittedly crude. Some persons will deem them too generous, others too stringent. Other criteria could be applied with much the same result. The income cut-off point at which no Federal income tax is required, for example, yielded an estimate for 1959 of 16 million children in low-income status, or 1 in every 4.[10] Recent

---

[8] The 1955 Department of Agriculture Food Consumption Survey found that, in terms of what it would cost to buy, 40 percent of the food used by farm families came from the home farm or garden. The purchased food, like that of the nonfarm families, averaged one-third of money income.

[9] As a working approximation, in the absence of current income data, the same proportion of children in subfamilies have been assumed in poverty status as the proportion of own children in families. The total number of children in subfamilies was estimated at 1.8 million, of whom 895,000 were living with the mother only, 725,000 with both parents, and close to 125,000 with the father only.

[10] Lenore A. Epstein, "Some Effects of Low Income on Children and Their Families," *Social Security Bulletin* (February 1961).

estimates of the number of persons of all ages with inadequate income have varied from 1 in every 5 to nearly 1 in 3.

Because of the diversity of conditions in this large country, and in acknowledgment of the differences in needs even among families similar in composition, one usually must select a procedure to maximize either specificity or validity. The method chosen may fail to do either; it will almost never do both. Thus one may elect to be so conservative that any family identified as poor will be unquestioningly acknowledged as such but others almost as bad off will not be counted. Or one can set such standards that no one truly poor will be missed in the screening process, but a number of others not truly in low-income status will be caught in the sieve as well. In the present instance the two estimates may well typify the two extremes, ranging from those undeniably in poverty status to those who risk deprivation because income is uncomfortably low.

By way of suggesting the level of living implied by the present approximation, the income required for a husband, wife, and two children not on a farm would be $3,165 by the more conservative measure, or $3,955 by the more liberal. The mother-and-two-child family, with allowance for the additional relative assumed to be living with the family, would require $2,945 or $3,680.

Some Factors Associated with Low Incomes

The 2¼ million families composed of a mother and her children today represent only one-twelfth of all families with children, yet they make up more than a fourth of all families classified as poor. Together with the 510,000 mothers who are currently living with their children as a subfamily in the home of a relative and who are even poorer, they are raising more than 6 million children. More than a fourth of these families are nonwhite—a reflection of the fact already cited that nonwhite children are more likely than white children to be brought up without a father. Of the families of children with both parents present, only 1 in every 12 is nonwhite.

When the statistics for white and nonwhite families are taken separately, they show, as expected, that the nonwhite families fare worse. Even the white mother raising her children without a father in the home usually does so, however, on a limited income. The median income was $2,675 for the white families and $1,665 for the nonwhite, but the nonwhite mothers had, on the average, nearly three children each and the white mothers slightly more than two.

Nonwhite families in general, despite their smaller incomes, are considerably larger. Three out of every 5 mother-child families with six or more children are nonwhite, but only 1 out of 5 among those with one child. A fourth of the husband-wife families with six or more children are nonwhite, in contrast to 7 percent of those with a single child.

The figures suggest, for both white and nonwhite families, that it is the poor who have more children—not that the family is poor because it has children.

TABLE 7 / INCOME IN 1961 OF FAMILIES WITH OWN CHILDREN UNDER AGE 18, BY RACE AND WORK STATUS OF FAMILY HEAD

| Total money income | Husband-wife families | | | | Families with female head | | | |
| | White | | Nonwhite | | White | | Nonwhite | |
	Head year-round full-time worker	Other	Head year-round full-time worker	Other	Head year-round full-time worker	Other	Head year-round full-time worker	Other
Total number of families (in thousands)	16,819	4,996	1,129	804	455	1,199	126	445
Number of own children per family	2.4	2.4	2.9	3.0	1.7	2.3	2.3	3.0
Percent	100.0	100.0	100.0	100.0	100.0	100.0	100.0	100.0
Under $1,000 ...	1.4	4.7	4.6	10.9	.7	29.2	6.7	26.4
$1,000-$1,999 ..	1.5	7.1	6.8	17.9	5.3	21.3	30.3	37.6
$2,000-$2,999 ..	2.9	11.1	12.8	24.4	17.0	17.4	23.6	18.6
$3,000-$3,999 ..	5.9	12.9	15.5	15.1	21.7	10.7	20.2	9.6
$4,000-$4,999 ..	9.3	14.6	15.0	10.8	20.0	9.7	2.2	3.4
$5,000-$5,999 ..	15.1	14.2	12.0	7.2	12.3	4.7	1.1	.9
$6,000-$6,999 ..	13.9	10.5	8.1	3.2	8.3	1.8	4.5	1.9
$7,000 and over .	50.0	24.8	25.3	10.6	14.7	5.2	11.2	1.6
Median income .	$7,005	$4,975	$4,610	$2,850	$4,285	$1,980	$2,340	$1,540

SOURCE: Derived from tabulations of *Current Population Survey* (March 1962), by the Bureau of the Census for the Social Security Administration.

Despite recent advances in school enrollment, in 1960 the mothers in broken families generally reported little education. Nonwhite mothers had considerably less; more than one-third had not finished the eighth grade, twice the proportion among the white mothers.

Finally, the nonwhite mother is somewhat less likely to work year round and full time, and when she does she earns much less than the white mother who works all year. The difficulty a mother has in raising children alone if she cannot hold down a regular full-time job is poignantly suggested by the figures in table 7. Women's earnings generally average less than men's, and those who must adapt their work schedule to the demands of child care find income markedly reduced. Two-fifths of the white mothers who did not work year round in 1961 and one-half of the nonwhite mothers had weekly incomes of less than $30.00 in 1961. As though to compound this handicap, the mothers without a full-time job were likely to have larger families to care for.

INCOME-SUPPORT PROGRAMS

Some of the mother-child families may be receiving aid from public programs, but those who must depend on them exclusively are likely to find themselves in low-income status. The public programs specifically designed to aid families that can no longer count on a father's earnings are old-age, survivors, and disability insurance and aid to families with dependent children. (A number of mothers and children also receive payments under Veterans Administration programs.)

The old-age, survivors, and disability insurance program cares for children with father dead or permanently disabled. It pays benefits without a means test, in amounts related to the father's previous earnings. Currently 2½ million children and their mothers are receiving payments under this program. In December 1961, benefits went to about 55 percent of all family groups consisting of a widowed mother and children and to 70 percent of all paternal orphans under age 18. An additional 80,000 widowed mothers could have been receiving benefits were it not for their earnings. The children of a deceased worker continue to receive their benefits even if their mother, through remarriage or because of her own earning capacity, no longer needs her benefit.

The amounts paid are not large, but they are, on the average, substantially better than those payable under public assistance in many States. A widowed mother and two or more children currently receive family benefits that average between $180 and $190 a month. Survivor families of three or more children, when the mother is not herself drawing benefits, receive an average of $160; the average is $125 when there are only two children. These amounts would hardly provide gracious living if they were the sole source of income.

With 9 out of 10 workers now covered by the Federal insurance program, the chances are almost that high that, when a father dies today (or becomes disabled), his child will be able to count on some regular income until he reaches age 18. On the other hand, for children bereft of support because the father and mother separate, divorce, or were never married—a much more common family crisis—the possibility of support under a public program is much more limited.

The program of aid to families with dependent children, which is the most applicable to this group, currently makes payments on behalf of children in nearly a million families. Three out of every 4 of these families have no father in the home. At the end of 1961, payments were going to some 625,-000 families with no father in the home—less than half the total estimated to be in need, and possibly not more than 4 in 10. To the extent that eligibility for participation in surplus-food-distribution or food-stamp programs is related to eligibility for public assistance, many of the needy mother-child families who receive no assistance may be barred from these also.

A recent University of Michigan study, with a more complex definition of poverty, arrived at a similar estimate.[11] The authors calculated that public assistance went to less than a fourth of all families defined as poor during 1959, and to 38 percent of those poor families composed of one parent and young children.

It may be worth noting that, although only 625,000 mother-child families were receiving aid to families with dependent children at the end of 1961, there were then about 900,000 mother-child families in which the mother did not work full time throughout the year and family income totaled less than $2,000 (table 7).

---

[11] James N. Morgan and others, *Income and Welfare in the United States* (New York: McGraw-Hill Book Co., Inc., 1962), p. 216.

With the low standards for aid to families with dependent children prevailing in many States, dependence on that program for support is in itself likely to put the recipient family in low-income status. Fifty percent of all payments of aid to families with dependent children go to family units of four or more, but only 29 percent of all the recipient families in the country draw $150 or more a month. Many States have limits on the maximum payment under aid to families with dependent children, and nine States will pay no more than $155 a month regardless of need. The average payment per family as reported in a study late in 1961 was only $112.[12]

Admittedly, some families have income from other sources besides aid to families with dependent children—income usually taken into account in figuring the size of their monthly assistance payment. The 1961 study indicates that the assistance payments represent four-fifths of the aggregate income of all recipient families. About every other family on the assistance rolls (45 percent) had some additional income (including income in kind); the average for all families amounted to $27, bringing total income per family—to support on the average one adult and three children—to $140 a month.

The overall poverty of the recipient families is suggested by the fact that, according to the standards set up in their own State, half of them are still in financial need even with the assistance payment. The average amount of such unmet need was $40 a month per family and ranged from a deficit of less than $20 in 13 percent of those whose requirements were not fully met to $75 or more in 6 percent.[13]

Inadequacy of Existing Programs

The data outlined for mother-child families as a group suggest how few of the benefits of our existing social programs, as administered, are likely to trickle down to them. In terms of economic progress, we may be well on the way to establishing

---

[12] Robert H. Mugge, "Aid to Families with Dependent Children: Initial Findings of the 1961 Report on the Characteristics of Recipients," *Social Security Bulletin* (March 1963).

[13] Welfare Administration, Bureau of Family Services, Division of Program Statistics and Analysis, *Characteristics of Families Receiving Aid to Families with Dependent Children, November-December 1961* (April 1963).

a "caste of untouchables," with mother-child families as the nucleus. Since most of the mothers in these families are separated, divorced from, or never married to the father of their children —rather than widowed—social insurance benefits to dependents of retired, deceased, or disabled workers are not available to them.

Many of these mothers work in private households, in retail stores, and in laundries and other service establishments not covered by Federal minimum wage laws or unemployment insurance. Three out of every 5 of the nonwhite mothers who are employed are working at service jobs, including domestic work in private households. Two out of 5 of the employed white mothers are clerical, sales, or kindred workers.

A number of these mothers work intermittently, with the result that their future old-age benefits will undoubtedly be minimal. Thus we may already be creating the old-age assistance caseload of the 1980's.

Although more than half the mothers are employed in the course of a year, often they do not hold down a regular full-time job. (Fifty-four percent of the mothers heading broken families were reported at work by the Bureau of the Census in April 1960, but only 1 in 4 of those interviewed in the Census sample for March 1962 had worked full time throughout 1961.)

With day care of young children largely unavailable or in any event beyond their means, the mothers' employment opportunities will be severely limited or children must be left unattended. Manpower and retraining programs up to now have offered little to the woman with as little formal education as most of these mothers have. Rehabilitation programs have seldom provided for child care while the mother is being trained.

Many of the same difficulties characterize the father in husband-wife families with inadequate income. Such families as a group can look to even less help from public programs than broken families can. It is perhaps the inability of the man to earn—particularly among nonwhites—that is conducive to the marriage disruption, or the failure ever to undertake legal marriage, that leaves so many mothers to bring up children without a father. Research now under way suggests that families with the father an unskilled laborer, as well as broken families, contribute much more than their proportionate share of high school freshmen who rank low in aptitude.

There are more children deprived by low family income of their rightful chance at making their way in society who live with both a father and mother than there are similarly deprived children living with the mother only. One of the ways to abate the problem of the low-income mother-child family is to take appropriate action while the family is still intact.

LEGACY OF POVERTY

A considerable body of data is being accumulated on the subject of transmission of poverty. Some of the results of current study are conflicting and difficult to interpret, and much research is still needed. There seems sufficient basis, however, for adopting as a working hypothesis that perhaps the single medium most conducive to the growth of poverty and dependency is poverty itself. The corollary might be that although adequate family income alone is not a sufficient condition to guarantee that children will escape low-income status as adults, it is usually a necessary one. There are people whose only legacy to their children is the same one of poverty and deprivation that they received from their own parents.

A recently released study of cases assisted by aid to families with dependent children shows that, for a nationwide sample of such families whose cases were closed early in 1961, "more than 40 percent of the mothers and/or fathers were raised in homes where some form of assistance had been received at some time." [14] Nearly half these cases had received aid to families with dependent children. This estimated proportion that received some type of aid is more than four times the almost 10 percent estimated for the total United States population. With education so important these days for any chance at a well-paying job, the educational attainment of children formerly receiving aid to families with dependent children fell well below that of the same age group in the general population. Thirteen percent of the total population aged 18-24 had not gone beyond the eighth grade, but in the sample of families receiving aid the corresponding proportion was twice as high.[15]

Similarly, the University of Michigan study reported that among all families with children no longer in school the children had gone through high school or beyond in 65 percent,

---

[14] M. Elaine Burgess and Daniel O. Price, *An American Dependency Challenge* (American Public Welfare Associaton, 1963), p. 21.
[15] *Ibid.*, p. 108.

but that in only 45 percent of the families defined as poor was this true.[16]

Poor families have been found in various studies not only to have less resources but much less often to have aspirations toward providing a college education for their children, despite the fact that education today is the key not only to a better job but to any job at all. A recent study of young people aged 16-24 in the labor force and no longer in school reported the relationship of unemployment to educational attainment, as shown below.[17]

Educational attainment	Percent unemployed
Not high school graduate	14
High school graduate, no college	7
Some college, not graduate	6
College graduate	3

Despite recent advances, it is still expected that almost 3 out of every 10 youths entering the labor force during the years ahead will not have completed high school and that a third of these—about 250,000 a year—will not even have gone through elementary school.[18] Almost surely, they will have to live out their lives and support their own children on only a minimum wage.

Children from the broken families who represent so large a proportion of the poor undoubtedly will often fall in the same unskilled category. The mothers with no education or cultural expectation for themselves, with little money to provide a home environment conducive to study, and needing the help of their older children's earnings to satisfy the bread-and-butter needs of the younger ones, often are in no position to encourage even gifted children to stay in school, though scholarships are available. The fact that schools in poor neighborhoods are likely to be short on counselors, books, and other tools needed by the student will serve to compound rather than mitigate the home deficiency.[19]

The deleterious effects of poverty on health, nutrition, and

---

[16] Morgan, p. 211.

[17] Bureau of the Census, *Farm Population*, ERS(P-27), No. 30 (August 1961), p. 28.

[18] Sar A. Levitan, *Youth Employment Act* (The W. E. Upjohn Institute for Employment Research, February 1963), p. 5.

[19] James Bryant Conant, *Slums and Suburbs* (New York: McGraw-Hill Book Co., Inc., 1961).

other living conditions have also been noted.[20] There is, to be sure, no unanimity on the question of inherited deprivation. Some feel that it is lack of motivation or an innate lack of ability that is transmitted rather than lack of opportunity. For some children an overlay of discrimination combines with low-income status to perpetuate the deprivation. In his Civil Rights Message of February 1963, President Kennedy said:

> The Negro baby born in America today—regardless of the section or State in which he is born—has about one-half as much chance of completing high school as a white baby born in the same place on the same day, one-third as much chance of becoming a professional man, twice as much chance of becoming unemployed, about one-seventh as much chance of earning $10,000 per year, a life expectancy which is seven years less, and the prospects of earning only half as much.

There is need for considerable refinement of the definition or standards by which poverty is to be measured, if we are to trace its course with assurance. Nevertheless, compelling evidence already suggests a lingering reservoir of self-perpetuating low-income status among particular population groups—toils the individual often is powerless to escape and a deprivation that falls in large part outside the scope of existing remedial programs. Along with the basic research into the cause and long-range cure for chronic low income, there is need for more thoroughgoing inquiry into the characteristics of those currently affected and a means of counteracting some of the more dire social consequences, at least for children.

If it be true that the children of the poor today are themselves destined to be the impoverished parents of tomorrow, then some social intervention is needed to break the cycle, to interrupt the circuits of hunger and hopelessness that link generation to generation. For the common benefit of all we must assure the security and well-being of all our children—at the same time the Nation's most precious and most perishable resource.

---

[20] Epstein, "Some Effects of Low Income."

@@@@@@@@@@@@@@@@@@@@@@@@@@@@@@@

OUT-OF-SCHOOL YOUTH,
FEBRUARY 1963

@@@@@@@@@@@@@@@@@@@@@@@@@@@@@@@

THOMAS E. SWANSTROM

Education and training requirements for entry jobs have stiff-
ened at a time when youth unemployment rates are on a high
plateau. Youths entering the labor force for the first time are
usually evaluated as prospective employees in terms of their
education and training, since they have little or no work experience. Consequently, it is useful to examine the dropouts' and
high school graduates' backgrounds as they relate to the problem of unemployment among young persons.[1]

CURRICULUM

The purpose of a vocational or commercial program in high
school is to better equip students who will look for jobs after

---

[1] This is the second of two articles based primarily on information from
supplementary questions in the February 1963 monthly survey of the labor
force, conducted for the Bureau of Labor Statistics by the Bureau of the
Census through its Current Population Survey.

Data in both reports relate to persons sixteen to twenty-one years of age
who were no longer in school, were not college graduates, and were in the
civilian noninstitutional population in the calendar week ending Feb. 16,
1963. Members of the Armed Forces and inmates of institutions are excluded.

Since the estimates resulting from this survey are based on a sample,
they may differ from the figures that would have been obtained from a
complete census. The sampling variability may be relatively large in cases
where the numbers are small. Because of the comparatively small size of
the group covered in this survey, the number of sample cases that could
be used was small. Consequently, numbers under 200,000 and percents
based on them should be used with caution.

they leave school. Only 30 percent of the youths who dropped out of high school followed such programs. It may be that the proportion with vocational or commercial programs would have been higher if more schools had offered these programs in the 9th and 10th grades—the highest grades attended by a majority of the high school dropouts included in the survey.

Among the young men who were high school graduates, about 38 percent had taken either of these programs, only a slightly higher proportion than for dropouts. But the differences in the proportions were more pronounced among the girls; 50 percent of the graduates had been enrolled in vocational or commercial programs, two-thirds again as high as for the dropouts. Since better educated and trained workers are more likely to be in the labor force, this variation may partially explain the higher post-school labor force participation rates of the female graduates. Probably a more important factor is the smaller proportion of graduates than dropouts who were married.

Even though most students do not follow a vocational or commercial program while in high school, almost 95 percent of the male graduates and about 70 percent of the dropouts completed at least one vocational or commercial course. As shown in the following tabulation, nearly the same proportion of dropouts as graduates had completed the most commonly given vocational courses despite the shorter period of time that dropouts had been in school.

	Proportions taking vocational or commercial courses	
Male	*Graduates*	*Dropouts*
Typing	54	18
Machine shop	37	28
Metal working	34	27
Carpentry	32	29
Agriculture	29	18
Bookkeeping	21	6
Female		
Typing	87	50
Home economics	73	76
Bookkeeping	52	21
Shorthand	51	15
Business machines	36	5

On the other hand, both the male and female graduates were much more likely than dropouts to have completed commercial courses, and this training doubtless gave the graduates an added advantage in finding clerical jobs; about 68 percent of the female graduates employed in February 1963 were employed in clerical jobs compared with only 20 percent of the female dropouts.

As part of their high school education, some students participate in a school-work program in which they attend school part time and work part time, while earning required school credit for their work. The outside work they do is directly related to the subject matter studied in school. These programs are given in comparatively few schools and primarily in the fields of distributive (sales) and business education. Only 7 percent of the graduates and 3 percent of the dropouts reported enrollment in a school-work program.

EMPLOYMENT GUIDANCE

Since the end of World War II, a sharp rise in employment has occurred in those occupations which require high levels of training and skill. Since 1947, the proportion employed in white-collar occupations has increased sharply while that for the unskilled jobs has decreased; these trends are expected to continue during the remainder of this decade.

Yet only four out of ten youths who had attended high school said they had received any guidance from a school official or from a State employment office about the kind of training they should have or the kind of work they should look for after leaving school;[2] a somewhat larger proportion of girls than boys had received such advice. Graduates were more likely than dropouts to have had guidance from their school or from the State employment service, as shown at top of page 88.

Job guidance from either the school or the employment service appeared to have had some beneficial results for the dropouts when they left school. Three out of ten of those who had received guidance had a job waiting when they left school, compared with about 2 out of 10 of those who had not received job guidance. Job guidance did not benefit the graduates to a similar extent; about one-third had a job waiting whether they had obtained guidance or not.

---

[2] Of course, some students may have received job guidance without recognizing it as such.

| | Both sexes | | Male | | Female | |
Source of job guidance	Drop-outs	Grad-uates	Drop-outs	Grad-uates	Drop-outs	Grad-uates
Total	100.0	100.0	100.0	100.0	100.0	100.0
Received guidance	22.4	56.1	20.3	51.1	24.0	58.9
School only	17.1	37.8	14.4	34.6	19.2	39.6
Employment service only	4.2	4.9	5.1	4.8	3.6	5.0
School and employment service	1.0	13.4	.8	11.7	1.2	14.3
Did not receive any guidance	77.6	43.9	79.7	48.9	76.0	41.1

TRAINING SINCE LEAVING SCHOOL

Youths were asked, "Since you left school, have you taken any training such as accounting, secretarial, electrician, laboratory technician, etc.?" It was found that high school graduates were much more likely than dropouts to have entered such training programs after leaving school—three out of ten graduates, but only one out of ten dropouts. Girl graduates were more likely to have entered a training program than boys, as shown in the following tabulation:

| | *Proportions with training* | | |
	Both sexes	*Male*	*Female*
Dropouts	9.5	9.8	9.3
Graduates	29.0	23.8	31.8

Many of the boys took training as mechanics, repairmen, or clerical workers; girls chiefly studied to be secretaries, clerical workers, or beauticians.

The most common sources of instruction for post-school training programs for both dropouts and graduates were special schools, such as technical institutes, and secretarial or barber schools (table 1). Male dropouts and graduates had training in special schools in roughly the same proportions—slightly over one-third of each group with training. Female graduates, on the other hand, were about twice as likely as dropouts to have attended special schools—about three-fourths of the graduates with training compared with 40 percent of the dropouts. On-the-job training programs were the second most important source of training for both young men and women.

TABLE 1 / Type of Training Institution Where Training Was Taken Since Leaving School, by Years of School Completed and Sex, February 1963

[Percent distribution of out-of-school youth, 16 to 21 years of age]

Type of training institution	Male			Female		
	Total	Years of school completed		Total	Years of school completed	
		Less than 4 years of high school	4 years of high school		Less than 4 years of high school	4 years of high school
Total: Number (thousands)	394	134	260	814	157	657
Percent	100.0	100.0	100.0	100.0	100.0	100.0
Special school or technical institute	37.4	35.6	37.6	67.6	39.2	73.5
On-the-job training program	28.3	20.0	31.8	13.1	19.0	12.6
Other company training program	1.0	—	1.6	4.7	7.6	3.8
Apprenticeship	10.6	14.1	8.6	.4	—	.5
Armed Forces	8.6	14.1	6.9			
Correspondence school	8.2	5.9	9.0	1.6	4.4	1.1
Other	6.0	10.4	4.5	12.5	29.7	8.5

Note: Because of rounding, sums of individual items may not equal totals.

A high proportion of the youths who had taken post-school training found jobs using their new skills. About two-thirds of the females and half the males who were no longer taking training used their training on a job. High school graduates were more successful than dropouts in obtaining jobs in their field of training, the ratios being 68 percent and 50 percent, respectively.

EMPLOYMENT WHILE IN SCHOOL

Many students work while they attend high school, some because of economic necessity and others to obtain extra spending money or for other reasons. Dropouts were much less likely than high school graduates to have worked while in school. Three out of five graduates had held a job as against one out of three dropouts. Of course, the graduates could be expected to have had more opportunity for employment since they were usually older at the time of leaving and probably had spent more time in school than the dropouts. The acquisition of a job may have enabled some youths to remain in high school until they graduated because it lessened the financial burden. This point is reinforced by the fact that one out of five dropouts reported they left school for economic reasons.

Male dropouts and graduates had worked in similar occupations while in school. One in four of each group had jobs as nonfarm laborers, while dropouts were somewhat more likely to take farm jobs than graduates. On the other hand, there were marked differences between the occupations at which female dropouts and graduates worked. A greater proportion of such dropouts worked as farm and as private household workers, whereas the graduates were more likely to have worked at sales jobs while in school.

Both graduates and dropouts who held jobs while in school fared better in the job market after leaving school than those who did not. Among the dropouts, 30 percent of those who had worked during their school years had jobs waiting when they withdrew from school, compared with only 17 percent of those who did not work. Graduates who held a job while in school were almost three times as likely as those who did not work to have a job waiting upon graduation—44 percent and 17 percent, respectively. In a substantial number of cases, the jobs waiting for those who had worked while in school may have been the same ones held while in school.

MOBILITY

About 40 percent of the males and 60 percent of the females who had been farm residents in their last semester of elementary or high school had moved to nonfarm areas by February 1963. The farm to nonfarm shift was made by about the same proportions of dropouts and graduates.

About seven out of ten males who moved from a farm area after leaving school did so for economic reasons (table 2). Among young men who had moved from one farm residence to another or from one city or town to another, only four out of ten did so for economic reasons. Among young women, however, only a small group moved because of economic considerations; the majority reported the causes as marriage or that their husbands needed to move. There were no differences in the proportions of graduates and dropouts who moved for economic reasons.

Migrants were less likely to be unemployed than those who had not moved. Among nonfarm residents at the time of the survey, the unemployment rate for dropouts who had moved, 23 percent, was significantly lower than that for those who had not moved, 31 percent (table 3). Even among those who had completed at least four years of high school, the unemployment rate was twice as high for nonmovers as for movers—15 and 8 percent, respectively.

Girls, both graduates and dropouts, who had moved since their last year of school were much less likely than nonmovers to be in the labor force in February 1963. This tendency probably reflected the large proportion who moved because they had married or because their husbands had to move.

PROFILE OF THE UNEMPLOYED

Some 850,000 (18.6 percent) of the young people in the labor force were unemployed in February 1963, and dropouts were twice as likely as graduates to be looking for work. One-third of the unemployed men and 40 percent of the women had never worked. Unemployed persons who had worked at some

TABLE 2 / REASON FOR MOVING TO CURRENT RESIDENCE FOR PERSONS WHO MOVED SINCE LAST YEAR OF SCHOOL, BY TYPE OF MOVE, YEARS OF SCHOOL COMPLETED, AND SEX, FEBRUARY 1963

[Percent distribution of out-of-school youth, 16 to 21 years of age]

Type of move, years of school completed, and sex	Total		Reasons for moving to current residence							
	Number (thousands)	Percent	Economic reasons				Family moved	Marriage	Husband related †	All other
			Total	To look for work	To obtain a job	Other*				
MALE										
All movers	609	100.0	49.4	14.7	25.4	9.3	14.2	4.6	—	31.8
Farm to nonfarm	213	100.0	71.8	10.8	44.1	16.9	9.2	8.2	—	10.8
All other	396	100.0	38.4	16.7	16.2	5.6	16.7	2.8	—	42.2
Less than 4 years of high school	356	100.0	48.8	14.8	20.7	13.3	15.1	1.2	—	34.9
Farm to nonfarm	127	100.0	71.6	11.0	30.3	30.3	12.8	3.7	—	11.9
All other	229	100.0	38.0	16.6	16.2	5.2	16.2		—	45.9
4 years of high school, or more	253	100.0	50.2	14.6	31.6	4.0	13.0	9.1	—	27.7
Farm to nonfarm	86	(‡)							—	
All other	167	100.0	38.9	16.8	16.2	6.0	17.4	6.6	—	37.1
FEMALE										
All movers	1,427	100.0	16.2	5.4	7.0	3.7	10.1	21.5	32.0	20.3
Farm to nonfarm	352	100.0	21.2	5.7	10.6	4.9	10.6	22.1	31.5	14.6
All other	1,075	100.0	14.5	5.3	5.8	3.3	9.9	21.3	32.1	22.2
Less than 4 years of high school	642	100.0	15.6	3.8	7.1	4.7	10.4	20.7	37.8	15.5
Farm to nonfarm	161	100.0	24.4	8.1	11.2	5.0	13.8	23.1	28.8	10.0
All other	481	100.0	12.7	2.3	5.7	4.7	9.3	19.9	40.8	17.3
4 years of high school, or more	785	100.0	16.6	6.8	7.0	2.8	9.8	22.2	27.0	24.4
Farm to nonfarm	191	100.0	18.5	3.7	10.1	4.8	7.9	21.2	33.9	18.5
All other	594	100.0	15.9	7.9	5.9	2.2	10.4	22.6	24.7	26.3

* Included, among others, wanted to work at new location, to earn more money, and transferred.

† Included, among others, husband transferred or found a job, to be with husband, husband stationed at location, and husband going to school.

‡ Percent not shown where base is less than 100,000.

NOTE: Because of rounding, sums of individual items may not equal totals.

TABLE 3 / LABOR FORCE STATUS OF NONFARM RESIDENTS IN FEBRUARY 1963, BY YEARS OF SCHOOL COMPLETED, MOBILITY STATUS SINCE LAST YEAR OF SCHOOL,* AND SEX

[Percent distribution of out-of-school youth, 16 to 21 years of age]

Mobility status, years of school completed, and sex	Total		In civilian labor force			Not in labor force	Unemployment rate †
	Number (thousands)	Percent	Total	Employed	Unemployed		
BOTH SEXES							
Less than 4 years of high school ‡	2,771	100.0	60.3	43.2	17.0	39.7	28.3
Moved	907	100.0	51.0	39.5	11.6	49.0	22.7
Did not move	1,827	100.0	65.2	45.1	20.1	34.8	30.9
4 years of high school ‡	2,963	100.0	75.7	65.7	9.9	24.3	13.1
Moved	858	100.0	61.7	56.6	5.0	38.3	8.1
Did not move	2,086	100.0	81.8	69.7	12.1	18.2	14.7
MALE							
Less than 4 years of high school ‡	1,216	100.0	91.1	64.4	26.7	8.9	29.3
Moved	307	100.0	93.2	70.0	23.1	6.8	24.8
Did not move	884	100.0	91.0	62.3	28.7	9.0	31.6
4 years of high school ‡	974	100.0	90.7	77.4	13.3	9.3	14.7
Moved	211	100.0	88.6	81.5	7.1	11.4	8.0
Did not move	751	100.0	91.7	76.4	15.3	8.3	16.7
FEMALE							
Less than 4 years of high school ‡	1,555	100.0	36.3	26.8	9.5	63.7	26.2
Moved	600	100.0	29.5	23.8	5.7	70.5	19.2
Did not move	943	100.0	41.2	29.0	12.1	58.8	29.4
4 years of high school ‡	1,989	100.0	68.3	60.0	8.3	31.7	12.1
Moved	647	100.0	52.9	48.5	4.3	47.1	8.2
Did not move	1,335	100.0	76.2	65.9	10.2	23.8	13.5

* Persons who moved to a different city or town from the one in which they were living in their last year of elementary or high school.

† Unemployed as a percent of the civilian labor force.

‡ Includes some persons for whom mobility status was not known.

NOTE: Because of rounding, sums of individual items may not equal totals.

TABLE 4 / REASONS UNEMPLOYED PERSONS LEFT THEIR LAST JOB, BY YEARS OF SCHOOL COMPLETED AND SEX, FEBRUARY 1963

[Percent distribution of out-of-school youth, 16 to 21 years of age]

Reason for leaving last job	Male			Female		
	Total	Years of school completed		Total	Years of school completed	
		Less than 4 years of high school	4 years of high school		Less than 4 years of high school	4 years of high school
Total: Number (thousands)	338	231	107	206	112	94
Percent	100.0	100.0	100.0	100.0	100.0	(°)
Economic	46.3	42.7	54.4	26.4	19.6	——
Improvement in status	18.0	19.1	15.5	14.7	16.8	——
Termination of temporary job †	11.0	14.2	3.9	24.9	16.8	——
Illness or disability	5.5	6.2	3.9	1.5	2.8	——
Household responsibilities	1.2	—	3.9	21.8	29.0	——
Fired	4.3	6.2	—			——
Other reasons‡	13.7	11.6	18.4	10.7	15.0	——

° Percent not shown where base is less than 100,000.

† Included, among others, slack work, no more work available, and the firm had moved or gone out of business.

‡ Included, among others, to earn more money, hours too long, work too hard or unpleasant, and to find a job where advancement opportunities were better.

NOTE: This table excludes unemployed persons who never worked. Because of rounding, sums of individual items may not equal totals.

time were asked why they had left their last job. About half of the boys and one-fourth of the girls said they had left for economic reasons—slack work, no more work available, or the firm had moved or gone out of business (table 4). Even though young workers have much difficulty in finding employment, one out of six quit their jobs to seek one where they could improve their status—to earn more money, work shorter hours, or better their chances for advancement, etc. The transitory nature of some of the jobs held by young women is illustrated by the high proportion (one-fourth) who left because their jobs were temporary. Nearly the same proportion of the girls had stopped working—at least temporarily—because of household responsibilities.

Many unemployed young people had to depend on members of their families for financial assistance since only a small minority received unemployment compensation. In February 1963, about half of all unemployed persons in the Nation were receiving unemployment benefits compared with only 14 percent of the unemployed out-of-school youth. Graduates were twice as likely as dropouts to be receiving unemployment benefits (19 and 9 percent, respectively). The prime reason for the wide variation in proportions may be that young workers, and especially dropouts, may not have worked long enough during the prior year to become eligible for benefits or may not have worked in industries or for employers covered by the unemployment insurance law.

In their search for work, both graduates and dropouts most frequently contacted their friends and relatives, employers other than those they had formerly worked for, and the State employment service (table 5). Male graduates tended to use more methods than dropouts, and they also applied to former employers and placed or answered advertisements to a more significant extent.

In response to the question, "What kind of work are you looking for?", 60 percent of the unemployed women graduates reported clerical jobs and approximately the same proportion of dropouts indicated service or operative jobs (chart 1). The percentages seeking these jobs were nearly the same as the actual proportion of jobs reported held by employed female graduates and dropouts. The job goals of the young men were not so well defined. About half of both the unemployed graduates and dropouts reported they would take "any kind" of job, thus suggesting they lacked specific skills.

TABLE 5 / METHODS USED BY UNEMPLOYED PERSONS TO FIND WORK, BY YEARS OF SCHOOL COMPLETED AND SEX, FEBRUARY 1963

[Percent distribution of out-of-school youth, 16 to 21 years of age]

Method used to find work	Male			Female		
	Total	Years of school completed		Total	Years of school completed	
		Less than 4 years of high school	4 years of high school		Less than 4 years of high school	4 years of high school
Total: Number (thousands)	488	340	148	340	156	184
Percent*	100.0	100.0	100.0	100.0	100.0	100.0
Former employers	32.4	27.1	44.6	14.7	14.7	14.6
Other employers	59.6	64.1	49.3	50.1	47.4	52.4
Friends or relatives	63.9	63.5	64.9	56.9	52.6	60.5
Advertisements	27.7	21.8	41.2	24.9	21.2	28.1
State employment office	48.2	43.5	58.8	46.0	41.7	49.7
Private employment agency	7.4	3.2	16.9	9.7	5.8	13.0
Union	5.7	2.1	14.2			
Other	10.0	9.4	11.5	14.1	14.7	13.5

* Since many persons indicated they had used more than one method to find work, the sum of the items adds to more than 100.0 percent.

Virtually all of the unemployed were looking for full-time jobs. In response to the question, "What is the lowest weekly wage or salary you will accept?", a greater proportion of the dropouts than graduates said that they would be willing to work for less than $40 a week on a full-time job. Among the dropouts, one-fourth of the males and one-half of the females would accept that little money, significantly greater proportions than among the respective graduates (chart 2). The chart also shows that the minimum wage and salary desired was not unrealistic when compared with earnings of employed persons in the same age group and with comparable education.

WORK EXPERIENCE IN 1962

Information was obtained on the extent of work experience and unemployment during 1962 for those persons who had not attended college and who had dropped out or graduated from school prior to January 1963. While about equal proportions (over 90 percent) of male dropouts and graduates had worked at some time during 1962, among the women, a much greater proportion of the graduates than dropouts had worked. Only half the female dropouts had worked, as compared with over eight out of ten graduates, primarily because a larger proportion of the dropouts were married and therefore had household responsibilities. Among dropouts who did work, two-thirds were employed for six months or less. Year-round employment at full-time jobs in 1962 was much more common among graduates even though a larger proportion of them had finished school during 1962 and therefore were not as likely as dropouts to have worked at such jobs all year.

Dropouts were more likely than graduates to have had unemployment during the course of a year. Among those in the labor force during the year, half the dropouts and about one-third of the graduates had been unemployed at one time or another in 1962. Greater proportions of males than females had at least 1 week of joblessness.

Among youths unemployed during the year were approximately a quarter of a million (60 percent of them dropouts) who had looked for work for at least one week but could not find any. Inability to find any work was particularly evident among female dropouts, with one out of four of the unemployed unable to find a job.

Of those who had worked at some time during the year but had also been unemployed, dropouts were twice as likely as graduates to have been jobless for a total of more than half a year. The percentage of dropouts with more than half a year of unemployment is especially striking since it was half again as large as the 15 percent of workers of all ages. The high proportion of dropouts with a substantial amount of unemployment may be attributed in part to the temporary nature of many of their jobs. Half of the dropouts had two or more periods of unemployment during 1962, compared with one-fourth of the graduates.

ACTIVITY SINCE LEAVING SCHOOL

In order to obtain a panoramic view of what the youth had done since leaving school, they were asked, "Looking back at the time since you last attended school, what were you doing most of the time?" Virtually all the young men—about nine out of ten—reported they had spent most of the time either working or looking for work. A somewhat higher proportion of graduates than dropouts had worked most of the time—79 percent and 72 percent, respectively. Dropouts were more likely to have worked at part-time jobs. A greater proportion of white graduates than dropouts worked most of the time, but among nonwhite males, there was virtually no difference in the proportions. About 17 percent of male dropouts had been unemployed most of the time since leaving school, compared with 11 percent of the graduates.

Of the 275,000 male graduates and dropouts who had been out of the labor force most of the time since leaving school, about 95,000 had been in the Armed Forces most of the time, 70,000 said they had been "doing nothing," and about 35,000 had taken job training. Dropouts were nearly three times as likely as graduates to have been "doing nothing." Virtually all of those who had spent their time in job training were graduates. The major activity was influenced to some extent both by the age of the youths and the length of time that had elapsed since leaving school, which was fairly recent for some.

A much larger proportion of the women (40 percent) than men had been out of the labor force most of the time since leaving school, primarily because of family responsibilities. Among the women, three out of five of the dropouts had not

CHART 1 / TYPES OF JOBS SOUGHT BY UNEMPLOYED DROP-
OUTS AND HIGH SCHOOL GRADUATES,° BY SEX, FEBRUARY 1963

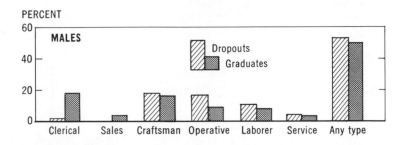

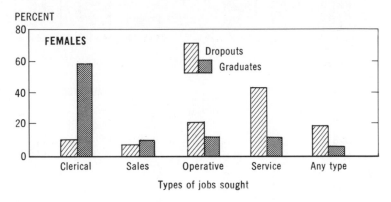

Types of jobs sought

° Persons aged 16 to 21 who did not attend college.

been in the labor force most of the time—a rate two and one-
half times that for graduates—reflecting mainly the greater
proportion who were married. Relatively twice as many
women graduates as dropouts had been working full time most
of the time, but the proportion of all the women who had
worked part time (9 percent) was about half that of the men.
The lower percentage of women who had worked part time
most of the time since leaving school did not reflect the full
extent to which they tend to be employed less than a whole
week. Many of the women who had spent a major portion of
their time out of the labor force probably had worked occasionally for a few hours a week.

The proportions of white and nonwhite women who had
been in the labor force most of the time since leaving school

CHART 2 / LOWEST FULL-TIME EARNINGS UNEMPLOYED DROPOUTS AND HIGH SCHOOL GRADUATES° WOULD ACCEPT COMPARED WITH EARNINGS OF EMPLOYED YOUTHS, BY SEX, FEBRUARY 1963

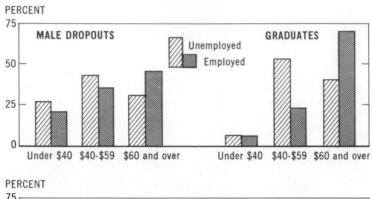

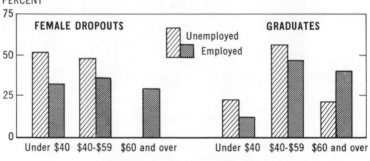

° Persons aged 16 to 21. Included among high school graduates were persons with some college training.

were the same. However, about 23 percent of the nonwhite women had been unemployed most of the time compared with only 6 percent of the white. The greater prevalence of unemployment among nonwhite girls emphasizes the handicaps they have when they enter the work force. A higher proportion of them had failed to graduate from high school and a smaller percentage had taken post-school vocational or commercial training. When they left school, relatively fewer nonwhite girls had a job waiting, and among all the girls who looked for a job, it took nonwhite girls longer to find one. Also, nonwhite girls were much more likely than white girls to work in occupation groups which had higher unemployment rates than those in which white girls were concentrated. A majority of the employed nonwhite girls were working in private household and other service occupations and a relatively small proportion in clerical jobs; for white girls the situation was reversed.

☙☙☙☙☙☙☙☙☙☙☙☙☙☙☙☙☙☙☙☙☙☙☙☙☙☙☙☙

REALITIES
OF THE JOB MARKET

For the High School Dropout

☙☙☙☙☙☙☙☙☙☙☙☙☙☙☙☙☙☙☙☙☙☙☙☙☙☙☙☙

HERBERT BIENSTOCK

The realities of the job market for the high school dropout are, tersely stated, bleak. At the present time, and with every prospect that these relationships will continue to intensify during the remainder of the 1960's, the high school dropout can expect to earn less than the graduate, experience unemployment more often, and, when employed, work in a lower-skill category. If the dropout is nonwhite, his relative position is worse.

There is much concern today, and properly so, with the school dropout problem. Frequently, however, it is misconceived as a problem created by an increase in the number of young people dropping out of school. This is not so in fact. The fact is that a smaller percentage of students are dropping out of school than ever before. What heightens our concern is that there are fewer job opportunities available when they drop out because, under the impact of the great and accelerating increases in automation and technological change, the number of jobs available for high school dropouts is rapidly declining. Indeed, job opportunities for the high school dropout are shrinking more rapidly than the high school dropout rate is declining.

It used to be true that if a boy or girl who wanted to work dropped out of school there was an unskilled job available. Increasingly, this is not the case. That is what complicates this problem. The unprecedented growth anticipated in the American labor force in the decade of the 1960's, particularly the vast influx into the labor market of large numbers of young persons, adds to the dimensions of the problem.

POPULATION AND LABOR FORCE TRENDS

Changes in Labor Force

To properly understand the reality of the job market for the high school dropout during the decade of the 1960's, we need first to take a look at the general manpower posture of the nation during this decade. The unprecedented growth in the labor force in prospect during the 1960's is one of the basic factors in any appraisal of the job outlook for high school dropouts. The number of workers in the United States is expected to rise by about 12.6 million between 1960 and 1970 (see Table 1).

The most dramatic change will occur in the age group 14 to 24, as the large number of youngsters born during the postwar baby boom begin to reach working age (see Table 2). During the 1960's the number of young workers under age 25 will increase by about 45 percent, compared with a 10.7 percent increase in the age group 25 to 34, an actual decline of 1.5 percent in age group 35 to 44, and an increase of 18.5 percent in the number of workers over 45 years of age. The decline in the number of workers 35 to 44 years of age reflects the impact of the low birth rates of the 1930's. The contraction in the number of workers age 35 to 44, the hard core years of working life, should provide young people with improved opportunities for moving ahead, particularly in the latter part of the 1960's. The increased demand for higher skills and greater education will,

TABLE 1 / CHANGES IN TOTAL LABOR FORCE BY AGE 1950 TO 1970

[in millions]

	Number			Change			
	Actual		Projected	1950-60		1960-70	
Age	1950	1960	1970	Number	Percent	Number	Percent
Under 25	13.3	13.7	19.9	0.4	2.7	6.2	45.0
25-34	15.1	15.1	16.7	0.1*	−0.3	1.6	10.7
35-44	14.1	16.8	16.5	2.7	18.8	−0.3	−1.5
Over 45	22.2	27.5	32.6	5.3	24.1	5.1	18.5

* Less than 100,000.

however, place an additional handicap on the high school dropout.

To understand the sheer magnitude of the large influx of young people into the world of work of the 1960's, we should compare the net increase of 6.2 million young persons under 25 into the nation's work force with the net increase of 400,000 in this age category recorded during the 1950's. The increase anticipated for the present decade is better than fifteen times greater than in the previous decade.

Since the beginning of this century, the proportion of the working population in the younger age groups has been declining steadily because of the significant and substantial drop in labor market participation among youth. Regulations concerning youth employment and lengthening years of attendance in school have been primarily responsible for this trend. Under the impact of the large influx of youngsters into the job market of the 1960's this long-term trend is being reversed, despite the continuing decline in labor market participation among youth as a result of increase in the number of years of school attendance.

The rate of increase among young male workers during the 1960's will be five times as great as the corresponding rate among male workers of other ages. The rate of increase among young female workers during the same period will be more than double the corresponding rate among female workers of other ages. As a result, the proportion of the total labor force made up of young people 14 to 24 years of age will rise to the point where they will account for almost one of every four workers in the United States in 1970. About one of every two new additions to the labor supply in the 1960's will come from the young age groups.

Results of 1947 Baby Crop

As a result of the sharp increase in the birth rate in 1947, following the end of World War II, the number of youngsters reaching 18 years of age—the age at which the first wave of entry into the labor force takes place—will jump by a full million between 1964 and 1965 (see Table 2).

TABLE 2 / NUMBER OF PERSONS REACHING 18 YEARS OF AGE

[in millions]

Year	Number
1950	2.2
1955	2.2
1960	2.6
1961	2.9
1962	2.8
1963	2.8
1964	2.8
1965	3.8
1966	3.6
1967	3.6
1968	3.6
1969	3.7
1970	3.8

SOURCE: U. S. Bureau of the Census.

Of particular concern is the fact that in 1963 the baby crop of 1947 reaches 16 years of age. Thus, in 1963, there were a full one million more youngsters reaching the age of 16 than in 1962, an increase of more than one-third in a single year. Age 16 holds particular significance to those concerned with the problems of the high school dropout since it represents the modal age at which youngsters leave school. Just about one out of every three high school dropouts falls out at age 16.

INDUSTRIAL AND OCCUPATIONAL PATTERNS

Significant shifts in the industrial and occupational composition of the nation's economy are not without pertinence to understanding the problems which concern the high school dropout in today's job world.

Distribution of Employment

Possibly the most dramatic shift in our economic structure in recent years has been the relative decline of employment in the goods-producing industries, including agriculture, manufacturing, mining, and construction, and the continued rapid expansion of the service sectors of the economy, especially trade, services, and state and local government (see Table 3).

TABLE 3 / PERCENT DISTRIBUTION OF EMPLOYMENT, BY INDUSTRY DIVISION 1947, 1957, AND 1962

Industry division	1947	1957	1962 °
Total †	100.0	100.0	100.0
Goods-producing industries	51.3	45.9	41.8
Manufacturing	29.8	29.0	27.7
Durable goods	16.1	16.7	15.6
Nondurable goods	13.7	12.4	12.1
Mining	1.8	1.4	1.1
Construction	3.8	4.9	4.5
Agriculture	15.8	10.5	8.6
Service-producing industries	48.7	54.1	58.2
Transportation and other utilities	8.0	7.2	6.5
Trade	17.2	18.4	19.1
Finance, insurance, and real estate	3.4	4.2	4.6
Services and miscellaneous	9.7	11.4	12.8
Government	10.5	12.9	15.2
Federal	3.6	3.7	3.9
State and local	6.9	9.1	11.3

° Preliminary.

† Represents wage and salary employment in nonfarm industries based on employers' payroll data, plus total employment in agriculture based on household survey data.

NOTE: Individual items may not add to totals because of rounding.

TABLE 4 / TRENDS IN 1930-70 PERCENT DISTRIBUTION OF
EMPLOYMENT BY GOODS- AND SERVICE-PRODUCING INDUSTRIES

Year	Goods producing	Service producing	Year	Goods producing	Service producing
1930	56	44	1955	47	53
1940	54	46	1960	45	55
1945	53	47	1965	44	56
1950	49	51	1970	43	57

Since 1930 the relative importance of the goods-producing and service-producing industries has just about reversed. In 1930 goods-producing industries accounted for 56 percent of all employment and service-producing, for 44 percent. In 1950 the service-producing industries for the first time began to provide more jobs for people in this country than the goods-producing industries. By 1960 the goods-producing industries accounted for 45 percent, with the service-producing industries accounting for 55 percent (see Table 4).

Some of the long-term trends date back a century or more, for example, the long-term decline in our farm employment. At the turn of this century about one out of every three persons in the labor force worked on a farm; today the proportion is less than one-tenth. This shift has continued to be an important factor in the labor market in recent years.

Major Occupational Changes

This trend is of considerable significance to the high school dropout since it is one of the major causes of his difficulties in the labor market. The high school dropout was not quite the economic liability on the farm that he is in the cities today. Indeed, on the farm where brawn and willingness to work hard were among the major job attributes, the high school dropout was an economic asset. Each year since the end of World War II, however, a net average of about 200,000 workers have shifted out of agricultural employment to nonfarm jobs or out of the labor force. For the decade ahead an additional loss of 1.2 million farm jobs is projected (see Table 5).

Changes in industrial structure also involve changes in occupational mix since industries vary considerably in occupational

TABLE 5 / EMPLOYMENT BY MAJOR OCCUPATIONAL GROUP 1950, 1960, AND PROJECTED 1970

Occupational group	Number (in millions)			Percent distribution		
	1950	1960	1970°	1950	1960	1970
All groups	59.7	66.7	80.5	100	100	100
White collar ...	22.4	28.8	37.5	38	43	47
Manual	23.3	24.3	27.6	39	36	34
Service	6.5	8.3	11.1	11	13	14
Farm	7.5	5.4	4.2	12	8	5

° Projected by Bureau of Labor Statistics. Because of rounding, sums of individual items may not equal totals.

composition. The major occupational change during the past half century has been away from the arduous, unskilled types of jobs toward occupations that require higher levels of skill, and therefore, education and training. The professional and other white-collar occupations have grown fastest over the past half century and this pattern is expected to continue in the years ahead (see Table 5). Employment of professional and technical workers as a group increased by 47 percent between 1950 and 1960, a growth rate more than three times the average for all occupational groups.

The clerical worker category, an important component of the total white-collar group, showed employment gains of 34 percent between 1950 and 1960, a rate of growth second only to that for professional workers. Sales workers were also among the occupational groups which expanded at an above-average rate, by 19 percent, during the 1950's. As a result the white-collar groups increased in relative proportion from 38 percent to 43 percent of total employment between 1950 and 1960 and are expected to continue to gain at a rapid pace. It is anticipated that by 1970 the white-collar categories will account for 47 percent of employment.

In contrast, the blue-collar or manual occupations declined in importance from 1950 to 1960 and are expected to continue to decline between 1960 and 1970. The craftsmen, foremen, and kindred worker group, which account for about one out of every three blue-collar jobs, rose by about 12 percent between 1950 and 1960, a rate below the average for employment generally. Operatives and kindred workers, one of the largest occupational groups in the labor force, did not change significantly in absolute numbers and thus declined in relative importance. The third major component of the blue-collar group, the industrial laborers, recorded an actual decline of 10 percent between 1950 and 1960. By 1970 the blue-collar group is expected to fall in relative importance to about 34 percent of total employment from a level of 39 percent in 1950. Service jobs are expected to increase quite rapidly, from 6.5 million in 1950 to a level of 11 million in 1970. In relative importance this group is expected to rise from 11 percent of total employment in 1950 to about 14 percent in 1970. By 1970 farm jobs are expected to account for only about one out of every twenty jobs in the nation.

IMPLICATIONS FOR THE
HIGH SCHOOL DROPOUT

Educational Attainment and Employment

It is increasingly apparent that the fastest expanding occupational sectors are those which typically require the highest degree of education and training and provide the least in the way of job opportunities for the high school dropout (see Table 6).

Compared with an over-all job gain of 21 percent projected for the period 1960 to 1970, the professional and technical worker category, in which persons presently employed average 16.2 years of school, is expected to register a gain of 43 percent. Less than two out of every hundred high school dropouts find employment in this occupational group.

In the clerical and kindred worker group, which is expected to register a 31 percent gain for the decade, educational attainment in March 1962 averaged 12.5 years. Less than seven out of every hundred high school dropouts find employment in this category.

On the other hand, just about half of all employed persons in March 1962 with less than twelve years of education were employed in blue-collar jobs. One out of every four such persons was employed as an operative or a kindred worker, a job area in which opportunities are in relative decline. Seven percent of all persons with less than a high school graduation in March 1962 were employed as industrial laborers, a category in which no increase in job opportunities is expected for the entire decade of the 1960's. The close relationship between level of educational attainment and occupational category of employment is clear.

TABLE 6 / EMPLOYMENT CHANGE, EDUCATIONAL ATTAINMENT, AND DISTRIBUTION OF EMPLOYED PERSONS BY OCCUPATIONAL GROUP

				March 1962 distribution of employed persons 18 years old and over by educational attainment		
	Change 1960-70		Median school years completed March 1962	Less than high school graduation	High school graduation	Some college education
Occupational group	Number (millions)	Percent				
All groups	13.8	21	12.1	100	100	100
White collar	8.7	30	..	22	54	84
Professional and technical workers	3.2	43	16.2	2	7	43
Managers and proprietors	1.5	21	12.5	9	12	17
Clerical and kindred workers.	3.0	31	12.5	7	27	15
Sales workers	1.0	23	12.5	4	8	8
Blue collar	3.3	14	..	50	32	10
Craftsmen and foremen	1.7	20	11.2	16	14	5
Operatives and kindred workers.	1.6	13	10.1	26	15	4
Laborers, except farm and mine ..	0	0	8.9	7	3	1
Service occupations..	2.8	34	10.3	18	10	5
Farm occupations ...	−1.2	−22	8.7	10	4	2

Occupational Distribution

The relatively bleak outlook for the high school dropout is put into sharper focus by the data presented in Table 7. Only 22 percent of white-collar workers in March 1962 had less than four years of high school, while 40 percent had some college education. In contrast, 65 percent of the blue-collar work force reported less than a high school education, with only 6 percent having some college education. Again we see the tendency for the high school dropout to make up a much larger component of that part of the work force which is expanding least rapidly.

TABLE 7 / OCCUPATIONAL DISTRIBUTION OF THE EMPLOYED 18 YEARS OLD AND OVER BY EDUCATIONAL ATTAINMENT, MARCH 1962

Occupational group	Less than high school graduation	High school graduation	Some college education	Total
All groups	46	32	22	100
White-collar occupations ..	22	38	40	100
Professional and technical workers	7	17	76	100
Managers and proprietors	33	34	33	100
Clerical and kindred workers	21	57	22	100
Sales workers	31	40	29	100
Blue-collar occupations ...	65	29	6	100
Craftsmen and foremen .	57	34	9	100
Operatives and kindred workers	68	27	5	100
Laborers, except farm and mine	75	21	4	100
Service occupations	65	27	8	100
Farm occupations	72	21	7	100

Major Occupation Groups

The kinds of jobs school dropouts obtain are much less desirable than those held by high school graduates. Nonwhite youth appear to be in an even less favorable position, whether they are graduates or dropouts. Table 8 indicates the occupational distribution of white and nonwhite high school dropouts and graduates during the period 1959 to 1961 in terms of their labor force status in October 1961. Better than four out of every ten white high school graduates were employed in the clerical and kindred worker category, compared with about one out of every ten of the white high school dropouts.

Relatively fewer nonwhite workers, whether high school graduates or dropouts, obtain clerical jobs. However, the differences between the employment pattern of white high school graduates and dropouts also hold true for nonwhite youth. While more than 16 percent of nonwhite high school graduates were employed as clerical and kindred workers in 1961, only 3 percent of the nonwhite school dropouts were employed in clerical jobs in 1961. From these data it is evident that the high school dropout can anticipate starting his journey in the world of work in a lower skilled category.

TABLE 8 / MAJOR OCCUPATION GROUP OF HIGH SCHOOL GRADUATES NOT ENROLLED IN COLLEGE BY YEAR OF HIGH SCHOOL GRADUATION AND OF SCHOOL DROPOUTS BY YEAR LAST ATTENDED SCHOOL, BY COLOR, OCTOBER 1961

[Percent distribution of persons 16 to 24 years of age]

	High school graduates		School dropouts			
	White	Non-white	White		Nonwhite	
Major occupation group of employed	1959 to 1961		1959 to 1961	Prior to 1961	1959 to 1961	Prior to 1959
All occupation groups:						
Number (thousands).	1,896	199	636	1,625	198	432
Percent	100.0	100.0	100.0	100.0	100.0	100.0
Professional, technical, and kindred workers	3.5	1.0	1.6	1.2	0.5	0.5
Farmers and farm managers	1.2	..	0.6	1.4	..	3.0
Managers, officials, and proprietors, except farm	1.8	1.0	1.2	1.8	..	0.9
Clerical and kindred workers	42.6	17.4	10.4	6.7	3.0	2.8
Sales workers	5.8	3.0	3.6	3.8	2.0	0.9
Craftsmen, foremen, and kindred workers	5.0	3.5	5.8	12.9	3.0	3.0
Operatives and kindred workers	19.0	23.9	31.0	39.4	13.4	23.2
Private household workers.	1.6	9.0	5.9	2.2	10.4	10.6
Service workers, except private household	8.8	21.4	12.5	10.8	15.9	18.3
Farm laborers and foremen	4.3	11.4	11.8	8.4	37.8	21.5
Laborers, except farm and mine	6.3	8.5	15.6	11.4	13.9	15.4

NOTE: Because of rounding, sums of individual items may not equal totals.

CHANGING LEVELS OF
OCCUPATIONAL ATTAINMENT

Trends in Educational Attainment

In Table 9 we see evidence of the educational advances since 1940 in the nation's work force. For the labor force, 18 years of age and over, the median years of schooling completed have lengthened from 9.1 years to 12.1 years, a gain of three full years in less than a quarter of a century.

TABLE 9   /   TRENDS IN EDUCATIONAL ATTAINMENT OF THE LABOR FORCE 18 YEARS OLD AND OVER, 1940-1962

| Year | Median school years completed | Percent distribution by years of school completed° | | |
		School dropouts	High school graduates	Some college
March 1962	12.1	46.2	32.1	21.7
March 1959	12.0	49.2	31.7	19.1
March 1957	11.7	51.5	30.5	18.0
October 1952	10.9	55.6	27.8	16.6
October 1948°	10.6	..	..	..
April 1940°	9.1	68.1	19.7	12.2

° Does not include persons 65 years old and over except for distribution for March 1962.

The proportion of high school dropouts in the nation's work force has declined accordingly. In April 1940 better than two out of every three American workers had an educational attainment of less than twelve years, with only 12.2 percent having been exposed to some college education. By March 1962 the percent of high school dropouts in the nation's work force had declined to less than half (46.2 percent) with more than one out of every five workers (21.7 percent) achieving some college education. The proportion of high school graduates in the nation's work force has risen steadily from 19.7 percent in April 1940 to 32.1 percent in March 1962.

Educational Status of Labor Force Entrants

With the rising level of educational attainment we are in fact holding more youngsters in school for longer periods of time than ever before. Despite this, however, the number of high school dropouts anticipated for the decade of the 1960's totals 7.5 million. Despite the declining dropout rate, the sharp increase in the number of persons in the younger age categories during the 1960's results in a growth in the total number of high school dropouts entering the labor force of from 7.2 million to 7.5 million (see Table 10).

TABLE 10 / EDUCATIONAL ATTAINMENT OF LABOR FORCE ENTRANTS IN THE 1950's AND THE 1960's

	1950's		1960's°	
Level of attainment	Number (millions)	Percent	Number (millions)	Percent
Completed 4 years high school or better ...	11.4	61.3	18.3	70.9
High school dropout	7.2	38.7	7.5	29.1
Total	18.6	100	25.8	100

° Projection.

Thus, close to 30 percent of the 26 million young people entering the work force of the 1960's will have dropped out of high school before graduation. In the context of what we have noted in terms of the rapid drying-up of opportunities for the high school dropout, one can begin to understand the nature of the problem.

UNEMPLOYMENT AND THE DROPOUT

Unemployment Rates

Unemployment has traditionally been substantially higher among young persons than among adults (see Table 11). In 1962, for example, the unemployment rate for young persons

14 to 19 years of age ran about 13 percent. For those in their early 20's the rate was 9 percent, while for adults 25 years and over it averaged somewhat over 4 percent. Although they represent only one-fifth of the total labor force, young persons under 25 account for a third of the unemployed. Typically, the teenage unemployment rate runs two and one-half to three times as high as the rate for persons over age 25. Very significant also is the fact that an average of more than twice as many male and female nonwhites as whites are unemployed.

TABLE 11 / UNEMPLOYMENT RATES, 1962, BY AGE, COLOR, AND SEX

	White		Nonwhite	
Age group	Male	Female	Male	Female
All ages	4.6	5.5	11.0	11.1
14-17	12.1	11.7	19.9	24.1
18-24	9.3	8.9	16.6	21.9
25-34	3.8	5.4	10.5	11.9
35-44	3.1	4.5	8.8	8.9
45 and over	3.8	3.6	9.1	5.7

There are some obvious reasons for the relatively higher rates of unemployment for these young people, since in this group are included a large proportion of the new entrants into the labor market who frequently have a period of unemployment associated with "shopping around" for a job. Young people also tend to change their jobs more frequently than older persons as they seek the "right" job. Furthermore, young people starting out on their working careers tend to be relatively vulnerable to layoffs because of lack of seniority and inexperience.

Long-Term Unemployment Rates

Of particular concern has been the sharp rise in the long-term unemployment rate for young people. In 1957 the age group 14 to 24 accounted for about 17 percent of the long-term unemployed (six months or longer). By 1962 this age group had risen to account for almost 23 percent of those unemployed for more than six months (see Table 12). Large numbers of youngsters out of school and out of work, some 700,000 of them in 1962, present the nation with a social problem of large dimensions.

TABLE 12 / LONG-TERM UNEMPLOYED: SIX MONTHS AND LONGER BY AGE AND SEX, 1957 AND 1962

Sex and age	1962	1957
Total	100.0	100.0
Male	69.8	70.7
14-24 years	15.0	11.7
25-44 years	23.0	21.8
45 years and over	31.9	37.2
Female	30.2	29.3
14-24 years	7.8	5.4
25-44 years	11.8	12.6
45 years and over	10.6	11.3

Comparative Unemployment Rates

Although the rate of unemployment is high among all young people, it is far higher for the high school dropout. Dropouts differ considerably from high school graduates in that a greater proportion are men, nonwhite, and come from farm areas. In a study of employment and unemployment experience of high school dropouts and their labor force status in October 1961, some striking differences in unemployment experience of dropouts and high school graduates were noted (see Table 13). Almost 27 percent of the dropouts who left school in 1961 were unemployed in October as compared with 18 percent of the high school graduates.

The rate of unemployment for both dropouts and graduates declined as they grew older and obtained more job experience. However, school dropouts are not able to overcome many of their disadvantages and continue to suffer from considerably more unemployment than graduates.

Those who dropped out of school in 1959 had a rate of unemployment in October 1961 nearly twice as high as that for the high school graduates of 1959. Altogether, a total of 500,000 dropouts 16 to 24 years old were unemployed in October 1961, accounting for about one-half of all persons in these ages who were unemployed and out of school.

The dropouts' limited education and the fact that they tend

to be younger than graduates help to explain their special difficulty in finding jobs. The dropouts are clustered in the 16 to 18 age group whereas most graduates tend to be at least 18 years or over.

TABLE 13 / UNEMPLOYMENT RATES, BY SEX, OCTOBER 1961 OF HIGH SCHOOL GRADUATES NOT ENROLLED IN COLLEGE BY YEAR OF HIGH SCHOOL GRADUATION AND OF SCHOOL DROPOUTS BY YEAR LAST ATTENDED SCHOOL

[Persons 16 to 24 years of age]

Graduation status and sex	1961°	1960	1959	Prior to 1959
Both sexes:				
High school graduates	17.9	11.6	8.3	7.4
School dropouts	26.8	17.2	17.0	12.7
Male:				
High school graduates	18.5	13.9	6.8	6.3
School dropouts	28.0	15.0	17.5	10.4
Female:				
High school graduates	17.6	9.9	9.7	8.7
School dropouts	(†)	22.1	16.1	17.9

° Data for graduates refer to June graduates only.
† Percent not shown where base is less than 100,000.

Educational Attainment

The close correlation between unemployment, experience, and level of educational attainment is dramatically shown in the data presented in Table 14. Unemployment rates for high school dropouts run more than half again as high as those for high school graduates, while those with some college education experience unemployment at less than one-third the rate of high school dropouts.

TABLE 14 / UNEMPLOYMENT RATE BY EDUCATIONAL ATTAINMENT, MARCH 1962

Years of school completed	Unemployment rate
Total	6.0
Less than high school graduation	8.1
High school graduation	5.1
Some college education	2.6

Occupational Groups

Another perspective of the reality of the job market for the high school dropout is shown in Table 15. The close correlation between the unemployment rate in occupational groups and the relative importance of high school dropouts in the labor force in each group is clear.

In 1962 unemployment in the professional and technical occupations was at a rate of 1.7 percent. Less than 7 percent of the professional, technical, and kindred worker group, however, consisted of high school dropouts. In contrast, the industrial laborers' unemployment rate was 12.4 percent in 1962 and the data show that three out of every four workers were high school dropouts.

TABLE 15 / UNEMPLOYMENT RATE BY OCCUPATIONAL GROUP AND PERCENT OF GROUP WITH LESS THAN HIGH SCHOOL GRADUATION

Occupational groups	Unemployment rate 1962	Percent high school dropouts March 1962
Professional, technical, and kindred workers	1.7	6.9
Clerical and kindred workers	3.9	21.2
Sales workers	4.1	31.2
Craftsmen, foremen, and kindred workers	5.1	56.9
Operatives and kindred workers	7.5	67.7
Laborers, except farm and mine	12.4	74.6

EARNINGS AND THE DROPOUT

Earnings and Education

Not only can the high school dropout expect to find employment in a relatively low skill occupation and experience a higher rate of unemployment but he can also look forward to a considerably lower level of lifetime earnings (see Table 16). As might be expected, additional years of schooling have little immediate impact on initial earnings. Inexperienced workers in most occupations start at a relatively low level of earnings which tend to increase as skill and experience are acquired.

Persons with a relatively low level of educational attainment, however, tend to reach their earning peak earlier in life and at a considerably lower level than persons at the upper end of the educational attainment range.

TABLE 16 / LIFETIME EARNINGS BY AMOUNT OF EDUCATION, MALES, BY YEARS OF SCHOOL COMPLETED, 1949 AND 1961

Years of school completed	1949	1961
Elementary		
Less than 8 years	$ 98,222	$124,930
8 years	132,683	168,810
High school		
1 to 3 years	$152,068	$193,082
4 years	185,279	224,417
College		
1 to 3 years	$209,282	$273,049
4 years or more	296,377	360,604

SOURCE: U. S. Bureau of the Census.

Estimates of lifetime income provide an insight into the financial rewards associated with education that cannot readily be obtained from the annual income data. Additional schooling is clearly associated with a very substantial increase in lifetime income. A study by Herman P. Miller of the U.S. Bureau of the Census revealed that over a lifetime the difference in earnings of men with one to three years of high school and those of a high school graduate is better than $31,000, while the difference in earnings between a high school graduate and a college graduate is about $136,000.

Earning Trends

Table 17 throws some additional light on earning trends in recent decades. Of males 45 to 54 years of age, those with four or more years of college reported increases in annual income of 66.2 percent between 1949 and 1958, compared with a 47.4 percent increase for high school graduates, a 40.9 percent in-

crease for persons with one to three years of high school, and a
25.9 percent increase for persons with less than eight years of
schooling. There appears to be a clear relationship between
level of educational attainment and rate of increase in annual
income for this period.

TABLE 17 / CHANGES IN INCOME BY EDUCATIONAL ATTAIN-
MENT FOR SELECTED POPULATION GROUPS, 1949-58 AND 1956-
58

	Years of school completed					
	Elementary		High school		College	
Population group	Less than 8 years	8 years	1 to 3 years	4 years	1 to 3 years	4 years or more
Males, 45 to 54 years:						
1949	$2,140	$2,912	$3,209	$3,687	$4,099	$5,549
1958	2,694	4,065	4,522	5,433	6,366	9,220
Percent change	25.9	39.6	40.9	47.4	55.3	66.2
Urban males, 14 years and over:						
1956	$2,654	$3,631	$3,858	$4,563	$4,526	$6,176
1958	2,504	3,594	3,840	4,702	4,921	6,780
Change	− $150	− $37	− $18	$139	$395	$604
Urban females, 14 years and over:						
1956	$830	$1,178	$1,111	$2,093	$1,775	$3,090
1958	845	1,055	1,101	2,181	2,085	3,447
Change	$15	− $123	− $10	$88	$310	$357

SOURCE: U. S. Bureau of the Census, Current Population Reports, Series
P-60, Nos. 33 and 27, and U. S. Census of Population, 1950, Special Report P-E, No. 5B.

Distribution of Family Income

In Table 18 we see evidence of the close relationship between
education of family head and family income in the year 1961.
While 78 percent of those with less than high school graduation
had family income under $3,000 a year, only 21 percent of
those earning $15,000 and over were in the less than high
school graduation category. At the upper end of the family income range, $15,000 and over, 58 percent of all family heads

had some college education, while in the under $3,000 category only 7 percent reported some college education.

TABLE 18 / PERCENT DISTRIBUTION OF FAMILY INCOME, 1961, BY YEARS OF SCHOOL COMPLETED BY HEAD

	Education of head		
Family income	Less than high school graduation	High school graduation	Some college
Total	55	26	20
Under $3,000	78	15	7
$3,000 to $4,999	62	26	10
$5,000 to $6,999	50	32	17
$7,000 to $9,999	42	32	26
$10,000 to $14,999	33	28	38
$15,000 and over	21	20	58

SOURCE: U. S. Bureau of the Census.

CHARACTERISTICS OF THE DROPOUT

Some Factors in Graduation Status

Recent studies of the Census Bureau reveal some interesting high lights on the characteristics of young people who reach the senior year of high school and of those who do not, and of high school seniors who graduate and those who fail to graduate. The findings are presented in Tables 19 to 21. More than 12 percent of high school seniors in 1959 did not graduate, nearly 16 percent of the boys and 9 percent of the girls. In both categories, the comparison of nonwhite seniors who did not graduate was much higher, for example, 24 percent of nonwhite males compared with 15 percent of white males. There appears to be some relationship to place of residence, with 14.1 percent of urban seniors not graduating, compared with 11.3 percent of seniors in the rural farm areas, and 8.9 percent of seniors in the rural nonfarm areas.

A close relationship with occupation of the household head appears to be evident (see Table 21). The proportion of October 1959 high school seniors who did not graduate varied from a low of 8.1 percent for youngsters coming from farm worker

TABLE 19 / GRADUATION STATUS IN 1960 OF OCTOBER 1959 HIGH SCHOOL SENIORS BY SELECTED DEMOGRAPHIC CHARACTERISTICS

[Based on persons reporting characteristics]

| | High school seniors in October 1959 | | |
| | | Percent who— | |
Subject	Number reporting	Graduated	Did not graduate
Color and Sex			
Total	2,057,000	87.7	12.3
Male	1,037,000	84.2	15.8
White	941,000	84.9	15.0
Nonwhite	96,000	76.0	24.0
Female	1,020,000	91.2	8.8
White	924,000	91.9	8.1
Nonwhite	96,000	84.4	15.6
Residence			
Urban	1,215,000	85.9	14.1
Rural nonfarm	549,000	91.1	8.9
Rural farm	293,000	88.7	11.3

SOURCE: U. S. Bureau of the Census. Series Census—ERS (P-27), No. 32.

families to 9.7 percent in families with white-collar worker heads, 13.2 percent with manual or service heads, and 23.2 percent of youngsters with heads of family unemployed or not in the labor force.

Family income, too, appears significant. Seniors from families earning under $6,000 experience a failure-to-graduate rate of about 17 percent compared with an approximately 7 percent rate in families with annual income of $6,000 and over. Table 20 shows the close relationship between IQ quartile and the ratio of graduates as well as close relationship to achievement. Interestingly enough, high school seniors in the general curriculum experience the higher dropout rate, 18.3 percent, compared with 12.7 percent in the commercial and vocational curriculum and 4.1 percent in the college preparatory curriculum.

SUMMARY

The realities of the job market for high school dropouts can be understood best in the framework of the basic patterns of population trend, labor force changes, industrial and occupational shifts, and the new patterns of educational attainment that are now characteristic.

Among the more significant developments to be considered are:

1. We are on the threshold of an unprecedented influx of 26 million youths into the labor market of the 1960's. The large expansion of the under-25 group in the labor force, at the same time that rapid advances in technological development

TABLE 20 / GRADUATION STATUS IN 1960 OF OCTOBER 1959 HIGH SCHOOL SENIORS BY SELECTED MEASURES OF ABILITY AND EDUCATIONAL PLANNING

[Based on persons reporting characteristics]

	High school seniors in October 1959		
		Percent who—	
Subject	Number reporting	Graduated	Did not graduate
Intelligence Quotient (IQ)			
Top quartile	552,000	94.7	5.3
Second quartile	491,000	93.5	6.5
Third quartile	300,000	88.0	12.0
Bottom quartile	343,000	79.9	20.1
Scholastic Standing			
Top quartile	462,000	97.4	2.6
Second quartile	419,000	96.7	3.3
Third quartile	402,000	95.3	4.7
Bottom quartile	475,000	80.5	19.5
High School Curriculum			
College preparatory	753,000	95.9	4.1
General	709,000	81.7	18.3
Commercial, vocational, and other	401,000	87.3	12.7

SOURCE: U. S. Bureau of the Census. Series Census—ERS (P-27), No. 32.

TABLE 21 / GRADUATION STATUS IN 1960 OF OCTOBER 1959 HIGH SCHOOL SENIORS BY SELECTED ECONOMIC CHARACTER-ISTICS

[Based on persons reporting characteristics]

| | High school seniors in October 1959 | | |
| | | Percent who— | |
Subject	Number reporting	Graduated	Did not graduate
Occupation of household head			
White-collar worker	713,000	90.3	9.7
Manual or service worker ...	1,005,000	86.8	13.2
Farm worker	185,000	91.9	8.1
Unemployed or not in labor force	155,000	76.8	23.2
Family income			
Under $4,000	289,000	84.4	15.6
$4,000 to $5,999	241,000	81.3	18.7
$6,000 to $9,999	266,000	93.6	6.4
$10,000 and over	123,000	91.1	8.9

SOURCE: U. S. Bureau of the Census. Series Census—ERS (P-27), No. 32.

in industry are taking place, presents some major barriers to any satisfactory labor force adjustment of the dropout.

2. Fifteen times as many young people under age 25 will enter the work force in the 1960's as did in the 1950's. About 30 percent of the 26 million will be high school dropouts.

3. Beginning in 1963 there will be about 1 million more young people each year reaching the typical dropout age of 16 than the average level for the five-year period of 1958-62.

4. Despite the increase in the total number of dropouts in the 1960's, the dropout rate is declining; educational attainment is rising and the proportion of high school dropouts in the labor force has recently fallen below the 50 percent mark.

5. Dramatic shifts in industry are taking place. Under the impact of rapid technological change, job opportunities on

the farms and in the factories are shrinking—job areas that typically provided employment opportunities to dropouts.

6. White-collar and service jobs are expanding rapidly; blue-collar and farm jobs are shrinking. It is evident that the major areas of job expansion in the decade of the 1960's and beyond will be in those occupational categories that require the highest degree of education and training. On balance, job opportunities for dropouts are contracting.

7. Unemployment is typically, at least in the United States, a problem of youth. Unemployment rates in the teenage years run two and one-half to three times the rate for workers over 25.

8. Unemployment hits the dropout even harder. The circle of relationship between level of educational attainment and occupation distribution of employment and unemployment closes in on the dropout with an unemployment rate that, good times or bad, runs considerably higher than for graduates.

9. Not only can the dropout expect to experience higher rates of unemployment and work in a lower skill level, but he can also anticipate lower annual and lifetime earnings.

10. There is evidence that among the significant factors determining *who* will become a dropout are: color, place of residence, education, occupation of family head, family income, IQ level, scholastic achievement, and course of study.

The outlook for the dropout in the world of work is bleak and will become increasingly so, unless new paths are found to bridge the gap between school and some of the expanding job areas within their reach, such as the service and skilled worker categories.

While the high school dropout may not represent, for the most part, college potential, the expanding occupations present a fruitful area for the development of training methods needed to move the dropout into some of the rapidly expanding areas of the economy. For smaller numbers, it may be possible to motivate them to extend their education and training to reach into the faster-growing job categories, the semiprofessional, technical, clerical, and sales occupations.

Unless such paths are found, it is clear that the realities of the job market for the high school dropout can mean only higher levels of unemployment, lower levels of earnings, and, when employed, work in jobs that are rapidly feeling the adverse impact of automation and technological development.

@@@@@@@@@@@@@@@@@@@@@@@@@@@@@@@@@

JOBS, DROPOUTS,
AND AUTOMATION

@@@@@@@@@@@@@@@@@@@@@@@@@@@@@@@@@

ELI GINZBERG

INTRODUCTION

During the past century our young people have spent an increasing number of years in school preparatory to starting work. The patterns of schooling have differed in various regions of the country, and access to and use of the available schooling has differed among various groups in the population. But beneath these diversities have been certain general trends: children and young people have tended to spend more years in school; the school year has been lengthened; the quality of the staff has been improved; the curriculum has been broadened and deepened to better meet the needs of an increasingly diversified school population; more and more young people have been graduating from high school and going on to college.

Today about four out of every six young people earn a high school diploma, and approximately half of these enter college. Once again, about half who enter college eventually earn their baccalaureate degree—that is, about one in every six in the age group. Put negatively, five out of six young people do not graduate from college: two leave high school; two stop with a high school diploma; one more leaves at some time in college.

In comparison, in 1900 only seventeen in a hundred earned a high school diploma; only seven in a hundred, a college degree. In 1930 the comparable figures were thirty-five in a hundred and thirteen in a hundred. For a great variety of reasons, including the belief that education is a good in itself, it is a mainspring of our democracy because it creates a literate electorate; it underpins our dynamic economy by helping to develop the potential and skill of future workers; it is a cornerstone of a mobile society because it offers the opportunity to youngsters born into low-income families to acquire the prerequisites by which they will be able to move up the occupational ladder; for these and other reasons, the American people have been willing to spend increasing sums on education and have been willing to delay the time when young people begin to work.

THE SCHOOL AS TRAINER

Our society has long considered the primary task of the school to be instruction in basic knowledge and reinforcement of basic social values. The school has the responsibility of the second stage of the socialization process—the family has responsibility for the initial effort. The school is the transitional environment between the sheltered family and the competitive work place. With this role, the school has always served as a preparatory training-ground for employment.

In addition to instructing children in the use of language and numbers and in familiarizing them with certain basic facts about the natural and social world, the school provides training in discipline, routines, cooperation, leadership and the other basic facets of adult life, particularly those reflected in the world of work.

THE CHANGING OCCUPATIONAL STRUCTURE

Whenever a basic social institution such as the public school has multiple functions to perform, it is inevitable that the professional leadership as well as concerned citizens will disagree about the exact emphasis which the institution should place on the accomplishment of one or another objective. No decade has been free of disagreements about the responsibility of the schools for preparing young people for gainful employment, and about the best ways to discharge this responsibility.

Rather than enter upon a review of this never-ending controversy, it might be more useful to make explicit some of the major changes in the relationship between education and employment that have characterized the recent past and those that are likely to be upon us before very long. First, with regard to the changes in the economy: the number of jobs which require little more than a strong back and a willingness to work long and hard has been declining rapidly. One generality that can be safely ventured here is that whenever a machine is invented that is capable of doing the tasks formerly performed by large numbers of persons, it is likely to be installed—even if the machine is costly and even if the workers were paid a low wage. The last several decades have seen more and more routine laboring jobs eliminated in agriculture, mining, construction, manufacturing and in the service sector of the economy.

At the same time, the economy has created opportunities for an increasing proportion of persons with professional, technical, or managerial skills—that is, individuals who have completed higher education.

Another development has been the rapid expansion of white-collar jobs below the professional and technical level—that is, in clerical and sales occupations. These are the jobs for which a high school diploma or junior college degree have increasingly become prerequisite.

THE RESPONSE OF THE SCHOOLS

We have noted that there has been a steady expansion in higher education reflected in the growing proportion of the population which attends and graduates from college. These are the young people who are filling the rapidly expanding professional and technical occupations. We also referred to the steady increases in the proportion who complete high school but do not go beyond—the source of supply for the rapidly expanding white-collar sector of the economy. For both of these groups, the schools have done well: they have been able to attract, hold, and educate an increasing proportion of the population for those occupational areas which have been undergoing the most rapid expansion.

But what about the one out of three young persons who leaves high school and then faces a relative and even absolute decline in the number of laboring positions available? The school-leaving age in most states remains sixteen, although a few states require attendance until seventeen or eighteen. In contrast, in some states young people can still get working papers at fourteen. In light of the steady upward drift in the educational and skill requirements for new workers, the question must be asked whether the educational authorities have been slow to respond to the changing demands of employers. The answer to this question hinges in considerable measure on the characteristics of the young people who now leave high school as soon as legally possible.

THE DROPOUTS

The number of years that a young person must remain in school is determined by law. But the number of years that he is able to profit from education is a function of a great many other variables including his genetic potential, his developed intelligence, his value structure, the influences exerted on him by family, community and peers, and by special circumstances that may dominate his life—such as trouble with the police, early parenthood, emotional instability.

The considerable effort that has been made in recent years to study the "dropout" has provided many, if not all, of the answers to the question of why a significant proportion of young people fail to complete high school. By far the most important reason is that by the time they reach school-leaving age, usually sixteen, many of them are several years behind schedule. Instead of being ready to enter the eleventh grade, they may be in the eighth or ninth grade. This usually reflects an early difficulty in mastering the curriculum which, in turn, caused the youngster to develop negative attitudes toward the school. Classes become uninteresting and the discipline increasingly burdensome. Small wonder that this group takes the first opportunity to escape from these constraints.

Another large group of dropouts are young men and women who have been able to make normal progress in their studies but have never become really interested in learning, and do not see much point in prolonging this experience until they acquire a diploma. Many of these young people are growing up in communities which place little importance on educational achievement, where the facilities and teaching staff are often inadequate; usually they are not encouraged by family or friends to continue in school. Their early withdrawal usually reflects a pervasive lack of interest.

The third group is a much more heterogeneous assemblage of young people, including some with special talents, who have major problems which make it difficult or impossible for them to continue in school. Some have run afoul of the law and are already in custodial institutions. Others are so disturbed that they cannot control themselves sufficiently to meet the minimum requirements of the educational system. A considerable number of young women withdraw because of marriage or pregnancy. Others, usually boys, are determined to get away from home at the earliest possible moment. Some young people, from very low-income families, are under pressure to become wage earners as early as possible. These groups, and other distinguishable groups of young people, when given the opportunity, prefer to leave school.

THE PRESENT DILEMMA

The term "dropout" has an insidious connotation until one realizes that in earlier generations it could have been applied to youngsters who did not complete elementary school, and that it is beginning to be applied to those who enter college but do not stay to earn a degree.

Despite the increasing public clamor for all young people to remain in high school until they graduate, the following realistic factors must be confronted. There is no point in forcing young people to remain in school if they have not acquired the skills with which to learn, and if they cannot relate their school experiences to their present or future life, they therefore do not make any effort to learn.

The ambitious national effort which would be required to insure that all young people graduate from high school can be justified only if the knowledge and skills they would acquire between their seventeenth and nineteenth years would significantly enhance their opportunities for employment or would add to their individual and social performance as adults. The incremental education—which would be about 20 percent more than they now have—might or might not prove worthwhile.

Moreover, the question must be faced whether the present reliance of many employers on a high school diploma as prerequisite for employment for new workers is an inexpensive screening device which has the additional effect of reducing the number of potential applicants from minority groups, or whether the knowledge and skills acquired in the last two years of high school actually add a necessary increment to the young person's personal capital. If underemployment prosperity, which has characterized the American economy since shortly after the end of the Korean War continues, it is likely that employers who must select new workers from among high school and post-high-school graduates will simply raise their criterion, and the young man with only a high school diploma will still be at the end of the queue.

It is not a high school diploma per se that qualifies a young person for work and for responsible citizenship. Rather, it is his acquisition during the years that he is growing up of a value orientation, social competences, intellectual knowledge and skills, and study and work habits that will enable him to find a place within our highly differentiated economy and society. Therefore, to appreciate the challenge to the schools it is necessary to look more closely at emerging social and economic trends.

THE SHAPE OF THE FUTURE

In a very few years the vast majority of the American people will be living in metropolitan areas. The modern city does not provide the type of protective environment that for a long time was characteristic of rural America, where the uneducated could survive at a modest level. Many of our most acute problems reflect the transfer of the rural population, white and Negro, from the low-income farm areas of the Southeast into the large urban centers. We are suddenly becoming aware of a two-generation gap between the education and skills of the new migrants and those of the settled urban population. It may not be necessary for the urban dweller of the future to be a high school graduate but it is difficult to see how he will be able to make his way unless he has the equivalent of at least ten years of effective schooling back of him.

The word "automation," like the word "dropout," is highly charged. Some writers proclaim that we are in the early stages of a revolution that will soon result in making work or workers obsolete. The new automated machines, with the help of a few programmers and maintenance workers, they say, will be able to turn out all the goods we need or desire. The critical questions, they claim, will be how to distribute income so that there will be an effective demand for all these goods, and how to turn our new leisure into constructive channels.

Others hold that nothing has changed; there is no revolution, nor is there likely to be one. They claim that a tremendous gap remains between what we want and need as individuals and as a society and our ability to produce the required goods and services. Prophecy is a poor platform for policy. The future will certainly be different from the past and yet the past gives us our best clue to the shape of the future, especially the near future. On this basis, we can be reasonably sure that agriculture will provide relatively very few new jobs and fewer will utilize unskilled labor. The President's First Report on Manpower indicated that nine out of ten young people now growing up on farms will have to find employment in other sectors of the economy.

The outlook for manufacturing is less clear. We know, however, that it was not until this year that total employment exceeded the peak reached in 1943 and that the proportion of blue-collar workers in manufacturing is considerably lower than in the early forties. A cautious estimate would see no significant absolute and surely no relative increases in manufacturing employment in the years ahead and would forecast, in any case, a shrinkage in semi-skilled jobs.

Technological advances in construction have been steady if not spectacular and this is the way it is likely to continue—although there is always the possibility of a radical breakthrough in prefabrication which would lead to a substantial substitution of machinery for labor.

Currently, two out of every three persons in the labor force is employed, not in the goods-producing sector, but in the service sector; that is, in trade, transportation and public utilities, finance, insurance and real estate, government services and other services. While it is unlikely that the machine will be able to displace labor at a rapid rate in some of these service fields, the potentialities of rapid development in others cannot be ruled out; in fact, it must be anticipated in light of the potency of the computer. Moreover, the machine is not the only factor that operates to economize in the use of labor; the growth of enterprises and markets, improvements in managerial effort, the upgrading of the work force itself all have this potential.

While the foregoing summary statement does not imply any extreme position about tremendous disemployment as a result of automation, it does point to the probability of a relative, and possibly even an absolute, reduction in unskilled jobs and a relative decline in the proportion of semi-skilled jobs. There is another aspect to automation that should be briefly mentioned. Although substantially enlarged resources are being devoted to research and development this will certainly result in the more rapid obsolescence of knowledge and skill. This creates a concomitant need for the expansion of educational and training opportunities for adults if the nation is to have a vital work force.

The outlook, then, is for further relative and even absolute declines in the unskilled and semi-skilled blue-collar jobs; a probable slowing up in the expansion of white-collar jobs in those sectors where the computer can be installed; a continued growth in professional and technical workers; a possible growing gap between the total number of jobs available and the total number of younger and older persons available for and interested in working.

THE OPTIONS WE CONFRONT

1. Acknowledging that the amount of education an individual has acquired has a significant influence on his prospects for employment, should we assume that all young people coming of working age will be employed if they have earned a high school diploma? If education is only one of the determinants of employability, how much effort should society devote to attempting to keep the dropout in high school? How much to other approaches aimed at expanding the demand for workers with limited competence?

2. To what extent can the high school solve the dropout problem, even with substantially enlarged resources? May it not be

necessary to seek fundamental improvements much earlier in the schooling process so that all young people acquire the reading and other skills which they will need if they are to make constructive use of four years of secondary education?

3. Since many high school students with average or even above-average ability drop out because they are not interested in their classes and do not understand the importance of acquiring additional education, could some of this group be encouraged to continue to graduation if more work-study programs were available? Would their exposure to real jobs, their association with adults, their earning of money, provide the stimulation and incentive which are now lacking? How practical is it for the schools to seek the cooperation of employers and trade unions to explore this dimension?

4. No matter what efforts are made to hold all adolescents in school or in school-corrected programs until they earn a high school diploma, some will continue to drop out. To what extent do these young people now have the opportunity to return to school or otherwise acquire a diploma? What steps might be taken to broaden their opportunities for a "second chance"?

5. Many employers have established the requirement of a high school diploma for all new members of their work force. Is this a reasonable requirement? If not, should efforts be made to encourage them to restudy this requirement in order to increase the opportunities of dropouts to obtain employment?

6. In light of the probable speedier obsolescence of knowledge and skills in the years ahead, what actions should be recommended to individuals, employers, and communities so that more adults will have the opportunity to continue their education and training?

7. The probable increasing proportion of jobs in professional and technical occupations in the future raises the question of whether there are serious barriers to entrance to college, junior college or other post-high school educational and training facilities for some qualified young people and what types of action may be recommended to reduce or eliminate these barriers.

8. Is there any danger that, as a result of the current concern with the future employability of many young people, the high

schools will slight or ignore other important goals? What, if anything, can be done to assure that this does not occur?

9. If more and more adults will need access to educational and training facilities, what steps should be taken by employers, governmental agencies, and other strategic groups in our society to help assure that the required facilities and personnel will be made available?

10. What actions can narrow the marked differences among regions in their ability and willingness to support education, and the substantial differences between urban and rural communities within the same region, as well as between the central cities and the suburban areas of large metropolitan centers? What additional actions are required to assure that each child has a reasonable opportunity to get a solid educational preparation for his later work and life?

11. The school builds on the foundation that the family lays. What special efforts should be made by the school systems in communities in which large numbers of children and young people are growing up under handicapping circumstances, including the particular handicap of not living with both parents? Should school boards attempt to persuade the American people that they should spend more money on children from low-income homes than on children from more privileged families? If this policy is sound, what adjustments are required in our system of taxation to accomplish this end? What programs are most likely to prove productive?

12. If the American people can be persuaded to make additional resources available for education in general, and for secondary education in particular, what adjustments are called for in the present variegated patterning of secondary education which includes academic, vocational and general curricula in comprehensive and specialized high schools?

CONCLUDING OBSERVATIONS

Many of the issues posed above are of long standing. Some go back to the earliest days of public education. But there are several new dimensions that should be borne in mind as these problems are studied, for the solutions must be attuned to them.

Educational preparation has come to play an increasingly important part in determining the work and careers of the population. This means that any serious deficiencies in the schools will have increasingly serious consequences for the productivity of the economy and the stability of the society. A significant minority of the population grows up in a family and community setting which fails to prepare them to profit from what the school has to offer. Hence, the school faces a special challenge to meet the needs of this disadvantaged minority.

No matter how effectively the schools discharge their responsibilities, not all of their graduates will necessarily secure employment. Full employment will be easier to approach if gross differences in educational background are reduced, but even if these differences are eliminated, to achieve full employment now requires additional changes.

But if the schools are to make their optimal contribution to the preparation of the population for work and life, they must meet the overriding challenge of awakening in all of their pupils an interest in learning and teaching them the basic skill of reading on which a lifetime of continued learning ultimately rests.

Part
Three

SOCIAL
AND
HISTORICAL
FACTORS

@@@@@@@@@@@@@@@@@@@@@@@@@@@@@@@@@@

INTRODUCTION

@@@@@@@@@@@@@@@@@@@@@@@@@@@@@@@@@

Dropout studies of every level of sophistication and from every locale of the country are virtually unanimous in finding dropout rates to run very significantly higher among lower-class youths—among youths from low-income families, and especially among underprivileged minority group youths. Hence, the sources of the dropout problem are deep, multiple, and complexly interwoven throughout the fabric and structure of American life. Suddenly the specters of automation and population expansion highlighted the existence of large segments of our society which technological advance was increasingly setting adrift. Yet this condition and climate of drift—or alienation, as so many of our authors call it—has been a longstanding, and, paradoxically, a significant feature of the structure of our society.

The problem is highly complex. It is not simply that a substantial segment of our society—the segment from which a preponderant proportion of dropouts derive—is alienated and isolated from the mainstream of American social and economic life. In many cases the effects the brutal experience of alienation has wrought upon its victims remain. And there seems little reason to expect that any amount of education can be really effective and meaningful so long as its claimant remains in an inferior relationship to the mainstream of society.

For S. M. Miller, the dropout problem is fundamentally a political problem. He finds that school is irrelevant for the majority of dropouts, since they have long had in mind job levels that require little formal education. Consequently, the immediate necessary steps are to increase the range of jobs available, to structure and ease access to them, and to improve the conditions on these jobs. But, Professor Miller says, these are fundamentally political not educational issues. And resolution of educational issues, he proposes, can only be realized within the context of a deeper and more inclusive economic and political resolution.

For Herman Long and Charles Willie, not even great improvements in economic and political conditions can be adequate, unless they are accompanied by certain crucial social improvements—above all, the end of racial segregation in all its forms. Professor Long recapitulates the history of the Negro's experience of isolation and alienation and the ways in which this experience has engendered severely depressed expectations. Professor Willie, echoing several other authors, argues that educational change can only follow upon a more vast social and institutional change: "To focus only on the deprived child without considering also the social system which alienates him and contributes to his deprivation may not solve even half of the problem and certainly not the whole."

IN SEARCH OF A FUTURE

EUNICE S. GRIER

BACKGROUND AND OBJECTIVES

This study of career-seeking experiences of selected Negro high school graduates in Washington, D. C. was undertaken by the Washington Center for Metropolitan Studies in an effort to provide knowledge helpful in solving one of the most critical problems facing urban America today.

At this crucial period in its history, America is becoming aware that its survival both as a world power and as a viable social and economic system may depend on the effectiveness with which it utilizes the human potential of all its citizens. Technological advance, essential to maintaining our international position, has created a growing mismatch between labor supply and job needs. Some skills are in critically short supply, and the shortages hamper further progress. At the same time, the economy has increasing difficulty utilizing persons with other skills, or with no skills at all. The resulting "hard-core" unemployment menaces the nation's economic stability at the same time as it brings hardship to the families directly involved.

The handicaps of inadequate educational preparation and restricted job opportunity, moreover, fall disproportionately upon certain groups in America's population. One of the most important of these groups is Negroes. And since they are concentrated overwhelmingly in certain geographic locations, the obstacles which hinder them tend to become burdens upon entire localities.

Particularly hard hit are the central cities of our major metropolitan areas where Negroes constitute an ever-larger proportion of the total; yet their political boundaries are usually static. As a result, the core municipalities of the metropolis encounter increasing difficulty in coping with the inevitable concomitants of Negroes' disadvantaged status: economic deprivation; problems of family life, children and youth; neighborhood deterioration; and growing political unrest. They must meet burgeoning human problems with declining resources.

In metropolitan Washington these problems are seen in particularly sharp contrast. Here, overall levels of education, occupation and income are among the highest in the nation; and yet shortages of certain key skills are already apparent and threaten to become more serious in the decade ahead. At the same time, a substantial fraction of the area's people, and especially of its Negro residents, lack the educational preparation necessary to take advantage of many of the job openings now going begging.

Overall unemployment is presently low in the National Capital Area; nonetheless, jobless rates are distressingly high among certain groups. At the time of the 1960 Census, for example, Negro males were unemployed over two and a half times as often as white males. Among Negro male youth under 20, over one-fifth were looking for work. Underemployment is a frequent problem as well. Family incomes among Negroes are substantially lower overall than those for whites, and at equivalent educational levels Negro workers usually earn less than their white counterparts.

With 85 percent of all Negroes in the metropolitan area residing within the District of Columbia, and the District's residents now well over half Negro, the City of Washington bears the brunt of the manifold and accumulated disadvantages of the metropolitan area's Negro population.

Further, the present situation holds sobering portents. For over 200,000 of the nearly half-million Negro residents of the metropolitan area in 1960 were under 21 years old. Most of these children and youth will enter the adult world of work and family responsibility in the next two decades.

In whatever context one views the problem—whether for the nation as a whole, for the 212 metropolitan areas where over two-thirds of America's population now resides, or for metropolitan Washington which is the nation's administrative heart and its principal showplace for the world—it becomes apparent that the full utilization of the potential contributions of youth is essential to continued social and economic health. It was with these matters in mind that the Washington Center, through its Commission on Human Resources, undertook the present study.

If America is to solve this problem, three critical areas demand attention. One is the educational system, which must prepare youth adequately and realistically for the responsibilities of a changing world. The second is the employment market; employers must recognize and anticipate their personnel needs, and must be ready and willing to take full advantage of the skills of all citizens in order to fill these needs.

The third area is the process of transition from schooling to ultimate career—a process which is largely accomplished, in our society, during the period of roughly a half dozen years between the time a youth leaves high school and the time he settles down finally to the general type of job he will probably pursue for the remainder of his working life. The study reported here focuses particularly upon this critical transition period.

For youth this is a time of testing and being tested, of exploring, of trial and often of error. No matter how adequate his educational preparation may be, no matter how bright the opportunities which beckon, this period will be instrumental in determining how well a youth makes use of his talents toward the betterment of himself and the nation in which he lives.

During this phase some young people go on to post-high school education; and with more or less sureness of aim they select from the wide range of educational fields the one to which they feel themselves best suited by ability and preference. Others, unequipped to pursue further training by financial resources, scholastic aptitude, or interest, make their choice from among those starting jobs available to persons with no preparation beyond high school.

In few if any stages of life are the decisions which must be faced more crucial. Yet little precise information is available about the events of this period of trial and their impact upon the individual. This, then, is a pilot study aimed at overcoming a few of the factual limitations to more effective action on problems confronting youth during the transition from school to career. It is an examination in some depth of the experiences of a selected group of Negro high school graduates in the District of Columbia during the five years immediately following their graduation.

In light of limited immediate resources and the general paucity of information on the subject, the study was viewed as an attempt to identify problems for further examination and experimental action—not as a definitive effort intended to produce final recommendations. Its general focus was upon the factors which might be impeding the ultimate achievement of such young people's full human potential. Two general kinds of obstacles were posed for examination: those which might exist in the job situation, and those which might reside in the youth themselves or in their background of experience in home, school and community.

THE YOUTH STUDIED

The youth whose experiences we examined included all male graduates of the class of 1956 from one District of Columbia high school who could be located five years after their graduation. There were forty-six young men in the sample, of whom thirty-nine were reached for personal interviews in considerable depth; seven more were contacted by mail. In addition to data on experience following graduation, the interviews sought considerable information on home and school background, initial aspirations and present outlook.

The five-year interval permitted a substantial time lapse in which the graduates had opportunity for experience in job seeking or post-high school training. At the same time, it allowed study of a group of graduates still reasonably contemporary with young people completing high school today, and who faced fairly comparable conditions in their efforts to find productive places in the adult world of work. The sample was limited to male graduates because of the traditional position of the male as the principal breadwinner in the American family.

It was also limited to youth who had attended a school whose coursework and orientation was aimed largely at preparation for college and whose student body was generally believed capable of pursuing education beyond the high school level. Graduates of this school were used to minimize the chance that any problems they encountered in seeking careers would be due to serious limitations in ability and interest.

There was no way of comparing this group with the general run of white or Negro graduates from District of Columbia high schools; when they were graduated, no standardized system-wide achievement testing existed in the District schools. It is, however, probably safe to characterize them as an above-average group of young men, though not one of blue-ribbon caliber. The male graduates of this class had generally lagged behind their female classmates in academic achievement; most had attained average grade records, but this performance was in the context of a school with higher-than-average expectations for its students.

Almost all were natives of the District of Columbia; even among the handful who had been born elsewhere, most had come to Washington at an early age and had received all of their formal education in District public schools.

THE FAMILY SITUATION

At the time they were interviewed for this study, five years after graduation from high school, the majority of the young men were unmarried and were still living at home with their parents. Their parents were better educated than the average of Washington area Negroes, for whom the median in 1960 was less than ten years of schooling. Only about ten percent reported that neither parent had graduated from high school, and almost half of the young men had at least one parent with some college training.

Most of the youth had grown up in stable, two-parent families, although there was a sizeable minority from broken households. In the latter cases it was usually the father who was missing from the family. A majority of the households were small or moderate in size.

The occupations of both fathers and mothers ranged from professional to unskilled laborer or service worker. Only a small minority of the parents were professionally employed, and almost all of these were schoolteachers. Most of the professionals, moreover, were mothers rather than fathers. This meant that only a few of the youth had a professionally employed parent of the same sex. Close to half of the fathers were engaged in semi-skilled or unskilled laboring or service jobs; almost the same proportion of mothers were service workers. Generally, however, parents' employment appeared to be steady, rather than on-and-off, by-the-day work.

On the basis of their parents' occupations and also the appearance of their homes, most of these youth seem to have come from families where incomes and living standards were modest. They were not slum dwellers from seriously deprived backgrounds; but neither were many of them well-to-do.

From the relatively high educational level achieved by the parents, it might be anticipated that they would have high hopes for their children's future. On the other hand, many of the parents might have difficulty in aiding their children financially during college; and also in providing them with concrete advice about the rewards, prerequisites and demands of the professional careers toward which most were taking the first step by attending an academic high school. That these things were generally the case, we shall see shortly.

INITIAL ASPIRATIONS

The youth themselves almost uniformly held high aspirations. At the time of their graduation, virtually all of them wished for a career in one of the professions. Even among those with no clearly formulated career goals, professional occupations were usually viewed as desirable; and they considered possibilities chiefly within this range.

Many of those concerned with the advancement of minority youth believe that one of their chief obstacles is predominantly low aspirations, aspirations presumably kept low by long acclimatization to the barriers of discrimination. Negro youth do not achieve much, it is held, partly because they do not aim very high. Several careful studies in recent years, however, have placed this assumption in question.[1] Our study found no evidence in conflict with such studies. Whatever difficulty the youth in our sample may have subsequently experienced in their search for careers was *not* due to initially low aspirations.

PURSUIT OF FURTHER TRAINING

In line with their attendance at an academic high school and their ambitions for personal attainment few of the young men stopped with a high school diploma. Of the forty-six graduates, thirty-nine took some form of post-high school training. Thirty-two entered colleges with degree-granting powers, and seven more attended schools for specialized technical training. Only seven took no post-high school training at all. So far, then, it would appear that most of the youth not only had high ambitions but were launched upon the path to fulfillment after leaving high school.

Five years later, most of the young men still possessed high aims, but comparatively few were very far along toward achievement. Furthermore, many had altered their specific career goals one or more times.

Of the seven who had entered schools for specialized technical skills, five were now employed in occupations directly related to their training. For the college-bound, however, the picture was quite different. Among the thirty-two who had entered degree-granting institutions, only seven had actually received bachelor's degrees.

Most of the rest had interrupted their studies at least once, and often twice or more. Very few of these, however, appeared to be permanent "college dropouts." Of the twenty-five young

---

[1] For example, see A. Antonovsky, and M. J. Lerner, "Negro and White Youth in Elmira," Chapter in *Discrimination and Low Incomes*, edited by A. Antonovsky and L. Lorwin (New York: State Commission Against Discrimination, 1958). See also Hylan Lewis, *Child Rearing Among Low-Income Families* (Washington, D. C.: Washington Center for Metropolitan Studies, 1961).

men who had some college, but had not yet been graduated when they were interviewed for this study, eighteen were presently enrolled. Four more said that they expected to register for the semester coming up shortly. For only three did the likelihood of completing college seem extremely slim at the time this study was made.

REASONS FOR INTERRUPTION

Precisely why these young men had interrupted their college careers was not entirely clear in all cases, and a number of the respondents appeared unable to report their own motivations with any great degree of clarity. Undoubtedly the reasons were seldom simple, and it is probably safe to state that there was often more than one contributing factor.

Difficulty with the pace of college coursework apparently played a role for some. Three of the youth reported that they had been suspended or expelled from college because of failing academic grades; all three had been reinstated, however, and were continuing their studies when they were interviewed.

Several of the dropouts indicated that they had done so in order to earn additional money which they needed to continue in college. Probing, however, suggested that the definition of inadequate funds ranged widely—from lack of money to cover the essentials of tuition and boarding expenses (obviously a severe need in a few cases), to funds adequate not only for academic requirements but also for such material acquisitions as cars and for the social events that are part of most campus life. Financial burdens due to early marriage apparently had little effect on progress in college, however; relatively few had married, and among these most had persisted in their studies.

THE "FLOUNDERING" PHENOMENON

The most frequent explanation given by students for leaving college was the presence of nagging questions in their own minds about the wisdom of the course they were following. Many stated, with varying phrasings, that they had become unsure of what they really wanted to do with their lives, and decided to drop out of college in order to have time to think more about their futures and about their ability and willingness to undertake the necessary preparations for professional careers.

One young man said: "I guess I wasn't ready for it [college]." Another stated that he "needed a break in school." A number of the respondents indicated that they had revised their career decisions after a period of searching self-evaluation.

Here, of course, we are dealing both with recollections of past events not easily verified and with a problem area which is highly subjective and emotion-laden. Nonetheless, the general validity of this explanation seems supported both by data on changes in career aspirations and major coursework, and by the frequency with which the young men later returned to college.

The desire for a career at the professional level was not lost by most, but the initial choice of a career often wavered and the students frequently underwent a period of great uncertainty and "floundering," during which many decided to drop out of college until their doubts were resolved.

Five years after graduation, when they were contacted for this study, most of the youth still wished to enter a profession. Only ten persons or about one-fourth of the total, however, had maintained their original choices.

Although no single career had stood out as the prime favorite at the time of their high school graduation, engineering or one of the physical sciences was reported as the choice of nine of the graduates. Five more said they had chosen medicine, and six said they had wished to be schoolteachers. Only four of the young men said they had been undecided about their careers.

By the time this study was made the emphasis had shifted substantially away from engineering, the physical sciences, teaching and medicine. There were now only two aspiring engineers, one chemist, two teachers and two doctors in the group. Interest in the social sciences and in the arts had picked up considerably.

Perhaps more significant, the number of respondents who indicated themselves as "undecided" about their future careers had doubled from four to eight. Asked what kind of work they expected to be doing ten years hence, these young men either replied that they did not know, or listed a range of possibilities so broad that it was obvious they had not narrowed their choices even to a general area of interest. The "undecideds" included not only some of those who had dropped out of college, but at least one respondent who had actually received a degree and was now in graduate school. The following is excerpted from the interviewer's record on this young man:

> Mr. C......... was graduated from college in 1960 with a degree in physical education. He is currently working for his master's degree in education because he feels it will benefit his chances of employment in the future. Ten years from now Mr. C......... hopes to be a practicing physician or in medical school. His plans for the immediate future are rather vague although he is contemplating entering the service in June 1962. He would like to join the aquatic division and possibly become a frogman. If he likes it, he will remain in the service; if he does not, he will attempt either to enter medical school or to pursue a career in some phase of physical education.

And from other interview notes:

> I asked Mr. L......... what he expects to be doing in another ten years. "That depends on the Army," he said. "I might go to school. If I found an electronics school near my Army base I would apply for entrance. Of course, the Army might put me in kitchen work because of my job experience [restaurant work] . . . Or, I might still be with the restaurant I'm working for now in another ten years. Or, I might get a job in government."

> After one semester in college, Mr. A......... changed his major from physical education to foreign relations. Asked why he made his change, he replied: "Well, I want to travel, and I like politics, and I am very fond of Oriental people." He said that his minister was interested in foreign relations and had done a great deal of traveling. Mr. A......... said that he guessed he would continue with foreign relations when he returns to college next year, but added, "I may switch to sociology. . . ." Ten years from now, Mr. A......... hopes to have his master's degree and to have a much better job than his present one.

The phenomenon described as "floundering" is known to be quite frequent among young people and particularly young males, as they struggle to grow out of adolescence and into adulthood. It is a period often fraught with uncertainties and with frequent changes of mind. Given the limitations of this present exploration as a pilot survey, we are hard put, nevertheless, to explain the unusually high degree of "floundering" which our group appeared to display, and the unusually high degree of persistence toward college which they apparently maintained in spite of interruptions. Some insight may be gained, however, from looking at the sources and kinds of career guidance which these young men received and their interpretation of this guidance.

SOURCES OF CAREER GUIDANCE:
FAMILY AND FRIENDS

Just as many of their aspirations appeared basically to be of a rather generalized nature—to enter a profession and achieve a high station in life—so also may have been much of the stimulation and encouragement which the youth received in their search for satisfying careers. Students were urged to aspire high, but recalled receiving little advice about what this injunction meant in concrete terms.

Most parents, for example, evidently wanted their sons to attend college and supported them both psychologically and, to the extent of their limited ability to do so, financially as well. But, according to the students' recollections of their parents' attitudes, "going to college" was the goal, rather than the undertaking of specific occupations. Probably more important, the family circle did not provide much advice about the rewards and requirements of specific occupations, let alone exert pressure to make a particular career choice. One respondent summed it up this way:

> I never felt any pressure from my parents in any specific direction except they expected I would attend college.

And others reported:

> My parents were always interested in my school experiences, and they talked to me about my schoolwork and my future ambitions. They said they wanted me to go to college and to be successful in whatever I decided to do. But the specific career choice was to be mine.

> My parents wanted me to go on to college although neither of them completed high school. They did try to discourage me somewhat from taking an engineering course. They suggested that a liberal arts course, like economics, would require less studying. But there was never any question about their wanting me to go to college.

> I knew my parents expected me to attend college and enter a profession.

> My mother was more concerned about my getting a college education than about a particular field. My father did not push me to-

ward a particular field, but emphasized the importance of a college education.

The only thing I'm sure of now is that I will continue my education because this is necessary for Negroes to compete successfully. My parents have impressed this fact upon their children and are committed to helping their children get a good education.

The last of these quotes may be particularly indicative. Of course, we are dealing here with the youths' interpretations of their parents' wishes as revealed in behavior recalled after the fact. Both memory and perception of another's motives intervene. While some caution is required for this reason, the strong thread of similarity among the responses gives some reason for believing that our data are meaningful. At the least, they probably yield a fairly accurate picture of the manner in which *the graduates viewed their parents' desires for them* at the time they were trying to arrive at career choices.

It would appear that parents urged further learning upon their children primarily as a means toward a general end: "success" in an occupation yielding both status and financial security. A college degree was viewed as a key to this success. But the choice of a particular occupation, with all that this choice involved in the way of specific educational preparation, was left largely to the youth himself.

There was, of course, the graduate whose parents tried to discourage him somewhat from pursuing engineering. Another, who aspired to a career in drama, reported being warned by his parents about its uncertain financial rewards. On the minority of occasions when parents (usually the mother) apparently expressed a positive preference for one career over others, it was usually for professions such as medicine and education which have traditionally been open to Negroes in the Washington area.

At this point it may be worthwhile to recall that, while the educational levels of the parents were considerably higher than for most Washington Negroes, only a small fraction were actually employed in a profession. In all, there were only twelve professionally employed persons among all the parents of the graduates under study. Only four fathers were professionals, compared to eight mothers; since all the respondents were male, this fact means that only about one-tenth had a professionally employed parent of the same sex.

The range of professions at which the parents worked, moreover, was very limited. Most were teachers, one of the very few professional-level jobs freely open to Negroes a generation ago. This might tend to limit parents' comprehension of the demands of other professions, but would not necessarily reduce these professions in their esteem. Thus, they might try to orient their children to a generalized desire to pursue a profession; but they would not, in many cases, be well equipped to give their children concrete advice on the wide variety of professions available.

The same factors which limited parents' experience would also tend to operate on most of the adults with whom these youths would normally come into close contact. For this reason, few would have available among their adult acquaintances a wide range of career models against which they could match their own predispositions.

SOURCES OF CAREER GUIDANCE:
THE SCHOOL

By their own account, the graduates were also strongly motivated toward higher education and professional careers by the high school which they attended. At that time, the school offered only an academic course, and the implication strongly received from teachers and others was that graduates should and would go on to college. One respondent told the interviewer: "The school constantly made students aware of the achievements of its college-trained alumni, and instilled in the students the feeling that they were expected to do likewise." Another graduate said: "The high school teachers encouraged students to prepare themselves for further education." Still another respondent recalled that he "was encouraged both at home and at school to attend college."

Many of the graduates undoubtedly were already motivated toward college when they elected to attend an academic high school. Nevertheless, there seems little question that both the history of the school's earlier graduates and the interest of the faculty could serve only to keep these motivations alive.

A review of various mimeographed materials distributed to the student body by the counseling staff during the period when these youth were in attendance reveals a strong emphasis on motivation toward college, and on preparation for college admission. "Counseling Newsletters," for example, contained admonitions to apply early; detailed information about entrance examinations and scholarship opportunities; and announcements of special coaching classes for College Board exams. Listings of guidance materials which students were urged to read were also long on college orientation.

Our sample of graduates recalled a variety of techniques employed by the school to expose students to concrete knowledge of various professions and to orient them in light of their own aptitudes. One device mentioned by a number of respondents, and which evidently left a deep impression on some, was the "career day" assemblies at which talks were given by persons who had achieved success in specific occupations. A few of the graduates recalled speakers whose careers resembled their own aspirations, either initially or at present. One aspiring engineer, for example, remembered hearing a professor of engineering from a local university: "I was very much impressed by the man, and decided that this would be a good career for me." Another, with ambitions to enter law, remembered "a middle-aged woman lawyer who spoke to the students."

The young men also recalled a variety of techniques used by the school to help the student recognize his own abilities and preferences. One of these was the administration of aptitude tests; the results of these tests were then discussed with the students. The school counseling office, some recalled, also provided numerous books and pamphlets on career choices and college requirements. One respondent said that the guidance counselors tried to locate part-time and summer employment for students going on to college, but that this endeavor "was usually not productive because of the dearth of such jobs."

We must await, of course, a systematic evaluation of the effectiveness of various counseling procedures both in high school and elsewhere. Some new techniques have been added to the career guidance arsenal since these young men left high school. In addition, some counseling undoubtedly took place which was not identified as such by the students.

In light of the actual post-graduation experience of the persons interviewed, however, it seems a fair statement that for these youth at least the counseling procedures were successful only to a very limited degree in producing a realistic orientation toward their life's work. This statement does not reflect in any way upon the efforts of counseling personnel in the context in which they were required to work. In the absence of strong and effective supportive efforts by both home and other community resources, the school had unusually stringent demands placed upon it to make up the deficit.

ROLE MODELS

Another source of inspiration and incentive toward specific careers, and perhaps the most influential, was a "role model" whom the youth wished to emulate. Seventeen of the graduates said that they had been influenced by such a model in their choice of career. In most cases, the model was someone they knew well, such as a relative, a family friend or a teacher.

One young man, for example, said that he had been influenced to enter dental school by his own dentist. Another, aspiring to a medical career, said that one of his uncles is a physician, and he has observed that medicine is "a lucrative occupation." And two other respondents pointed to teachers who had been sources of inspiration to them. One youth, who now wishes to become a high school physical education teacher and coach, expressed great admiration for one of the coaches at the college he attended; the other decided to pursue a career in drama because of the example of the faculty advisor of the high school dramatic club.

Still another graduate, whose early ambition was to be a teacher, said that he now hopes to follow the example of James Baldwin, whose works he has read with great interest. While he still anticipates doing some teaching, he hopes to find a job in Africa which will provide him with an income and will also enable him to "explore the myth that is the Negro." Such an experience, he said, would enable him "to sense and feel new things so that I can speak as a Negro, not just to Negroes, but to the whole world."

Several persons have hopes of going their model one better. One respondent, for example, attributed his interest in social work to his mother's volunteer activities as sponsor of a home for dependent children. Another, whose brickmason father built the family home himself, is currently studying to be an architect.

ON-THE-JOB EXPERIENCES AS
GUIDES TO CAREERS

The analysis also included the question of how much career guidance was obtained from on-the-job experiences. For six of the informants, such experience was clearly decisive; these six reported that they had arrived at their present career choice as a result of job experience in similar situations. For five out of the six, this experience was gained while in military service.

One young man, who had been given teaching assignments in his Army reserve unit, has decided to combine teaching with his earlier interest in science and to become a science teacher. Another has decided to study foreign languages, with the aim of becoming an interpreter, as a result of a two-year sojourn with the Army in Germany. While abroad, he learned to read and speak German quite fluently and decided to continue his study, adding other languages to his repertoire. Two other young men attended special Army schools for training as electronics technicians and are now employed in similar capacities in civilian agencies; eventually, both would like to get degrees in engineering. The fifth respondent with military experience was trained by the Army as a teletype operator; he would like to continue in this occupation, but has been unable to find a similar job as a civilian.

Outside of military service only one of the interviewees reported that a job experience was of any use in helping him decide on a career. Although he was wavering at the time of interview, he was considering switching his college major to sociology as a result of a highly satisfying work experience with mentally retarded children.

For many of the graduates, however, neither personal experience nor the experience of others whom they knew well had been adequate and varied enough to provide sufficient guidance to the choice of a satisfying field of work. A number of those who had found such first- or second-hand experience valuable in their decisions had done so only after a lengthy period of uncertainty or wasted effort.

With these facts in mind, it may be well to look at the employment history of this group since leaving high school.

POST-HIGH SCHOOL EMPLOYMENT

All but one of the forty-six young men in our sample had had some work experience following high school graduation. At the time they were contacted for this study, most were gainfully employed. Twenty-five were working full-time, and ten more were employed either in part-time or summer jobs. Eight were unemployed, however, and all but one of these were actively looking for work. The unemployed amounted to 18 percent of the total sample, a surprisingly high proportion for an area which has an unemployment rate substantially below that for the nation as a whole. And these were not dropouts but high school graduates, most of whom had some college training as well.

Of the twenty-five who had full-time jobs, only three were working in positions closely related to their present career aspirations. One was a commercial artist, and two were the electronics technicians mentioned earlier. The rest viewed themselves as merely marking time until they were able to fulfill their true ambitions. This was five years after their graduation from high school, when they had reached a median age of 23 years.

Since their graduation from high school, the young men had held among them a total of fifty-six full-time jobs. While some of these jobs were used chiefly as a means for building up cash reserves for college expenses, they were neither part-time nor temporary in nature. Most of these full-time jobs fell into two broad occupational categories: clerical and service. Almost all of the twenty-four clerical positions were in governmental agencies; and they were heavily concentrated in the U. S. Postal Service. Nineteen of the full-time jobs were in service occupations, most being distinctly menial in character. For example, five of the jobs were as dishwashers, four as porters and three as busboys. One of the youths had worked as an unskilled laborer, and four as cab drivers or parking-lot attendants.

The median income reported for these full-time jobs was about $70 weekly. The high was $100, and the low was $25. Had not a substantial proportion of the positions been with the Federal government, the average would have been much lower. Most of the service jobs paid $1 per hour, and some even less.

The part-time and summer jobs, which had been taken mostly with an aim to obtaining funds for college, were about on a par with the full-time jobs, except that fewer of them were with government.

Many of the jobs, whether full-time, part-time or temporary, provided little in the way of useful experience which could be applied to later career opportunities. Nor were they useful in exposing these youth to the wide variety of occupations and fields of work which are available. Furthermore, the pay was generally low in accord with the low-skilled nature of the work; after deducting living costs, it is doubtful that many of the youth were able to build up any sizeable bankroll against college expenses.

CHANNELS TO EMPLOYMENT

The young men were asked how they had obtained each of the jobs they had held. The findings in this respect may also be indicative. Overall, by far the most important source of referrals was a relative or friend, usually a person who worked for the same employer or was a personal friend of the employer. Almost half the jobs were found in this way. Eleven of the jobs were obtained by a door-to-door canvass of employers believed to have openings. Civil Service examinations were an important route to jobs in the Federal government. Newspaper ads led to only seven jobs; private employment agencies provided only five; and the United States Employment Service only two.

It is well known that personal contacts furnished by relatives or friends are one of the most frequent sources of job opportunities for the population as a whole. Nevertheless, the heavy reliance upon relatives and friends among these youth meant, of course, referrals predominantly by persons who themselves were Negro. Many of them were of an older generation. To the extent that those who made the referrals had themselves been restricted in their job advancement as a result of direct discrimination or of inadequate educational preparation, their own disadvantages would tend to be reflected in the opportunities of the youth they advised. In this way, of course, past discrimination may have cast its shadow on the present generation.

Yet the results of the study do not support the conclusion that carry-over of past disadvantages was *all* that operated to hamper these youth in achieving their full potential. There is some evidence also from the interviews that a number of the youth deliberately avoided employers whose hiring policy toward Negroes was not known to them. To some degree they may have been restricting their own horizons in an effort to avoid the humiliation of a racial rebuff.

A number of the young men, however, did not restrict their job explorations in this way, and their overall employment pattern did not differ significantly from the rest. Experiences directly indicative of discrimination were relatively infrequent in the recollections of the graduates interviewed; rarely did they recall race being mentioned as the reason for rejection, although there were many refusals. Nonetheless, the overall pattern of employment experience for this group of above-average high school graduates is suggestive of strong restrictions upon job opportunities: restrictions both of level and of range. Only through operation of discriminatory barriers, however covert and subtle, can their limited job achievement logically be explained.

ⓔⓔⓔⓔⓔⓔⓔⓔⓔⓔⓔⓔⓔⓔⓔⓔⓔⓔⓔⓔⓔⓔⓔⓔⓔⓔⓔ

NO HIDING PLACE:
THE NEGRO SEARCH

ⓔⓔⓔⓔⓔⓔⓔⓔⓔⓔⓔⓔⓔⓔⓔⓔⓔⓔⓔⓔⓔⓔⓔⓔ

HERMAN H. LONG

Around the turn of the century a noted social scientist predicted, on the basis of studies he had made of Negro mortality, that the problem of the Negro in American society would be solved eventually by the virtual extinction of the Negro through his inability to survive biologically. Time was all that was needed—perhaps two or three generations—to provide the answer to the problems of health, education, and civil status then looming in almost hopeless magnitude less than twenty years after Reconstruction. The accuracy of such a prediction is not even of academic significance by now, but it serves to illustrate both the great contrast between the status of the Negro population sixty years ago and now and the presence of an attitude toward the prospect of the Negro in America which has persisted through the years. It is an attitude which, if not the sum and substance of American social policy toward the Negro, is at least in part its source. If the Negro could be forgotten or effectively isolated from the mainstream of common experience and contact, then the rest of the American community could go its way without this continually embarrassing distraction.

ISOLATION OF THE NEGRO

Segregation, both benign and vicious, legal and extralegal, assured a measure of isolation—physical, social, and psychological—that was effective enough over the next thirty or more years to produce a range of separate institutions so encompassing as to place the Negro effectually outside the common society. From the "Negro quarters" on the broad expanses of plantation land, with their all-purpose school, lodge hall, and church structures, to the "cross the tracks" houses huddled in town and city ghettos, the pattern of dissociation remained constant. So constant it was, in fact, that for most white Americans the Negro became only an abstraction, almost never a real and vital personal experience. There were mixtures in the abstraction, sometimes threat, sometimes curiosity, but it remained above all, a gross caricature, a vehicle of personal and social distance. And while both Negroes and whites came to be for each other what Copeland calls "contrast conceptions," the Negro "got to know white folks" (as the expression goes) perhaps somewhat better, because his role in the system and the necessity for his survival in it required that he do so.

Factors Preventing Total Isolation

However effective segregation may have been in setting the general pattern, it was not 100 percent efficient and did not produce complete isolation. Both groups were dependent upon a common economic system, and while this constituted one important intervening influence, its effect was substantially negated by the drawing of caste lines in the job and occupational structure which limited Negro upward mobility in the economic scale and rutted both aspiration and talent. It was an isolation of a sort—or perhaps, better, segmentation—no less real because of the fact that it was not physical. The racial division of labor and reward which it prescribed was best suited for the farm and plantation economy, but it was adapted to the industrial economy of succeeding years. And in spite of the wide range of talent and the changing character of skills required for an expanding industrial technology, it has remained as a drug in the new system.

Two other mediating influences appear to be of greater effect, at least at the stage of the early decades after 1900, in preventing a more complete isolation of the Negro. Both fall into the category of the accidental. One is the development of a system of free public education, undoubtedly the most important leveling influence in American society; and the other is the fact that the Negro began to move in accelerating and unbelievable magnitude away from his rural moorings to the cities of the region and to the big metropolitan centers of the North. (Indeed, the crescendo seems unending!) Ravages of the boll weevil, crop shortages, continuing low wages and poverty, lynchings and expanding patterns of violence, injustice and intimidation, entrance of large numbers of Negro men into the armed services during World War I—these and other forces literally wrenched the Negro from his traditional bondage to the rural South. Beginning around 1915, the "Great Migration" rumbled into existence; it became the most powerful impersonal factor in the history and drama of modern Negro life.

But let us turn to the institution of the public school for a moment, since it has the most immediate bearing upon our concern with what we have come to call "dropouts" and the special interest of this paper with the Negro aspect of that phenomenon.

THE PUBLIC SCHOOL IN THE SOUTH

The historical roots of southern education were essentially aristocratic, and it was not until after the advent of the Reconstruction state governments, which established the principle of universal free education, that the public school institution grew permanent roots. There were more private academies in the South in 1850—2,640—than there were public high schools some fifty years later—1,013; and by 1900 less than 40 percent of the children of school age were receiving regular instruction. Of this number, only 1 out of 10 managed to reach the fifth grade. With complete collapse of Reconstruction by 1883 and the later "separate but equal" Supreme Court decision, the development of the public education followed a tragic, racially distinct course which accentuated the existing lag in public education and made more or less permanent the considerably greater lag in the education of Negro children. Segregated schools provided the avenue for Negro educational discrimination, and it became standard practice for Negro per capita allotments based on school population to be diverted to the white schools. By 1916, Louis Harlan points out that the rate of such racial discrimination in school funds varied from 100 percent in North Carolina to 1,000 percent in South Carolina. Although white students generally were only 20 percent more numerous than Negro students, they were 3,000 percent more numerous in state-supported high school facilities.

The Rural Negro School

A limping, weak, makeshift institution was thus spawned in the Negro public school of the South, and its hereditary defects were transmitted to succeeding generations cumulatively. Nevertheless, it was the only institution the Negro had in common with the general society and culture—even though only a carbon copy—and it constituted the primary means through which the democratic and common cultural values were transmitted to the Negro child. Both the institutional adaptation and the process of transmitting meanings and values from the larger culture were faulty. Even the printed language and the context out of which it came bore a strangeness, and education became largely a rote process relying more on mechanical memorization than on reasoning. The form and the symbols of the mainstream of the general culture and lore were present, but not the substance and relevance. The adaptation was largely to a folk culture which shaped the institution to its own form.

Isolation and the context of life almost totally geared to the cultivation of cotton imposed, as Charles S. Johnson observed in *Shadow of the Plantation*,[1] "relentless demand for children's labor" and exacted a "forced growth upon children from the moment of birth." Every aspect of life seemed to urge toward the earliest possible attainment of adulthood. School had little relation to the demands of planting, hoeing, and picking cotton, except as it might help one to "count and figure" a little bit, and it was impossible to grasp, except vaguely, the meaning it had for the broader life outside from which one was excluded and rejected. Life was survival, and possible disaster was constantly at the threshold. School was a luxury, fine for the young ones too tender for hoeing, and it was a good place for the older ones to go once the crop was in. By and large it was as much a matter of "dropins" as of "dropouts."

The Urban Negro School

The growing center of public school education in the South was its urban environment. Here the Negro school had a little better chance, for it was less isolated and closer to the industrial demand. But it was only a slight modification of its rural counterpart, and industrial discrimination limited both entrance to and mobility in the occupation and job structure. A species of vocational education emerged in the Negro schools under stimulus of the Booker T. Washington philosophy and the Tuskegee experience, which had some meaning to immediate life needs and new opportunities. However, as the "noble idea" came to be applied by school boards and superintendents, it devolved into nothing more than preparing Negro children to fit only into the menial categories of the job market. There was a surfeit of courses in cooking, dressmaking, tailoring, home management, shoe repairing, and beauty shop operation; almost none in bookkeeping, mechanical drawing, sheet metal

---

[1] Charles S. Johnson, *Shadow of the Plantation* (Chicago: University of Chicago Press, 1936).

work, electricity, the machine operations and related skills required for use and adaptation to the industrial performances. Except for a few small shop operators of restaurant, beauty shop, tailoring, and shoe repair establishments, the Negro schools produced no new corps of artisans and skilled workers. In addition, by this time, the unions had closed the doors to apprenticeship training. The Negro student, in his newly achieved urban sophistication and frustration, soon said to himself, his teachers, and parents that there was no need to go to school only to become a maid or janitor.

Inadequacy of the Negro School

Education failed to become the way out of the cul-de-sac in which the masses of Negroes were caught during this first generation around the turn of the century. It provided for a few, however, the first step into the cultural mainstream, and it is out of this segment that the basis was formed for the distinct and sizable Negro middle class of today. For the sons and daughters of the sharecropper or tenant family it could hardly be called functional, and for those thrown into the harshly competitive and demanding urban job market it was only slightly more relevant. The task of education in the area of Negro experience, I would argue, has always been, and remains, that of making itself relevant and functional. While education served as a primary means of social and occupational mobility in the American "open" society, it could not achieve entrance into the society for the Negro or provide adequate and meaningful incentives. These are limitations, of course, for which it is not responsible.

NEGRO MIGRATION

Large-scale migration achieved for the Negro a kind of physical freedom and mobility, even though limited, which education and other influences were unable to effect. It was essentially a means of adjustment to adversity, and in its cumulative effects, changed to a profound degree what might be called the typography of the Negro population. Fifty years after the dire prediction of Negro population regression, the Negro population had almost doubled its size, reaching a little over 15 million in 1950. At the same time, two major displacements occurred as the result of migration which altered the traditional southern and rural character of its location. Movement from rural areas of the South to the cities within the region and a concomitant movement from the South to the urban centers of the North made the Negro, in 1950, a predominantly urban population. It was apparent also that a northward shift in population concentration of almost astounding proportions had taken place.

There were some 4.8 million Negroes now living outside the South, and this represented a total more than four times greater than the number of such residents in 1910 (slightly over a million) and falling slightly short of doubling the number in 1930 —2.5 million. Five northern states—Illinois, Michigan, New York, Ohio, and Pennsylvania—accounted for half of the total Negro population increase over this period. In 1910 they had together only 566,000 Negro residents, but by 1950 the total had jumped to 3.2 million. The net effect of this increase was a Negro population which had shifted from about 16 percent urban in 1900 to 61 percent urban in 1950, and which had changed from approximately 10 percent northern to almost a third northern over the fifty-year period.

With increased industrialization of the South, the raising of standards of living, and a slight lessening of the most extreme forms of Negro exploitation, it seemed likely that Negro northward movements in the 1950's would show signs of decline. Not so. By 1960 the total nonwhite population nationally reached almost 19 million, and it was estimated that the southern segment of this group had declined to the surprising level of 58 percent. This meant that almost half the Negro population was now residing in the North and West—somewhere around 8.6 million. The South lost 1,457,000 through net migration and the northeastern, north central, and western areas had net gains from the same source of 26, 24, and 39 percent, respectively. It was evident that the Negro population had assumed a distribution no longer predominantly southern but distinctly national in character.

Urban Migration

But while a broader geographic spread of Negro residence was accomplished, greater concentration in the major metropolitan centers of the country also took place. The Negro population had become more than 72 percent urban; and waves of incoming migrants, together with an equally persistent movement of white families to suburban areas, doubled and tripled the previous Negro proportions among the total inhabitants of the big cities. Chicago, with the largest numerical increase of any city—328,219 between 1950 and 1960—saw its Negro segment become 23 percent of the total residents. In Philadelphia the proportion was 26 percent; in St. Louis, Detroit, and Cleveland, 29 percent; in Cincinnati, 22 percent; in Baltimore, 35 percent; and in Washington, D. C., 54 percent. New York became the first city with a Negro population of a million; and Los Angeles, with 326,589 Negroes, saw the proportion of this segment grow from about 4.5 percent in 1940 to 13.5 percent in 1960. Similar trends obtained in the big southern cities where, for example, the Negro proportions ranged up to a high of 37 and 38 percent in Memphis and Atlanta, respectively.

Although some expansion in the areas of Negro residence within the cities necessarily occurred in response to these tremendous changes in size of Negro population, studies of this aspect of the problem consistently show an increasing pattern of Negro containment within a limited number of residence areas of the central city. It is a story of heightened segregation developing concurrently with Negro population growth in the urban centers, and even more it is a story of continued life in areas of deepening blight, decay, and social disorganization. Freedom from the isolation and hopelessness of the plantation South which movement to the city and to the North had given the Negro seems now, ironically, to have led to a new kind of immobility. The plantation has been supplanted by the city ghetto, and although the boundaries and limitations are less severe, the prospect of escape to the middle-class world for the masses of Negroes is only minutely better. A full cycle has passed in less than three generations in the social history of the Negro.

Changes in Family Patterns

But the more dismal aspects of this history lie beyond the mere physical factors of geographic and local residence. While undoubtedly the movement to cities and to the North had important positive effects upon the educational, occupational, and economic status of the Negro, it did not fully compensate for the original disabilities with which the Negro began, once he achieved freedom, and those which accumulated in succeeding generations because of weakness in the very institutions upon which improvement depended. The family and the school were two of the most crucial institutions and both have retained, over most of the period of Negro migration history, vestigial marks of their rural and adverse origins. Slavery and the later plantation economy gave the Negro family a dominant maternal character. Held together more by ties of sentiment, affection, and the immediate exigencies of life rather than by strong male leadership, its very structure made it easily amenable to dissolution in the new urban environment.

Frazier thus described the city as a "place of destruction," pointing up the high rates of desertion and separation which followed the weakening of sentimental ties and other alienating influences of the city which played upon the Negro male. Migration history thus has been paralleled by a process of family disorganization followed by reorganization as residence became permanent, economic status improved, and other stabilizing influences began to have an effect.

We must remember, however, that what we are describing covers, by and large, the experience of not quite three full generations of Negro families. It must be emphasized, too, that migration has been persistent and cumulative, and the processes of disorganization and reorganization are continuous in this history. Samples of Negro families drawn at random today would reveal family types caught at various stages of this process in relation to length of residence and migrancy status. Large proportions of families with female heads, of families with no males present, and of families broken by separation, divorce, and desertion would abound among residents of shorter urban history. And the opposite trend would dominate among the older migrant group—the second and third generations—which had opportunity to achieve the equalitarian and middle-class prototype. It would be interesting, and possibly useful, to speculate on the effects upon Negro youngsters of the absence of a strong male image in the Negro family and community. Psychological, psychiatric, and sociological investigations are either missing or fragmentary in this area, and yet they might open the door to understanding the basic motivational problem involved in our concern with school persistence, life and career expectations.

EDUCATION AND THE NEGRO

When slavery ended, practically all Negroes were illiterate, but the succeeding history has been one of accelerating improvement. By 1880 approximately 40 percent were able to read and write, by 1900 the proportion had increased to more than a half, and by 1950 it rose to 90 percent. Even though Negro rates of school attendance at the elementary school level approached that of whites by 1960, conspicuous and serious differences nevertheless remained in average grade achievement and in rates of attendance at the high school and college levels. Negroes remained about three grades behind whites in average educational achievement; five times as many of them, percentage-wise, failed to go beyond the fifth grade; half as many managed to complete high school; and only a third as many Negroes as whites graduated from college. One of the best illustrations of the continuing educational lag is that in 1959 the number of Negro young men in the 25-29 age group who graduated from high school did not reach the proportion which similarly aged white young men had attained almost twenty years earlier—in 1940. Moreover, the rate of Negro male college graduation in 1959 was only three-fourths the rate obtaining for their white counterparts in this age group in 1940. It is worth pointing out that these Negro young men were born, on the average, about the year 1932, and that their parents were part of the generation just making the adjustments involved in the early phases of great migration cityward and northward. In spite of great absolute improvement over his own previous educational status, a lag of major proportions still remains, and not only in achievement but in incentive to overcome relative deprivation.

Opportunities for the Negro

Add to this the severe complication that while the Negro youngster is faced with the task of catching up this generaional gap, the entire educational and occupational process undergoes a radical upgrading of demands and expectations. The jobs which his parents and those of his peers have performed— the unskilled hand operations—are dropping out of the market, accompanied by unemployment rates among Negro workers which remain chronic and run twice as high as those for white workers. By 1970 these jobs are expected to drop to a point below their proportion in the labor market of 1910. Meanwhile, professional and technical jobs are expected to double, and the clerical and sales, proprietal and managerial jobs are predicted to grow by 50 and 38 percent, respectively. Long-term trends which have indicated a gradual diminishing in the differentials of income and occupation between the Negro and white segments of the population since 1900 have shown, since the 1950 period, unfortunate signs of widening. The expanding sectors of the economy and the job market have no need for unskilled workers, and the Negro worker, as Dr. Irvin Sobel has expressed it, "finds himself caught on a sinking ship." In the non-white 18-19 age group of 1960, two-thirds were found to have left school, and one out of every four who entered the labor force was unemployed—a rate twice that for white youth of the same age.

In a recent comment on trends revealed by the 1960 census, Talcott Parsons points out that the rapid increase of the lower-class nonwhite element into the cities is the latest phase of a long-standing process through which upwardly mobile groups have entered the urban world. This latest phase, he predicts, is likely to be the last of the "series of peasant infusions into the American urban community," and he expects that it will be temporary because of the proven absorptive power of the metropolitan-industrial complex and the increasing predominance of middle-class patterns of life. The social history of the Negro—at least those aspects of that history selected for review in this account—certainly fits into the general perspective of Parsons' observations. But however promising ultimate Negro absorption and adjustment may appear in the long run, it is with the present "temporary" stage and its ill-fittings and dysfunctions that we must deal. The racial problem is a special case, and the difficulties involved in the Negro's following the general pattern typical of immigrant experience should not be underestimated. It is the response of the Negro youngster in the urban ghetto, vaguely aware of a history which he can only sense in the limitations, struggles, and frustrations of his parents, but keenly conscious of the chasm standing between him and real opportunity, which we must confront. Charles E. Silberman, in his *Fortune* magazine article entitled "The City and the Negro," has described the problem eloquently and well. He puts it this way:

> But among the great mass of working-class Negroes and a large part of the middle class, apathy exists side by side with a growing, festering resentment of their lot. These Negroes are more and more convinced that they should have a better life; they are less and less convinced that they themselves can do anything about it.
>
> The danger is not violence but something much deeper and harder to combat: a sense of permanent alienation from American society.[2]

THE PROBLEM OF THE NEGRO DROPOUT

All of what has been said in these remarks is by way of commentary on the problem of school dropouts as it relates to Negro youth. Its message is implicit rather than explicit, and because of the rather large framework in which it has been placed some additional pointing up is undoubtedly called for. Perhaps more than anything else the implied thesis is that the special problem of dropouts is for the Negro youngster only a symptom of a much more encompassing malady which is bound up, on the one hand, with the alienating influences of lower-class life in the urban ghetto, and on the other, with a set of depressed aspirations and expectations engendered by Negro social and cultural experience in America. The former of these factors the Negro shares in common with other lower-class urban youth, but the latter are, in the nature of the case, unique to his own outlook. Together the two circumstances are mutually reinforcing, possibly adding up to the dimension of an endemic pathology. Education for the Negro has always lacked relevance to life, and quitting school has been, in the context of Negro social and cultural history, normal.

Education as a Personal Encounter

If this assessment is valid—substantially if not entirely—the conclusion may seem warranted that the task of teachers and

---

[2] Charles E. Silberman, "The City and the Negro," *Fortune,* Vol. 63 (March 1963), pp. 88-91.

educational leaders in making an effective attack upon Negro educational attrition is doomed to defeat. Fortunately this is not necessarily the case, because what has been described is a general phenomenon and situation. Education, after all, is a personal encounter, and the effects of the interaction between teachers and learners, especially where there is warmth, empathy, and sincerity, cannot be overestimated.

No one can predict how and by whom the defenses of a sensitive and unresponding student may be led to fall, opening the door to new self-insight and aspiration. This is the wonder and magic of education—and it is its ultimate validation. But the conclusion does clearly emerge that expediencies and gimmicks will not suffice; that better, newer, and more sharply directed use of school and social work resources is required; that education of the Negro urban and lower-class youngster must be somehow related to the totality of his situation and his needs if it is to be meaningful.

I would not presume to say how this may be done, but such radical departure as new forms and types of organization in the traditional public school enterprise may be attempted—at least experimentally. Especially pertinent to such measures are those families which the social work agencies are beginning to identify as the "multiproblem families." An effort to involve both parents and their children in the same educational experience, in the same classrooms and grade levels, might also seem worthy of exploration.

Determinative Factors for the Dropout

The dropout studies all point up to a complex of factors as determinative; and my impression is that they show the Negro youngster to be characterized by either a greater amount of these social debilities or a more consistent configuration of them. This would seem to require a remedial program which proceeds to deal with all facts of the complex at the same time. And while an approach of this sort strongly commends itself, the demands of personnel, organization, and finance which it would require appear staggering if not impracticable. We are left, therefore, with the necessity of finding that factor or set of factors in which we have the best confidence as being most determinative and which, at the same time, might have an effect upon other elements in the complex of possible causality.

If this identification can be made, then the path into which the major part of our efforts, resources, and inventiveness should go would be more clearly indicated.

It is perhaps irresponsible to suggest what such a path might be in the absence of adequate and sufficiently persuasive evidence. But I cannot resist a hunch, which can only be tentative and provocative at this juncture, that points in the direction of job recruitment, job placement, and work experience arrangements systematically carried out by the schools in cooperative planning with employment agencies, business, and industry. I am not thinking only of the vocational schools and programs in this regard, and I would underscore the recruitment and placement aspects of this possibility. The lower-class student, and especially the minority group for whom attendance in school beyond the compulsory age is a calculated risk, must discover and know that education will make a real and immediate difference. Evidence from an increasing number of sources strongly urges the crucial importance of the problem of employment in the situation confronting urban lower-class families of Negro and other minority groups.

Relationships Between Economic Factors and Dropouts

The study of Connecticut youngsters, by Dr. Henry G. Stetler,[3] which explored among other considerations the relationship between economic factors and dropouts, is pertinent and revealing in this connection. Stetler compared Negro and white dropouts with each other and with similar samples of nondropouts in the four major Connecticut cities, in regard to a number of family, social, economic, and attitudinal characteristics. As might be expected, the Negro and white dropouts revealed the same general pattern of factors in relation to indices of family structure, education, income, and occupation, except that the Negro group had higher proportions in those categories which were indicative of a background of disorganization, poverty, and low income and occupational achievement. It is not surprising, too, that the same general Negro-white differences obtained in the nondropout group. But the significant thing is that

---

[3] Henry G. Stetler, *Comparative Study of Negro and White Dropouts in Selected Connecticut High Schools* (Hartford, Conn.: State of Connecticut Commission on Civil Rights, 1959).

the factors of parental education, income, and occupational level clearly differentiated the white dropouts from the white nondropouts but failed to identify consistent and substantial differences between the Negro groups leaving and staying in school. In other words, it did not appear generally to matter a great deal whether the Negro parents had high educational achievement, high incomes, and were in the skilled and above categories; but these were extremely sensitive factors in the case of the two white groups. In addition, Stetler found that the income distribution of white families whose parents had only an eighth-grade education or less was almost exactly equal to that of Negro families on the high school and college graduate levels.

෧෧෧෧෧ ෧෧෧෧෧෧෧෧෧෧෧෧෧෧෧෧෧෧෧෧෧෧෧෧

DEPRIVATION AND ALIENATION:

A COMPOUNDED SITUATION

෧෧෧෧෧෧෧෧෧෧෧෧෧෧෧෧෧෧෧෧෧෧෧෧෧෧෧

CHARLES V. WILLIE

We have just completed a study of juvenile delinquency in Washington, D. C.[1] Eighty-five per cent of the youth referred to Juvenile Court during the course of a year are Negro, although Negro youngsters represent only about 66 per cent of the total population 10-17 years of age. Nevertheless, our report to the President's Committee on Juvenile Delinquency and

---

[1] *Washington Action for Youth* (Washington, D. C.: United Planning Organization Board of Directors on Juvenile Delinquency, 1964, mimeographed).

Youth Crime stated that no association exists between juvenile delinquency and race that cannot be explained by the unequal experiences of deprivation and alienation of Negro and white children in the nation's capital. Negro children are deprived in that 68 per cent of their parents, as compared with only 18 per cent of the white parents in the District of Columbia, live in neighborhoods that are below average in socio-economic status with more than half of the households having incomes of less than $4,000. Negro children are alienated in that 76 per cent of the nonwhite population are restricted to a segregated ghetto-type area in which 90 per cent of the population are nonwhite according to the 1960 census.

WHO ARE THE DEPRIVED?

We consider a person or a category of persons to be deprived when their financial resources are insufficient to obtain the goods and services considered necessary for a normal standard of living in the local community. Deprivation is a condition of life relative to the local situation. We consider a person or a category of persons to be alienated when they are cut off from the mainstream of a society and the helpful supports of a community. Racial segregation as practiced in the United States for more than a century has been a powerful form of alienation, cutting off Negro youth from the helpful assistance of the society at large. There are other forms of deprivation and alienation, but economic and racial forms are what we shall discuss today.

Our report to the President's Committee indicated that juvenile delinquency and other forms of antisocial behavior are highest in the deprived areas of Washington. The delinquency rate for the total low-income area based on youth referred to Juvenile Court is twice as large as the citywide rate of 29 per 1,000 youth 10-17 years of age. A few neighborhoods of poverty in the center of the city offer their youth a 50-50 chance of obtaining a court record before attaining adulthood.

Our report also stated that if the District of Columbia were interested in doing something about delinquency and antisocial behavior it had to do something about both deprivation and alienation. We contend that any program designed to upgrade the Negro population economically will experience only short-term success and is doomed ultimately unless it also deals with the corresponding problems of segregation and alienation. In short, racial segregation and discrimination breed economic deprivation.

The same statement can be made of our schools. Racially segregated institutions are associated with economically deprived youth. This, of course, is the hooker on which many communities strike out. They are willing to help Negro youth become upwardly mobile so long as they remain in "their place" which is, of course, a contradiction. But the rationalization for discrimination is strange. Even Dr. James B. Conant swung at this bad pitch in his book *Slums and Suburbs,* published in 1961. He counseled "those who are agitating for the deliberate mixing of children to accept *de facto* segregated schools as a consequence of a present housing situation and to work for the improvement of slum schools whether Negro or white." [2] The fact is that most slum schools serve a predominantly Negro population and in general, communities unwilling to desegregate their Negro population have been unwilling to upgrade it economically. We have several decades of empirical evidence that the doctrine of "separate but equal" does not work. It cannot work. The reason for separating the races in the first place is to accord them differential treatment. Anyone who ignores this fact is whistling in the dark.

As Dr. Conant has said, "more money is needed in slum schools." [3] But more money will never be spent in slum schools so long as they are schools reserved for minorities who are unwelcome in the mainstream of community life. Consider the programs designed to upgrade slum schools throughout the nation; they are largely supported by foundation funds that originate outside the community. While some localities have provided matching funds, by and large there is an absence of large-scale commitment to expending a disproportionate amount of the school budget in slum schools. I do not expect this situation to change for the better so long as slum schools are part of the overall community pattern of racial segregation, *de facto* or deliberate.

You may detect from these initial remarks that this discussion will deal with problems of deprivation and alienation not so much as they are confronted by the teacher in the classroom

---

[2] James Bryant Conant, *Slums and Suburbs* (New York: McGraw-Hill Book Co., Inc., 1961), p. 31.

[3] *Ibid,* pp. 145-146.

but as they are fostered by the community at large. The major thesis of this discussion is that deprivation is a function of alienation. You cannot solve the former without solving the latter.

SCHOOLS IN WASHINGTON, D. C.

Our Washington experience is a prototype of what may be experienced in many big cities of the nation. The best high school in the community is in a predominantly white neighborhood; the poorest high school in the community is in a predominantly Negro neighborhood.

Washington, D. C. schools operate on a track system in which children within a specific grade are grouped according to their ability. The tracks range from basic, general, and college preparatory, to honors. Yet one senior high school in the predominantly Negro slum section of that city had no honors track. What happens to the bright students in that school who deserve advanced study?

In another school district in the predominantly Negro slum section of the city, one-third of the grade-school students attend elementary schools erected before 1900, as compared with only one-sixth of the citywide enrollment at this level in the District of Columbia. Also, 16 per cent of the elementary children attend school on a part-time schedule because of overcrowding, as compared with only 3 per cent of the citywide elementary school population. In this same predominantly Negro slum section, 26 per cent of the elementary school children are in classes of 36 or more children, as compared with 18 per cent of the elementary school children in the citywide population.[4]

It is true that in some localities the conscience of the community has been pricked by the current civil rights revolution. A few new schools have been built in Negro neighborhoods. These one or two schools have not upset the pattern. I would admonish you to keep your eye on the pattern. It is also true that selected schools in predominantly Negro neighborhoods have been singled out for "higher horizons" programs. This is a laudable beginning, if it is clearly understood as a beginning. Until higher horizons schools are the rule rather than the exception in slum sections of the city, they still will not have trans-

---

[4] *Washington Action for Youth*, p. 19.

formed the pattern of a poor quality of education in slum schools.

In his book, *The Affluent Society,* Dr. John Galbraith states that "we [ought to] invest more than proportionately in the children of the poor community. It is there that high-quality schools . . . are most needed to compensate for the very low investment which families are able to make in their off-spring . . ." [5]

We ought to do this. But are we likely to do so when it is recognized that many of the poor are Negro and that for several years our institutions have deliberately separated Negroes and other minorities from the mainstream of community life so that they could be treated differently?

CAN NEIGHBORHOOD SCHOOLS SUCCEED?

In 1961, Dr. Conant publicly endorsed the statement of a city superintendent of schools who insisted that "he was in the education business and should not become involved in attempts to correct the consequences of voluntary segregated housing." [6] Viewed historically, one hardly could call racially segregated housing in the United States voluntary. But that is another issue. The main point of this school superintendent is that he is in the business of overcoming deprivation, not alienation, as if deprivation because of race could be solved within the framework of existing racial alienation.

At one point Dr. Conant believed this could be done, though now he has some doubts. In 1961, his published position was that *de facto* segregation should be accepted as a consequence of the present housing situation and that groups agitating for the deliberate mixing of schools could spend their energies best working for the improvement of slum schools, whether Negro or white. In February 1964, in a Chicago news conference, Dr. Conant altered his views and allegedly said, according to the Associated Press, "I was clearly wrong when I suggested several years ago that busing high school youngsters around a big city was impractical." He allegedly further said that big cities should strive to have as many racially and economically mixed

---

[5] John Kenneth Galbraith, *The Affluent Society* (New York: Mentor Books, 1958), pp. 256-258.
[6] Conant, p. 30.

high schools as possible and that the comprehensive high school should become truly comprehensive.[7]

Although the statement in *Slums and Suburbs* has probably been used by some communities as the basis for attempting to do something about deprivation without altering community patterns of segregation and alienation, even then, back in 1961, Dr. Conant approached the subject with ambivalence. In that same book, he observed that for "nearly a hundred years our ancestors—North and South, East and West—accepted, almost without protest, the transformation of the status of the Negro from that of a slave into that of a member of a lower, quite separate caste." And then he admits that "we now recognize so plainly, but so belatedly, a caste system finds its clearest manifestation in an educational system." [8] Persons unprepared to do something about the school and racial segregation ignore this section of Dr. Conant's book. But we ignore it today at our own peril. This is what the civil rights revolution is all about. It is concerned with the mainstream of American society, and the abrogation of a semi-caste system. This is why we call deprivation and alienation a compounded situation. To eliminate deprivation, we must eliminate alienation.

How do we go about eliminating the compounded problems of deprivation and alienation? First, we must begin to identify the problem as it is and do away with a lot of camouflaging verbiage.

The reason that Negro children were one to two years behind white children in some subjects when the Washington, D. C. schools desegregated in 1954 is because Negro children for many years had received the short end of the deal. For years, Negro youngsters in that community and in other communities have been segregated, discriminated against, and herded into a separate caste-like status. As Dr. Conant points out, "a caste system finds its clearest manifestation in an educational system." [9]

---

[7] *Associated Press,* news story (February 11, 1964).
[8] Conant, pp. 11-12.
[9] *Ibid.*

JOBS AND ATTITUDES

I am reminded of a young social scientist in Washington who came to us for financial assistance for his project designed to teach Negro youth good work attitudes so that they could find jobs. Here was a purveyor of a project who knew but tried to ignore the fact that the unemployment rate is twice as high among Negro males as it is among white males because, on the one hand, Negroes have less opportunity than whites to learn marketable skills, and on the other hand, white employers are inclined to hire white workers first. It seemed to us that the primary problem was not to expend our energy developing good work attitudes but to redouble our efforts to provide a meaningful education for these youth, providing them with marketable skills, and to eliminate discrimination against them. The opportunity to earn money is usually a good antidote for poor work attitudes.

As a matter of fact, we proved this during the summer of 1963. Washington Action for Youth, in cooperation with the D. C. Public Schools, the D. C. Recreation Department, the U. S. Employment Service, and the Washington Urban League, sponsored a summer job program for deprived youth. Jobs were obtained in government and in private business for approximately 1,100 youth 16-18 years of age. Most youth earned $1.25 per hour for a period of eight weeks with wages being paid by the employing organizations. Seventy-two per cent of the youth lived in poor neighborhoods. Two-thirds came from families in which the head was a manual worker. Eighty per cent had not worked previously. About 6 per cent had parents currently receiving public welfare. Ten to 15 per cent had court records. These were deprived youth who had experienced limited opportunity in the past. In general, they turned in high-level performances when the opportunity to work was provided.

At the close of the summer, employers were requested to evaluate the performance of each youth and to indicate whether he would hire the youth again. Eighty-seven per cent of the youth achieved job performance ratings of average to excellent and employers were sufficiently satisfied to state that they would rehire three out of every four youth. Nearly all of the youth were Negro.

So the phrases "poor motivation" and "poor attitude" are but camouflaging verbiage that cover up the poor effort of the adult affluent society to reach out to deprived youth and to provide opportunities for them in the mainstream of society. When this is done in good faith, our experience is that these youngsters respond well.

Low aspiration is another camouflaging phrase that covers up the fact that in our society all are encouraged to succeed but some are denied the opportunity. We know that low-income Negro families are acquainted with the good life and want it for their children. In the summer of 1963, we surveyed a randomly selected sample of 1,000 households in a deprived and predominantly Negro neighborhood in Washington. Respondents were asked: "What do you hope your child will do when he grows up?" About half replied that job preference is for the child to decide. Of the remaining number who had specific occupational preferences, 90 per cent wanted their child to be a professional worker such as a doctor, lawyer, engineer, minister, teacher, nurse, or social worker. Moreover, these low-income, unskilled or unemployed workers in our sample were aware of the educational requirements for professional work. Two-thirds thought their children would need a college education. These families have dreamed no small dreams. Their aspirations are high. But their means for fulfilling these aspirations are few. Their financial resources are small. Their experience of discrimination is great. In summary, the opportunity system is blocked.

Parenthetically, probably the best example of camouflage at the national level is the reasoning that prevailed in the United States for so many years prior to 1960 that a person of Catholic religious faith could not adequately perform his duties as President of the United States because he would be subject to political control from the Pope in Rome. We now know in 1964 that this reasoning was but rationalization of personal prejudice.

SHIFTING THE ONUS

We tend to attribute to others the problems that are our own. Thus, youth who are pushed out of school because schools are not flexible enough and sufficiently creative to accommodate their special needs are labelled "dropouts." This label places the onus on the youth and not on the school. Poor, fearful, lower-class, Negro families that are rejected by community social service agencies are classified as "uncooperative clients" who do not want to be helped. This label places the responsibility on the family and not on the agency. These and other techniques we have used to rationalize the inadequacies of an affluent society that cares but does not care enough for the poor, oppressed, and the afflicted. The time is at hand when we must call a spade a spade. Deprivation is closely associated with discrimination. We cannot eliminate one and keep the other.

After facing up to the problem as it actually is, the next task is to devise an appropriate methodology for solving it. In general, two alternatives lie before us—one, change the individual, and the other, change the system. Attempts to change the individual are easier because a person is malleable, vulnerable, and defenseless. Attempts to change the system are more difficult because institutions are rigid and time-honored. But change the institutional system we must, if school people are to be more than a band-aid brigade.

Helping deprived youth is necessary and essential. However, these efforts must be viewed in proper perspective as acts of rehabilitation. Changing the system that generates segregation, alienation, and deprivation is an act of prevention. While tackling the backlog of past misdeeds requires much of our time and may appear to be overwhelming, we must at the same time assign part of our energy to preventive activities if the same problems we are working so hard to overcome today are not to be visited upon future generations.

The deprivation of the present was contributed to by the social system of the past. Dr. Conant recognized this when he said that "public schools for Negroes and whites together might have softened the caste lines," had these been established long ago when slavery had just vanished.[10]

Of crime control, Dr. Leslie Wilkins of Great Britain has reminded us of the limitation of our approach. Like other community efforts, those designed to suppress crime have focused largely on individuals. As Dr. Wilkins points out in the book *Society Problems and Methods of Study*, it is easy to say of the criminal "He did it—deal with him." Dr. Wilkins points out that "crime has *not* been considered as a failure of social controls but has been simplified to the wrongdoing of single per-

---

10 *Ibid.*

sons or gangs." "It should be clear," he concludes, "that dealing with him has not solved the problem of crime and seems unlikely to do so. . . ." He points out that there are social as well as personal control mechanisms, and . . . "to operate on only half of the problem (that is, the personal component) may not solve even half of it, let alone the whole." [11]

The same may be said of problems of deprivation in the school. To focus only on the deprived child without considering also the social system which alienates him and contributes to his deprivation may not solve even half of the problem and certainly not the whole.

DEPLOY STUDENTS

It seems to me that one of the major system changes the school must make if it desires to overcome deprivation due to alienating racial segregation is to renounce commitment to the concept of the neighborhood school. With reference to elementary schools, I am uncertain as to the importance of the neighborhood school. But at the secondary level, the concept of a neighborhood school contributes to segregation; and on this basis, it cannot be justified.

No one argued about the virtues of the neighborhood high school in Dallas, Texas nearly twenty-five years ago when I attended Lincoln High School for Negroes in that city. Although my family lived in the western sector of Dallas, in a neighborhood called Oak Cliff, my brothers and sister and all of our playmates traveled by bus several miles to the southern sector of Dallas to attend high school; and we paid our own bus fare. The only other high school for Negroes was in the northern sector. This was during the days of segregation. Then, the neighborhood school was not exalted.

There were, of course, high schools in the western sector of the city where I lived. One might call these neighborhood schools. But enrollment in these schools was limited to white children. The concept of the neighborhood high school, therefore, was not relevant in the city of my youth. Had the little Willie boys and girl attended the neighborhood high school in

---

[11] Leslie T. Wilkins, "Criminology: An Operational Research Approach," in A. T. Welford, Michael Argyle, D. V. Glass, J. N. Morris, eds., *Society Problems and Methods of Study* (London: Routledge and Kegan Paul, Ltd., no date), p. 329.

Dallas in the 1930's, 1940's, and early 1950's there would have been unmistakable racial integration. As the Negro population in urban areas has increased during the past quarter of the century and as this increase in population has been limited to ghetto-like neighborhoods in the center of the city, the concept of the neighborhood school has assumed greater relevance in education. One suspects that the concept of the neighborhood school has been assuming increasing importance since the Supreme Court's decision in 1954 which ruled illegal officially segregated public schools.

I have still another reason for suspecting the concept of the neighborhood school is not as great as it is said to be. It seems the concept of the neighborhood school is most rigidly adhered to in lower class and in lower middle class neighborhoods, but is more flexible and relaxed for residents of the affluent neighborhoods. In Washington, D. C., for example, one of the better elementary schools is the Amidon school in southwest Washington. The superintendent of the city school system has a special interest in that school and its curriculum. In fact, he has written a book about the beneficial effects of its curriculum and the method of teaching that goes on there. The principal of the school has a doctor's degree and some of the finest teachers in Washington are employed at the Amidon School. Amidon is an open school. Children attend it from all over the city. By taxi, late model car, and other means of transportation, well-dressed children from all over the city descend each day on Amidon. For these more affluent children it would appear that the quality of education they receive is considered to be more important by their parents than the geographic location of the school.

Even another example is the boarding school. Some of the presidents of this country graduated from these schools. Boarding schools certainly are not neighborhood schools. Yet, they turn out persons of good character and sound mind. But boarding schools are for the affluent. Could it be that neighborhood schools are recommended for the alienated and poor? The concept of the neighborhood school should remain an open issue in public education. It is in need of more study and analysis, particularly from the point of view of its association, if any, with segregation, alienation, and deprivation.

DEPLOY STAFF

Another kind of change in the current system of schools and education could be in the deployment of personnel. The racial composition of the teaching staff in many big city schools tends to reflect the racial composition of the neighborhoods in which these schools are located. In Washington, D. C., for example, there are high school principals who are Negro; but none are principals of schools in predominantly white neighborhoods. Moreover, the high schools in predominantly Negro neighborhoods have predominantly Negro faculties and the high schools in predominantly white neighborhoods have predominantly white faculties. The argument is frequently given that teachers prefer to teach in schools that are near their homes. This reasoning suggests that one of the primary variables in education is the residential location of the instructor. I beg to differ with this reasoning. No reliable study has found any correlation between the teaching talents of an instructor and his residential address. Furthermore, a diversified teaching staff is a distinct educational experience for the student. Every school within the city could have an integrated teaching staff of white and Negro teachers. This is within the power of most school administrations; and they should integrate teaching staffs with all deliberate speed. What better way to teach children that Negro and white persons should live together as brothers and sisters than to show them daily that Negro and white persons work together as teaching colleagues.

These and other changes in the school as a system we must make to overcome the festering problem of deprivation compounded by alienating segregation. Changes in the behavior of an individual may or may not affect the institutional systems of a community. But changes in the institutional system usually produce changes in individual behavior. This kind of change tends to be more enduring because it is sanctioned and supported. The time has come not only to redeem the individual who has fallen but to modify the system that contributed to his downfall.

Teachers and administrators are not expected to remake the world. But they can certainly influence the direction in which it is moving by demonstrating what is attainable within the institution in which they work.[12] If a caste system finds its clearest manifestation in an educational system, then the schools are a good place to start in eliminating racial segregation, alienation, and deprivation.

ᘓᘓᘓᘓᘓᘓᘓᘓᘓᘓᘓᘓᘓᘓᘓᘓᘓᘓᘓᘓᘓᘓᘓᘓᘓᘓ

DROPOUTS—

A POLITICAL PROBLEM

ᘓᘓᘓᘓᘓᘓᘓᘓᘓᘓᘓᘓᘓᘓᘓᘓᘓᘓᘓᘓᘓᘓᘓᘓᘓᘓ

S. M. MILLER

Discussions about dropouts are too broad and too narrow. They are too broad because they seem to assume that the category of dropouts is a homogeneous one and that little variation exists within the category. The discussions are too narrow because they do not adequately look upon the problems of dropouts as economic and political issues, but mainly as educational ones. It is the purpose of this paper to redress the balance.

VARIATIONS AMONG DROPOUTS

Adequate information on school dropouts is lacking. The best available estimate is that presently one-third of all youths will never finish high school. This rate varies considerably from region to region—by degree of urbanization, by character of community, and the like. New York City is not America; nor is Muncie. Conditions vary tremendously from community to

---

[12] Charles V. Willie, "Anti-Social Behavior Among Disadvantaged Youth: Some Observations on Prevention for Teachers," *The Journal of Negro Education*, XXXIII (Spring 1964), 180-181.

community and have marked effects on dropout rates. Rates for one community cannot be extrapolated to produce national trends. The preconditions and later experiences of dropouts are not the same in different communities.

Contrary to some popular beliefs, dropouts are not exclusively from working-class and lower-class or low-income families. In Syracuse, New York, for example, 30 percent of the parents of dropouts were in white-collar occupations.

Similarly the ecological distribution of Syracuse male dropouts shows that at least one-fifth come from "fair" or "good" neighborhoods.[1]

A reanalysis of data collected by the Bureau of the Census suggests that 70 percent of all dropouts come from families whose income is below $5,000 a year.[2] While this under $5,000 group is, of course, overrepresented among dropouts, the surprising result is the large percentage of dropouts who do not come from the poorest families.

Another way of analyzing the data is to study the percentage of stay-ins. Of low-income youth (under $5,000 family income) perhaps 60 percent do graduate from high school. Thus, not all dropouts are from low-income families, nor do all low-income youth become dropouts.

These data strongly underline the heterogeneity of those called dropouts. Instead of discussing *"the* dropout," it is necessary to analyze the etiology and experience of different types of dropouts. Of course, different strategies may be required for each type.

The fourfold table below linking class and school level attendance indicates cells that are frequently overlooked in discussions of social class and dropouts:

Social Class	School Situation	
	Dropout—	*Graduate*+
Working and lower classes	− −(1)	− +(2)
Middle classes	+ −(3)	+ +(4)

---

[1] Our Syracuse data indicate that not all recent dropouts are having job problems. Perhaps 40 percent of white males have been able to obtain fairly good jobs (white-collar and skilled manual) two years after dropping out.

[2] The following data should be regarded as only indicative of general trends because of a number of problems of classification in the original data.

The preceding data indicate that cell (3), the middle-class dropout, is overlooked in discussions of dropouts as is cell (2), the working- and lower-class graduate.

The middle-class dropout has not been analyzed as such.[3] The likelihood is that there is considerable variation among middle-class dropouts. Three types seem to emerge: (a) the dropout with school-related emotional difficulties, (b) the emotionally disturbed dropout whose difficulties are not directly related to school, and (c) the dropout from a family which is economically and/or educationally marginal to the middle class. The latter type, I would guess, makes up the bulk of middle-class dropouts.

In this paper I am not developing this typology because I want to keep the focus on the dropouts of the low-income families, including those from families "old" or "new" to urban manual life and those from working-class and "lower-class" homes. But it might prove worthwhile to expend research effort on the middle-class dropout. Probably more important would be studies of the working-class and lower-class high school graduate, for in seeing the factors that lead many to stay, we may be better able to depict ways of helping others.

THE LOW-INCOME DROPOUT

I would suggest four types of low-income dropouts: (a) school-inadequate, (b) school-rejecting, (c) school-perplexed, and (d) school-irrelevant. While few pure types exist, it seems worthwhile to isolate the different sets of pressures which operate.

The School-Inadequate Dropout

The school-inadequate category refers to those who may have difficulty in completing school because of low intellectual functioning or disturbing emotional functioning. This category is probably much smaller than generally assumed. The data on

---

[3] Solomon O. Lichter, and others, *The Drop-Outs: A Treatment Study of Intellectually Capable Students Who Drop Out of High School* (Glencoe, Ill.: Free Press, 1962).

The Lichter book is the one exception, but here only a particular slice of middle-class dropouts have been studied.

IQ show considerable overlap between working class and middle class. Siller's study demonstrates that if a few extreme cases of low IQ performance are disregarded, the class differences are small. Further, a recent census study has a surprising result and suggests that intellectual inability to function in school may not be an important reason for dropping out. One-third of the dropouts leave school in their senior year; put another way, 10 percent of students entering their senior year dropped out before the end of it. These figures may be too high since some of these nongraduates may return to complete school.[4] But even if these figures are reduced considerably, it is still shocking that so many come close to completing high school but do not make it. It may be that senior level work is more exacting than earlier school and that many students are not prepared to handle it; it is doubtful, however, if 30 percent (those dropping out before the senior year and those dropping out in the senior year) of our youth are incapable of handling it. Something is wrong here.

The School-Rejecting Dropout

The second type of low-income dropout is propelled by a push away from school. Not a few find school as presently conducted confining, unuseful, ego-destructive. They want to get away from this negative, boring experience, and in many cases the school would like them to get away. In a group of boys who had dropped out and were unable to get jobs, most of them, we found, claimed that they did not voluntarily withdraw from school—they asserted that they were pushed out and frequently in a fairly direct way.

I doubt if most low-income dropouts leave school because of a pure dislike of it. Three conditions indicate the likelihood that the push from school is not omnipotent among low-income dropouts. First, most dropouts do not leave school as soon as they are legally eligible. Second, many dropouts, as pointed out earlier, withdraw in the senior year. Third, our Syracuse "unemployable" dropouts, who should be likely candidates for posts of school critics, had a generally favorable attitude toward school: they asserted that they had a positive feeling

---

[4] Daniel Schreiber has informed me that the NEA data show a lower rate of senior dropouts.

about at least some teachers; they thought teachers were generally fair, and they missed school because of its social aspects —such as meeting friends during the school day. This attitude may be a nostalgic glow for a past which appears in retrospect more attractive than a difficult present, but the absence of a deep, pervasive antipathy toward school is surprising in a group which had problems of "adjustment" in school and conducted itself, or was conducted, out of it.

The School-Perplexed Dropout

The school-perplexed dropout has been largely ignored in the emphasis on cultural values operating as barriers to school achievement among those of low income. It is widely assumed that all or most low-income families and youth have very little interest in school or in high-level occupational achievement. A variety of studies shows, however, that this is not the case, at least for low-income Negroes. At the same income levels, Negroes voice much more interest and concern about education than whites. Many Negroes see education—as Patricia Sexton has pointed out to me—in power and prestige terms, as giving them a standing and protection in a discriminatory world. But it is not Negroes alone who are concerned about education. The Reiss-Rhodes study in Nashville reports that less well-off youth are much more likely to say that education has overwhelming importance than do youth from better-off families.[5]

I find that when I report such data, the reaction is that low-income youth and their families are unrealistic in their aspirations. This may be true—although Lockwood's Baltimore study reports for high-school students (all classes) that only 5 percent overestimate their occupational potentials while more than 35 percent underestimate them!—but this contention is a far cry from the previous assertion that aspirations are too low. If aspirations are very low, then we are told cultural barriers inhibit educational achievement; if aspirations are high, then we are informed that they are unrealistic. I think that we are saying that we do not know how to deal with the kinds of edu-

---

[5] Frank Riessman, *The Culturally Deprived Child* (New York: Harper & Brothers, 1962).

In his chapter, "Are the Culturally Deprived Interested in Education," Riessman summarizes a number of studies which are in the same direction as our conclusion.

cational concerns and problems many low-income families and youth have. For many low-income youth and families, a complete and unrelieved rejection of school does not exist. We have to recognize that many come to school with some personal or family concerns about it but become perplexed, lost, and sometimes reactive against the school experience, ending up as dropouts.

I would guess that neither of the first two categories is large, that the third category is growing, and that the bulk of low income dropouts find school largely irrelevant. I will concentrate consequently on the latter dropout type.

The School-Irrelevant Dropout

Many prospective dropouts never have expected to graduate —they have a job level in mind which does not require much education. Since they see education instrumentally, they are not interested in school as such, and the school's inability to interest them compounds the problem. They may be described as having "low aspirations," but they may not see themselves in that light. Is having "high aspirations" a desirable goal and achievement? Does graduating from high school really provide entry into higher-level jobs?

Let us examine this latter question. The long-term data on education and income indicate that the general rise in the level of income has not reduced the importance of education; it has shifted upward the breaking point where education leads to high or low income.

It is certainly better to be a high school graduate than a dropout, but it is much better to be a college graduate. As Vance Packard has pointed out, the "diploma elite" is clearly advantaged. The differences in annual income between high school graduates and high school dropouts are less than those between high school graduates and college graduates, and the gap between those with a high school diploma and those with a college diploma is increasing.

Nor are occupational differences between high school graduates and dropouts starkly in favor of the graduates, as is commonly believed. While one out of six graduates does distinctively better than the dropout, the advantage is not overwhelming. Putting the data differently reveals that there is great occupational overlap for the majority of dropouts and graduates, so that the advantage of graduating from high school is not immediately obvious.

Comparisons of the occupational experiences of dropouts and graduates do not attempt to hold social class constant. Many noncollege-going high school graduates are from middle-class homes; their occupational achievement may be influenced by this social class variable rather than by the graduation variable. It is my guess that social class *does* make a big difference among high-school graduates. The higher the social class level of the graduate's family, the more likely it is that he will obtain a high-level job. Graduates from working-class and lower-class families are not at all as likely to do well. I suspect that if we could parcel out family status in viewing the relation of graduation to occupation, we would find that graduation does not make a great difference for the boys from the working classes; it is the linkage of graduation with prior middle-class status that makes the difference in the over-all results of the relation of high-school diplomas to occupations.

I do not have good evidence to support this hunch. As far as I know, there are no national data which report occupational level by level of education and occupation of parent. I have made some very rough computations by manipulating census data; these calculations suggest that at least one-quarter of high school graduating, noncollege-going, working-class sons end up in low-level, low-income jobs. This is the picture soon after graduation: it undoubtedly improves in later years. Less than 10 percent end up in fairly high-level jobs soon after graduation. High school graduation helps working-class and lower-class boys, but the aid may not be great nor immediately apparent.

I suggest that, at some level, many lower- and working-class boys have some awareness of the facts about them. Consequently, they are not particularly interested in doing something about school—to say that they are "culturally deprived" or "unmotivated" is choosing the wrong target. It is not clear what they should be motivated to, if the chances of getting a good job are not great. To say—as one of my colleagues has—that getting a 10 percent or 15 percent or 20 percent advantage by graduating from high school is still a distinct improvement, is to ignore the fact that, by the same token, for perhaps 8 out of 10 working-class boys graduation is not going to produce much.

Improving economic prospects may not have an immediate

effect nor an all-powerful effect in reducing dropouts. But without such improvement in prospects, various tactics for encouraging dropouts to stay in school are not likely to be effective. And, as I shall point out, it may be better that these tactics fail.

THE LABOR MARKET AND
ECONOMIC GROWTH

The concern for dropouts is great because of the confluence of four factors: (a) an anarchic, unorganized, inefficient labor market prevails; (b) technological change is occurring at a rapid clip; (c) economic growth is limited (an unusual event during a period of technological innovation); and (d) the push from the rural and agricultural areas is leading new migrants to the large cities.

The impact of technological change would not be so dangerous if the other three factors were not also operative. Similarly, the anarchic labor market would not have ill effects if economic growth were taking place. From the point of view of change and public policy, it is obvious that we are not going to attempt to slow up the processes of technological change and urbanization involved in (b) or (d). The labor market and economic growth—(a) and (c)—become fundamental axes of public policy.

In former years, with the operation of apprenticeship systems, there was orderly progression through the job structure. Today this is not true. Indeed, Harold Wilensky has gone so far as to argue that for many blue-collar people, it is erroneous to talk of "occupational career" since there is no progression or clarity to occupational movement.

It would be helpful if there were a rational labor market in which job opportunities were charitable, the roads to them clear and accessible, and the movement into the niches serviceable. There is no clear optimal way of obtaining jobs today because a rational procedure for making jobs available does not exist. The academic world is a familiar and horrible example of irrational and nonrational ways of sorting people and jobs. What is needed, among other things, is an adequate sorting device in terms of employment exchanges.

Needed are new substitutes for apprenticeships. "Workshops" have been suggested by Kohler and Friedman—some orderly,

regular system by which one is inducted into a job and progresses to higher-level occupations. Probably much on-the-job
training would be involved.

An anarchic labor market creates problems at any time;
but when it coexists with low economic growth, difficulties are
compounded. We are attempting makeshift devices because of
an ineffective economic steering mechanism in this country. We
should not forget that great economic growth would probably
eliminate all but the thorniest of our dropout problems.

Considering the nasty things that are said about education,
high-school diplomas do not magically transmute their holders
into intellectual giants. To a large extent, social attitudes toward dropouts and the excess labor supply, rather than dropouts' actual incapacities, are the important limiting factors for
dropouts.

We are increasingly living in a "credential society" where we
do not evaluate people on the basis of performance but on the
basis of credentials ("He's a Harvard man"). People who have
unusual ability—as Admiral Rickover pointed out in relation to
teaching credentials—but who have not had certain courses or
formal licensure-type qualifications, cannot attain jobs, especially high-level jobs. Could a Richard Titmuss, Britain's prem-
ier social welfare expert—a holder of a chair at the London
School of Economics but a man without a bachelor's degree—
have been able to secure a post in the United States if he were
an American? This emphasis on formal education as the union
card for jobs is unfortunate, for it reduces the utilization of
alternative routes to competence and emphasizes "sponsored"
or "guided" mobility in which social acceptance of the aspirant
is important.

SELECTIVE MOBILITY

Gans has referred to "guided individual mobility" and
Turner, to "sponsored" mobility. What seems to be happening
with the increased emphasis on education is that we are co-
opting people for "success" if they perform in certain socially
acceptable ways. High-level intelligence may forge its own
way; but for the more ordinary ascendant, a certain social cast
is required—for educational advance and then occupational
admission. It is this cast Friedenberg and Goodman detest.
Much can be said about this mold and its effects. I want to

point up some neglected and perplexing (social) issues and consequences.

I suspect that the sociological emphasis on the functional necessity of "occupational socialization"—i.e., absorbing the social values, stance, and outlook associated with a job—is very much overdone. Many, many jobs can be well done without this socialization. Job competence, not job socialization, is the target. We are frequently getting socialization without economic advance; perhaps we need more economic advance without socialization. Providing the former may deliver the minimal social quantities which may be desired.

In emphasizing efforts to encourage students to graduate from high school and in making special efforts to locate talented youth and encouraging them to move ahead, some important considerations may have been ignored. An emphasis on such programs as Project Talent can be a way of attempting to go around the problem of educational discrimination rather than breaking through it. For it is obviously possible to make strenuous efforts to locate potential graduates without breaking down existing practices of discrimination in terms of de facto segregation and the distribution of educational resources. Helping the talented few is not solving problems of discrimination, and it avoids direct confrontation with a basic issue of contemporary American education.

It may well be that our efforts at guided individual mobility may result in providing enough mobility to enough people so that pressure for real, basic, pervasive social change will not take place. We could be providing sops rather than solutions.

Parallel to this possibility is the lack of concern for those who will not be "making it." What about those left behind by the educationally mobile? Those who are left behind will be filling a variety of low-paying, low-skill jobs. There should be considerable effort to improve the conditions of these jobs in terms of pay, rationalization (to reduce layoffs), working conditions, and the like. Legislation (a minimum wage which provides a floor which makes sense in terms of today's cost of living), more effective union organization, and concentrated local planning may be necessary to decasualize the labor force and improve working conditions. These aims are minimal and a necessary prelude to any effort to provide the kind of job meaning with which Paul Goodman has rightly been concerned.

As a youth advances in the mobility route, whatever the reason for his being selected or the nature of the route, what happens to the community from which he comes? If we become more concerned with those left behind, we have to consider questions such as these: Is it possible to have guided individual mobility that improves the chances for improvement of those who do not move ahead? Should an effort be made to encourage those who have moved ahead to attempt to help those who do not? Should they be made to feel that going up does not mean opting out of the plights of their former mates? Does social mobility necessarily mean that potential leaders are lost to the group which fathered them?

Do we want to change the conditions of a lot of people a little or greatly change the conditions of a small number of people? In medical care with its present state of economic organization, the general purpose is to improve a lot the condition of a few. Certainly this is true of the orientation of private psychiatry and even community mental health programs supported by tax funds, as Paul Hoch, New York State commissioner of mental health, has pointed out. Whenever a shortage of professional talent occurs, the emphasis is upon upgrading professional talent to provide really high-level personnel, thereby restricting the supply rather than trying to see how the tasks can be subdivided so that more adequate service can be given to a greater number of persons.

Programs of social action which are oriented to facilitating the upward mobility of individuals (i.e., not through collective action or through improved conditions of the group as a group) are probably devoted to the principle of greatly changing the conditions of a few. Is this our overriding social value?

Every decision is a death; a choice means that we cannot pursue other possibilities. The price of every act is the loss of alternative opportunities. The economist knows this well and talks of opportunity costs: What other utilities are foregone in achieving a particular utility? Have we adequately assayed the opportunity costs of our present-day efforts?

I do not intend these questions to be rhetorical ones, for I am not sure of the answers, but I think that they reflect important issues that are not currently discussed. Of one thing, however, I am obviously convinced. It is that we have to concern ourselves with social change—not only with individual change. In the earnest attempt to do something about dropouts, should our efforts perhaps be directed more toward FEPC and full employment than toward publicity aimed at encouraging youth to stay in school?

A Historical Note

If job opportunities are improved, then perhaps in the next generation a great number of the children of the new working classes may make real moves to improve their conditions. It is not sufficiently realized that former disprivileged ethnic groups did not improve their conditions mainly by education, but through business and political employments. The Irish and Italians did not initially have a heavy emphasis on education as vehicles for improvements. It was usually after the parents had made some economic stake—frequently through business—that Irish and Italian youth began to go to college. The Jews were different in that more of their ascent was through education; the emphasis on literacy and learning among Jews has been noted as important in their movement. Ignored has been the fact that in the "old country" many of them were petty traders and small businessmen so that they came to this nation with more varied experience than do the new working classes of today. Moreover, the Jews, like many other ascending ethnic groups, but unlike Negroes and Puerto Ricans, had religious values which maintained male importance and family solidarity.

The new working classes—if they wish to be mobile—face the special condition of having to go increasingly through the educational blender with neither the special background of the Jews nor the minor business successes of the Irish and Italians. Their way is more limited and they are being put through the school sifter at a time when heightened demands are being made for higher-level performance in the educational system.

STRATEGIES OF CHANGE

My emphasis on economic factors is a result of the feeling that attitudinal factors have been overstressed. It may be that a great surge in educational attainments of the low-income group might lead to a great demand for economic expansion—in turn leading to the production of more jobs. I rather doubt this. A great educational surge is more likely to lead to unrest, unemployment, underemployment. How that unrest would become crystallized is unclear, Frank Riessman contends. It could be a

dangerous road—made less threatening, however, by the likelihood that the campaigns to persuade youth to stay in school
will not succeed.

The varied campaigns to get youth to stay in school can only
be successful if they are unsuccessful; for if everyone went on
to graduate from high school and if many went on to college,
there would not be enough appropriate jobs available. It is
dangerous to raise aspirations if we cannot be sure of a payoff
for the additional effort involved. I doubt if these campaigns
will gain many new recruits for high school diplomas. Those
who see school as irrelevant to their lives—because of its inability to deliver occupationally or esthetically, as Friedenberg and
Goodman contend—are unlikely to find the propaganda of a
campaign an irresistible siren song. It should be noted too, as
Maurice Connery has pointed out, that the campaigns may
have some boomerang effects in lowering the self-esteem and
enterprising efforts of dropouts by convincing them that they
have no occupational chances at all.

Another possibility is that there would be some increase in
opportunities; this increase would be followed by a large increase in educational achievement and expectations. Then, we
would again have the problem of whether opportunities match
the supply of labor.

Other possibilities abound. But what is worrisome in the situation is not the lack of aspirations and desires but the likely
absence of opportunity. Aspirations may lag beyond opportunity, but that is usually a short-run phenomenon.

In American life, it has been customary to offer "education"
as the panacea for all problems, whether those of racial prejudice, sexual unhappiness, or economic conflict—and I suppose
that "research" frequently is the proffered answer when we are
afraid of taking action. I have the feeling that to the problems
of discrimination, inadequate economic functioning, and poverty, we are again offering the reply of "education." In doing
so, we are essentially making it a bootstrap operation—telling
those who have the most strikes against them that they have to
do the most work to improve the situation.

These remarks, negative as they are, are not to say that all
kinds of educational programs and experiments to improve
schooling and its attractiveness are not a priority item. Nor do
they argue that subjective attitudes play little role. I am questioning how effective this present-day emphasis is for the
school-irrelevant dropout and in the attack on the overdeter-

mined *social* problem of youth, unemployment, discrimination, and poverty.

Goodman and Friedenberg are saying that schools today desiccate humanity; I am saying that schools and education cannot be expected to solve the blight of poverty and inhumanity: the entire society and economy are implicated. And, it may be that, by our stress on eliminating dropouts, we are not politicalizing the important issues. At the same time, we may be giving people a comfortable way to forget about the corrosive character of much of our social and economic life.

We are in danger of making dropouts a problem of personal inadequacy, subcultural values, and the like: most dropouts are neither knights nor "hoods." We should be aiming to make the problem of unemployment and unsatisfactory employment a problem of politics—of citizenship rights, of economic rights, of social rights. In the sophistication that has made sociology the substitute for socialism, we should remember that even in sociology the structure of institutional forces and opportunities play an important role.

Part
Four

EARLY
CHILDHOOD

INTRODUCTION

The establishment of Operation Head Start during the summer of 1965—a preschool educational program for more than half a million disadvantaged four- and five-year-old children—signaled the opening of a new area for exploration of the root sources of "cultural disadvantage" and underachievement. There is little question that the reformation of the schools (which in one way or another all our authors call for), is crucially important, for the schools need to be drastically renovated to meet the full range of challenges posed by their pupils. Simultaneously though, research has turned toward an exploration of factors within the child himself and within the culture he is raised in, which may be important and relevant to his later school achievement. The aim of such research is to determine which factors in the child's early environment might be manipulated to provide him with better ability to cope within a school setting. Similarly, the long-range aim of special preschool programs for disadvantaged children, such as Operation Head Start, is to provide these children with the basic skills necessary for school achievement, which they, unlike middle-class children, do not acquire in their home environments.

Martin Deutsch, who has been a leading figure in the field of early childhood education research, raises a number of issues and problems confronting educators who attempt to design programs to compensate for the inadequacy of the child's home educational background and prepare him for the demands the school will make upon him.

Bruno Bettelheim, in reviewing Benjamin S. Bloom's conclusions, suggests that the crucial factors of cultural disadvantage which later lead to poor school performance, and which have to do with family background and with relations between parents and child, cannot often be significantly influenced or changed in the school setting. In Bettelheim's mind, the child must be reached through his parents, in his home, during the very earliest stages of his development:

> Thus if we were really serious about doing something for the intellectual development of underprivileged children, we would have to make our influence felt in their homes, by encouraging parents to change their intellectual expectations and aspirations for their children as well as their own language habits, and to make learning supplies, periodicals, and books available.

Robert Hess's paper describes a study whose objective is to explore the language, teaching patterns, and customs of poverty populations and to discover means of intervening constructively in the earliest "educational" exchanges between mother and child. Here, then, is a tentative effort, based upon the theories of the English sociologist, Basil Bernstein, to by-pass the symptoms in which cultural disadvantage displays itself and to affect the child's structure of cognition at its most intimate origin.

@@@@@@@@@@@@@@@@@@@@@@@@@@@@@@@@@@@@

EARLY SOCIAL ENVIRONMENT:

Its Influence on
School Adaptation

@@@@@@@@@@@@@@@@@@@@@@@@@@@@@@@@@@

MARTIN DEUTSCH

This paper will make no attempt to incorporate the total complex of social institutions involved in school failure, for this can
lead only to a loss of the direction necessary to the carving out
of relevant and malleable chunks of the problem. For this reason, the focus will be largely on the school, an institution that
in itself cannot initiate major social change, but one which can
play a determining role in orienting its products. The school is,
after all, the only social institution which has some contact with
all children.

There is variation (a) in the impact of this contact from
group to group, fostered through the preparation by the parents of the child for the first school contact; (b) in the general
meaning of the school to the economic substance of the community; and (c) in the expectations of the school and the appropriateness of the curriculum for the child. These differences
in the interaction among the child, the school, and the community, are determined, among other things, by social attitudes
toward education, stability of community, social class and ethnic membership of family, and sex of child.

THE CHILD'S PREPARATION FOR SCHOOL

Generally speaking, the middle-class child is more likely than
others to have the importance of school imprinted in his con-

sciousness from the earliest possible age. This is not necessarily bad or good for the child or the school, but it is very different from the preparation of the lower social status child. I have never seen a school curriculum that is organized on the basis of the existence of these differences. Though these differences are sometimes acknowledged, both sets of children nevertheless are asked to climb the same mountain at the same rate, as if they had similar prior experience and training.

The lower-class child, because of poorer preparation, is at a real disadvantage in this mountain climbing, though it is the middle-class child who probably has more personal anxiety about the success of his climb. However, the middle-class child has available to him other avenues for handling the school situation. There is more likely to be contiguity of the school-faculty orientation with his home-family orientation. Failure can be interpreted to him in appropriate and familiar terms, and methods of coping with it can be incorporated—increasing the motivation or offering the necessary rewards, goals, or punishments to effect the desired change in performance. For the middle-class child, the school is very central and is continuous with the totality of his life experiences. As a result, there are few incongruities between his school experiences and any others he is likely to have had, and there are intrinsic motivating and molding properties in the school situation to which he has been highly sensitized.

For the lower-class child there is not the same contiguity or continuity, and he does not have the same coping mechanisms for internalizing success or psychologically surviving failure in the formal learning setting. If the lower-class child starts to fail, he does not have the same kinds of operationally significant and functionally relevant support from his family or community—or from the school—that his counterpart has. Furthermore, because of the differences in preparation, he is more likely to experience failure. It might even be that both groups are equally motivated, in terms of quantity of motivation, but failure or lack of recognition for the middle-class child might only serve to channel his energies more narrowly, while for the lower-class child it early becomes dysfunctional, with the effect of converting the original motivation into a rejection of intellectual striving.

EFFECTS OF SCHOOL FAILURE
ON THE CHILD

Failure in school for the middle-class child can be more personally disorganizing because the continuity of values from home to school insures that such a child will be considered a failure in both places. However, as was already pointed out, there are also more resources available for helping the child to cope with the failure and to recover from it, and to mitigate its degree.

For the lower-class child, school failure may result in less personal upset or disturbance but may be more final, both in terms of recovery of adequate functioning in school and in terms of occupational choices. Such failure may have the result of gradually but nevertheless effectively alienating the child from the school and the structure of opportunity which is associated with it.

In addition, though these parents may or may not be opposed to the specific act involved in the child's leaving school prematurely, they may have shared with the child their own personal affect regarding their experiences with social institutions. Particularly the minority group lower-class parent is likely to explain, rationalize, and attribute job and economic frustration—both correctly and incorrectly—to the operation of impersonal societal institutions. He may thus identify, accurately and inaccurately, these same institutions with his child's experience in school. This negative affect can rapidly and perhaps inadvertently be generalized to the whole school learning process.

This kind of constellation has particular significance where the school system operates as a bureaucratic mechanism, isolated from the community, and unable to counteract the consequences of inadequate preparation for functioning in the school factory. So the school, at the time the child decides to leave it, has little influence with either the child or the parent, and even if it did, it is frequently just not programed for interpreting process to nonmiddle-class children and adults.

ALIENATION OR INCREASING RAPPORT?

Thus, if the school is to influence the continued attendance of children, the influence must begin and the channels for its transmission must be opened well before the school failure and the dropout problem arise.[1] This brings us to the first contact of the child and his parents with the school. The process of alienation or, on the other hand, of increasing rapport, begins here. It is at this level that certain crucial questions must be asked.

Points to Be Considered

First, is the child intellectually and psychologically ready for the school experience, for the specific curriculum, and for the demands of comprehension, communication, motor control, and timing made by the school? The reference here is not to specific "readiness" as the term has been characteristically used in educational circles but, rather, to the sociocognitive preparations and anticipations of the child for this new experience. Next, are the parents helped to become aware of the school's purpose, the nature of its demands on the child, and how they—even if uneducated—can play a meaningful role in the education of their child? Is the school accessible to these parents? In other words, is it a place which stimulates embarrassment for their ignorance and fear of its power, or is it a center for comfortable contact and a sharing of their interest in their child?

In this interaction among three elements, what about the school itself—the third element? Is it a structure that the community can be proud of, and where staff can share this pride? Do its teachers and administrators see a challenge, or are they

---

[1] Of course, not all dropouts are school failures (and there might even be instances when high-performance creative children *should* drop out of school—but that would make another paper), but the evidence suggests that the majority are. Similarly, of course, all dropouts are not lower-status children, but again the majority are; and I would postulate that with middle-class children there is a higher incidence among dropouts of psychological malfunctioning, while with lower-status children it is more likely to be associated with sociocognitive dissonance and general problems of communication.

interested only in securing discipline and in surviving the day? Do they have some understanding of the social backgrounds of their children, the temporary limitations that might have been imposed by these backgrounds (in terms of good schoolwork)? Is there a reasonable amount of staff stability, particularly in the early years? And is there some attempt to adjust the curriculum and primers to current life realities?

Considered, But . . .

The answers to these questions we all really know. The experiences of the child from the disadvantaged background simply do not prepare him for successful school performance. The teacher has, more often than not, *not* been trained in the sociology of learning, and also, more often than not, her training fails to give her a sense of challenge in teaching children, particularly those who start out with handicaps. Usually she prefers—both by training and personal inclination—the immediately bright, responsive child who also most probably places a type of demand on her professional skills which is more congruent with the orientation of her training.

The schools are more likely than not to be underequipped, closed to the children for after-school experimentation with extracurricular books and arts and crafts, and closed to the community as evening centers for learning and socializing. More likely than not, nobody explains to the parents how they can help or be important factors in the education of their child, and the whole process of their child's education—even for the few who become active in the PTA's—remains foreign and alien, and often their contact with the school carries a condescending quality. The early curriculum is likely to be unfamiliar, experientially discontinuous, while the primer, despite all criticism, is still most likely to be boring, repetitious, suburban, and altogether too white.

What we have stated here, of course, are some of the major problems of getting a grip on children from social and cultural backgrounds which do not participate in the middle-class values of the school. These problems are raised here not because it is now fashionable to lay at their door all of our current social difficulties, but because to me it is inconceivable to consider the problem of the high school dropout without focusing on the early relationship among the child, the family, and the school, and the transition between the preschool environment and the school.

Considering all these combinations, factors, and circumstances, it is amazing that as many children as do still find sufficient relevance in the school experience to remain. In this context it might be noted parenthetically that the real occupational expectations of these children are more congruent with their homes and community experiences than they are with the school setting. It might be that only as school is perceived as being more functionally relevant to adult occupations can early negative experiences become decreasingly influential in the decision to leave school. Here is not meant the Conant solution of simply more vocational high schools but, rather, the *same opportunity distribution for all populations,* regardless of subgroup membership.

IMPORTANCE OF A PRESCHOOL
TRAINING PROGRAM

There are many possible avenues through which solutions for these problems might be evolved. But none of them exists independently, and any successful solution would have to involve a confluence of institutional changes on the level of the child, of the curriculum, of teacher preparation, adequate economic school support, and community-school bridges with two-way traffic. Nevertheless, there are certain possibilities for social intervention on the child-focused level that may open individual escape hatches and that might require minimal structural and process change in the current school operation. The most important of these areas of social intervention, and one that comes least into conflict with existing institutionalized barricades to change, would be that of an intensive, highly focused, preschool training program.

There are no data at the present time to prove that a preschool program could reduce the incidence of later dropout (though such data would not be difficult to collect), so this paper must be considered a speculative discussion. We have some preliminary data on this which indicate that preschool, kindergarten, or day-care experience, or a combination of these, is associated with higher group intelligence test scores. The scores are higher in the first grade, and the differential tends to be accentuated in a fifth-grade population; apparently this differential holds when social class is controlled.[2]

From present data it cannot be said definitely that there is any direct relationship between the early school experience and the school dropout, but I would hypothesize a very strong relationship between the first school experiences of the child and academic success or failure, and that the more invariant the school experience, the more important the early experience would be to the academic success of the child. I would also hypothesize that children who have had a preschool and kindergarten experience are more likely to cope appropriately with the kinds of things the school demands intellectually than are children who have not had this experience. This would be particularly true for children from lower socioeconomic groups, and would be most true for children who come from the most peripheral groups in our society.

Early Preparation or Later Failure?

For example, what happens when a child from these groups comes to school for the first time in the first grade? If he has not had experience with books; with the kinds of perceptual and developmental demands that are made by the school; with the kinds of language demands implicit in the nature of the communication that comes from the teacher to the child? That child's chances of starting to fail within the school situation are greatly enhanced. It is common in the first grade for a teacher to talk to the class for a period of ten minutes or so. Yet very often these children have never before experienced a ten-minute-long speech sequence coming from an adult to a child. So, in school, at the very beginning the child experiences this "foreign" information coming in at a rapid rate, requiring complex auditory differentiations for which life has not programed him.

What is likely to happen in this process, and fairly immediately, is that the child will start to look upon school as a place where he doesn't understand and where he experiences much failure. Perhaps more important, the teacher often starts to

---

[2] These data, which are currently being analyzed, were gathered by the Institute for Developmental Studies and will be separately reported as part of a larger study.

build in expectations of the child's failing. It is likely that at a very early age, the child perceives this expectation of failure. And the children who are most likely to have these expectations directed toward them are children who come with the fewest aptitudes for a middle-class life oriented situation. They are likely to be the most poorly dressed, to have a dialect, to come to school somewhat late, and, in general, are likely not to fit naturally into the kinds of middle-class strictures and constrictions that are established within the school system.

The child who comes to school with very few of the kinds of intellectual cognitive structures that school demands will be basically the most susceptible to this process of failing and will be the least likely to start communicating with the teacher. The critical question, then, is whether a child can at least start the educational process by learning the basic skills. In order to accomplish this for children from socially marginal backgrounds, I would say that some kind of antecedent experience that would compensate for the inadequacies within the home and in the social structure would be very beneficial and would be likely to help the child to achieve a positive adjustment to the demands of the school. (The use of the term "adjustment" here is not meant to imply adjustment to the social aspects of the school process or to the conformity pressures of the school—those questions are beyond the scope of this paper.)

What Can a Good Preschool Program Do?

A good preschool program would attempt to give the child the antecedent preparations for school that the home, community, and at least relative affluence give to the middle-class child. Such programs could be set up only after intensive training of teachers and staff to work on the problems of communicating with the parents as well as developing methods and techniques for compensating the child for a narrowness of experiential variation. The attempt would be to enrich those developmental areas most functional and operative in the school learning situation, thereby establishing both cognitive and attitudinal continuity between the preschool and the school years. Hopefully, knowing that the child is most responsive to acquiring basic skills in the preschool and early-school years, these skills can be fostered, and their acquisition can thus help lay the basis for a reduction in school failure experiences and an increase in school success.

The skills referred to here would include, for example, the visual and auditory perception which underlie reading, language skills, spatial and temporal orientation, general information, familiarity with books, toys, games, and the development of a sustained curiosity. In addition, the attempt must be made to engage the child as an active participant in the learning process rather than as a passive recipient of a school experience.

Establishing a good base. In facilitating the learning process in these children, the school must expect frequently to do a portion of the job traditionally assigned to the home, and curriculum must be reorganized to provide for establishing a good base.

The child, from the time he enters school and is exposed to assumptions about him derived from experience with the middle-class child, has few success experiences and much failure and generalized frustration. The frustration inherent in not understanding, not succeeding, and not being stimulated in the school, while being regulated by it, creates a basis for the further development of negative self-images and low evaluations of individual competencies.

It is important to emphasize that the early training to counteract this process is not a matter of inculcating middle-class values but, rather, of reinforcing the development of those underlying skills that are operationally appropriate and necessary for both successful and psychologically pleasant school learning experiences. The fact that these skills are almost routinely stimulated in middle-class homes does not mean that in content they are middle class: e.g., there is nothing fundamentally culturally loaded in a good or poor memory, but it can be awfully important in preparing for an examination.

Interpreting an appropriate behavior. Another question must be considered, and that is how the child's first anticipations are developed toward the school. It is often stated that among Negro parents there is low motivation toward school accomplishment. I have not found this so: I've found a great degree of motivation, but a lack of understanding of how instrumentally to make this operative for the child. The problem then, is to interpret for the child the kind of behavior that will make it possible to function and cope with the school mechanisms.

One way this could be handled is through a direct relationship between the teacher and the community. For example, there are some communities where the school is seen as the resource center—where it is kept open in the evening; where there are library books that can be taken out; and where generally there is an attempt to have the school seen as a place of social transition. When the school is a real part of his life and of his community, the child can more normally have the opportunity someday to decide if he wishes to go toward a learning experience consistent with the demands of the school, if he wants to stop off with a lower level of education, or if he wishes to go toward advancement in some other type of vocation with skills less closely related to the formal school demands.

To return more directly to the problem of anticipations toward the school, I do think that the sense of failure that often develops at an early stage projects itself through the total experiences of the child, not only temporally, in terms of his reaction to the demands of the school, but also in terms of his whole concept of self-identification, of a positive self-concept, of the development of a sense of dignity. This sense of dignity, I think, is closely related to how much money, how much concern, how much institutional modification we are willing to put into the school. In neighborhoods where most schools have practically every window broken, there are some protected schools which are beautifully kept: there is a reciprocal feedback, as if the institution and the children were working and cooperating with one another—and there is a sense of mutual respect that goes along with it. Here too, of course, is where teacher training in community sociology and mental health becomes a very important question.

Developing the child's inner self. Horizons and goals are stimulated early in life, and if the parents have had low ceilings in terms of variety of experiences, with the intensity being in terms of job insecurity, negotiations with welfare and landlords, and the like, there is not much left to give the child a sense of identifying the self with goals that take individual impetus and disciplining. This problem, in a larger context, is societal, and has its analogous aspects in the routinized existence of middle-class suburbia, rigid schedules, automated work, and cities and suburbs that share a sameness and drabness. Sometimes the excitement to be sparked in a child must reach his subjective self, his imagination and individual poetry. After this, he might make discriminations and differentiations not seen by his peers in the external world. This development of the inner self can certainly start soon after the development of language, and can be an intrinsic part of the preschool experience, and possibly a basis for much later motivation.

THE FEMALE DROPOUT

It is often in school that another element of the dropout problem related to another type of discrimination takes place— and it is an element that is often ignored. That is, the female dropout. Too often, discussions of dropouts deal with all cases as an undifferentiated totality or concentrate on males, without recognizing that many of the elements responsible for such a high dropout rate among Indian Americans, Negro Americans, etc., are similar in the case of females. Through a preschool program, it was hoped that the increased preparation of the child would also modify the anticipations of the teacher, in that the child's increased responsiveness will create higher expectations of him by the teacher, and thereby feed back to the child. Here we were referring to children generally, to the whole area of teachers' expectations, and the tendency of children to either reach or bend for them.

At some undefined point, our social expectations, as reflected through our teachers, change in regard to anticipating differential intellectual behavior from boys and girls. This is probably not always a conscious distinction, but males of any social class are more or less expected to have to use their intellects in the business of preparing to make a living. For females this assumption is less likely to be made, and the antecedent attitudes and seedlings are probably manifested in the preschool and kindergarten. I know of no data for this, but there is no other known area of strongly ingrained social attitudes and expectations which is completely discontinuous with earlier, though not necessarily discernible, orientations, and it is unlikely that these expectations would have developed only later in the school years.

I would expect that a high proportion of female school dropouts are intellectually average girls who have, proportionate to the boys, more academic success but who feel that intellectual development and their personal futures go along divergent paths. With society increasingly needing skilled people, the distinction between male and female intellectual roles must be explicitly eliminated early in the learning process, if the later effects are to be minimized and school is to offer the same potential to children regardless of sex.

PROSPECTS FOR A PRESCHOOL PROGRAM

The emphasis in this paper on the preschool program as a means of accommodation between the school and the child and his family represents, it is felt, a necessary approach to the dropout problem. It is beyond the scope of this paper to examine it from the other end of the continuum: the problem of the motivation of the high school student to join the labor force when the opportunities available to him may not be numerous or productive. Further, the high incidence of minority group dropouts makes necessary a consideration of prejudice in employment patterns. But these are broad societal problems, to be attacked and solved in the social arena. And if they were solved, the individual problems of the unprepared child coming into the unpreparing school would assume even greater importance. Developmentally, it would seem that this is one of the first areas in which to approach the problem, and one for which there may be less resistance.

There seems to be great need in mid-twentieth-century America to thoroughly discuss all problems, investigate their causes, delineate possible solutions, and implement only those solutions that have been sufficiently skeletonized so that they no longer represent threats to the status quo. The danger to the approach discussed here is that it will be put into the context of the stress-free, quasi-"purposeful" play, psychologically supportive, momistically oriented, de-intellectualized, sterile enclosures where much of early childhood education is located. If such takes place, social experimentation in this area could have the fate previously indicated. But if the social scientists and educators undertake such a project jointly in a spirit of experimentation and with bovicidal collaboration against the accumulated sacred cows, the possibilities of success are greatly enhanced.

HOW MUCH CAN MAN CHANGE?

BRUNO BETTELHEIM

How much can man change and at what age is it too late to hope for very much change? It has been important that we know, but we had no means of doing so. Now thanks to Professor Benjamin Bloom's study of *Stability and Change in Human Characteristics* we do know, and the implications for social planning are vast indeed.

The dialectic process never stops. Only recently has American social science adopted the psychoanalytic view of man: hence the widespread conviction that human personality is shaped in infancy, and that the early characteristics are extremely resistant to change. Nevertheless, we find our social scene flooded with statements on how this or that form of social engineering is going to change personality at an age when (according to psychoanalytic theory) personality can hardly be changed short of long-term therapy or some influence of equal depth.

If it is not already plain, I am speaking, among other things, about the present controversy over school integration. Mixing children of different backgrounds is supposed to change the outlook on life of the culturally deprived child and to improve his academic progress, as if both were not determined before he entered kindergarten or first grade. We are told that the attitude toward learning is such a superficial characteristic that it depends merely on what happens in class, or with whom one goes to school. Often the same social scientist who believes on the one hand that infant rearing shapes personality, claims on the other that the intellectual virtues are superficial enough to be conditioned by chance experiences in class. But, in fact, psychoanalytic theory holds that the attitudes formed in infancy are what condition the classroom experience.

More recent revisions of psychoanalytic theory deny that the basic personality, on which the child's view of learning depends, is essentially formed with the resolution of the Oedipus complex. According to the most important revision of the Freudian system, that of Erik Erikson, basic trust is the ground rock of all later trust in others (including one's teachers) and in oneself (so vital in attacking problems) and depends on the very earliest experiences of life. If these have not been favorable, they may condition, inversely, a life-long distrust of others (including one's teachers and what they teach) and of oneself.

As if this were not bad enough, our autonomy—including the qualities required to attack intellectual problems—depends on experiences we have only slightly later in life, and so does our ability to take initiative in meeting problems. When school age finally comes, it is the combination of trust, autonomy, and initiative that will condition whether or not we are capable of the industry so important for learning. Conversely, if our preschool experience has bred mistrust, shame, doubt, or guilt into the personality, the school experience will reflect not industry, but inferiority.

If Erikson is correct, then the school experience of one kind of child will stand under the triad of trust, initiative, and industry, characteristics which will send an intelligent child brought up in good cultural circumstances to the head of the class no matter what. The school experience of another child will stand under that other triad of mistrust, shame, and doubt, and will lead to inferiority. Every experienced teacher knows that if these qualities are present, even in fairly pure culture, paired with good intelligence, they will make learning and teaching impossible. They are what characterize the personality of the nonlearner or, in milder form, the underachiever. They are the characteristics found dominant in children from culturally deprived homes or disadvantaged ones. True, they are also found in children from very different homes, but such children are exceptions; among children from deprived homes, these characteristics are endemic.

If these theories on human development are correct, and if the characteristics most needed for school achievement are those stated, no Supreme Court dictum saying that academic achievement depends on how children are grouped in school can help. The facts of human nature cannot be changed by a court dictum; not, at least, without our also creating conditions that would allow it to be effective.

But suppose these theories are not valid. Suppose that how a child fares in school does not depend on his personality, but on what happens to him there. Perhaps these issues are too important for decisions about them to be based on psychoanalytic theories. Once more we confront the sterile controversy of nature versus nurture: Is man the result of his environment or his inheritance?—but with the difference that inheritance has been largely replaced by early experience. Thus today's controversy seems to center on the question: Is man the result of his earliest or his later experiences? Or to put it within the context at hand, is human personality and achievement the result of preschool or inschool experience? Whether we can expect different schooling to matter much or little will depend on how this controversy is resolved.

If we decide that different schooling will matter little, we may still wish to press for integrated schools as a matter of social justice, but this will not help the child coming from a disadvantaged home to lift himself out of his dreary background. We must recognize that as far as helping the socially and culturally deprived is concerned, the fight for integrated schools is a kind of shadowboxing which obscures the fact that we fail to do the social engineering where it counts, during the first few years of life. Of course, if we decide that we can radically change central aspects of the personality after age six by simply giving the child a different school experience, then we must concentrate our social engineering there, and can forget about the earliest years of life. If so, we shall also have to scrap the psychoanalytic theory of personality, because it has misled us with its claim of the vast importance of earliest experience. Here the two archenemies, psychoanalysis and the Catholic Church, see eye to eye. Witness the Jesuits' conviction that if they are given the child up to the age of seven, they do not fear for the child's future development.

There have been some straws in the wind suggesting that both the Jesuits, and several centuries later, the psychoanalysts, were right. For example, studies of children who achieved differently in reading reveal that success, or the lack of it, depended on the attitudes they brought with them to school. If on entering school they thought of themselves as readers, were convinced of the value of reading, convinced that they could learn to read easily (that is, had trust in themselves and initiative in tackling learning), then they had an easy time learning to read. Those who came to school doubting the value of reading, and doubting that they could learn to read, failed by and large, even though they shared the same classrooms and were exposed to the same stimulation. The identical setting gave them an experience exactly opposite to what the good learners had.

Still, this was merely a straw in the wind. What was needed was greater certainty, more precise evidence that would stand up under the most careful scientific scrutiny. In matters of such complexity, bearing so crucially on what is today the greatest issue in the nation, such evidence was a great deal to expect. But it has now been provided in Professor Bloom's scholarly book. Because it is a technical study with many statistical graphs, tables, and charts, it is to be feared that it may be less widely read than it deserves to be. That it is a statistical study may make it forbidding reading to some, but it cannot be overlooked by anyone concerned with education. Those who cannot follow the intricacies of statistical analysis will still be richly rewarded by the eminently readable text. For the substantive findings and the marvelously thorough analysis of this study have tremendous implications for our social and educational planning.

Benjamin Bloom brings the highest credentials to his task. He is Professor of Education at the University of Chicago and was for many years its university examiner. A life-long student of educational achievement and its evaluation, he is currently President of the Association for Educational Research and a member of the standing committee of the International Study of Educational Achievement. In his book he surveys and synthesizes the findings of all major longitudinal studies of youngsters, some of which have followed particular children for ten or more years, and compares them with other relevant research on human intelligence and achievement. His methods allow him to answer questions like the following: Under which conditions can human development be altered and how do different environmental conditions affect the growth and development of human characteristics? How much can environmental forces affect the development of a characteristic, and what are the limits for affecting a characteristic by educational or other environmental forces.

Though none of the longitudinal studies which are analyzed in this book were based on psychoanalytic thinking, Professor

Bloom finds that characteristics acquired early in life are the most stable of all, thus corroborating psychoanalysts' hypotheses on the importance of the first years of life. No other study, based on highly objective data and subjected to the most rigorous statistical analysis, has so powerfully supported the speculations of Freud and his followers. More than this, Professor Bloom shows that characteristics developed in a short time are not very stable, which suggests that we should be dubious of stories describing far-reaching changes in human characteristics that are achieved within months. He too finds what psychoanalysis has taught us: that while the basic characteristics are very stable, the symptoms that express them are not. Yet despite these conclusions we still direct most of our social engineering, in problems like juvenile delinquency, school dropouts, etc., toward changing the symptoms instead of the characteristics behind them.

Probably the broadest implications of Professor Bloom's findings are those bearing on intelligence and academic achievement. His analysis of studies of identical twins shows that when children are brought up from shortly after birth in radically different environments, their intelligence varies markedly. If one twin was reared in an environment that was highly nutritive both to his intelligence and his emotional life, and the other grew up in an opposite kind of environment, then their I.Q.s varied at maturity by as much as twenty points. As Bloom says, these twenty points

> . . . could mean the difference between a life in an institution for the feeble-minded or a productive life in society. It could mean the difference between a professional career and an occupation which is at the semi-skilled or unskilled level. A society which places great emphasis on verbal learning and rational problem solving and which greatly needs highly skilled and well-trained individuals to carry on political-social-economic functions in an increasingly complex world cannot ignore the enormous consequences of deprivation as it affects the development of general intelligence.

On the surface, this seems to be an argument for the impact of environment on intelligence as voiced by those who say children should be shifted from one school to another to improve their academic achievement. But the shift in schools does not help much because it appears that only during the first four years of life does the I.Q. change markedly with environment —up to two-and-a-half points per year. From ages eight to seventeen (school age) the highest average effect that even the most radical change in environment produces is not more than 0.4 I.Q. points per year. In ten years this does not exceed a change of four I.Q. points, far too little to make a real difference. The conclusion must be that though it is tremendously important to provide infants with the most favorable environment during the first four years of their lives, the influence of the environment on intelligence becomes smaller and smaller with each year after the fourth, and by school age is insignificant.

Equally crucial is the research that compares children, born and raised in Philadelphia, who maintained about the same I.Q. score throughout grade school, and their Negro classmates, who were born in the South and moved to Philadelphia at different ages. If school integration pays off in change of intelligence, the scores of the Negro children should have improved with their move to these schools. But the only real improvement was made by children who changed their environment before school age, those who moved to Philadelphia before six. These children gained an average of six-and-a-half I.Q. points during the first to ninth grades, showing the cumulative effect of more favorable conditions and a more intellectually nutritive environment. Unfortunately, a change of six-and-a-half points in I.Q., though quite marked, has little practical effect. An improvement of twenty points, on the other hand, can make a tremendous difference. Such an improvement seems to be impossible, however, unless the change in environment is made soon after birth, since half of this gain (ten points) would have to be made during the first four years of life. Even the six-and-a-half points were gained only by children who moved to a better environment long before school age. Children who were born in the South and moved to Philadelphia when they were in the fourth grade gained only about three I.Q. points during the rest of their school career, while children who did not come till the sixth grade gained only two I.Q. points. Thus we see a marked decrease in the effect of better environment as children grow older: The greatest changes happen during the first few years of life, and the next greatest during the first few years in the new environment.

This is true of all children, not only those who move from a culturally deprived environment to a better one. In analyzing all research on developing intelligence, Professor Bloom found that half of all the growth in intelligence takes place between birth and age four. The next 30 per cent increase in intelligence is made between the ages of four and eight. Between eight and seventeen, when the child is of school age, intelligence increases only about 20 per cent. In short, just as much intelligence develops in the first four years of life as in the next thirteen years, and there is very little growth after eighteen.

What are the specific factors in an environment that have so much influence on the growth of intelligence? Professor Bloom and his co-workers identified thirteen such factors, all relating to family background or to the relations between parents and children. Seven of these factors are process variables indicative of the parents' response to the child and his capacities—their intellectual aspirations for him, the rewards they offer for intellectual growth, the opportunities they provide for learning inside and outside the home (not including school), and the nature and amount of help they give to extend learning in a wide variety of situations. The other six factors tend to be more stable: they are characteristics of the parents and the home. Among them are the parents' use of language in a variety of situations; the opportunities in the home for enlarging vocabulary and the quality of the language used; whether there is emphasis on correct use of language; the availability of books, periodicals, and library facilities. These thirteen factors account for two-thirds of all intelligence development, a process that is completed before the child even enters school. Thus if we were really serious about doing something for the intellectual development of underprivileged children, we would have to make our influence felt in their homes by encouraging parents to change their intellectual expectations and aspirations for their children as well as their own language habits, and to make learning supplies, periodicals, and books available.

So much for the intelligence we suppose to be inborn. What about achievement in school? Even for general achievement, such as reading comprehension, the ground is laid long before the child enters school. A full third of whatever the child will achieve later in school is developed by the time he gets there, probably because so much of it depends on vocabulary development and language comprehension.

The home environment is very significant not only because of the large amount of educational growth which has already taken place before the child enters the first grade but also because of the influence of the home during the elementary school period.

By the time the child has reached an age when the home influence is waning, when he is old enough to strike out on his own—that is, by the end of grade school—a full 75 per cent of all his academic achievement has already been made. Thus efforts in behalf of the child after that time can only influence 25 per cent of his total academic achievement. In other words, if we could stimulate a student to do 20 per cent better in high school (a tremendous gain, if achieved), it would improve his overall achievement only 5 per cent, a rather insignificant gain.

The home environment not only conditions the level of achievement the child reaches when he enters school, but continues as a powerful influence no matter what his school experience. Children coming from different homes were matched in respect to their reading achievement at second grade. When they were retested at the eighth grade, the children with fathers in occupations requiring higher education were on the average 2.25 grade levels ahead of those whose fathers' occupations required less than a high school education. Thus even if children go to the same type of school and start out in second grade at the same level of achievement, whether or not the home supports the school's educational efforts will make all the difference in the child's final achievement.

Besides the implication for educational planning, this study also contains much fascinating information on the incredible stability of early acquired human characteristics. For example, whether and to what degree a boy will be aggressive (so important a factor in juvenile delinquency, to mention only one consideration) is more or less set when he is three, for by this time he has reached the half-way mark in the development of this characteristic. The inversely corresponding characteristic of dependence reaches its half-way mark in girls by the age of four. This is also true of both general intelligence in boys and girls, as I have noted earlier, and for the equally important characteristic of intellectuality.

Why then are we so blind to the fact that all our educational planning for the underprivileged begins when for all practical purposes it is too late? And this despite all that psychoanalysis has taught us. One answer is that so few psychoanalysts are interested in or knowledgeable about education, and that they concentrate their interest on the development of the emotions, not the intellect. But there is another answer, as Professor Bloom points out.

The prolongation of the period of dependency for youth in the Western cultures has undoubtedly been a factor in desensitizing parents, school workers, and behavior scientists to the full importance of the very early environmental and experiential influences.

By keeping youth in school so many years we have made ourselves believe that added years of schooling will make a difference: Witness the present efforts to keep dropouts in school, as if at sixteen one or two more years in school could influence their intelligence or academic achievement.

But while we try to add more schooling at the end, "a central finding in this work is that for selected characteristics [intelligence, academic achievement, aggression, etc.] there is a negatively accelerated curve of development which reaches its midpoint before age five. We have reasoned that the environment would have its greatest effect on a characteristic during the period of its most rapid development." This means that if we want to raise the intelligence of children by the possible maximum of twenty I.Q. points (the rest of their intelligence is conditioned by inheritance) we must change their environment long before they come of school age. To do this we will have to free ourselves of a few of our most widely held prejudices— that the child is the private property of his parents to do with as they please, that we are therefore powerless to change the environment he grows up in, and that human beings are infinitely improvable, at any age, no matter what the home environment of their childhood. Or, in the unemotional language of the scholar who wrote this book:

> There appears to be an implicit assumption running through the culture that change in behavior and personality can take place at any age or stage in development and that the developments at one age or stage are not more significant than those which take place at another.

Will we heed the advice implied in this remark? Will we base our planning for all children, privileged or not, on the unassailable facts he presents? If so, there must be radical reform in the lives of children between the ages of two to four or five. Or will we continue to fool ourselves by thinking that we can change the lives of underprivileged children in school, when it is much too late for everything that really counts? I believe that reform must be concentrated where it most matters—

on the conditions of life at home—if we are to give these children what they most need.

௸௸௸௸௸௸௸௸௸௸௸௸௸௸௸௸௸௸௸௸௸௸௸௸௸௸௸௸

MATERNAL TEACHING STYLES AND EDUCATIONAL RETARDATION

௸௸௸௸௸௸௸௸௸௸௸௸௸௸௸௸௸௸௸௸௸௸௸௸௸௸௸௸

ROBERT D. HESS

The view I wish to present is that the dropout syndrome has its origins at the preschool level in the nature of the communicative and interactive modes that develop between mother and child. The affective, regulatory, and disciplinary aspects of mother-child interaction are traditional topics for research and theory, but the importance of the cognitive components of these early experiences has not been fully recognized. The argument of this paper is that inadequacy in the cognitive features of early mother-child exchange fosters later alienation of the child and adolescent from the educative processes and other basic sectors and institutions of society.[1]

Within the last year I've had two experiences which illustrate vividly the problems arising from educational inadequacy, particularly those of adults in urban areas. Last spring [1962], I started working with a community group attempting to develop a retraining program for adults in an economically depressed

---

[1] The various circumstances involved in alienation of youth are described in a paper by R. J. Havighurst and L. J. Stiles, "A Statement of National Policy for Alienated Youth," *Phi Delta Kappan* (April 1961). In this paper, I am adopting their definition of the term.

section of Chicago. In preparing our proposal, we inquired of the appropriate agencies about the success of established training programs for adults. We discovered that one of the difficulties these programs encounter is a frequent failure of applicants to pass qualifying exams for the program; of twenty persons who apply, about three pass the tests which qualify them to enter courses of training that are now available.

The problem of semiliteracy in adults in the United States, although usually ignored, is not new. Our method of dealing with adult illiteracy has been through education of children in the public schools so that illiteracy would gradually and eventually disappear from our society. However, our attempts to raise the general level of education of populations in economically depressed areas of this country are, at the present time, inadequate. Although it is difficult to get firm data (primarily through the reluctance of school boards to release achievement test results and other performance indices on schools located in culturally deprived areas), there is reason to believe that many, if not most, of our high school students in economically disadvantaged areas are semiliterate when they drop out or graduate from high school. Moreover, given current population and migration trends, the average level of functioning education in our major cities may be decreasing. The dropout syndrome is part of a larger, critical problem of education in the urban context.

The second experience that illustrates another dimension of this total educational issue was a series of conversations with teachers and principals in several schools in three of our large cities. These professionals were aware of the extent of illiteracy at adult levels in depressed urban areas but were more concerned about a situation at the other end of the age range—one not so well known. They agreed that in some areas of the large cities one-half to two-thirds of the children are educationally retarded when they enter the first grade. That is, on opening day in many schools there may be as few as one-third of the first grade class who are ready to start a typical first grade curriculum.

What is behind the circumstances that prevent vast numbers of young people in working-class areas of urban regions from taking advantage of opportunities offered by the institutions of the city and community? What are the implications of this situation in view of skills that youth must develop to be fitted for occupational and other roles in our society?

It is my thesis that it is necessary to examine the early experiences of urban youth and to study the origins of attitudes that create educational retardation if we are to be effective in an intervention program. The problems of junior high school and high school students are fairly well known. We have much less information about the kinds of conditions that operate to produce them nor do we have adequate information about the skills that are lacking when children come to kindergarten and first grade. In the hope of finding some answers to these questions, we began a project at the University of Chicago which I would like to describe. It inquires into the origins of motivational attitudes and behavior leading to dropout and other educational failure.

Orientation for this research goes back to the well-documented relation between social class and both academic performance and intelligence, which consistently shows test scores to be relatively low in working-class groups, especially in that socioeconomic level we now term "culturally deprived." This relative deficit in scholastic competence and educability is the essential problem that is facing the schools in metropolitan areas of the United States.

The question our study presents is this: in what way does social class experience affect mental development? What happens in the cultural environment that produces behavior which by grade 7, 8, or 9 results in educational retardation of two to three years? Part of the theory for the project comes from Basil Bernstein of the University of London, who takes the position that the effect of cultural disadvantage is understandable if we consider social class experience as a set of conditions or variables involving a wide variety of effects that impinge upon the young child.[2] In order to deal with the problems of social class and learning, we need to understand what occurs in the interchange between the child and his cultural setting. It is essential to break these experiences down to small bits—to their basic component parts—and to analyze social class and cognitive deprivation in specific and manageable terms.

In this context, the underlying hypothesis of our research is this: in cultural deprivation, the pattern of communcation that develops between mother and child has an effect upon the

---

[2] For a full statement of his position see Basil Bernstein, "Social Class and Linguistic Development: A Theory of Social Learning," in A. H. Halsey, Jean Floud, and C. Arnold Anderson, eds., *Education, Economy, and Society* (Glencoe, Ill.: Free Press, 1961).

child's cognitive equipment which handicaps him when he begins his school program. This is not so much a theory of deficit as an argument that there are cognitive patterns of responsive behavior and ways of interpreting stimuli from the external world that these children learn in interaction with their families. These patterns are not adaptive or functional for academic learning and may prevent the child from taking advantage of cognitive experiences available in a classroom.

In Bernstein's view, language structures and conditions what the child learns and how he learns, setting limits within which future learning may take place. He identifies two forms of communication codes or styles of verbal behavior: *restrictive* and *elaborate*.[3] Restrictive codes are stereotyped, limited and condensed, lacking in specificity and the exactness needed for precise conceptualization and differentiation. Sentences are short, simple, often unfinished; there is little use of subordinate clauses for elaborating the content of the sentence; it is a language of implicit meaning, easily understood and commonly shared. It is the language form often used in impersonal situations when the intent is to promote solidarity or reduce tension. Restrictive codes are nonspecific clichés, statements or observations about events, made in general terms that will be readily understood. The basic quality of this mode is to limit the range and detail of concept and information involved. Elaborate codes, however, are those in which communication is individualized and the message is specific to a particular situation topic and person. It is more particular, more differentiated, and more precise. It permits expression of a wider and more complex range of thought, tending toward discrimination among cognitive and affective content.

Let us consider two possible examples of mother-child communication using these two types of codes. Assume that the emotional climate of two homes is approximately the same; the significant difference is in style of communication. A child is playing in the kitchen with some pots and pans when the telephone rings. In one home the mother says, "Be quiet," or "Shut up," or any one of several other short, peremptory commands, and she answers the phone while the child sits still on the floor. In the other home the mother says, "I'd rather you kept quiet

---

[3] Bernstein has used different terms for these two communication modes. In his chapter in Halsey, et al., he calls them "public" (restrictive) and "formal" (elaborate). The terms used in this summary come from more recent papers.

while I answer the phone, dear." The question our study poses is this: what inner response is elicited in the child, what is the effect upon his developing cognitive network of concepts and meaning in each of these two situations. In one instance, the child is not asked for any kind of mental response. He is asked simply to do something; he is not called upon to reflect or make mental discriminations. In the other example, the child is required to follow two or three ideas. He is asked to relate his behavior to a time dimension; he must think of his behavior in relation to what happens to another person, and is called upon to attend to how the mother thinks and how she feels. He has to perform a more complicated task to follow the communication of his mother in that his relationship to her is mediated in part through concepts and shared ideas; his mind is stimulated or exercised (in an elementary fashion) by a more elaborate and complex verbal communication initiated by the mother. As objects of these two divergent communication styles, repeated in various ways, in similar situations and circumstances during the preschool years, these two imaginary children would be expected to develop significantly different verbal facility and cognitive equipment by the time they entered the public school system.

The orientation of our project is to view the child as an organism which receives a great deal of information of many kinds, much more than he can accommodate. Even as adults, we respond to only a small part of the total stimulation we receive in a typically active working moment. What the child responds to, how he interprets stimuli, and how he responds are learned in interaction with the environment. He is taught what to attend to, how to interpret messages, and how to respond. These patterns of cognitive response are socialized in early experience in the home, and become the basis upon which further cognitive development proceeds.

Operating within this basic rationale, our project attacked this problem: if children from working-class homes come to school unprepared to do the level of work the classroom demands, and if middle-class children, for the most part, come to school adequately prepared, what facilitating experiences are present in middle-class homes that typically do not occur in the working-class homes?

To study this problem, we selected 160 mothers and their four-year-old children: forty from upper middle-class backgrounds, forty working-class mothers from skilled occupational levels, forty from unskilled occupational levels, and forty mothers on public assistance. All families are intact, except those on public aid.[4] We are studying these mothers along several dimensions: 1) the mother's self-concept and her view of herself in relation to the community and to the school, 2) the attitudes the mother has developed toward the school as an institution and toward learning as an experience, 3) the cognitive aspects of communication process between mother and child, and 4) the affective aspects of interaction, to enable us to examine what it is (in addition to the information that the mother passes to the child) that affects learning.

It is in terms of self-concept and motivational structure that we find some of our largest differences among the mothers of our research group. The aspiration levels that mothers have for their children vary, of course, both within the social classes as well as between social classes. However, it is not at all uncommon for a working-class mother to respond to the question "What would you like Johnny to do when he grows up?" with the comment: "I want him to be a doctor." Then if the interviewer asks, "What do you think he'll really do?" she is likely to offer a completely different choice: "Oh, maybe he'll end up working in a steel mill." Or if she is asked about her daughter, she will say, "I want her to be a teacher," and later, say she expects her to be a clerk in a dime store. There is often a large gap between what they feel is a desirable occupation level and what they think their children are going to do.

Think of this view of the world in terms of its effect upon the self-concept of both mother and child. In a society that offers a wide range of opportunities, the mother is convinced that the child is not going to reach desirable goals, either through lack of opportunity, lack of schooling or ability. If we ask these mothers about their own educational and occupational experience we obtain a similar response—less preparation than needed, much higher aspirations than can be achieved.

We find also that in economically depressed sections of the city the mother's interaction with the community tends to iso-

---

[4] These mothers are all Negroes, so selected because of the significant representation of Negroes in economically depressed areas of Chicago. Obviously, cultural deprivation in the United States occurs in several different national and racial groups, including Indians, Mexicans, Puerto Ricans, and whites. An added advantage is that this will provide one of the few research opportunities to study social class differences in maternal behavior and cognitive development among Negroes.

late her from the world in which she lives so that her view may become one of "family against the world." Her interaction with the school, with other agencies, particularly agencies that have to do with public welfare, reveals a great deal of ambivalence. Anyone who has worked with families that have been subject to the various regulations of public housing, of public assistance programs, or of other programs which subject their clients to suspicious scrutiny can easily observe the negative effect this treatment has on dignity and self-confidence. Our research interest is in the resulting impact on the child's sense of confidence and competence as he approaches public school.

Another area, that of achievement motivation, and of the acquisition of attitudes toward school, approaches the socialization of educability from another vector. One technique we used was to ask the mother to tell us what she would say to her child as she sent him away on the first day of school. We get quite different responses within and between classes. The typical pattern in a working-class home is something like this: "I tell him to do what the teacher says, not to get into trouble, not get into any fights, be sure to come home after school, and don't get lost." This is a view of the school as raising issues of dealing with authority and with peers, rather than presenting educational content. There are occasional references to learning, but if so, they are presented almost inadvertently. Such a response is in contrast to the upper middle-class families where the mother is more likely to say: "Well, the teacher, is sort of like your mother, you learn from her; if you have any problems, go to her; you are going to learn to read and write." This approach views experience in school in terms of the child's learning experience.

We also asked the subjects to tell a story about a picture showing a teacher and mother in conference. In our preliminary data, the working-class mothers most often say that the mother has been called in by the school over some disciplinary problem; the upper middle-class mother more frequently sees the conference as one in which the mother is coming to consult with the teacher about a learning problem.

The major difference between these two types of response is in the view of the school as an institution with which the child must cope, as contrasted with a view of the school as a place for learning. The lower-class child approaches school not oriented toward learning but attuned to the need to get along with the institution. The experience is defined to him as a problem of adapting to the teacher and to the peer situation. This presents a misconception of the school's purpose with a heavy emphasis upon conformity and upon physical behavior, rather than mental activity.

The most critical part of our project is a detailed study of the cognitive exchange between mother and child—how the mother teaches the child; as a secondary point, we will study the ways these teaching styles may be related to the child's school performance. In our project, the mothers are brought to the University Nursery School where they're taught three simple tasks by our staff. One is to sort some plastic toys (cars, spoons, and chairs) by color and function; another is to sort some varying-shaped and colored blocks by size and marking; and the third is to draw designs on an etch-a-sketch toy. An etch-a-sketch is a small screen with two knobs. Underneath the screen is a lever which draws a line on the screen and which can be operated by moving the knobs. One knob handle controls the vertical movement; the other controls the horizontal movement. The mother is instructed to operate one knob and the child the other. Together they are to make a series of designs which increase in complexity. We first teach the mother how to do each of these tasks, then ask her to teach or work with her child. Our object is to observe the interaction between her and the child in this teaching situation. What is her teaching style and how does it affect the cognitive development of her child?

The variation in styles of maternal teaching can be illustrated by one of the tasks we used in the pilot phase of the study. We had a jigsaw puzzle with fish of various size and color. The mother was asked to teach her child how to put the puzzle together. Mothers showed a great deal of variation in their approach to teaching their children this problem. One mother, for example, took the puzzle and said to her child: "This is a jigsaw puzzle. You've never seen one before. We take the pieces out and then put them back together. See where all the pieces are and look at the colors; look at the size so you'll know where they go." She had defined the task. She had told the child how to proceed. Then she spilled out the pieces, gave the equipment to the child and was able to guide him, by verbal direction, to respond to visual clues needed to solve the problem. Another mother, equally supportive of her child (according to our interviewers who saw her in her home), took the puzzle and dumped it out on the table in front of the child without a word and then said: "Now, you do it." Then she watched and as the child would pick up a piece and try to put it in place, the mother would say, "Turn it around; turn it around." Thirty-five times she repeated the instruction: "Turn it around." Finally, in frustration and defeat, the child said to her, "You do it."

Although this mother was trying to help the child, she did not know how to teach, and was unable to convey the concepts needed to solve this simple problem. It is apparent that the ability to communicate concepts, to share information, and to program a simple task is often not offered in the family situation. However, this is not the only important outcome of a situation of this kind. Imagine the child in repeated interaction with his mother coming upon situations which he tries to solve, but through lack of maternal assistance, finds it impossible. The reaction of defeat ("You do it") is likely to recur and be magnified many times, and develop in the child an orientation, toward both the world and toward certain kinds of problems, that sees difficulties as not solvable. Compare his response with that of the first child in our example who did not know more about the puzzle to begin with, but who, through experience, realized that with some guidance there was a way to reach a solution. Upon this kind of motivational base, attitudes toward new learning may very well emerge.[5]

Difficulty arises when the mother is not able to transmit to the child the kinds of things prerequisite to success even at this very early level. If the young child experiences success in mental tasks in the home so that there is positive reinforcement, some reward for learning, his natural curiosity can then take him through most of the early stages.

From our experience, it seems likely that many mothers can be taught to develop these cognitive faculties of their children. We are now in the planning stage of a program to prepare mothers in educationally disadvantaged homes to teach preschool children the basic cognitive skills they need for the first grade curriculum.

The next area we have been exploring in these interaction

---

[5] We have been surprised at the resources of motivation and energy these mothers display. They try—they try very hard, indeed. We thought that an abstract task like sorting blocks might bore mother and child. On the contrary, we have seen four-year-olds stay with a task for twenty minutes with the mother concentrating upon her efforts to help and to teach.

situations is the role of emotional support and achievement pressure in the teaching process. Our learning situations thus include: 1) the amount of information the mother can transmit; 2) the amount of support she gives the child in the learning situation; and 3) the pressure she puts on the child to achieve. The way a mother uses information, support, and pressure not only reveals her teaching style, but may have systematic effects upon the child's approach to learning and problem solving. That is, it seems likely that if a mother offers support to the child in learning situations but gives little information about how to solve problems and little pressure to complete tasks or achieve, the child will respond with a casual attitude toward learning and toward achievement; a mother who puts a great deal of pressure on a child to achieve and perform, but who is unable to supply the information necessary for successful learning, may well induce disappointment and frustration in the child and inhibit curiosity; the mother who offers information and pressure without effectively supporting the child may arouse undue anxiety around learning and performance situations. The focus of our study is to examine the effects of these various maternal teaching styles on the educability of the child, both with respect to his cognitive ability and with regard to his motivation for learning.

One important requisite is the need to involve the community and home in a task of this kind. The problem of strategy on a long-range basis should be to shift as much responsibility and participation to the community level as possible. The participation of community organizations and institutions, particularly of the family and mothers in this sort of program, offers an opportunity to improve communication between school and mother, and to give the mother a different concept of the school and what the school can do. It may also give her a new view of how she may work with the school to provide for the child the precondition for successful learning. This kind of co-ordinated effort in urban areas may, in time, make conferences of this sort unnecessary.

SELECTED READINGS

1. BERNSTEIN, B. "Social Class and Linguistic Development," in Anderson, A., Floud, J., and Halsey, H., *Society, Economy and Education.* Glencoe, Ill.: Free Press, 1961.

2. Brooks, D. "A Study to Determine the Literacy Level of Able-Bodied Persons Receiving Public Assistance." Cook County Department of Public Aid. 1962.

3. Bruner, J. S. "The Cognitive Consequences of Early Sensory Deprivation," in *Sensory Deprivation*. Cambridge: Harvard University Press, 1961.

4. Conant, J. B. *Slums and Suburbs*. New York: McGraw-Hill, 1961.

5. Davis, A. *Social Class Influences upon Learning*. Cambridge: Harvard University Press, 1948.

6. Havighurst, R. J. "Education and Social Problems of Big Cities," New City, I (February 1, 1963), 9-12.

7. Havighurst, R. J. and Stiles, L. J. "A Statement of National Policy for Alienated Youth," *Phi Delta Kappan*, April, 1961.

8. Hess, R. D. and Shipman, V. "Cognitive Environments of Urban Pre-school Children," Progress Report, Urban Child Center, University of Chicago, December 1963 (mimeographed).

9. Luria, A. R. "The Role of Speech and the Regulation of Normal and Abnormal Behavior," U. S. Department of Health, Education and Welfare, 1960.

10. Rosen, B. C. and Andrade, R. B. "The Psychosocial Origins of Achievement Motivation," *American Sociological Review*, XXII (1959), 185-218.

Part
Five

PROGRAMS: PRESENT AND FUTURE

INTRODUCTION

The constant and repeated failure of large numbers of students who have spent ten or more years in school to attain functional literacy, interrelated as it is with their inability to get and hold jobs, or to enter the armed services, created a crisis in society. Faced by an eruptive situation which threatened to destroy the public school system as it exists today, educators and school administrators were forced to critically examine the entire school setting. Axiomatic truths concerning the nature of learning, the curriculum, the organization of the classroom, and the school itself are being challenged. The preparation of teachers, both pre-service and in-service, is being scrutinized and evaluated. Crucial decisions will have to be made if the severe and intense pressures for change bearing down on the schools are to be lessened. The time for innovation, modification, and change has come, for to continue the kind of "educational programs which typify the majority of our inner-city classrooms is to march irrevocably toward explosive failure." (Niemeyer)

Because there are no alternatives, except the need to change, the banner of innovation flies high over every school system. But innovative practices vary, depending on the size of the system, the sophistication of the staff, and the desire for real change. They can be something entirely new, something never tried out before; they can be an integration of discrete programs focussing on a particular problem; they can be the introduction of programs tried and proved elsewhere; or, they can be old programs under a new name. Regardless of what they are, the pace of real change is slow and uncertain. Few, if any, school systems have adopted a practice that the space industry found useful and productive, namely an ongoing program of evaluation and research. Under this system defects can be quickly spotted and changes and modifications made expeditiously and effectively.

The authors of the articles in this section believe that these children and youths can learn. Daniel Schreiber states that though many may lack the competency, they are capable of doing sustained, efficient work. Because children and family have a culture not attuned to the school, and because the school is not attuned to the culture, Carl L. Byerly believes that there is a need for materials depicting realistic situations in urban areas. In addition, others believe that the use of indigenous personnel in the classroom (Pearl) and the introduction of topics dealing with interpersonal relationships will help (Niemeyer).

The writers recognize that teachers feel their effectiveness is vitiated by the demoralizing influence of the home and community; that too often their role is one of baby-sitter, guardian, and jailor. This attitude may be due to the middle-class values the teacher brings to the job, or it may be due to the lack of basic preparation offered by the schools of education. Pearl states that many teachers believe their primary role in working with these children is to "repair" them and deal with their handicaps. He challenges them to examine their current practices and to truly test their theories. Teachers have to accept the responsibility for teaching human beings to learn. A teacher must say "I'm here to teach and you are here to learn," and then perform.

The curriculum is attacked because it consists of meaningless material totally removed from the life experiences of the child, affords no linkage with the future, and provides no gratification to the child for being successful. Frank Riessman states that children do not verbalize in response to words alone but to things they see and do. Yet the curriculum is based primarily on the written or spoken word.

The programs presented range from preschool programs to work-experience programs for dropouts. Schreiber states that since work is the hallmark of adulthood and since the best preparation for work is work itself, the school must offer work experiences for such youths. He describes the different kinds of work-experience programs and stresses the need for alert and constant supervision and guidance.

Arthur Pearl deplores the "all or nothing" nature of teacher training, and the lack of intermediate step-off points. He sees this as the school's failure to respond to society's need for new careers and the failure to link up the population that needs jobs with the jobs that need doing. Riessman stresses the training of disadvantaged youths as sub-professionals, teacher aides, recreational aides, and health aides.

Team teaching, nongraded primary classes, extended school day or school year are mentioned as possible solutions. The use of audio-visual materials as a means of closing the gap between the world of the child and the outside world is discussed. Teaching machines, which are impersonal and permit a child to progress at his own speed, are mentioned. Byerly points out that dependence on the machine alone may lead to disaster and that the teacher must be assiduously attentive and modify the machine when necessary if the child is to receive optimum value from its use. Furthermore Byerly maintains that these innovations in teaching and learning should enable the school to do what it has been trying to do for years, namely, to individualize instruction. And to the extent that a school is willing and able to rearrange and modify its curriculum, its organization, and its methodology, then to that extent will it be successful. This is particularly true for the alienated child, the potential dropout, who must achieve some measure of school success if his ego is to be rebuilt and talents salvaged.

There is some disagreement among the authors about the size and complexity of the problem and the best method of introducing programs which offer the possibility of solution. Should demonstration projects be set up as prospective beachheads from which more extensive efforts can be launched? Or is it too late for demonstration projects, and should full programs be immediately initiated? However there is complete unanimity that the school must assume a new role if it is to fulfill its promise to educate all the children that cross its threshold.

WORK-EXPERIENCE PROGRAMS

DANIEL SCHREIBER

THE SCHOOL SETTING

Alienated youth comprise a sizable portion of the school drop-out population, but all dropouts are not necessarily alienated. Some have the good fortune to escape alienation.

Youth's attempts to gain peer recognition and approval, self-esteem, and feelings of accomplishment may take the form of deviant acts which are disruptive or illegal. Rather than describe and discuss such attempts, let me quote from a series of taped interviews with school dropouts, which were taped at the Syracuse University Youth Development Center. The young men who came to the Center for help in finding a job had been unemployed for some time; they were restless, had definite ideas of work, had at least one major delinquency, came from broken homes, and had dropped out of school during the ninth grade.

INTERVIEWER: Did you have any teacher you didn't like?
DROPOUT: No. Up to a certain point.
INTERVIEWER: Well, tell me about it.
DROPOUT: He was a man, too. Ah, I was doing my best work, you know, and he always kept telling me I hadda do better and he kept after me. So one day, I told him off and walked out of the class and never came back.

* * * *

INTERVIEWER: Tell me about school. What did you like about school?
DROPOUT: Well, you know. I got used to school real fast. Then, you see I was in about the sixth grade, well, you know. Then I met up with the fellows and we used to sit in the back of the room, always made sure that

	I got in the back of the room. We used to pass the bottle.
INTERVIEWER:	What bottle?
DROPOUT:	Wine bottle.
INTERVIEWER:	Why did you drop out of school?
DROPOUT:	I didn't drop out of school. I was put in reform school.

      ❊   ❊   ❊   ❊

INTERVIEWER:	Why did you drop out of school?
DROPOUT:	I didn't drop out. They dropped me.
INTERVIEWER:	Why did they drop you?
DROPOUT:	Well, when they dropped me there were a few other boys. . . . Oh, it was impossible for me to stay in school. No, I quit. I went to school in September. I started in September. I guess it was just about the end of the month, I quit and then . . . the reason why I quit was that my mother wanted me to help her out. So I went to work and I lost a job. I was laid off. So then I couldn't find another job. My mother asked me to go back to school so she could get welfare assistance for me. So I went back to school. . . . And then when I went back to school, I didn't care too much about it. After that I didn't feel like doing my work or anything. I wanted to go to work.

Too frequently, the school, caught between the vortex of compulsory school attendance laws and defiant, uninterested, hostile youth, seeks a quick and ready solution to its problems. The solution is obvious and patently simple, expeditious, and painless; namely, get rid of him, regardless of his age or competence, through expulsion or suspension from school. Propelled unceremoniously, and without skills, into the world of work, alienated youth finds that there is no place for him there either. A game of volleyball ensues—with the alienated youth as the ball. Society, not knowing what to do with him but knowing that the evidence of crime, welfare payments, and illegitimacy is increasing, suggests training programs. Eventually, the suggestion is made that these problems can best be resolved in school; and, hence, the way to force the schools to resolve them is to extend the compulsory school attendance to high-school graduation or to age eighteen. Both solutions are irrelevant and nondeterminative, for as Wattenberg has pointed out, "Juvenile delinquency is now seen as one symptom of a cluster of problems related to alienation." Alienation is not parthenogenetic. It is fertilized by the social pathology that exists in the community and incubates during the child's school-age years.

Responsibility of the School

Havighurst and Stiles in their excellent paper, "A Statement of National Policy for Alienated Youth," [1] stress the objective and subjective need of youth to achieve success and confident self-identity. The function of the school is to provide the means for them to do so by offering alternatives to the academic program. If work experience is important in the success of growing up, and many educators believe that it is, the schools have the responsibility of making work-experience programs available to those pupils who want and need them.

Definition of work experience.—A work-experience program at the secondary-school level is a program in which the pupil is released from classes or school during part of the day, or a whole day, to work. The work may be done in school or out of school; it may be for pay or without pay; it may or may not carry course credit toward graduation. In some cases, study and work may be closely related, while in others the school simply makes it possible for those who want to work to do so. Hunt enumerates six different types of work-experience programs. There are:

1. In-school, nonremunerative general education work-experience programs.
2. Out-of-school, nonremunerative general education work-experience programs.
3. Remunerative general education work-experience programs at the junior high school level.
4. Remunerative general education work-experience programs at the senior high school level.
5. Remunerative vocational work-experience programs in senior high schools not subsidized by federal vocational-education funds.
6. Remunerative vocational work-experience programs in high schools subsidized from vocational-education funds.[2]

---

[1] Robert J. Havighurst and Lindley J. Stiles, "A Statement of National Policy for Alienated Youth," *Phi Delta Kappan,* XLII, No. 7 (April 1961), 283.

[2] DeWitt Hunt, *Work Experience Education Programs in American Secondary Schools,* United States Office of Education, Bulletin No. 5,

An additional type of work-experience program will be added to this list by the Economic Opportunity Act of 1964. Title 1B of the Act, Public Laws 88-452, enacted August 20, 1964, permits the Secretary of Labor to set up work-training programs. These programs, which will be known as the Neighborhood Youth Corps, will provide useful work-experience opportunities for unemployed young men and women in order to increase their employability or to enable them to continue or resume their education.

FUNCTIONS OF WORK EXPERIENCE IN
THE LIVES OF MALADJUSTED YOUTH

Importance of the Role of Work

As industry and work become more complex and sophisticated, employers will demand not only higher levels of education but also higher levels of work skills from entry workers. The *Washington Report,* a United States Chamber of Commerce newsletter, reported on September 4, 1964, that the Dallas, Texas, Chamber had concluded, after a survey of job requirements, that in ten years the minimum requirement for any job in the Dallas area will be at least one or two years of post-secondary-school education.

Too many young men and women find it extremely difficult to bridge the gap between school and work. The opportunities for work that existed in a less urban society are fast disappearing, and family chores are no longer part of a young man's development. In the labor market, the rate of unemployment of boys, ages 14-17, is twice that of older boys and four times that of adult men. As recently as 1953, boys who left school could find work. At that time, the unemployment rate for males, ages 14-19, was approximately 6 per cent for white and 7 per cent for nonwhite. Since 1958, the unemployment rate for this age group has not fallen below 12 per cent for whites nor below 20 per cent for nonwhites. Yet, work is still the hallmark of adulthood, and if work experience cannot be obtained elsewhere, the schools must offer it. For maladjusted youth, the best preparation for work is work itself.

1957 (Washington: Department of Health, Education, and Welfare).

Difficulties Encountered in
Gaining Work Experience

School dropouts, particularly alienated youth, encounter great difficulty in gaining work experience. First, their age, usually sixteen years, operates against them. Miller found that the age of the dropout was more important to the employer than *the actual grade* completed.[3]

A study made by the Bureau of Census for the Department of Labor showed unemployment for the year 1961 among the various age groups in the male labor force as follows:[4]

Age Groups	Percentage
16 through 17	21.5
18 through 19	15.2
20 through 21	10.6

Second, those with less education have always had more difficulty in finding jobs. In 1952, the educational level of the unemployed was slightly less than 10 years (of school completed), while all workers had a level of approximately 11 years; in 1962, the levels were 10.6 years and 12.1 years, respectively. Third, there is a surplus of unskilled workers in the labor market. The per cent of unemployed in the civilian labor force has not fallen below 5 per cent during the past five years. Fourth, the cost of machinery and plant equipment has risen steadily in the past decade, and employers are reluctant to let inexperienced teen-agers work on expensive machines. Fifth, many dropouts lack the accepted credentials of employability —a high-school diploma, school references, or job references.

In addition, quite often an alienated youth has a police or court record which militates against his being hired. And, lastly, he lacks the basic work skills necessary to perform satisfactorily. In a study on industry's practices and policies relating to youth employment, Freedman states:

---

[3] S. M. Miller, *The Syracuse Dropout* (Syracuse, New York: Syracuse University Youth Development Center, 1963).

[4] *Counseling and Employment Service for Youth* (Washington: United States Department of Labor, Bureau of Employment Security, November 1962).

Persistent tendency is to oversimplify qualifications . . . and those who do not meet the requirement of high-school graduation are suspect. The diploma becomes a screening device even where the job does not require it. . . . One employer gave as his reason for not hiring dropouts, "We cannot use cowboys." . . . A large group stressed social acceptability and good appearance.[5]

HYPOTHESES

Because work is basic to the existence of any society, it is difficult, if not impossible, to think of an individual fitting into society without a work role. "When a man's occupation is known, a great deal about him may be immediately deduced with a high degree of accuracy; until it is known, little can be said about the role he is playing or about his status in either his own eyes or those of *his fellows*." [6] If a man has no occupation and is not working, he performs no function in or for society. At best, his relations with others are marginal; at worst, he is alienated from them.

Since work is the hallmark of maturity, many educators believe that work-experience programs should be made available to maladjusted youth. They hypothesize that:

1. Work experience gives direct and indirect satisfaction to maladjusted youth which reduces the likelihood of delinquent activities on their part.
2. Work experience can prevent serious delinquent behavior.
3. Work experience can rehabilitate the maladjusted.

WHEN SHOULD WORK EXPERIENCE BEGIN?

A study made in Minneapolis by the Health and Welfare Council shows that almost one-third (31 per cent) of the male contacts with the Crime Prevention Bureau occurred by age thirteen, and one-fourth (24 per cent) of the female contacts took place by that age. In a run-down, dilapidated neighborhood, known as the Target Area, the police contacts for all

---

[5] "Getting Hired, Getting Trained," New York National Committee on Employment of Youth, August 1964, mimeographed.

[6] W. F. Cottrell, *The Railroader* (Palo Alto: Stanford University Press, 1940).

youth, ages 10-17, was 9.8 per cent as against 4.9 per cent for the city; and, of these contacts, the per cents of contacts with males and females, ages thirteen and under, were 36.5 (city, 30.8) and 33.9 (city, 23.9), respectively. More than one-half (55 per cent) of contacts by the Crime Prevention Bureau for the year 1963 were with youth who had had previous contacts.

A study done in Harlem by HARYOU showed similar results —10.9 per cent delinquency rate for Harlem as against 4.6 per cent for New York City. In addition, an analysis of reading achievement showed that, whereas 30 per cent of Harlem's schoolchildren were below grade level at the third grade, 80 per cent were below grade level at the sixth grade. More than one-half (55 per cent) of the pupils who went on to senior high schools from the four junior high schools in Harlem dropped out before graduating. A sampling study done by the Urban League in New York found that more than one-fourth of the boy dropouts were "invited" to leave, and almost one-fifth were sent to correctional institutions.

Unmistakably, these two studies, and there are others, highlight the necessity of starting work-experience programs in the seventh grade of the junior high school. They should continue through senior high school and lead to graduation.

In order that there be a proper sequential development of the program, staffs of the junior and senior high schools, working co-operatively, should develop the curriculum and kinds of work experience. This joint undertaking will insure that the senior high school will give school credit for Grade IX work experience. Hopefully, it will reduce to a minimum the unnecessary repetitive aspects of the curriculum, such as completing a job-application form every term.

Age, sixteen plus.—Not all maladjusted youth are identified by age thirteen. In a study involving Minneapolis youth, it was found that the modal age of police contacts for males was sixteen and for females, fifteen. Many who were making a satisfactory adjustment in elementary and junior high school became alienated at age sixteen when they entered senior high school. The school is larger, the teacher demands more, pressures to conform are greater, and college-preparatory courses prove to be more difficult. Those youngsters who are failing academically should be offered an alternative at that time, before truancy and delinquency set in. One alternative to dropping out is enrolment in a work-experience program, hopefully geared to the needs of sixteen-year-olds.

In addition, youth who have left school before graduating, or who have been "invited" to leave, and who are unemployed, should be encouraged to return to school. They, too, can be assigned to a work-experience program. Hopefully, Title 1A and 1B of the Economic Opportunity Act of 1964 will encourage many to do just this. (These programs are described in greater detail later on.)

OVERVIEW OF WORK-EXPERIENCE PROGRAMS

The work-experience program should be an integral part of the public school program and under the supervision of the board of education. Classes in the academic subjects may be held in a regular school building, a special school building, or in rented space near the work stations. The work performed may be in school, in public institutions, or in private industry. Youth may or may not receive wages for their work. For some youth, depending on age, social maturity, and competence, the work experience may stress basic work disciplines while for others the stress may be on vocational skills.

Difficulties Encountered

Many maladjusted and alienated youth lack the competence —not the capability—to do sustained, efficient work. Their work habits are poor; their early experiences taught them to cheat, and it is possible to "cheat" on any job—for example, painting over unprepared surfaces or filing papers under the wrong letter. They tend to see the foreman as the enemy and want to "tell him off" when things become difficult or his orders become insistent. They are aggressive, impulsive, and erupt in loud, vile language when baffled by a job. One boy, assigned to work with the baker in the school cafeteria, reacted violently after the baker had asked him for the fourth time whether he had put the salt in the dough-mix. The baker knew, but the boy did not, that if the salt were omitted the rolls would be flat and tasteless. Needless to say, the work station was lost for the remainder of the school year.

Many of the boys who are dishonest see their placement in business establishments as affording them an opportunity to steal with impunity. Small tools, left lying about, disappear.

Two boys assigned to work as stock boys in a supermarket were not told of security measures taken by the market. They took several expensive cuts of meat, wrapped them in paper, placed them near the doorway, intending to walk out with the package at the end of the day. The assistant manager found the package, questioned the boys, fired them summarily, and the school lost two work stations.

In addition, many youths lack the social competence to succeed on a job unless helped. They must be taught formal greetings—good morning, good-bye—how to shake hands, and the like. Their ability to communicate properly and effectively with the foreman and adult workers is impaired by their slovenly and slurred speech patterns, the paucity of their vocabulary, and their inability to comprehend orders.

Too often, they lack an understanding of the nature of the working relationship—an appreciation of the fact that the foreman's job is to see that the work is done, that a worker who is late or absent may prevent other workers from doing their jobs, or that his absence or lateness will throw an additional burden on his co-workers. The statement by one young man best describes this attitude: "What difference does it make to him. I lost a day's pay, not him."

Employer Expectancy

Unless the school, through its work-counselors, explains fully and honestly the aims and goals of the program to the prospective employer and foreman, the program will fail. The employer will expect one type of youth (a counterpart of his regular workers) and he will get another type (a maladjusted youth). Where explanation has been given, the employer is less apt to discharge the youngster for an egregious act. Instead, he will call the work-counselor who will talk with and guide the youngster. In another supermarket, not far from the one described earlier, a similar occurrence took place. The manager phoned the counselor who went immediately to the store and spoke to the boy. The boy was suspended from his job for a week—note, he was not discharged—and after several individual guidance sessions was sent back to the supermarket where he remained for the rest of the school year. The work-experience station was not lost.

Other Difficulties

Before seeking and asking for work stations, the school should be fully cognizant of the child labor laws. When can a child work? How many hours can he work? At what age can he work in manufacturing plants? What health examinations, if any, are necessary for food handlers? Also, will the employer have to pay minimum wages? Does the fact that certain plants engage in interstate commerce affect employment of youth? Must the youngster be covered by workmen's compensation? If so, who will pay the additional premium?

These problems are not impossible to solve. Experience has shown that they can be resolved satisfactorily, to both the employer and the school. The major problem is finding a sufficient number of work stations in private industry. In September, 1963, the Greater Hartford (Connecticut) Chamber of Commerce established a work-study committee consisting of representatives from private industry, labor, schools, social agencies, and governments. After an elaborate screening program, 124 potential dropouts were selected, but only 45 were actually placed. Apparently, it was more difficult to find work stations than even this committee had anticipated.

Since there may be a dearth of jobs in private industry, the school must look for stations in its own organization as well as in other public and private nonprofit organizations. Here, too, the work to be performed must be real and meaningful.

In response to the question, "What have been the major difficulties encountered in the operation of STEP (School to Employment Program)?" the Buffalo (New York) Board of Education replied as follows:

1. Finding opportunities for private employment.
2. Stipends were deducted from welfare recipients.
3. Patterns of academic failure were, at times, too deeply ingrained to effect changes in academic outlook.
4. Difficulty in promoting interest in home study because of low parental expectations, impoverished cultural environment, and lack of physical facilities conducive to study.[7]

---

[7] See "District Progress Report 1962-63 to New York State Department of Education" (Buffalo, New York: Buffalo Board of Education, July 1963, mimeographed).

CONSTRUCTIVE USE OF WORK EXPERIENCE

Some educators believe that all types of maladjusted youth can benefit from a public school work-experience program and should be given the opportunity to engage in one. Others believe that the nature of a work-relationship precludes certain types—the sociopath and the extremely disturbed personality —from engaging in it successfully. It is felt that youth who can be described as simple aggressive, hostile aggressive, withdrawn, or as privated can use work experience constructively.

Caution should be exercised in assigning the hostile aggressive. If too many of this type are assigned to the same place, group dynamics may operate to vitiate the positive aspects of the program. Five hostile-aggressive youth were assigned to work as dishwashers in a hotel in California. Halfway through their job, two of the young men got into an argument and started throwing dishes at each other. This triggered off a dish-breaking scene engaged in by all. The loss was $200 for the dishes and all work stations at the hotel.

GIRLS AND WORK EXPERIENCE

Because so many work-experience programs have been initiated and developed specifically for boys, it is disappointing to find very few programs developed particularly for girls. Perhaps this should not be too surprising, considering the role of the male in American society—the provider of food, clothing, and shelter for his wife and family. Yet, to assume that because of the dominant role of the male, the female will not be active in the labor market, is contrary to fact.

The United States Department of Labor, in its report on women workers, found that more than one out of every three workers in the labor market in December, 1964, was a woman. In total, women accounted for 26 million workers—24.7 million of whom were employed and 1.3 million unemployed. Also, the number of women workers is increasing faster than the number of women in the population. In 1940, females constituted 50 per cent of the population; 25 per cent of all workers were women and 28 per cent of all women were in the labor force. In 1964, they constituted 51 per cent of the population and 35 per cent of all workers; 37 per cent of all women were in the labor force.[8] It is pertinent to note that more than half (56 per cent) of the women workers are married, 23 per cent are single, and 21 per cent are widowed, divorced, or separated, and that one-half of the 4.6 million women who are heads of families are in the labor force.[9]

Since girl dropouts are "nicer" than boy dropouts—represent fewer school disciplinary cases, include fewer adjudicated delinquents, read better (in Pocatello, Idaho, girl dropouts read as well as boy stay-ins), have recorded higher I.Q.'s, receive better scholastic grades, have fewer grade retentions—it appears probable that work-experience programs for girls should be in the so-called middle-class range of jobs. Jobs in which the worker comes in contact with other persons appear to offer the greatest opportunity. Training should be provided for secretarial work; for positions in retail sales and in service trades; and for subprofessionals, such as nurse's aides, recreation aides, and teacher aides for prekindergarten and kindergarten classes. Because each one of these occupations has a career line, a young woman who is successful in her "entry job" can, by application, study, and further education, obtain promotion to higher-level positions—for example, from nurse's aide to practical nurse, and eventually, to registered nurse.

The federal government under Title 1A of the Economic Opportunity Act has set up Urban Job Corps centers for women, ages 16-21. It is hoped that 13,000 young women will be enrolled the first year, and 30,000 by 1967. In addition, opportunities for work experience exist in the Neighborhood Youth Corps and Community Action projects.

EVALUATED PROGRAMS OF
WORK EXPERIENCE

When, in 1961, Phi Delta Kappa asked its members to report on work-study programs, over 1,500 were identified. Since then, the number has increased. The work-experience programs reported in this chapter are representative of those through

---

[8] *Summary of Current Economic Facts and Labor Force Data— Women Workers* (Washington: United States Department of Labor, January 1965).
[9] *Ibid.*

which national and local government, schools, and private organizations are coping with maladjusted youth.

Many of the programs that will be described in this chapter represent pioneer efforts to serve a selected group of deviants or potential deviants in a particular neighborhood in a particular city. Some have proved to be successful and have been expanded; some have proved to be successful and have been adopted by other groups. But, at the time this article was written, many programs had not been in existence long enough—some were still in the experimental and study stages—to show conclusively whether or not a particular program would reduce the number of or help maladjusted, alienated youth.

Programs at the Junior High School Level

Kansas City work-study program.[10]—Since September, 1961, the Kansas City public schools have been engaged in the initial phase of a work-study experiment, testing the hypothesis that boys having difficulty in school will be less likely to drop out and/or become delinquent if they are provided with systematic and supervised work experience commencing at age thirteen or fourteen and continuing until they reach the age of seventeen or eighteen. This longitudinal research is planned to extend over a six-year period, 1961-68.

Two groups of about 200 boys each were selected in the spring of 1961 and of 1962 in Grade VII on the basis of school maladjustment and average or below-average ability. The racial composition of Group I was approximately 60 per cent Negro and 40 per cent white, while the second group was approximately 50 per cent Negro and 50 per cent white. Three of the four junior high schools from which youngsters were selected were located in low-socioeconomic neighborhoods. Each boy was assigned to either an experimental or a control group. Members of the control group did not receive training beyond

---

[10] The work-study program is a co-operative venture of the Public Schools (Kansas City, Missouri), the Kansas City Association of Trusts and Foundations, and the Ford Foundation. Three progress reports have been published; the first in May, 1961, describing the screening procedures and group-work activities; the second in November, 1962, focused on the first year's operation; and the third in July, 1964, compared, tentatively, the experimental and control boys and described problems of transition faced by the boys as they go from junior to senior high school.

normal class instruction, while a systematic three-stage work-study curriculum was provided those of the experimental group.

Work Stage I, for boys 13-15 years of age, was planned to carry on socially useful work in groups of ten to twenty-five boys under the direction of a skilled work supervisor. Included among the tasks in this phase were unskilled yard-landscape work and small-scale repair jobs. Among these were cutting grass and weeds along school fences, raking leaves, cultivating around shrubs, painting packing stalls, and refinishing school desks and tables. The remaining half of each pupil's schedule was spent in an academic program geared to his abilities, interests, and temperament. This program was designed to provide a basic mental preparation for the roles of citizen, worker, and parent.

From ages fifteen to seventeen, the boys spent their half-days of labor in the employ of local business or industry. Close contact between school and employer was maintained during this second phase of the program in order to insure pupil adjustment to the personal and vocational demands of working for hire. Tasks during Stage II did not differ greatly from those of Stage I except that they represented an investment of private capital. Even more investment was involved in Stage III, during which the boys, aged sixteen to eighteen, concentrated on full-time successful employment as their major objective. Employment co-ordinators counseled with them during this period regarding job shifts or adjustments.

Enrollees in the work-study program during all three stages did not receive sufficient credits for high-school graduation. A special work certificate was given them indicating successful participation in the program throughout the five years of work-study experience. Provision was made that any experimental-group member could return to the regular school program if he and his parents so desired. If a teacher found that a boy's work improved and it was possible for him to do regular school work, then a recommendation could be made to the parents that the youngster return to a regular program.

As of May, 1964, almost all of the boys in Group I were sixteen years of age and most of them were in Grade X. In the second group, most of the boys were in Grade IX, a little more than half were fifteen years of age, and 5 per cent were between sixteen and seventeen years old.

It is understandable that few findings were available at the time of the progress report in 1964, since none of the boys had advanced to the final phase of the program. Especially the report could present few findings with regard to differences between control and experimental groups on aspects of delinquency, social adjustment, and school retention. Still some evidence at that early date, although not conclusive, was available. For example, the hypothesis that boys enrolled in the program would stay in school longer than similar type youngsters not enrolled was partially confirmed as shown by the 7 per cent differential in drop-out rates between the experimental and control groups in Group I and the 4 per cent differential for such groups in Group II.

The hypothesis that juvenile delinquency will be reduced when boys prone to delinquency are provided with work experience over a five-year period is, of course, still open to question. Data are continuously and systematically being collected from the police and juvenile courts, but any inference drawn at the present time must be considered quite tentative. The number of officially recorded police contacts had *not* been reduced among the first experimental group as a whole during the first two and a half years of the work-study program. In fact, the number and per cent of contacts were greater for the experimental group than for the control group. The results for Group II were similar.

Although there was no less delinquency in the experimental group as compared with the control group during Phase I of the program, there are indications that the second phase may show a difference in favor of the experimental group. As of February 1, 1964, approximately 33 per cent of 49 experimental boys in both Groups I and II had had some experience in Phase II. Eighteen had five or more months in supervised paid employment, and of these 18 boys, 8 had from nine months' to a year's experience. Of this total group, 22 had a total of 56 police contacts during Stage I; but only 2 of the 49 boys had a police contact during the time they were working in Phase II.

Of the 92 job placements made, 57 (or 64 per cent) were terminated; and almost 70 per cent of these terminations, divided equally, came about either by the employer discharging the boy or by the boy quitting the job or failing to appear for work. The reasons employers gave for discharging the boys relate to the same kinds of problems that characterized many work-study boys at the beginning of the program. The reasons boys gave for quitting their jobs were divided between legiti-

TABLE 1 / POLICE CONTACTS FOR EXPERIMENTAL AND CONTROL GROUPS

[Group I —September 1, 1961 to February 1, 1964]
[Group II—September 1, 1962 to February 1, 1964]

Group	Number of boys	Boys Contacted		Contacts	
		Number	Percent	Number	Average number
X_1	69	36	52.0	133	3.7
C_1	89	31	35.1	113	3.6
X_2	93	35	38.0	85	2.4
C_2	91	19	21.0	36	1.9

mate reasons and reasons reflecting poor work orientation and poor social adjustment.

It is interesting to note that many of the boys who failed on their first jobs made good adjustments on their second jobs, after they had been counseled by the school employment coordinator. More careful job placement also contributed to their success on the second job.

Program of the Milwaukee Public Schools and Jewish Vocational Service.—In 1962, the Jewish Vocational Service of Milwaukee, Wisconsin, together with the city's public schools and the Probation Department of Children's Court, received a grant of $400,000 from the National Institute of Mental Health to conduct a five-year research and demonstration project in the field of delinquency prevention.

The major aim of this program was to demonstrate that a half-time work experience in combination with half-time school attendance would diminish the antisocial conduct of adolescents who previously had displayed delinquent behavior. Using empirical data from related research on the probability of recurrent delinquent behavior, the project, as a corollary goal, hoped to identify three groups: (a) those individuals who would not be involved in further delinquent behavior whether they participated in the project or not; (b) those individuals who would be involved in delinquent behavior whether they participated in the program or not; (c) those individuals who would not be involved in delinquent behavior while or after participating in the program but who probably would have been involved in such behavior had they not participated in the program.

The rationale for the project stemmed from an observation

that lack of achievement, as well as lack of motivation for academic schoolwork, contributes to a feeling of frustration and inferiority. Adolescents, especially delinquents, are recognized as having a strong need for achievement of status, for strivings for adulthood, and for identity with assertive adult figures. These needs, at times, go unmet in a formal classroom setting because of teacher-pupil difference in values and cultural orientation.

The project offered an alternative to the formal academic school program. Shop supervisors (who functioned as work foremen) were selected in order to provide a suitable ego model with which to identify. Work was stressed as a symbol of adulthood and maturity. Supervisors were oriented to accepting behavior that most employers would normally not accept and to using this behavior to teach good social- and vocational-role behavior. Principles of group dynamics were studied, and problems relating to industrial situations were utilized.

Included in the study were 120 youths, 14-15 years of age, who had at least two contacts with police. Chosen by the Milwaukee public schools for this project, half were assigned to a control group. The control group remained in school full time and received services that were regularly available from the schools and other agencies.

Youngsters of the experimental group spent half of each day in school and the other half at the Jewish Vocational Service, where they participated in a controlled work-experience program. The work they did was obtained through subcontract from local industries and was supervised by the workshop staff, trained and experienced in working with teen-age delinquents. Psychological counseling was also available to the adolescents of the experimental group and their families.

Youths assigned to the experimental group were permitted to participate in this program for a maximum period of three years. Assistance in vocational planning and in finding a job was available. In most cases, efforts were made to encourage individuals to obtain further schooling, either academic or vocational.

Each year an additional group of pupils was added to the project. Upon termination of the program in 1967, an attempt will be made to compare results achieved with the experimental group with those of the control group. The major criteria for determining differences between the groups will include: presence or absence of delinquent behavior during and immediately subsequent to the period of participation in the project and educational, vocational, and psychological adjustment.

Programs for the Sixteen-Plus Age Level (Continuous School Membership and Returnees to School)

Municipal Co-operative Education Program of New York City.—The establishment of New York City's Municipal Co-operative Education Program marked the first time that a civil service of a municipal government became involved in a joint effort with public schools. This five-year experiment (1961-66), the first two years of which was financed by a Ford grant, had a dual purpose. A primary objective was to locate or create job opportunities through which it was hoped to reduce the rate of dropout in low-income neighborhoods. Many youngsters coming from this type of background were Negroes or Puerto Ricans, who would ordinarily face an added burden of job discrimination. A second objective was to develop new recruitment sources for city jobs which required skills that are in short supply.

A youngster participating in the program, which involved ten city agencies, worked one week and went to school one week, rotating with another student so that together their mutual job was always filled. Beginning in 1961 with 271 pupils sharing 131 jobs, the program involved 1,000 workers on 500 jobs in 1965. While one student worked, his counterpart was taking an accelerated school program, which included courses related to his job. Credit also was given for the work experience.

The students worked as clerks, typists, business-machine operators, stenographers, laboratory helpers, and public health aides in such city departments and agencies as hospitals, finance, housing, real estate, youth board, transit authority, welfare, and personnel. Each pair of pupils shared a city position budgeted for $2,750 annually. For the five-year period, it was estimated that pupil salaries would cost the city an estimated $55 million.

The teen-age participants, selected by the Board of Education, were drawn from low-socioeconomic areas of the city, from families of limited background. They came chiefly from communities and neighborhoods characterized by an indiffer-

ence to education; from families that had been denied or
largely denied the benefits of an education. Because of the inability of these teen-agers to interpret schoolwork in terms of
their future job expectations, they might easily have felt that
there was no reason to remain in school. Then, too, such youngsters came from homes in which economic circumstances
might, without a part-time job, have precluded completion of
high school.

Most of the evaluation was observational in nature rather
than objective, since empirical data were not collected by the
Manpower Utilization Council at the termination of the program. The Ford Foundation has already granted $26,000 for
the 1966 evaluation "to be undertaken through a university or
other qualified institutions selected in agreement with the
Foundation."

The results now available appear promising. At the completion of the 1964-65, school year, some forty-seven out of sev-
enty graduating seniors working in the Welfare Department
remained there as regular employees. Many students reported
that the program had provided them a splendid opportunity
for developing employment potential. City department heads
indicated that student help had served both to expedite work
and to provide a pool for staff recruitment. To the extent it was
successful in reducing dropouts, the project helped defuse the
"social dynamite" which Conant insists is piling up in America's largest cities.

San Francisco School District and Housing Authority.—The
San Francisco Unified School District and the City's Housing
Authority have developed a co-operative work-experience education program designed to encourage the growth of vocational
interests among teen-agers through part-time employment in
various offices of San Francisco's Housing Authority. This program was primarily designed to assist two particular types of
youngsters: (*a*) those who wished to continue their schooling
but who, without a job, might find it economically impossible;
and (*b*) the potential dropouts who needed to recognize the
significance of further education. It was hoped that the experience might foster in all trainees desirable work habits, dignity,
and self-respect.

Accommodating some one hundred trainees annually, the
program required participating young men and women to be
residents of projects within the Housing Authority, be sixteen
years of age or older, and to have completed Grade X. Selected

from the senior high schools of San Francisco, each prospective trainee had to meet satisfactory standards of attendance, deportment, and scholarship. For those chosen as trainees, the school system provided a special course focusing attention on development of job skills, which included applying for work, grooming, attitudes, and the improvement of job responsibility, dependability, working relationships with supervisors, and punctuality.

A trainee's daily schedule included four hours of classes and four hours of work. In some cases this was reversed—work in the morning and classes during the afternoon. Some of the various job classifications in which youngsters functioned were those of typist, machine operator, file clerk, receptionist, inventory clerk, gardener, janitor, and laborer. In addition to $1.25 per hour, pupils received five semester credits in "work experience" for their on-the-job training.

Housing Authority personnel in co-operation with work-experience co-ordinators from the school system supervised student employment activities. Together, these persons evaluated student performance for report-card purposes. Satisfactory progress both at school and at work was a requirement for continuance in the program. Upon completion of the work-study Youth Training Program, school employment counselors and vocational counselors assumed active leadership in securing full-time employment for graduates.

San Francisco School District and Safeway Stores, Inc.—Although this program was not designed to serve deviant youth, it had one feature which deserves inclusion in this report. One of the serious difficulties faced in implementing work-experience programs is the opposition of labor unions who fear that such work may be used to undercut union wages and increase unemployment. In Racine, Wisconsin, the J. I. Case Corporation and the local union agreed that students could work only in nonbargaining positions, and this practice is generally followed in most cities.

But in San Francisco, the Retail Clerks Union No. 648, Safeway Stores, Inc., and the School District developed a new classification titled *Student Clerks*. The contract states:

SECTION 20—STUDENT CLERKS

A student clerk is hereby defined as a person who is enrolled in high school or college, and as such is a regular member of the Union or has applied for membership in the Union in compliance with the provisions of this Agreement.

He shall be sixteen (16) years of age or over and shall have complied with all the rules and regulations of the Board of Education in regard to minors securing permits to work.

Tacoma-Pierce County (Washington) Program of Co-operative Educational Services.—The Tacoma-Pierce County Program of Co-operative Educational Services was developed by six school districts in response to the concern of school personnel about the life plans of mentally retarded adolescents for whom the usual coursework at the secondary level is inappropriate. From this attempt to develop curricular experience that would be realistic and helpful, both in the eyes of pupil and teacher, emerged a community-laboratory concept.

Basic to the community-laboratory concept was the rationale that often, for adolescents with handicaps, there are social and personal factors which prevent acceptable work in academic subjects. Those initiating the program believed that adolescents with handicaps, if left to their own resources in making the transition from school to the adult community, would experience difficulty and exploitation by others and would possibly require the expenditure of additional public funds to effect a reasonable life arrangement. Finally, those educators involved agreed that the resources and opportunities for education do not lie solely within the walls of our schools but can be found in abundance in the community of which the school is a part.

Pupils in this program attended classes in the morning and worked, without pay, during afternoons in bakeries, furniture or hardware stores, body and fender shops, churches, and service stations. These students were "nonacademic"; many had experienced difficulty in school. At last report the project was placing some forty pupils each semester in community-laboratory situations.

Both morning and afternoon programs were the responsibility of the teacher who had been assigned a group of not more than eighteen adolescents. During the afternoon the teacher worked in the corners of the community laboratory in which her pupils were to be found. A strong relationship was established with each community-laboratory associate, usually a businessman or employer who had agreed to participate in providing learning experiences for a handicapped adolescent. The third member of the team was the co-ordinator of the total program who worked with each teacher in finding appropriate

community-laboratory opportunities and in modifying placement when it was deemed advisable.

Architects of the Tacoma Project were reticent to evaluate
their efforts at the time this chapter was prepared since they
believed that an intelligent appraisal of its impact could not be
made earlier than after an elapse of five to ten years. It should
be mentioned, however, that a kind of continuous evaluation
was made as the experience of the boy and what was learned
about him in the afternoon work session was fed into the scholastic morning program at the high school, and what was
learned about him in the morning program was fed into the
afternoon laboratory experience.

Programs for the Sixteen-Plus Age Level
(Returnees to Special Classes)

Detroit Job-upgrading Program.—The Detroit public schools
and the City's Council for Youth Service, in 1949, began a job-
upgrading program to offer out-of-school, unemployed youth,
aged 16-20, an opportunity to continue preparation toward becoming self-supporting citizens. Now a regular part of the
school program, the job-upgrading project annually services
more than 1,000 dropouts who are referred by the schools,
community agencies, and interested individuals.

Since most of the youngsters have low ability and inadequate
education and come from poor economic and social backgrounds, they very often are not aware of proper procedures in
job seeking. Nor do they know their own assets or what assets
would fit into paid employment. Therefore, for three hours
each morning of the first six weeks of their program, youth
meet with a counselor to attack these basic problems. Each individual's needs are considered as he receives help in self-
appraisal of interests, attitudes, and abilities; in the development of an understanding of employer-employee relations; in
personal budgeting; in developing work habits; and in learning
techniques for job hunting.

Many of the more adaptable young people find employment
within a few weeks after entering the program. Others who
need the benefit of work experience to become employable
are placed on subsidized work-experience tasks in social agencies, city departments (recreation, hospital), and private busi-

ness organizations. In these, they acquire on-the-job experience coupled with the sympathetic supervision and understanding arising from the close co-ordination between the work supervisor and the teacher-co-ordinator.

During the first six months following placement, the teacher-co-ordinator makes frequent calls at the place of employment to see how the youngster is adjusting to his job. Through these visits, the worker continues to receive counsel and assistance in making the change from school to work. In most cases, the young people feel more secure and develop self-assurance because of these continued contacts. When he has demonstrated ability to hold a full-time job and has had at least six months of satisfactory work experience, he is on his own.

The accomplishments of Detroit's Upgrading Program are significant. In a typical year, for every 1,000 who are in the program, the records show that 410 are in jobs, 290 are in the process of upgrading, 40 return to regular school, and 260 leave the program voluntarily or for reasons beyond their control. The figures seem to indicate that many dropouts will readily accept a chance to make the transition from deprivation to dignity.

Double EE Program (Chicago Board of Education and Carson, Pirie, Scott and Company).—The Double EE (Education and Employment) Program of Chicago, initiated in 1961 by Carson, Pirie, Scott and Company in conjunction with the city's public schools, is an example of what can be done when the dropout problem is considered a communal responsibility. This large department store agreed to provide jobs for a group of dropouts (60) between the ages of sixteen to twenty-one, if the Board of Education would insure the continued education of these potential employees. Under a grant of $50,000 from the Ford Foundation, four Chicago teachers were assigned to the project.

Volunteer students of the program, accompanied by their parents, began Double EE training by attending a dinner at which the rationale and procedure of the venture were explained. Familial support has proved to be a vital factor in student success. After the orientation meeting, students embarked on a three-week pre-employment course in such subjects as how to prepare for an interview, how to improve basic skills, and the importance of good grooming. Public school teachers and guest speakers from the company served as the instructional staff for the pre-employment sequence.

After the first three weeks, Carson's Personnel Department made an appraisal of each student's interests, abilities, and job potential. On the basis of this appraisal, the student was assigned, initially at the rate of $1.15 per hour, to one of numerous positions, such as selling, stock handling, display, merchandise receiving, checking and marking, or food service. Each job was a regularly requisitioned one, rather than one created for student employment.

Two students were assigned to one six-days-a-week job with each student working on an alternate schedule of three days at work and two days in classes. The courses, given ten months a year, were in the areas of English, social studies, business, and essential mathematics. An attempt was made to relate the content to the jobs of students. For example, mathematics dealt with price items on sales slips, totaling amounts of money, and with the computation of salaries, withholding taxes, and social security payments. Spelling and reading included content not encountered in the student's work department.

Special workshops, taught by the public school teachers, provided opportunity for independent study by those individual students who could be encouraged and assisted toward completing the work for a high-school diploma through completing required subjects or electives which for lack of sufficient demand were not offered in regular classes. High-school credit was given for all courses. Evaluation and motivation were inextricably intertwined. Each youngster was assigned a "big brother" or "big sister"—a junior executive, usually a college graduate, who had volunteered to be a liaison in the supervisor-pupil-teacher relationship. There was close co-operation between the teacher and the supervisor or "big brother," so that course content could be geared toward removing those deficiencies that became apparent at work.

Because of the program's initial success—90 per cent of the students received merit increases, and more than half remained on in the store—the program was continued, and other business establishments were invited to join. Students are working as order clerks, telephone operators, and addressograph operators at Bell Telephone, Sears Roebuck, the Conrad Hilton Hotel, and many other places. But, in this program, too, the problem that plagues many expanded work-experience programs exists, namely, the shortage of job stations. Some of the students are now working in jobs created by the Board of Education.

Although the Double EE was set up as a work-study program, there is some doubt as to whether this was clear to all the participants. Merit increases by the store bore no relation to the student's schoolwork. Regardless of whether his schoolwork and attendance were satisfactory or unsatisfactory, a student could receive a salary increase if his storework was satisfactory. What is even more to the point, the school personnel were not consulted prior to the giving of raises. Hence, the strong possibility exists that the students saw no relationship between school and the job, and, therefore, no need for continuing education.

Government Programs

Mobilization for Youth.—New York City's Mobilization for Youth is a nonprofit corporation of representatives of settlement houses, welfare agencies, religious institutions, and other groups on the Lower East Side. In 1962, armed with an experimental three-year blueprint and $13 million, MFY began, in a 67-block area of high juvenile-delinquency rate, a practical and spirited attempt to salvage youngsters from a life of poverty. It was the first organization to receive a grant from the President's Committee on Juvenile Delinquency and Youth Crime.

One of the most conspicuous parts of this project is the unit, Urban Corps, which is seeking to prepare both high-school graduates and dropouts for the world of work. Presently the Corps services over 1,000 youth who, because of lack of skills, or because of their attitudes, grooming habits, speech, fear of discrimination, or other factors, are not deemed "employable" by business or industry. Depending on their past experience, adolescents may be assigned to one of the three program phases: work exploration, work projects, or on-the-job training.

The most elemental phase, work exploration, is designed for those having little or no work experience. Over a four-week period, participants are paid 75 cents an hour and they have an opportunity to try out a number of job types to determine their vocational choice. Work projects is the second phase, during which job skills are acquired under the direction of experienced supervisors. Some students work in the gas station, restaurant, or woodwork shop that are owned and operated by MFY. They receive $1.25 per hour. Others, at the same hourly rate, take part in projects carried on at nonprofit agencies on a contract basis. In these cases, boys might be members of crews assigned to work in masonry, carpentry, or construction. Wherever their work takes them during this phase, pupils are regularly visited by the MFY training officer and vocational counselor so that any adjustment problems or any serious learning difficulties requiring remedial instruction may be resolved. Male youths might find it necessary to take courses in arithmetic or geometry, while girls often require speed typing or spelling for clerical work.

A final stage is on-the-job training in such enterprises as gas stations, auto-parts stores, and business offices. All jobs are on a contract basis, with MFY sharing half of the expense for wages of the workers. On completion of on-the-job training, it is hoped that employers will hire trainees for steady employment. Where no permanent jobs are available, MFY assists youngsters in locating a job through its relationship with New York State Employment Service. One measure of the effectiveness of this program is the increasing number of applicants and trainees.

Another measure, a statistical one, more somber and less hopeful, is reported by Richard A. Cloward, director of research and evaluation for Mobilization for Youth, as follows:

> Between October, 1962 (when the work programs opened), and December, 1963, approximately 1,700 young people applied for assistance. Of these, roughly one in four eventually achieved competitive employment as a direct result of the program. For the bulk of those placed, the jobs are in marginal occupations at relatively low wages, and their subsequent job histories are not characterized by much stability, or continuity.

Jersey City, New Jersey (CANDO).—CANDO, short for Community and Neighborhood Development Organization, was conceived by a handful of men as a project to salvage high-school dropouts, who, lacking even the most rudimentary skills, are virtually unemployable. They formed a private nonprofit corporation in order to qualify for federal grants, and following a three-day period of rioting in the Negro section of Jersey City in August, 1964, moved quickly to get this aid. The federal government approved a grant of $328,000 payable in six installments, and the city appropriated $30,000 as its share. The program began in November, 1964.

The criteria used to select participants included age, school-leaving, and education. To be eligible for admission to the program, applicants must be between sixteen and twenty-one years of age and must have been out of school for at least one year. Preference is given to those with the least amount of formal schooling.

Ninety-five youngsters, seventy-five boys and twenty girls, were assigned to various city departments for a six-month period. Their educational level determined their job assignment in the police department, medical center, public works department, and city hall.

In order to encourage achievement and to reward successful work, the six-month period was divided into three phases of two months each. During Phase I, the boys and girls were paid $25 a week; in Phase II, they received $30, and in Phase III, their salaries were $35 a week.

Since this report was written when the program had been in existence for only two months, it was still too early to have any objective evaluative measurements. However, the director of the project, the participants, and the civil service supervisors are enthusiastic.

Private Nonprofit

Howard University—Community Apprentice Program.[11]—In March, 1964, the Center for Youth and Community Studies of Howard University in Washington, D.C., initiated a pilot program to train disadvantaged youth for new careers in "human" services. (This project was supported with funds from the National Institute of Mental Health and the Office of Juvenile Delinquency, Department of Health, Education, and Welfare.) This experimental research-and-training program grew out of the Center's concern with two problems of modern American society: (a) the lack of useful and meaningful jobs and the difficulties of rehabilitating disadvantaged youth, and (b) the shortage of trained personnel in the helping professions. The Center staff was interested in whether or not such youth could adequately perform the jobs that needed to be done, what kind of training was required, and the effects of such a program on the attitudes and behavior of the youth.

---

11 Based on personal correspondence between Dr. Arthur Pearl, director of the Howard University Center for Youth and Community Studies, and the writer.

Ten young people, from sixteen to twenty years of age, were trained over a three-month period as aides in the fields of day care, recreation, and research. Seven of these aides were boys, and three were girls. Several of the boys had arrest records while two of the girls were unwed mothers. All came from socially and economically deprived backgrounds and met the minimal requirements set for this program: they were unemployed, had no pending court action, were physically fit, had not completed high school, and could fill out an application form keyed to the fifth-grade reading level. The ten were selected at random from a group of twenty-eight referred by local agencies. Additionally, seven of the twenty-eight were selected as a control group matched to seven of the aides.

The twelve-week training course began in April, 1964. The course was designed to give the aides specialized training in recreation, research, and day care; to provide a core of general knowledge so that the aides might be able to assume a variety of roles; and to develop the values and behavior required to hold the jobs for which they were being trained.

During the first two weeks of the program, all ten aides were oriented to each of the job areas. In research, they learned to use a desk calculator, the rudiments of interviewing, group-process recording, and the administration of sociometric measures. In day care, they learned some basic principles of growth and development and specific games and activities for young children. In recreation, they learned rules of games, supervisory techniques for older children and adolescents, and record-keeping. At the end of this two-week period, the aides were given the opportunity to pick their own job assignments. Three boys and one girl selected day care; a similar group went to recreation, and one boy and one girl to research.

For the next four weeks, while receiving a stipend of $20 per week, the aides worked five half-days a week at local agencies (a recreation center for problem youth, a day-care center in a neighborhood settlement house, and the research division of the Center for Youth and Community Studies). The other five half-days were spent by all the aides daily in a core training group. During these sessions, under the guidance of a leader, the aides discussed problems that arose on the job, such as discipline, relationships with supervisors and other aides, and their own functioning as a group. They also considered more general matters of interest that arose from their discussions, such as the work of community agencies, civil rights, current events, and the legal process. The aides also attended bi-weekly specialty workshops, conducted by professional personnel, on the theory and techniques necessary to the individual jobs.

Thus, although the training was centered on ongoing job experiences, it also was designed to help develop a basic understanding of human behavior and to present ways to solve and analyze problems, as well as to enhance group and individual responsibility. Additionally, the training program offered a number of opportunities for practice in reading, writing, and arithmetic. Many "remedial" exercises were initiated by the aides themselves as they began to see the relevance of improved skills to their daily work. At the end of six weeks, the salaries of the aides were increased to $40 per week. They then worked for another six weeks as full-time staff members in the agencies in which they had been training, while continuing to meet for approximately eight hours per week in both the core-group and specialty training programs.

Given such a small number, it is difficult to draw any firm conclusions as to the effects of this program on individual behavior. Some tentative findings, however, can be reported. Of the ten aides, several of whom had had prior difficulty with the law, only one became involved in a minor offense during the course of the training program and the ensuing months of employment. This is in contrast to three members of the control group who were arrested during this period. Even more significantly, however, all ten aides remained in the program, despite their past histories of school and employment failure. They all received good to excellent performance ratings from job supervisors. They became increasingly responsible, prompt, and neat. Despite differences in past history and accomplishment, there was no appreciable distinction among them in terms of job performance. Several have returned to high school on a part-time basis or have taken special courses. All ten are now (some ten months after the beginning of the program) working in community agencies.

The Center for Youth and Community Studies is now conducting further experimental programs of the type described to help evaluate both the problems and the promise of new careers for disadvantaged youth. More research and careful investigation in this area needs to be done.

North Richmond (California) Neighborhood House.—Recruiting out-of-school, unemployed boys—in their homes, on the streets, and in the pool halls—has been the task of North Richmond's Neighborhood House since 1960. The object of seeking out boys who have been failures at school, in their homes, and in the community was to encourage and provide training for them in job preparation. The three-year project, financed by a $25,500 grant from the Rosenberg Foundation, was purposely designed to help unmotivated youth, since these adolescents—perhaps more than any other group—are most in need and least often the recipients of any positive attention.

From the beginning, with an initial group of twenty-four boys, the program has consistently emphasized motivation. In addition to providing a study hall and tutoring service in mathematics and reading, provision was also made to have the boys meet twice weekly to discuss and study problems associated with their status. Heavy emphasis is placed on group discussion and on examining problems such as the role of the Negro in our society, the worth of the individual, and the responsibilities and fulfilment of employment. In these sessions, conducted by a counselor, there is opportunity to vent deep-seated feelings of hostility, bitterness, and despair. Also important is the experience of filling out sample application forms, listening to local employers who serve as guest speakers, and watching movies on proper dress and conduct.

Because these young men have lived so long without a future, they cannot understand nor accept volunteering in order to gain work experience. Neighborhood House, therefore, promoted the concept of supervised work stations. Although local employers were offered reimbursement of $15 weekly to hire one of the adolescents on a part-time basis for a minimum of six weeks, most employers declined any remuneration. Each employer is required to provide firm, yet understanding, supervision and to submit realistic evaluations to be used in counseling. The boys work in the Veterans Hospital, for a local construction company, and for numerous civil service agencies. To expand the job-training section of the program, Neighborhood House has begun a course in janitorial training and service. The youths are hired to provide such services for offices and small businesses on a contractual basis.

FEDERAL GOVERNMENT PROGRAMS

On August 20, 1964, the Economic Opportunity Act was signed into law. Two parts of the Act, involving work-experience programs, are of direct interest to us. Although neither part is concerned with the rehabilitation of delinquents or youthful criminals—in fact, delinquents and criminals are excluded from participation—an understanding of the provisions of the Act and its implementation is important. Because 300,-000 young men and women will be involved, the chances are that there will be a temporary, possibly a permanent, reduction in the incidence of crime.

Job Corps

The purpose of Title 1A, Job Corps, is to prepare young men and women, ages 16-21, for the responsibilities of citizenship and to increase their employability by providing them, in residential centers, with education, vocational training, useful work experience, and other activities. The Job Corps consists of conservation camps for men only and training centers, for men and women (not co-educational). It was hoped that 40,000 youth, 40 per cent in conservation camps, 30 per cent in men's training centers, and 30 per cent in women's centers, would be enrolled by the end of the first year. But the multiplicity and complexities of problems faced by the newly organized agency made this achievement impossible. Enrolment in the Corps is voluntary, and an enrollee may leave at any time.

Conservation camps.—In conservation camps, young men with problems of attitude and who resist or have resisted learning receive basic skill training, as well as instruction in elementary reading, writing, and arithmetic. The camps which are operated by the Job Corps in conjunction with Forestry Service are limited to 200 enrollees each. The unifying force in the camp is a counseling program, dealing with every aspect of the experience—living, working, education, and recreation. Each center has a complement of approximately twenty-five professionals—directors, teachers, and work supervisors.

At the time this was written, few camps had been opened,

and in those that had been opened, only a small number of youth had begun their training.

Training centers (men).—One unusual feature of Title 1A is that the Director is permitted to enter into agreements with any public agency or private organization for the operation of a training center. This provision has led some of the giant corporations to submit proposals. One reason for their interest in training disadvantaged youth is that they will be allowed to make a profit on the operation. For example, one company's contract calls for a profit of 4.7 per cent on the total cost of approximately $10 million. Although it is too early to tell what the final outcome will be, there is sufficient evidence on hand to indicate that the training centers will be operated by such corporations in conjunction with a university. The corporation is responsible for the logistics, supply services, and vocational training, while the university is responsible for basic education, guidance, and counseling. Sometimes the university is the prime contractor and the corporation is the major subcontractor. Examples of such arrangements, with the prime contractor mentioned first, are: Federal Electric Company (a division of International Telegraph and Telephone) and Rutgers University; the University of Oregon and Philco Radio (a division of Ford Motor Company); Litton Industries, Inc., and the University of California at Berkeley; Southern Illinois University and General Electric.

The men's training centers enrol from 1,000 to 2,500 youth, and the major emphases are upon vocational training, job experience, and basic educational improvement in preparation for permanent employment. The total cost per enrollee is approximately $400 per month for the first year of operation.

At the time this is written it is impossible to evaluate the results of the program. Although six contracts have been signed, only one training center is in operation—and that one on a limited scale. Of the fifty-five young men who were assigned to the centers, fifty-one entered the program. In order to reduce problems of orientation and adjustment, approximately 200 youth are to be placed in the center each month until it reaches its full capacity. Hopefully, this lead time will permit the training center to make provision for individual differences.

That there is enthusiastic interest in enrolling in the Job Corps is shown by the fact that 26,000 young men sent in applications during the month of January, 1965. As of February, 1965, there were more than 72,000 applications on file.

Training centers (women).—These centers are planned to be smaller than the men's centers—a maximum of 300 women as compared to 2,500 men; they, too, will be operated by private organizations. As of February 1, 1965, none is in operation and none is contracted for, although negotiations are under way. Unlike the men's centers, these will be located in the cities. Although the girls will be prepared for permanent employment, the major emphasis will be on family living, on preparing the girl for a productive and fruitful life as a wife and mother.

Work-Training Programs

The purpose of Title 1B, Work-Training Programs, known as the Neighborhood Youth Corps, is to provide useful work-experience opportunities for unemployed youth through participation in state and community work programs, to the end that their employability may be increased or their education resumed or continued. In-school as well as out-of-school boys and girls are eligible. However, unlike the Job Corps enrollees, these youth will live at home. Although this section is part of the Economic Opportunity Act, it will be administered by the United States Department of Labor.

Under the Act, contracts also will be signed with public and private *nonprofit* agencies (private organizations are excluded) to conduct work programs. These agencies receive grants up to 90 per cent of the cost of the proposed costs. Youth who are assigned to a program will receive $1.25 an hour. In-school youth will work a maximum of 15 hours per week, and out-of-school youth will work a maximum of 30 hours per week. Preference is given to those agencies which are intimately associated with community action programs.

The Neighborhood Youth Corps cannot be evaluated as of February 1, 1965, because no programs are in being. Approximately 25 contracts were signed in January and more than 300 applications are on file awaiting final decision.

CONCLUSION

The failure to secure and hold a job is a severe blow to anyone; and, the blow is more severe to the dropout, to the school failure, to alienated youth. When he was in school, he learned that he was good *at* nothing, now he is told in no uncertain terms that he is good *for* nothing.

The redemption of these lives requires inventiveness, energy, and dedication, for the crux of the matter is not simply that so many sink but that so few have learned to swim. Work-experience programs manifest a school's willingness to sponsor and to engage in activities that hold promise of giving dignity and assurance to *every* child who crosses its threshold.

School-based work-experience programs are second-chance opportunities for maladjusted, alienated youth to become a part of the mainstream of American life. The programs described in this chapter possess common elements which enhance the possibility of successfully helping, either to rehabilitate youth or to prevent their maladjustment. In common, these programs:

1. Encourage and permit alienated youth to improve their self-images and self-concepts.
2. Enable them to learn and exercise self-discipline and to develop proper work habits and work attitudes.
3. Enable them to attain at least minimum levels of education and work skills which are marketable.
4. Offer alienated youth opportunities to relate themselves with and to other persons and encourage them to do so.
5. Give direct and indirect satisfaction to the individual in knowing that he can both undertake and complete a job satisfactorily.

But because most of these programs are new, the findings and conclusions must be considered inconclusive and, at best, tentative. However, we can optimistically predict that these programs will bring about a reduction in police and court contacts in the immediate future. They are good. They put money into the pockets of some youth. They permit youth to perform useful work. They promote the development of self-dignity and self-esteem. They involve guidance and counseling help. They remove large numbers of youth from their neighborhoods and place them in the healthy environment of residential centers. And, at the very least, these programs permit communities to have a much-needed breathing spell.

SELECTED READINGS

BURCHILL, GEORGE W. *Work-Study Programs for Alienated Youth.*
Chicago: Science Research Associates, Inc., 1962.

Guidance and the School Dropout. Edited by Daniel Schreiber.
Washington: National Education Association and American Personnel and Guidance Association, 1964.

MILLER, S. M. "The Meaning of Work," *Proceedings,* Allenberry
Conference on Mental Health in Industry, pp. 2-13. Harrisburg:
Pennsylvania Department of Mental Health, 1961.

One-third of a Nation. Washington: The President's Task Force on
Manpower Conservation, January, 1964.

The School Dropout. Edited by Daniel Schreiber. Washington: National Education Association, 1964.

SCHREIBER, DANIEL. "Juvenile Delinquency and the School Dropout
Problem," *Federal Probation* (September, 1963), pp. 15-19.

"Social Dynamite," *Report of the Conference on Unemployed, Out-of-School Youth in Urban Areas.* Washington: National Committee for Children and Youth, 1961.

"STEP, School to Employment Program, Second Annual Report
1962-63." Albany, New York: State Education Department, Bureau of Guidance, 1964 (mimeographed).

UNITED STATES HOUSE OF REPRESENTATIVES: Committee on Education and Labor. *Economic Opportunity Act of 1964.* Report No.
1458, 88th Congress, 2nd Session. Washington: Government
Printing Office, 1965.

UNITED STATES SENATE: Committee on Labor and Public Welfare.
Economic Opportunity Act of 1964. A compilation of materials
relevant to S. 2642. Washington: Government Printing Office,
1965.

Youth Development Demonstration Project: A Proposal. Minneapolis: Minnesota Community Health and Welfare Council of Hennepin County, Inc., April, 1964.

Youth in the Ghetto. New York: Harlem Youth Opportunities Unlimited, Inc., 1964.

A SCHOOL CURRICULUM FOR
PREVENTION AND REMEDIATION
OF DEVIANCY

CARL L. BYERLY

The agency which should assume primary responsibility for alleviating the problems of deviant youth is the public school. It is a responsibility which authorities have been inclined to ignore for various reasons. However, the social climate is changing, as the public becomes aware of the loss of human resources and the drag on the economy attributable to this oversight.

While social deviancy occurs at all levels of society, this chapter will concern itself largely with the development of a school program in those lower-class areas in which most children of school age are alienated and special handling of them is needed to salvage their talents, rebuild their egos, and launch them safely into the main stream of adult living on a productive level.

The term currently used to describe this kind of school program is "compensatory education." This kind of education is expensive. Solving social problems costs money, but *not* solving them will be even more costly.

THE CASE FOR COMPENSATORY EDUCATION

In its essence, the provision of compensatory education is an attempt to provide, for socially disadvantaged children, the experiential background which is the normal expectation of a

middle-class environment. Disadvantaged children tend to reflect the low educational level of their parents. They are further
handicapped by a lack of appreciation for education, low family income, and little or no experience of the wider community
outside the environment in which they have lived. Poor housing, poor health conditions, and broken or incomplete families
are among the factors adversely affecting these children. Such
socially disadvantaged children may be whites or Negroes or
members of a minority group of any race. If they are Negroes
or members of a minority group of a different race, they also
are affected by a whole complex of problems and attitudes relating to race.

These children may come to school almost entirely unready
for the usual school experiences, even at the kindergarten level.
Some do not know their own names, and many have never held
a pencil. Their speech may be so different from that of the
teachers and so unrelated to the language of the primers they
are given that they almost have a new language to learn. They
have had little experience in discriminating sounds, colors, or
shapes which is a part of the everyday experience of middle-
class preschool children whose families supply toys, endless explanations, and stories from books.

These children and their families have a culture, but it is not
attuned to the school nor is the school attuned to it. By the time
the child is admitted to school, generally at about six years of
age, it is likely that he may already have absorbed a climate of
low expectations, developed unfavorable opinions about himself, and acquired a concept of the school as an alien and un-
friendly place. Very rarely is the school itself well prepared to
counteract the child's attitudes and opinions or even to understand the approach of the disadvantaged child to school situations.

Recent research has placed more and more emphasis on the
learning disadvantages suffered by these children, as compared
to middle-class children, that are attributable to the home environment. For example, a recent publication discusses four
specific factors which handicap children in a deprived environment:

1. Poor speech habits and language patterns in the home discourage language development and restrict the number and variety
   of words which the child recognizes; this contributes to lower
   scores on I.Q. tests and lower school achievement, especially
   in reading.

2. Families have less time, opportunity, or know-how to take their children on expeditions to zoos, museums, stores, or different neighborhoods; the children also have fewer indirect experiences with the world around them through books, pictures, films, and the like. Such experiences not only increase verbal facility but help in making distinctions and in comparing objects, ideas, and so on, all important not only for I.Q. tests but for learning itself.
3. Children in these "disadvantaged" homes have fewer opportunities for solving problems or for thinking about a variety of issues, as compared with children in more abundant environments. Their parents do not have the habit of encouraging children to ask questions or to think things out for themselves.
4. There is less interaction generally between adults and children. Discipline tends to be authoritarian, and the "good" child is quiet and out of the way. This, too, limits the background of experience and language which the child brings to school.[1]

The Problem of Communication

Bernstein, also, has studied the differences in language and sentence structure of lower- and middle-class groups and has concluded that these patterns affect the way children think and the ways in which they set about solving problems.[2] All these differences are likely to be seen by teachers as evidences of slowness or even stupidity. In his book, *Crisis in Black and White*,[3] Silberman says that the slum child often lacks a sense of auditory discrimination. This sense is most important in reading because it enables the child to distinguish very subtle differences and nuances in sound. In a house where several people live closely together, the noise level tends to be so high that a child is forced to learn how *not* to listen. He learns to tune out his surroundings, to wall himself off from them. Thus, he does not learn how to distinguish between relevant and ir-

---

[1] The four statements are based on the discussion and annotations presented in Benjamin S. Bloom, Allison Davis, and Robert Hess, *Compensatory Education for Cultural Deprivation*. Based on working papers contributed by participants in the Research Conference on Education and Cultural Deprivation (New York: Holt, Rinehart & Winston, Inc., 1965).

[2] Basil Bernstein, "Social Class and Linguistic Development: A Theory of Social Learning," in A. H. Halsey, Jean Floud, and C. Arnold Anderson, eds., *Education, Economy, and Society* (Glencoe, Ill.: Free Press, 1961).

[3] Charles E. Silberman, *Crisis in Black and White* (New York: Random House, Inc., 1965).

relevant noises. For instance, if a truck rumbles by while the teacher is talking, the lower-class pupil hears only one big jumble of sound; the middle-class pupil has the ability to screen out the irrelevant noise of the truck and to listen only to the teacher.

The lower-class child tends to have a poor attention span and to have great difficulty in following the teacher's orders. The reason is that he generally comes from a nonverbal household. Adults speak in short sentences. When they give orders to a child, it is usually in monosyllables—"Get this," "Bring that." The child has never been obliged nor privileged to listen to several lengthy sentences spoken consecutively.

The middle-class teacher who rambles on for several sentences might just as well be talking another language. Lower-class children do not look upon an adult as a person of whom they ask questions and from whom they may get answers. Yet school, for the most part, is based on the assumption that children who do not understand will ask. This, these children will not do without the creation of a situation in which the teacher leads them to do so spontaneously and without coercion.

Antecedents

The research in the field of compensatory education is limited and inconclusive, but several abortive movements of the past supply valuable leads to the development of school programs which will more adequately fulfil the needs of the alienated youth of today. Pratt's "Play School" (*circa* 1920), Cane's "Walden School," and the Comings' "Fairhope Schools" were early expressions of a philosophy which is valid today. That the creative impulse is within the child himself was proclaimed by Rugg and Shumaker in *The Child-centered School*. "No educational discovery of our generation has had such far-reaching implications. It has a two-fold significance: first, that every child is born with the power to create; second, that the task of the school is to surround the child with an environment which will draw out this creative power." [4]

Two later efforts, also abortive, provide patterns and proce-

_____

[4] Harold Rugg and Ann Shumaker, *The Child-centered School: An Appraisal of the New Education* (Yonkers-on-Hudson, New York: World Book Co., 1928), Chap. V.

dures for dealing with atypical youth although they were not designed for this purpose. The "Eight-Year Study" of the Progressive Education Association and the "Life Adjustment Education" project growing out of the Prosser resolution (1945) made valiant attempts to adapt the schools to the needs of youth at the secondary level.

More currently, the "Great Cities Program for School Improvement" spearheaded by Superintendent Benjamin Willis, with the aid of the Ford Foundation, has initiated pilot programs and experimentation in fourteen of the largest cities of the United States with the object of finding better ways to meet the needs of socially and economically disadvantaged children and youth. Significant programs have been developed in Chicago, Detroit, St. Louis, Baltimore, Milwaukee, Pittsburgh, and Houston. In New York City, a variety of approaches have been and are being made to meet specific needs of children and youth:

For the Elementary Schools
    Early Identification and Prevention Program (1959)
    All-day Neighborhood Schools (1942)
    Junior Guidance Classes (1960)
For the Junior High Schools
    BRIDGE (Building Resources of Instruction) (1961)
    Summer Schools (1962)
    Aspirational Inventory (1964)
    Career Guidance (1958)
    Reading Counseling Service Centers (1962)
    Hunter College Student Teaching Project (1962)
    Fundamental Concepts and Skills in Mathematics (1962)
    Special Reading Programs (1958)
    Programed Instruction in Reading (1958)
In the Elementary and Junior High Schools
    Mobilization for Youth (1963)
For the Senior High Schools
    Job Education Program (Project III) (1960)
    Operation Return (1962)
    Summer Evening High Schools (1946)
    Joint High School Placement Service (1960)
    Work-Evening High School Program (Project II) (1960)
    Cooperative Education in Municipal Government (1961)
    Probject ABLE (1961)
    STEP (School to Employment) (1955)
    College Discovery Program (1964)
    Speech Approach to Basic Literacy (1963)

For the Elementary, Junior, and Senior High Schools
  Higher Horizons (1959)
For Emotionally Disturbed Children and Youth
  "600" Schools (Grades I-XII) (1947)

Other noteworthy centers of curriculum ferment are Boston, Oakland, and New Haven. Significant experimentation with preschool education is under way in New York, Baltimore, Cleveland, and Detroit. Research data and findings from all of this activity may be forthcoming eventually, but they are not available at this time. There is general agreement, however, on the areas of emphasis:

1. Building flexibility of various kinds into the program so that individual or group needs may be met when they occur. This may include length of periods, sequence of learning experiences, size of classes, combinations of content subjects, access to special services, and so on.
2. Adaptation of both materials and procedures of instruction to the understanding, the cognitive level, of the children concerned. This is recognition that intelligence, rather than being already fixed by genetic factors at birth, emerges as it is nurtured. Each stage of development carries with it possibilities for the acquisition of new abilities, new ways of processing information.
3. Strengthening the ego, building a positive self-image, as a primary objective of the school and its program. This means that each student has some successful learning experiences each day and that recognition is given when tasks are performed successfully. Teachers demonstrate confidence in and respect for the individuals in their classes.
4. Mustering the resources of social service agencies and professionals from other disciplines that are recognized as a necessary adjunct to bolster and undergird the work of the school. This is recognition that (*a*) the competencies of the social worker, the psychologist, the psychiatrist, and the guidance counselor are needed to supplement the skill and abilities of teachers, and (*b*) that the home and the community provide a learning environment which may conspire to defeat the necessarily limited effort of the school unless a conscious effort is made to counteract their influences.

IMPROVED PRACTICES IN PROGRAMING

Several variations in programing reflect significant advances in understanding the needs of children, particularly at the elementary level. Improvement of the learning environment serves to mitigate tendencies toward alienation, but it also brings the deviant into sharper focus so that the need for remediation becomes apparent. Thus, improved programing practices, viewed not as administrative devices but as a means of better meeting the needs of learners, offer much in the prevention and remediation of potentially maladjusted children.

Nongraded instruction.—Variously known as "ungraded primary," "primary unit," or "continuous progression," nongraded instruction is finding its greatest acceptance in the first three or four years of the elementary school, but there is a growing acceptance of the nongraded philosophy through the later years of the public schools. Its greatest virtue is its potential for the accommodation of the different maturity levels found in a given age group. It provides the security of continuous progress at a rate commensurate with a pupil's maturation and readiness; it removes the pressure—the threat of failure or repetition during the most impressionable years at which time self-image and identity are becoming firmly implanted. In such a program, teachers must become adept students of child growth and development and, invariably, more conscious of the problems and needs of individual children.

Grouping in various forms.—After weathering many attacks from inside and outside the teaching profession, ability grouping is gaining respectability and general acceptance. It takes many forms from the time-honored division into "blue birds" and "larks" in the first grade to the organization of "advanced placement" classes in the upper years of high school. Along with general ability grouping are to be found such features as reduced size of classes for slow-learning groups; large-group instruction, involving team-teaching or the use of teacher-aides; ability grouping for specific subjects, such as algebra or foreign languages; and the automatic grouping which goes along with choice of course of study to be followed.

Ability grouping is effective in the prevention of maladjustment because the focus is on providing educational experiences which recognize that children differ in many ways and that there are several respectable paths to learning and growing up. It is a laudable attempt to accommodate individual differences within the framework of group instruction.

Remediation.—While grouping may be a mass method of dealing with non-normal learners, remediation is generally restricted to smaller groups or to individuals for a varying but relatively short period of time. Remediation almost invariably requires the involvement of specially trained teachers, who may employ unusual equipment and teaching aids. Probably the most important need of the remedial teacher is the ability to sustain the ego of the child while the learning difficulty is being overcome. It is obvious that the most effective remediation is that which is supplied at the earliest detection of deviation. Its importance to the prevention of social maladjustment can hardly be overemphasized.

Other improved practices.—Other program modifications tend to be variations or extensions of the three already listed. The provision of a sheltered environment is a form of grouping which may prove to be efficacious in instances in which the number of social deviants justify and the availability of trained professionals make possible this plan. . . . The adoption of differentiated pupil-teacher ratios for groups in which the incidence of deviancy is high is another administrative procedure which is finding some favor and may be justified as providing "compensatory instruction" for children or youth who need extra attention. This, too, is a variation of remediation on a group basis. The provision of trained guidance personnel at all levels has increasing support in the profession, but it is an ineffective solution unless other supportive services are provided to supplement their efforts.

MODIFICATION OF TEACHING AND LEARNING EXPERIENCES

The preceding section has dealt with programing procedures which require administrative sanction for their use. There is another type of modification which stems from the skill of the individual teacher in adapting instruction to the needs of pupils.

Individualization.—Even in a group situation, a skilled teacher, with an adequate supply of instructional materials, can achieve a large measure of individualization of instruction. The recent movement in the direction of "individualized reading" is evidence of this professional concern. Good teachers with an understanding of their children's background and interests have always capitalized on this knowledge in making differential assignments no matter what subject was being taught.[5]

Progression into advanced instruction.—The factor of "readiness" is all-important for success in the mastery of advanced learning. Readiness is an individual matter and it may be as much an emotional as an intellectual factor. While textual materials and courses of study are presumed to provide a natural progression of learning experiences, they, from their nature, can only be a general aid to the teacher and not a substitute for perception and inventiveness on his part if further gradation or augmentation is needed for the group or the individual that he is teaching.

Use of mechanical, visual, and manipulative aids.—The era of the single textbook and rote learning should now be history, but vestiges of it still remain. The use of workbooks may be justified in skill subjects for which repetition and drill are needed to reinforce learning, but they tend to be a crutch for the teacher and an inadequate substitute for teaching which is sensitive to individual needs. The use of manipulative and visual aids not only broadens and deepens understandings but such aids frequently reach the deviant learner who fails to get meaning or understanding from textual materials or from the oral explanations of the teacher. Teaching machines, or programed instruction for individual pupils, undoubtedly have some values in the teaching of reluctant learners, but these devices are in their infancy and need further validation.

There is such a plethora of commercial aids and resources available to the teacher today that the problem becomes one of selecting those which are most appropriate for his purposes. Frequently, the adaptations by the teacher become more important than the aid selected. This means, in effect, that whatever mechanical or manipulative or visual or aural aid is utilized, the teacher's assiduous attention to and modification of it is necessary if children are to receive optimum value from its use.

Use of community resources.—The relating of learning expe-

[5] *Individualizing Instruction.* Sixty-first Yearbook of the National Society for the Study of Education, Part I. Nelson B. Henry, ed. (Chicago: University of Chicago Press, 1962).

riences to the life of the student is the essence of good instruction. Abstract and esoteric knowledge is not the fare for the average learner. It is especially indigestible in the case of reluctant learners. Thus, every attempt should be made to "tie in" the learning experience with what children know and with what they see about them. This points up the importance of community resources and of field trips, which may be anything from a visit to the nearest grocery or fire department to a visit to the city council or to local industries. Ordinarily, there will be a tremendous difference in the experiential background of a class of children even though they live in the same community. The excursions which broaden the cultural knowledge of those whose horizons have been circumscribed provide an opportunity for the school and the teacher "to reach" a group of children who, because of their environment, are already potential dropouts.

Another way of using community resources is to bring into the school and the classroom individuals who can explain their work, their unusual experiences, and their success in life in terms of its relation to what children learn in school. The use of eminent or successful members of minority groups as speakers is especially effective as a means of providing a better "role expectancy" or success image for children whose background tends to provide a negative or defeatist attitude toward their future careers.

Use of "built-in" success experiences.—When teachers are confronted with pupils who have experienced failure and defeat so often that it becomes almost an automatic expectation, a simple device is frequently effective in securing a change of attitude. The teacher makes individual assignments which he knows the pupil can master. These assignments are made within the regular framework of classroom procedure so that they do not appear to be contrived. A succession of sucessful performances, each a little more demanding than the previous one, recreates the confidence that is necessary to compete with the group and to achieve status and identify as an individual of worth.

This procedure is especially effective with slow-learning groups, but in the hands of skilful teachers, it can be utilized just as effectively in heterogeneous classes.

Adapting other curricular experiences as therapeutic aids.— In working with difficult children or those who promise to be difficult, it is important, in a general therapy program, to exploit the nonacademic features of the school program. Sometimes this requires a team approach, which is always desirable when specialized teachers are assigned for art, music, and physical education. Frequently, in such subject areas, a child achieves identity which carries over into his other classes. Participation in co-curricular activities, when the door is opened by judicious arrangement, may enable a youngster to salvage his self-esteem and his faith in society. Such measures as these, plus a host of others which may be provided in a typical school, may be utilized to prevent a retreat into "privatism"—the unconscious rejection of normal social behavior—which usually marks the social deviant.

CREATING A CLIMATE FOR LEARNING

The principal.—There is a consensus, among those who have studied the problem, that children from lower-class homes "have to be controlled before they can be taught." Control, in order to be productive, cannot be authoritarian but should derive from understanding and respect. Instead of the typical "academically oriented" school which further alienates these children, "behaviorally oriented" schools and classrooms are needed. They are needed to capture the interests, to develop motivations, and to lead the child to a recognition of the value and purpose of schooling and education as a means to fulfilment of individual (and societal) goals. The principal of the school is the key figure in determining the climate of the school. This has been observed over and over again in experimental programs of the Great Cities Program for School Improvement.

The difference between a successful and an unsuccessful school in a culturally deprived neighborhood lies to a very high degree in the kind of leadership exercised by the principal in developing and maintaining the morale and supportive attitudes of the teaching staff. Research is needed to identify these several attributes of leadership, both personal and professional. There is no question, however, that the principal's ability to organize, his ability to convey to his staff an enthusiasm for the special challenge of teaching these children, and his conviction that these children have talents and ability and can be helped to achieve success are all-important in establishing the learning climate of the school. Principals possessing these abilities and convictions provide realistic goals and intelligent direction toward the achievement of those goals. They have respect for the competence and ability of the teachers assigned to them and demonstrate a willingness to let teachers try out their ideas; they encourage innovative practices and procedures and are supportive whether or not the innovation proves to be efficacious.

The teacher.—In many ways the teacher responds to and reflects the climate of the school, but his effectiveness is circumscribed by the knowledge, skills, attitudes, and value patterns which he brings to his assignment. As Kvaraceus[6] points out,

> . . . every teacher plays many roles in his school day. He is a person "who knows"; he is a motivator and a "brother"; he is a guide in the selection of learning activities; he is a mediator of middle-class culture; he is an adult authority; he is a counselor; and last he is a judge and evaluator. Obviously, some of these are conflicting roles. They may also affect the norm violator as confusing roles. . . . The teacher's part in helping the delinquent is always crucial and potentially beneficial, but it is never simple and easy.

In order "to reach" the children from deprived neighborhoods, an entirely new dimension must be added to training programs designed for them. Teachers, as a group, tend to come from middle-class homes; they represent, generally, the conforming element of society and reflect a value system quite different from, if not alien to, that of the social stratum which these children represent. A more adequate background in anthropology, in sociology (related to urban living), and in human relations is imperative for success in teaching in a culturally deprived school. This background should include actual experience in deprived neighborhoods—in community agencies or in the schools themselves—and should culminate in a practice-teaching assignment in one of these schools under the sponsorship of a master teacher who has demonstrated his effectiveness in working with socially disadvantaged children.

For teachers already in service, a concentrated effort is needed to provide them with insights and understandings, mostly of a social and psychological nature, through workshops

---

[6] William C. Kvaraceus and others, *Delinquent Behavior: Principles and Practices* (Washington: National Education Association, 1959), p. 52.

and seminars, reading and discussion, and field trips into the environs of the school. Such a background of understanding is necessary to give meaning and significance to the learning experiences provided in the classroom and in the school program in general.

Staffing.—A significant aspect of compensatory education is the need for a much reduced pupil-teacher ratio in schools in which socially disadvantaged children predominate. These pupils need so much individual attention that twenty-five pupils in a classroom should be considered the maximum. A lower ratio should be provided, if possible. Also, depending upon the size of the school, additional auxiliary staffing should be provided. For a school with a thousand pupils the auxiliary staff should include two or three master teachers, a full-time visiting teacher (school social worker), a remedial specialist, a psychologist, and a school-community co-ordinator, the latter to provide liaison with parents and with community leaders and agencies. In addition, because of the high incidence of health and physical disabilities among these children, a full-time teacher-nurse should be a member of the staff.

Part-time teacher-aides should be recruited from the community to facilitate the work of the school. These may be either volunteer or paid personnel and should have responsibilities other than those of the clerical staff required for the operation of the school.

INSTRUCTIONAL MATERIALS

It has long been observed that the nature, style, and content of the textual and supplementary materials used in the classroom have a great deal to do with their acceptance or usefulness as vehicles for learning—for bringing about changes in attitudes and behavior. Recognizing that much of the instructional material presently on the market falls short of meeting the needs of a large sector of urban youth, the Research Council of the Great Cities Program for School Improvement appointed the Committee on Instructional Materials to work with the American Textbook Publishers Institute in the establishment of criteria and guidelines for materials for use in urban elementary and secondary schools. Among the considerations listed in their report on the selection of content and the approach of textbooks and instructional materials are the following:[7]

1. *Need for materials depicting realistic situations in urban areas.*
   Basically, textbooks and instructional materials must be concerned with the diversity of people who make up the society in urban areas, the highly mobile and transient population, the differences in social and economic status between the different groups in each community, and the changes in economic, educational, political, social and family life.
2. *Concern for the pluralistic nature of society in urban areas.*
   Big cities, by the very nature of their complexity, represent many different groups of people who must unite their efforts toward strengthening their community, city, state, and nation, rather than becoming compartmentalized into divisive cultures.

   Materials of instruction should avoid emphasizing the separateness of minorities when attempting to recognize their special needs. The materials should include references to cultural and ethnic groups as they arise naturally in descriptions of the overall urban community and should indicate appreciation for their contributions and achievements without undue emphasis.
3. *Concern for the identification of urban young people with events and people depicted in American history.* There is a pressing national need to stimulate new thinking about imaginative ways of presenting the American past for those who are handicapped by limitations of environment and beset with the problems which arise from differences in social class or racial background. The young person in the sprawling urban complex needs to see himself as part of ongoing American history. An awareness of the part played in history by people like himself can help him in this identification.
4. *Need for materials to help develop vital skills of communication.* Materials are needed which provide specific suggestions for teaching literature, reading skills, and listening skills, and which will contribute to speech improvement and communication in general. There is need to understand the characteristics of the young people who use these materials and of the problems teachers face in the classroom situation.[8]

---

[7] "Instructional Materials To Meet the Needs of Urban Youth" (Chicago: Research Council of the Great Cities Program for School Improvement, 228 North LaSalle St., 1965). (Note: The following paragraphs, in many instances, are not exact quotations. The author, who was a member of the Committee which prepared the report, was given permission to adapt its text for publication in this chapter. He has quoted extensively, paraphrased, rearranged, and summarized the statements formulated by the Committee.)

[8] *Ibid.*

The Committee on Instructional Materials for the Great Cities Research Council proceeded to provide examples of needed instructional material without reference to specific grade levels, but with the suggestion that each concept should be developed in "a progressive order on the basis of increasing pupil maturity."

Social Studies

In the social-studies area it is proposed that considerably more attention be given to urban problems and their impact upon the individuals who compose the urban society. Five major concepts are proposed to help the individual student identify properly with his urban environment.

Contemporary and Realistic Aspects of an Urban Society. Constantly changing conditions, plus the mobility of the American people, combine to require that all individuals must be capable of adjustment in the society. It is almost a condition of survival for people to realize that change is natural and that it may involve basic alterations in their lives. Thus, it is important that social-studies content and procedures include situations that show ways in which people live and work together in an urban community and that provide an understanding of community services that help a community function.

It is suggested, for instance, that the pupils should use the problem-solving approach to learn about the urban complex. As an illustration, pupils may study about the way in which big cities solve the problem of providing adequate water supplies. This kind of study would involve finding information about population density and dispersal, proper utilization of natural resources, physical environment and water resources, and uses of water in industrial development. It is quite in order to utilize contemporary situations to describe urban problems, such as population movements, population make-up, and difference in cultures.

The social problems created by the group in the exercise of civil rights in newly integrated neighborhoods may be pointed out. It is only fair to provide realistic treatment of the problems faced by the high-school student when he enters the adult world in a newly integrated neighborhood. In a very objective manner, it is quite possible to describe the events leading to the passage of civil rights laws and the problems still to be faced in discrimination in housing, employment, and the use of public facilities. In this connection, it is important to help the pupil apply the principles of critical thinking to the choices he must make between violence and civil disobedience and the orderly legislative processes in solving the problems of discrimination.

Complexity of Urban Areas as Group of Communities and Neighborhoods. The need to belong is difficult to satisfy in a megalopolis. Young people should receive help in developing an understanding of the causes of rootlessness: occupational transiency; economic instability; lack of identification with the city; problems arising from short-term acquaintances; and the resultant disinterest in community needs.

It is desirable to provide students with understanding of the various kinds of neighborhoods and community settings, such as areas of single-family dwellings, neighborhood shops, shopping centers, light industry, heavy industry, small business establishments, civic centers, and the relation of school and social service agencies to the various kinds of communities.

An awareness needs to be developed of the common problems of urban centers, such as traffic, utility services, and protection of health and property, as well as the support of public education. In this connection, it is also important to note the relationship of suburbs and rural communities to the metropolitan center, including such items as economic factors relating to production of goods, the market, financial operations, and policies concerned with public welfare.

Youth may be guided into an understanding of the function of youth organizations and agencies as they help individuals develop a sense of usefulness, worth, and belonging.

On a more personal basis, it is possible to develop an understanding of the conflicts arising in the young person who must adapt to new friends, standards, values, and goals as he grows up and as he moves from place to place. Positive suggestions may be provided for the solution of the problems of rootlessness by identifying community workers and agencies available for assistance. It may be pointed out in this connection how gang and club activities may be positively directed in efforts to improve the neighborhood, to participate in constructive community endeavors, and to make responsible use of recreational facilities.

Diverse Backgrounds of Groups Living in the Urban Complex. Young people need to understand that society in an urban complex consists of many elements. They must be made aware of its diversity, strengths, shortcomings, and contributions. To this end, students must learn to accept the existence of differing sets of values, to understand and avoid stereotypes, and to recognize the common goals of all elements of a pluralistic society, despite the diversity of races, religions, and cultures.

The pluralistic make-up of a megalopolis needs to be noted. It is profitable to explore the development of cultural pockets or islands and to note the contributions and the problems which are created by them. The interdependence of people living in large urban complexes needs to be emphasized and the realization of how our life is constantly being enriched by the influences of other cultures, traditions, and the heritage of the past. The problems created by prejudice and discrimination need to be portrayed honestly along with an understanding of the ways in which the young person can recognize them and work to overcome them.

Desirable Attitudes toward and Respect for the Law. The need to develop respect for the law as a cornerstone of society is of particular concern to responsible citizens and leaders in a megalopolis. Growing lawlessness and hostility toward law-enforcement officials must be countered by emphasis on the positive, protective role of the law and reliance on lawful group action.

It is necessary to develop an understanding and appreciation of, as well as a respect for, those persons who have responsibility for maintaining law and order, safeguarding health and safety, and developing the character of youth, such as policemen, school personnel, probation officers and welfare workers, religious leaders, and leaders of youth clubs. It is important for the pupil to recognize that resentment of law enforcement represents rebellion against authority in general and that such an attitude endangers society. Emphasis should be given to the need to resist peer group pressures when they contribute to violation of standards of behavior accepted by the community. Positive activities can provide wholesome outlets for the group.

Under this heading it is also possible to illustrate the constructive roles of government and law in such fields as labor, traffic, health and sanitation, education, and licensing regulations. Here, also, young people may be led to understand the psychological cause and *effect* of mob action and the excesses to which people may go when under such influences.

Occupational Opportunities Available in the Urban Area and the Need for Skills and Training. Instructional materials supplied to young people should help to develop a recognition of an appreciation for the dignity of all honest labor and of satisfaction gained from a job well done. The urban complex, with its greater specializations and the lack of identification of an employee with the finished product, makes this goal difficult to attain. All young people, especially those of cultural minorities living in large urban areas, need to learn and experience the satisfaction of a job well done and to appreciate its significance as a contribution to the community as well as to personal achievement.

Instructional materials and classroom activities should emphasize the importance of all types of occupations without building up the status of the professionally trained person to the extent that a young person would think he is a second-rate person if he cannot aspire to a profession. The important thing is to have each youngster set realistic goals for himself as related to his future career. To do this, information must be provided about occupational opportunities, the training needed to take advantage of them, the value of developing talent and special abilities, and the importance of education. Teachers have an opportunity to help students examine their goals in life and to begin to discriminate between false and real values, ideas concerning status, and conceptions of success. A realization needs to be developed as to how job opportunities increase for the young person who is properly trained and prepared and who has set high standards of workmanship and achievement for himself.

For members of minority groups it is increasingly important to stress the job opportunities which have opened to them because of progress in civil rights.

An appeal to the self-image is necessarily involved when evidence is provided that opportunities for self-employment exist everywhere for young people of initiative who are responsible, well trained, and unafraid of long hours of hard work. It may be pointed out that rewards, non-monetary as well as monetary, may be great in self-employment.[9]

American History

Urban children, particularly those growing up in depressed areas of large cities, have "difficulty in identifying [themselves] with the events and the people depicted in American history. For large numbers of urban children, particularly those who are members of cultural minorities, American history must be made more meaningful, with greater stress upon the fact that history is made by all peoples." In addition to the usual factual information, instructional materials are needed which:

Deal with leaders of minority groups who have made real contributions to the scientific, political, and social development of our country, and which thus help members of these groups develop pride in their ancestry.

Help the pupil to develop pride in his own country; understanding and appreciation of the American heritage, its traditions, and the many people who have contributed to the democratic way of life, and a respect for the innate worth and dignity of all human beings.

Show the part played in United States history by our national leaders; by the "less-than-epic" heroes, such as reformers, social

[9] *Ibid.*

workers, civic leaders, inventors, teachers, scientists, and artists; and by the other people from every walk of life who make up the community.

Point out the roles in American history of prominent and famous people from all ethnic groups.

Provide due consideration of well-known contemporary figures who have transcended minority group barriers and with whom minority group youngsters can relate and accept as models upon which to base their own behavior.

Describe contributions of lesser-known persons of ethnic and cultural minorities who have served their country.

Develop an appreciation of all nations and their leaders, without a loss of devotion to American ideals of democracy, by providing biographical accounts of heroes of other nations as well as American leaders.

Provide accurate and frank portrayals of current problems and changing conditions as influences in shaping the future.[10]

Communication Skills Materials

As far as schools are concerned, reading is the basic communication skill. The difficulty of teaching culturally deprived or culturally different pupils to read arises from several causes which have been described earlier in this chapter.

Reading is not prized in the home. . . . Many adults over twenty-five years of age have completed *no* years of school; great numbers of others have completed four years or less. Children in families with such backgrounds do not associate with anyone whom they value who uses books, magazines, or newspapers as a regular part of his life.

Connected discourse (conversation) is all but unknown to many children. Martin Deutsch points out that words and phrases constitute the only verbal diet familiar to large numbers of boys and girls in the poorest sections of cities. These children have had no preschool experience with the expression of abstractions. Discourse at home has been a series of directions, instructions, and expletives delivered with the greatest possible economy. [Only people who have an understanding of this situation should be entrusted to write materials to be used in classroom instruction for these children.]

1. *Literature: Fiction, Drama, Poetry, Articles.* There should be a variation of reading levels so that material is available for children who represent a wide range of reading abilities. Some

---

10 *Ibid.*

materials are needed for junior high schools with reading levels from second to fifth grade and for senior high schools with reading levels from second to eighth grade. However, the need for reading materials of this type does not mean there should be a lack of sophistication in content. Often subject matter of considerable maturity can be handled in easy-reading books. It is also important to point out that for many children it is desirable for books and stories to be short.

The content of reading materials should more adequately reflect the lives and characteristics of the young people who use them to learn to read. Clinical psychologists and psychiatrists should be consulted in determining the kind of image with which deprived or otherwise different children can identify, or at least not reject; then characters of this type should be depicted in pupil materials. Both the language and ideas expressed in the content of readers need to be considered. The speech patterns and some of the actual vocabulary used in real-life situations should be utilized in the contents of the readers.

Young people usually are more interested in books which portray life situations like their own and which therefore, seem real. They are less interested in an unfamiliar, seemingly artificial society and way of living, but a few themes are so exciting that unfamiliar settings are acceptable. These include adventure, the struggle for survival, and life on the frontier.

The success story, or "Horatio Alger" narrative, will appeal to pupils of low socioeconomic status if presented in a realistic contemporary context. Books of this kind can help raise pupils' aspirations when a poor self-image needs to be overcome.

If a book arouses a genuine emotional response in the reader, it may help modify his attitudes, values, and behavior. [It should be pointed out, however, that overt preaching or didacticism will defeat its own purpose.]

The content of books for teenagers, from the upper elementary school grades through senior high school, should have strong and immediate appeal. Some specific suggestions include:

For all boys:	Adventure, danger, survival, athletics, animals
For all girls:	Dating, jobs for girls, school, activities, mysteries
For both boys and girls:	Science fiction, mystery and detective stories, humor
For high school boys:	Jobs, cars, military service, dating

Whenever appropriate, the reader should have an opportunity to make value judgments based on realistic behavior of characters, and his sympathies and emotions should be stirred in desirable directions. Success in modifying a reader's attitudes, judgments, values, and actions through literature depends on the emotional impact of the writing, the genuineness of the situations portrayed, and the skill in presentation. Overt moralizing will defeat its own purpose.

[Because such instructional aids are largely non-existent some suggestions are provided for the setting and the characters for stories which would appeal to children and youth from lower socioeconomic surroundings.] Stories usually should have the central part of the big city as their setting. Suburban settings sometimes should be used, but less often than in current teenage literature. In addition, exciting adventures with settings in outer space, in Alaska, on the American frontier, and under water are acceptable.

Some stories should take place in segregated, one-race neighborhoods, and some in integrated, multiethnic neighborhoods. In books about multiethnic neighborhoods, it is especially important to avoid stereotyping. There should be some intergroup friction, some intergroup friendliness, and some friction between members of the same ethnic group. Intergroup relations may sometimes be the main theme of stories, especially in those with settings in changing neighborhoods, but should more often be used as background for a plot which is not concerned with intergroup relations.

In materials prepared for pupils in upper elementary school grades and junior and senior high schools, characters portrayed should be adolescents or adults, but not young children.

Characters should sometimes live in multiple dwellings, tenements, housing projects, and rundown one-family houses; less frequently, they should live in homes representing high-income levels.

The tendency to stereotype the "middle class" and "middle-class values" should be avoided. The socioeconomic status of the main characters should usually be of the lower-lower and upper-lower classes, occasionally of the lower-middle class, and much less frequently of the upper class. Poverty, moonlighting, homes in which both parents are working, the matriarchal home, unemployment, and seasonal employment, as well as prosperity and regular employment, sometimes should be depicted.

Home life of people in low socioeconomic groups often should be depicted as wholesome, although *not because* of deprivation. Some one-parent homes should be presented. Both the hardships and wholesomeness which characterize such homes should be portrayed.

Some "success stories" about characters who have risen socially, economically, or culturally are desirable. Again, preaching should be avoided.

Adult characters in stories should usually be blue-collar workers portrayed with admiration; they sometimes should be unskilled or semi-skilled workers portrayed without condescension; sometimes, they should be high-skilled workers or business or professional men.

Minority group members should occupy a variety of economic and vocational levels, including the highest. In some stories, they should be self-employed or own their own businesses, and demonstrate pride in their independence.

At every vocational level, persons should be portrayed as feeling pride of workmanship and as accepting the dignity of labor of all types.

Socioeconomic background and vocational status should be sketched in subtly, without preaching or didacticism.

In considering themes and plots for stories which would have strong appeal these would seem to be especially desirable: the need to belong to a group, the need to be accepted by peers, the need to succeed at something, the need to believe that the individual is important, and the need to feel satisfied about the status of parents.

Stories may sometimes portray intergroup prejudice and may deal with the current civil rights activities. The treatment should be candid and realistic but fair and not sensationalized.

Stories might sometimes show effects of automation on adults in such ways as job loss or fear of job loss; they may also portray the effects of changes in work technology in such ways as to emphasize the need to retrain, to take night school courses, or to move to a new locality.

Plots may sometimes revolve around problems resulting from change, such as the following:

1. Change of housing because of slum clearance or freeway built through residential section.
2. New neighbor who comes from another state or nation, or who is a member of another ethnic group.
3. New job in large, impersonal plant rather than in small neighborhood business.

Plots may sometimes involve dropouts as main or minor characters. The frustrations, resentments, emotional disturbances, and negative attitudes toward teachers and toward education should be shown from the dropout's point of view. The hardships faced by dropouts should be indicated without exaggeration or didacticism. No easy, unrealistic solutions should be proposed.

Unfinished problem stories ending with a question to be resolved might create interest and motivate discussion.

Plots may sometimes involve realistic attitudes in adolescents toward law enforcement officers. They should, in general, be shown performing difficult and dangerous duties as part of the day's work, but the officers should not be pictured as paragons of heroism.

Delinquents should not be glorified. On the other hand, neither should they be *preached* against; if there is any sermon, it should take the form of presenting cause and effect.[11]

Speech-Improvement Materials for Culturally Different Pupils

[Particularly at the elementary-school level,] linguistic barriers present one of the major handicaps to instruction of the in-migrant, the child in a home where a foreign language is spoken, and the child of parents who retain foreign-language idioms despite assimilation of and into the local culture [and children who come from regions of our own country with decided speech variations]. . . .

After children have been sensitized to . . . the discrepancies of the sounds which they hear at home (or in the home they left to come to the city) and with the sounds which they hear the teacher producing, they then should be able to read with much greater speed than is now possible.

Practice materials of some type, preferably consisting of pictures with some additional nonverbal stimulus, are needed to help children acquire both the pattern (grammar or structure) and the pronunciation used by the people in the community where they reside. This will be a difficult and expensive task, since the materials need to be prepared in terms of at least the broad phonetic elements representative of the geographic areas from which major cities obtain their populations.

[At the junior high level it is] suggested that a series of exercises, with related tapes, records, and other types of materials, be designed to develop articulate responses of young people. These exercises should provide practice in acceptable American-English pronunciation, enunciation, intonation, and speaking rhythm.

Colloquial expressions might be "translated" into standard American-English with no insinuation that the language used by the pupils and their parents is inferior. It is important that pupils learn that there are different American dialects and that most communication in school and business is conducted in standard American-English.

Techniques similar to those used in developing materials for teaching a foreign language might be utilized. Communication, facility in the use of language, fluency in articulation, and improvement of speech patterns should be emphasized. Interesting

---

[11] *Ibid.*

and realistic situations of appropriate maturity should be depicted in the content.[12]

Other Content Areas

While the foregoing sections have dealt largely with the social studies and language arts spectrums of the curriculum, it is not to be construed that other areas should remain untouched. The same principles apply in developing materials in these other areas: adapt the materials to the reading level and the apperceptive backround of the student; and provide a continuous "success pattern" in meeting more difficult concepts as the youngsters grow in knowledge and maturity, and so on. As indicated earlier, these youngsters bring with them latent talents in art and music which, if cultivated and developed, can frequently be made use of in helping them build an improved self-image and to achieve status among their peers.

In the field of vocational education, which is important in helping these young persons develop self-sufficiency, a whole new list of opportunities presents itself to the secondary school if it will use imagination in applying the provisions of the Vocational Education Act of 1963, the Economic Opportunity Act of 1964, and whatever new federal legislation may be forthcoming. Among the provisions of these acts, one of the most important is that of "earning while learning." For many years, highly motivated youngsters with definite goals for themselves have been able to "earn while they learn" in the co-operative education classes provided under the Smith-Hughes Act and its later revisions. Only now are the schools able to provide in school for paid work experience which is not tied to retailing, office training, or diversified occupations. Illustrations are provided later in this chapter of imaginative programs which are representative of a general trend that should be accentuated. It is almost axiomatic that schools which adopt the policy of providing paid work experience must also modify the "related subject instruction" which the youngster is expected to pursue while he is in the school.

---

[12] *Ibid.*

PRESCHOOL AND NURSERY EDUCATION

Among the various types of compensatory education programs which are being attempted, the preschool or nursery-school program leads the list by far in popularity. The majority of community-action programs submitted thus far, under the Federal Anti-Poverty Act, have included plans for preschool children. As an example, New York City, which in 1964 began prekindergarten classes for nearly 1,500 children from underprivileged areas, planned to increase the enrolment to 7,000 in 1965. Of the first eighteen cities or communities using Office of Economic Opportunity funds for education, fifteen included preschool programs as all or part of their project. Without discounting in any way the potential value of such programs, it is unreasonable to expect them to solve all the problems of the disadvantaged or delinquency-prone children.

As pointed out by Martin Deutsch, director of the Institute for Developmental Studies, Department of Psychiatry, New York Medical College, "there is more interest in preschool programs than is supported by the knowledge we now have." Programs are being set up in many places without adequate preparation, without well-trained teachers, and without a well-developed curriculum. The greatest need at present is for a few prototype centers to be operated on an experimental basis for research and development and for demonstration of enrichment classes. One such program has been in operation at the University of Chicago for some time under the direction of Robert D. Hess, where a plan has been developed for a pilot program of enrichment in nursery schools. The emphasis is upon cognitive processes and language development of children (three years of age or older) from low-socioeconomic groups. It would seem that such a program should provide a developmental basis for achievement in kindergarten and school, but there will have to be additional programs in the kindergarten and the early elementary grades. A larger project involving more children has been in operation in the city of Baltimore since February, 1963, through a grant by the Ford Foundation. From this project, we may expect a well-validated curriculum from preschool work. In New York City, Deutsch, a recognized leader in the development of prekindergarten programs, is heading a five-year project to develop a "therapeutic curriculum" for children from underprivileged areas. Wherever these programs exist there seems to be agreement on several aspects of the procedure. First, in the content area, there is an effort to increase the familiarity of the child with cultural objects, symbols, and intellectual modes of relating and classifying objects and symbols, and, at the same time, to enhance his vocabulary and his ability to express himself with adequate facility. Second, there is an attempt to involve the parents in the learning process, to familiarize them with the responsibilities of the home in stimulating the children to learn. Third, there is use of volunteers or teacher-aides, who may be recruited from the community, from among the parents, or from agencies. With the professional teacher, these volunteers form a team to work with children as individuals or as groups.

The primary development of the child at ages three or four is physical, emotional, and social. During the time that the children are in nursery schools, the teachers should give most of their attention to providing an environment in which the child may learn (*a*) to use his body, (*b*) to direct and control his emotions toward authority figures and peers, and (*c*) to develop his identity with an age group and to learn the various forms of social participation.

An element in the preschool program which Allison Davis identifies as being especially important is the establishment of a strong relationship of trust and mutual acceptance on the part of the pupil and the teacher. The feeling of liking for the teacher develops into respect and the desire to win her approval. It is just this step which is missing in the early school life of the child from low-socioeconomic groups and which must be built into it at the preschool and primary level. A bridge between the culture of the teacher and that of the low-status child can be established through informal activities, such as story reading, songs, dances, little plays, games, and the child's freedom to tell stories about his own life or fantasies, in whatever words he knows. Across this bridge, says Davis, the teacher can lead the child into new learning, new behavior; into a new world of letters and numbers and writing, which now becomes invested with the importance and cathexis which the child attaches to the teacher in whatever he values. From the good relationship with the teacher comes interest in the school.

PROMISING PRACTICES IN
CURRICULUM REVISION

In many cities, attempts are being made to restructure the school program to meet the needs of culturally handicapped and alienated children and youth. While there are some common threads among these promising practices, the variety of approaches is noteworthy. As a result of experience with these many separate attempts to solve a complex problem, there is a growing conviction that any significant or large-scale improvement of the school curriculum for alienated youth will result from a multipronged effort—probably a combination of some of the selected practices which have proved effective. In selecting the examples that are to be described in the following paragraphs, no attempt has been made to be comprehensive. The examples cited illustrate the broad spectrum of experimental effort to provide compensatory education.

While the costs of these projects vary considerably, in almost every case a subsidy was provided from an outside source. In each case, however, the local administration was trying to develop improved practices and procedures which could be financed within the local school budget when their validity had been established.

Baltimore, Maryland

Early admission of children to the school program.—This is a highly structured experimental project which is attempting to determine whether early admission to school can overcome any of the barriers to learning which environmental factors seem to impose. Attempts are being made to measure both immediate and long-range effects of the program. After the collection of comprehensive knowledge about each child and after orientation of the staff members to be involved, study is being made to determine what constitutes a foundation for continuity of experiences. A major attempt is being made to promote parental understanding of the growth and development of children and of the role of parents in relation to this change. Other features include the use of many volunteers from various social agencies and colleges.

Buffalo, New York

A program adapted to the needs of the culturally different.—
In five elementary schools with a combined enrolment of more
than 3,000 pupils and located in the heart of a seriously disadvantaged section of the city, an attempt is being made to develop a program of education and community interaction with
an educational process geared to meet the needs of the pupils
and to develop their abilities and talents. The program extends
into the homes, the neighborhoods, and other aspects of the
environment of the children. The following personnel were
added to the regular staff: (*a*) a reading specialist to work with
teachers, (*b*) a remedial reading teacher to work with selected
low-achievers in reading, (*c*) a speech therapist to analyze the
needs of the children and to take corrective measures, (*d*) additional art teachers to act as both teachers of children and
consultants for teachers, (*e*) additional music teachers to work
with both pupils and teachers, (*f*) a part-time coaching teacher
to help children with arithmetic, (*g*) a school social worker,
and (*h*) a school nurse. Many trips are provided for both children and parents.

Chicago, Illinois

The experimental summer schools.—These schools, started in
1960, differ from the regular elementary schools in having
lighter class loads (25 per class), more generous auxiliary services, and a time schedule which permits daily, continuous planning by the staff as a whole and in special groups. Teachers are
especially selected for these schools, children are grouped according to ability level, and teachers eat lunch with their pupils. The pupils come from a number of schools, and the areas
served include slow, average, and gifted children. Through
1963, approximately 600 pupils were enrolled in each summer
school, 100 at each level in Grades I through VI. In the summer
of 1964, some of the twenty experimental summer schools included kindergarten groups, and several also had a four-year-
old group. In addition to the full-time teacher-nurse, librarian,
psychologist, and physical-education teacher, the 1964 schools
were assigned a parent-co-ordinator to establish contact with

the parents, to develop classes for them, and, in other ways, to enlist their aid in helping their children get more out of their education.

District Eleven Special Project.—This is a special project designed to meet the needs of boys and girls who are fourteen years of age or over and who have not graduated from the eighth grade. Basically, the program involves special grouping of these boys and girls, on the basis of achievement in reading and arithmetic ability in nongraded classes of about twenty students each. Individualization of the instructional program and a personalized but firm relationship between pupil and teacher (both made possible by the reduced class size), the intensive counseling and guidance services available in the vocational guidance center, and the knowledge on the part of the pupil that he may move ahead as rapidly as he develops the necessary skills, have proven to be important factors in changing the attitude of the pupil, improving his motivation, accelerating his entrance to high school, and increasing the probability of his continuing in school until graduation.

Cleveland, Ohio

Addison Junior High Project.—A program having some rather unique features has been developed in one of the "most difficult" junior high schools in the city. These features include: (a) An internship program is provided for prospective teachers to allow undergraduate college students to work in a school situation before entering the formal teacher-training program in the college. (b) Transition classes are organized for pupils entering from elementary schools. These represent a serious attempt to articulate more closely the work of the elementary school and the junior high school. (c) Drop-out prevention program classes are provided through the industrial arts and home economics departments for pupils with the most serious problems. It is hoped that significant changes in attitude can be accomplished by selected teachers, curriculum revision, and extending the time for work. (d) Preschool orientation of new teachers is provided. New staff members assigned to the school are given an extensive briefing on the school, the pupils, and the community, with the object of making them more knowledgeable and appreciative of the problems which they will be facing in the classroom. (e) A secondary reading program is provided. It is, in effect, an in-service reading program designed to help teachers develop skills in teaching reading in all subject areas. Instruction is given through workshop seminars, on Saturdays, and occasionally during the school hours on school days. (*f*) A home visitation program is provided. Ten certificated teachers serve as home visitors. They keep the parents apprised of the child's adjustment in school and provide information to the teaching staff concerning the home situation. From this information, teachers gain insights and understandings of the problems facing the children of the community.

Detroit, Michigan

Great Cities Program for School Improvement.—This experimental project, covering four years, involved seven schools—both elementary and secondary—approximately five hundred teachers, and more than ten thousand pupils. In each school, additional supportive staff members are supplied: (*a*) a school-community agent, a trained social worker who works with parents and acts as a liaison between the home and school and community agencies, (*b*) a coaching teacher or reading specialist who works with both pupils and teachers to improve their skills, (*c*) a visiting teacher who works with children who have home problems or social or psychological problems which add to their difficulties in school, and (*d*) additional secretarial personnel. Much emphasis is placed upon after-school club activities for children, trips into the community, and the use of the school building as a community center, with a complete program of activities for parents. One of the major emphases is to help parents realize the supporting role they must play in the work of the school and how the school can be an agent for upward mobility.

Additional features of the Detroit program include keeping the school library open two afternoons a week and making it a lending library for the children of that school. The library is also used as a place for study for the children who have no place to study at home. Also noteworthy is the summer-school program which is offered in each building and which tends to offset the academic recession which generally occurs during summer. The summer school serves as a test bed for curriculum modification, a laboratory in which drastic changes can be wrought in the teaching style. Summer sessions are shorter, more informal, more relaxed, and more to the point. Since much of the "filler" and the repetition which many teachers use in lieu of real teaching is cut away, interest and motivation are maintained at a higher level. The traditional barriers between teachers and students tend to drop and even disappear. Classes are smaller, teachers less anxious. Where pressure exists, if it exists at all, it is self-initiated. Individual students receive more attention, whether it be in remedial-enrichment classes or in recreation and club programs. In addition to certified teachers, many college students with special abilities are employed to work with children in such areas as foreign language, instrumental music, art, dramatics, and various club activities.

In Detroit, the project schools are open from eight in the morning until late at night. Attention is focused upon involving the parents and the community. After-school and evening classes ranging from the basic "how-to-read" type of class to those which require considerable manual skill or intellectual endeavor are provided.

Houston, Texas

Talent preservation project.—Twenty classroom teachers were employed at regular salaries during the month of August to stimulate a back-to-school drive. They screened the records of students and visited homes of 1,400 students, urging parents and students to plan early for such matters as the physical examinations, vaccinations, and clothing. They also attempted to help parents realize the importance of further education for their children. Records show that 94 per cent of the project students returned to school in September, 1963. Two hundred dropouts are known to have returned to school, some after an absence of more than two years.

Los Angeles, California

SCOPE (School Community Opportunity Project in Education).—One SCOPE project is the student tutorial education project, which is experimental in nature and uses volunteer college students to tutor "educationally disadvantaged" high-school students. Staffing and housing are provided by the Los Angeles City School Unified District.

Another program, "Workreation," is provided in co-operation with the Los Angeles City Department of Recreation and Parks. It was designed to provide work, study, and recreation activities for high-school dropouts. Many of these boys not only gained skills leading to employment but were able to make up academic work needed for continuation in high school.

Another special pilot program was established to provide job opportunities for individuals of limited employment possibilities. This was set up at the Manual Arts and Jefferson High Adult School. It was designed to provide intensified training in specific fields for persons who traditionally find it difficult to find employment—members of various minority groups or youth from culturally disadvantaged areas. It was designed particularly for young people who had finished high school but were not pursuing any type of post-high-school training.

Milwaukee, Wisconsin

Orientation for in-migrant and transient children.—The use of an "induction center" in the Milwaukee program made it possible to place pupils in small classes where they could be taught by selected teachers. Teachers and supervisors, using special-help techniques, gave intensive assistance to individuals and small groups. After a short time, children from the in-migrant classes made a satisfactory academic adjustment to the regular class. Behavior problems and negative attitudes were minimized if not eradicated by placing pupils in the orientation-center classes in which they could succeed. This change of behavior was evident at both the elementary- and secondary-school levels.

New York City Public Schools

Career guidance program.—This program, aimed at Grades VII-IX, was designed to instil in the pupils hope for the future by making them conscious of their intrinsic worth and dignity. Emphasis was placed on (*a*) creating positive attitudes toward self and society, (*b*) corrective work in the three R's, (*c*) a specially designed curriculum, and (*d*) occupational information and part-time job placement. The program was guidance oriented. Each child met at least once a week with a guidance adviser who was assigned full time to each school. Enrolment in each class was limited to fifteen children.

Co-operative education in municipal government.—This program was designed for youth sixteen years of age or over, or who were juniors or seniors in high school. The aim was to provide for socioeconomic needs and to prevent dropping out of high school, to emphasize the placement of minority groups, and to help youth realize that a trainee must be able to produce on the job. Student trainees were placed in municipal government offices by the board of education. Schedules required them to work alternate one- or two-week periods. Students were enrolled on a twelve-month basis. Supervision was provided by school co-ordinators. Ratings by employers became part of the school records.

Early identification and prevention program.—This program was provided for children, kindergarten through third grade, with some follow-up service in the higher grades. It was designed to identify early the children's abilities, talents, and problems, to determine the incidence and nature of children's problems, and to find out the extent to which maladjustment could be prevented through creation of a sound mental hygiene educational climate. It also sought to identify individual school and community patterns indicative of probable success or failure in adjustment; to refine techniques for identification of abilities, talent, and maladjustment; to provide consultive assistance and to interpret children's behavior to the school staff; and to develop evaluative instruments for appraising the effectiveness of the integrated approach. It also provided specialized service by a guidance team composed of a counselor, a part-time social worker, a part-time psychologist, and a psychiatric consultant. Each team within an individual school developed a pattern of implementation suitable to the needs of that school.

Higher Horizons.—This was a program of enrichment, and of adjustment when necessary, for children from kindergarten through high school. It extended services to bright, average, and slow children in an attempt to make it possible for each child to receive an optimum education. It was designed to identify each child's abilities, interests, and needs and to stimulate him to attain achievement levels commensurate with his abilities. It provided appropriate guidance and counseling. It enlisted the assistance of the parents and the community.

Remedial services were provided. Improvement in reading was emphasized. To give cultural enrichment, trips were provided on a liberal scale. Class size was reduced, and clinical services were established.

One month pre-employment course for dropouts.—This was for students, from Grades IX-XII. Its aims were to help students achieve clear, realistic vocational goals; to prepare them for employment; to assist them in job adjustment; and to provide further guidance and help. Students attended the pre-employment course full time for twenty consecutive school days. They were then placed in employment and followed up on the job (at least once a month) until they reached the age of seventeen; those who lost their jobs were returned to school for job placement or for further instruction.

STEP—School to Employment Program.—This was a program, primarily for youth of fifteen years of age, designed to motivate potential dropouts to continue with their education until graduation, or to otherwise prepare potential dropouts for employment. The program combined school work in the morning, with daily work experience in private industry or a school-work assignment in the afternoon. Close supervision, teaching, and counseling were given on the assigned job by the teacher-co-ordinator. Except in special cases, students remained in the program for one year and were then returned to their regular school program.

Philadelphia, Pennsylvania

The school-community co-ordinator.—Lay people were chosen from among the adults in the community (preferably parents of children in the project schools) to serve as school-community liaison agents. These co-ordinators worked under the direction of the principal. They enlisted the participation of parents in school activities and helped develop leadership in the community. They also referred parents with particular problems to the proper school personnel—nurse, principal, or assistant. In project schools in which a majority of the children were from Spanish-speaking homes, an extra co-ordinator was employed. He carried the usual responsibilities of the co-ordinator and also served as interpreter.

The language-arts teacher.—The position of the language-arts teacher was created in an attempt to meet more effectively the needs of the child who comes to school lacking the experiential supports and communication skills necessary for successful school achievement. These teachers provided an enrichment program for ungraded groups of intermediate children who were considered potentially academically talented. They also developed a program for "late bloomers" at the primary level. This program provided for intensive work in listening and speech, in aural and visual discrimination, and in reading. The language-arts teachers were responsible for developing literature programs, for organizing a program of classroom demonstration for in-service training, and for directing a highly structured reading program in the project schools.

Special tutorial program for suspension cases and discipline problems.—Students who are suspended from a high school, although not reassignable to that school, may be given, with the approval of the district director, a second chance in another regular high school. Extremely difficult first offenders and cases of second and third suspensions may be assigned to the special tutorial program. Such students may continue their high-school programs by attending special classes of approximately ten students, scheduled from 3:30 to 6:30, in the new Technical High School. Students attend two days a week and may take a maximum of two accredited academic and one shop course per semester. Courses of study are the same as those in the regular high school. Students are assigned homework. All written work is carefully checked and much attention is given to the individual. Successful students may apply to the suspension committee for reassignment to a regular high school.

San Francisco, California

School-community improvement program.—This program, which involves several thousand students in six schools, has the following goals:

1. To improve language-arts skills of pupils.
2. To improve human relations and interpersonal situations for pupils, teachers, parents, and members of the community.

3. To increase school participation on the part of parents and members of the community.
4. To improve the training of teachers to better prepare them to meet the needs of culturally deprived pupils.
5. To improve pupil preparation for work.
6. To increase community awareness of the responsibility for employing youth.

Twelve additional staff members were assigned to work with the regular staff of these schools. Special help was provided students with reading problems. Cultural and educational enrichment experiences were provided, such as trips to opera, symphony, ballet, a ranch, and so on. Volunteers were used as teacher-aides and storytellers. College-trained women provided additional help in the classroom. Talents of volunteers were also utilized in art and music. Private and public agencies, churches, and social agencies co-operated to provide programs for pupils and parents.

The drama demonstration project.—This project was designed to show that drama, as an integral part of school curriculum and agency group-work programing, is an effective medium for motivating and then teaching the culturally deprived or disadvantaged child. The project sought to demonstrate that the child so motivated and equipped with learning skills will significantly raise his cultural and vocational aspirations. The in-school program provided opportunity for 112 seventh- and eighth-graders to participate in curriculum activities designed to inspire greater academic achievement. Liaison with community agencies made possible assignments related to the theatrical production. These assignments involved stagecraft, costume-making, puppetry, and dancing. Rehearsal of plays improved reading ability, vocabulary, diction, poise, and interest in school.

CONCLUSION

The focus of public attention on children and youth who are victims of environmental deprivation and the provision of unprecedented amounts of ear-marked funds to find solutions for the problems of dropout, unemployment of youth, and delinquency means inevitably that schools and public education must become involved. Schools must assume new roles. These roles require that the schools alter their objectives and procedures. In essence, schools must really adapt their programs to meet the needs of the pupils to be served rather than require the pupil to adapt to whatever the school may provide.

. . . Kvaraceus points out the inadequacies of the pilot and experimental programs for early discovery and prevention of deviancy and the lack of definitive conclusions as to the efficacy of specific programs. In the relatively few programs attempted in the public schools, there is little uniformity in approach or procedure. There is a tendency toward a consensus on an early approach—the preschool program—but little is known as to what this program should be or how it should be carried out. For the adolescent, there is a tendency toward a consensus on "work oriented" programs—practical training as opposed to academic education. No matter what age group is involved, there is a tendency for the school program (a) to involve parents in some manner, (b) to co-operate with other community agencies, and (c) to call upon the specialists of other disciplines (psychologists, psychiatrists, and social workers) to augment the work of the professional educators.

In the school systems where experimental programs have been attempted, there is a general recognition that new emphases are required in teacher education, both at the preservice and the in-service levels, if a program is to attain any success in reaching alienated children and youth. It is further recognized that the problem is so vast and complex that in spite of public clamor and the expenditure of huge funds no dramatic improvement is likely in the near future.

It is encouraging that public schools are recognizing that they have a responsibility for the deprived and maladjusted that cannot be shifted to any other agency. Only school systems can provide a continuous program over a long period of time—preschool to adult employment—which seems to be essential to achieving any measure of success with delinquency-prone children and youth.

SELECTED READINGS

BERTOLAET, FRED. *Promising Practices from the Projects for the Culturally Deprived.* Chicago: Research Council of the Great Cities Program for School Improvement, 1964.

BROWN, B. FRANK. *The Nongraded High School.* Englewood Cliffs, New Jersey: Prentice-Hall, Inc., 1963.

BURCHILL, GEORGE W. *Work-Study Programs for Alienated Youth.* Chicago: Science Research Associates, Inc., 1962.

COMBS, ARTHUR W. (Chairman of Yearbook Committee), *Perceiving Behaving Becoming.* Yearbook of the Association for Supervision and Curriculum Development. Washington: National Education Association, 1962.

Development: Another Look. Edited by A. Harry Passow and Robert R. Leeper. Report of ASCD Research Institute. Washington: National Education Association, 1964.

GOLDEN, RUTH I. *Improving Patterns of Language Usage.* Detroit, Michigan: Wayne State University Press, 1950.

GOODLAD, JOHN I., and ANDERSON, ROBERT H. *The Nongraded Elementary School.* New York: Harcourt, Brace & World, Inc., 1963.

HARRIS, IRVING D. *Emotional Blocks to Learning.* New York: Free Press of Glencoe, 1961.

HAVIGHURST, ROBERT J. *The Public Schools of Chicago, A Survey for the Board of Education.* Chicago: Board of Education, 1964.

Improving English Skills of Culturally Different Youth in Large Cities. Edited by Arno Jewett, Joseph Mersad, and Doris V. Gunderson. Washington: Office of Education, United States Department of Health, Education, and Welfare, 1964.

Individualizing Instruction. Edited by Nelson B. Henry. Sixty-first Yearbook of the National Society for the Study of Education, Part I. Chicago: University of Chicago Press, 1962.

KVARACEUS, WILLIAM C., and ULRICH, WILLIAM E. *Delinquent Behavior: Principles and Practices.* Washington: National Education Association, 1959.

MORSE, WILLIAM C.; CUTLER, RICHARD L.; and FINK, ALBERT H. *An Analysis of Public School Classes for the Emotionally Handicapped.* A Project of the Council for Exceptional Children of the National Education Association. Ann Arbor: School of Education, University of Michigan, 1964.

SLIM AND NONE—

THE POOR'S TWO CHANCES

ARTHUR PEARL

> *"Loyalty to petrified opinion never yet
> broke a chain or freed a human soul"*
> —MARK TWAIN

Current theory underlying most compensatory programs set up
to help disadvantaged children assumes that their learning
difficulties result from lack of basic preparation—that is, they
are inadequately socialized, haven't sufficient male figures in
their lives, have no books in their homes, can't delay gratification, suffer from accumulated environmental and cultural deficits, etc., etc. Therefore, teachers believe their primary role in
working with these children is to "repair" them and deal with
their handicaps. Programs are based on the premise that poor
children are out-of-step and need reshaping. On the basis of
such orientation, programs are generated that reinforce the inequality of education and the humiliation of the children.

There is an alternative explanation for the inability of the
poor to negotiate the educational system. They fail because
they are never given a chance. The alleged dysfunctionality of
disadvantaged youth is the *result* of being locked out of society,
and lack of motivation and apathy are the *consequences* of de-
nial of opportunity. Education fails with the poor because programs emphasize failure, inadequacy, and thus continue to
stigmatize and spoil the self-image of the youth.[1] Disadvantaged youth are denied opportunities to belong, to help others
and to salvage *themselves*. Educators take a myopic view of

---

[1] See Erving Goffman, *Stigma* (Englewood Cliffs, N. J.: Prentice-Hall,
Inc., 1963), for further elaboration of the spoiled image concept.

school difficulty. They fail to perceive the barriers which stand in the way of the poor students' success—barriers which they have constructed and which they daily reinforce.

Social scientists for some time have noted the difference between the socialization patterns of the poor and the non-poor. The poor are supposed to operate on the pleasure principle— they don't know how to delay need gratification. They have to get their kicks right now. On the other hand, we good middle-class people, who have been adequately socialized, operate on the reality principle—we delay our gratifications for future reward. We never buy a house until we save $20,000 and we never buy a car until we save $3,000. But the poor just aren't like that. . . . What is not understood in this formulation is that the poor don't suffer from a lack of future orientation— they suffer from a lack of future.

There must be a restructuring of employment opportunities so that the poor can find a place. Our schools must provide a learning experience which gives children a sense of contribution, of personal worth, a feeling of anticipation about the future and a certainty that they have a place in it. This is not happening now for the poor youth. The school is an alien land from which he "cuts out." This exclusion leads to another exclusion from a society which cannot employ him because he didn't learn. Without change, we face a frightening prospect of millions of people who are literally expendable—totally unnecessary to the functioning of the society and living with the terrible self-destructive knowledge that they are leaving no imprint on the sands of time, that they are "nobody" and functioning "no place."

Our education system can build in a future for our children only if educators look for what's wrong with current practice and start to truly test their theories. Is a child's non-commitment to education, is his dropping out of school the result of prior handicap—or are these things due to lack of choice, to lack of future, to being locked out? There is a very important difference. If the handicap thesis is fraudulent, everything we're doing makes little sense—whether it's the Job Corps program, the Neighborhood Youth Corps, or the compensatory programs in the schools. More and more the evidence supports the contention that opening up opportunities has a greater impact on poor children than do programs to "repair" them.

WHY EDUCATION IS SO IMPORTANT TODAY

Around the turn of the century, about 94 percent of our people didn't graduate from high school. It caused little concern because there was a variety of absorption systems—albeit imperfect—available to the poor. But today, at least four years of education beyond high school are necessary for upward movement in our economic system—and this becomes increasingly more true as traditional ways of making a living become obsolete. At one time there were many possibilities for entrance and upward mobility for most of our citizens.

(a) First, they could market their unskilled labor, learn on the job and move up. But today, machines are replacing men. Despite the fact that we've had well over a 30 percent increase in productivity over the past five years, there are no more people turning out products than there were five years ago. And the better jobs demand credentials.

(b) Another entrance was farming. But today agriculture is our most automated industry—over a million jobs have been eaten up by machines in the last six or seven years, despite the fact that agricultural surpluses continue to grow, and another million jobs will be destroyed in the next decade.

(c) Still another possibility was entrepreneurial enterprise. But today, the street peddler cannot compete seriously with a department store, nor the small machinist with the major auto companies.

(d) Finally, the fields of education, welfare, recreation were available to the poor because there were not the prerequisites for education which are currently demanded. Ralph Bunche says that the teacher who had the most profound effect on him had an eighth grade education when she began to teach.

These absorption systems are today closed off. Two fundamental things have affected dramatically the way we can be absorbed into society: (1) automation—eating up the jobs or dead-ending them and (2) the need for a credential to get into the largest and fastest-growing industries.

The biggest, fastest-growing industry in the country is education. It has to be the biggest ten years from now because by 1975 there will be 40 million more people in the country, and the median age will be less than twenty-five. With preschool education, fewer dropouts, more people going to college, the lowering of the teacher-pupil ratio, the 2.3 million teachers we now have could easily be expanded to 5 or even 10 million. The equivalent is true in medicine, recreation, welfare—for all the human services and for all the skilled jobs for which the system demands a college education for any significant involvement.[2]

Without credentials for the professions and for the new skilled and managerial jobs in private industry, the poor are locked out of participation in the economic life of the country. And yet, the poor need education more than anyone else. It wasn't a great tragedy that Barry Goldwater couldn't get through the first year of college because his family could find things for him to do around the store. But the poor have no such resources—they must have an education. *Education is the only equalizer they have.* Nevertheless, because of the way education is now structured, it's unlikely that very many of the poor will get the credential. Why?

WHAT HAPPENS TO DISADVANTAGED YOUTH IN SCHOOL

(a) *We "sort."*

The teachers' responsibility is to teach, but instead we engage in self-fulfilling prophecy. We decide that certain people cannot be educated; we refuse to educate them; they grow up uneducated; and we pride ourselves on our exceedingly accurate predictive index. This sorting principle puts a stamp on pupils very early in the game which follows them all the way through the production line until they come out labeled "dumb" or "smart" because there has been very little done to change the initial judgment. This distorts the educational function—teachers are supposed to *change* persons; they are not there only to sort and stamp.

(b) *We refuse to educate the poor.*

Very few of the poor will get a chance to get the all-important credential because very few will be placed in tracks which lead to a college degree. As an example, consider the schools in Washington, D. C.

In a school where middle-class white students go, where the

---

[2] For a full discussion on how to create millions of jobs in the human services, read: Arthur Pearl and Frank Riessman, *New Careers for the Poor* (New York: Free Press of Glencoe, Inc., 1965).

median income for the parents is over $10,000 a year, 92 percent of all students are in college-bound tracks. In another school in Washington, D. C., where 100 percent of the students are Negro and parents make less than $4,000 a year, 85 percent are in non-college-bound tracks.[3] In other words, almost 9 out of 10 of the Negro youth are being told they are not college material (and thus they cannot get a credential). In effect, these youths are being told that they have no future except possibly in menial service occupations. Thus, selective education imposes a rigid class structure upon the poor—especially the Negro poor. . . . At the present time, the *best* predictor of a future college education is the occupation of the student's father. If the student has a parent with less than a college education, who works at a blue-collar job if he works at all, and is Negro, Mexican or Indian, the probability of being a dropout is more than three times as great as a student who is reared by professional, well-educated, "white" parents.

(c) *We discriminate.*

How do we appraise peoples' intelligence or lack of it? If they talk like we do, or act like we do, obviously they have to be intelligent. If they don't, equally obviously, they must be non-intelligent. Nothing could be more logical. So we establish a series of tests that we devise for us, standardize on us, administer in situations in which we feel comfortable, and on this basis, we determine who is educable or non-educable. And then we spend millions of dollars—because some people think this process isn't really fair—to look for that culture-free or culture-fair test. It's a totally unrealizable goal, and yet there is little questioning whether it is essential to find this kind of test at all. Why is it really important to label children "dumb" or "smart" early in the game?

This is not to say that all people are equal, but rather, that no valid measures of intellectual capacity have been developed, and perhaps it doesn't really matter, since few of us function anywhere near capacity.

The argument for homogeneous grouping reduces to convenience for the teacher. The teacher takes the position, quite logically, that they all have different abilities. But, even in homogeneous groups, the children are not all identical. No matter how you group them, they're different people. They just hap-

---

[3] Elias Blake, "Teaching in Washington, D. C. Schools," *Integrated Education* (June 1965).

pen to be somewhat similar on a particular score, but they're different in background, sex, learning styles, tempo and timing. Only one variable has been isolated as a result of this grouping, but the teacher believes her job will be easier because she can operate at the same pace.

By the same token, however, we begin to water down the curriculum successively as we begin to label people as slower learners or less able. Those who learn slower are going to get less. Those in the second track are going to get a second-class education, and a third-class education will be offered those in the third track.

Evidence, however, doesn't support the thesis. No evidence shows that homogeneous groupings work better *for the students*. Both here and in England,[4] it appears that a bright child learns no better when placed with similar children than when grouped heterogeneously. And the poor children—the so-called "dumb kids"—*are* hurt by the grouping. They end up doing worse than the so-called "dumbbell" left in a heterogeneous group. Grouping doesn't help the educational process. Most of these kids aren't stupid, despite our judgment. They know who's being grouped with whom even if the labeling is couched innocuously as "bluebirds." If *they* don't know, the other students will tell them. They soon learn to fulfill the role expected of them and—most destructive of all—learn to believe in the "truth" of the school's judgment of them.

If you're put in basic tracks, if you're given watered-down curriculum, if you're treated as if you're dumb, there is not much you can get from school.

Although evidence does not support homogeneous grouping as educationally valid, it *is* definitely discriminatory. There's no question that the child who goes into the smart track tends to be the youth whose parents are well educated. Those who go into the dumb class are those who didn't choose their parents very well. The track system is a discriminatory process—and it reinstitutes a segregated school system within the school. There are interracial schools in this country where almost all the students on the honor track are "white" and almost all the kids in the lowest tracks are Negro or Spanish-speaking. This is not a "racially balanced" school. It's a totally segregated school, but

---

4 See for example J. W. B. Douglas, "Streaming by Ability," *New Society* (February 6, 1964), p. 6.

the segregation takes place within a building. The segregation is just as intense, just as invidious, just as pernicious as if it were a racially exclusive school.

WHY ARE THE SCHOOLS ALIEN TO THE POOR?

The Rules.

There is no logic or rationale for most school rules. There is a minimum tolerance for differences—and much more tolerance if you're non-poor than if you're poor. For example, if students don't dress or wear their hair in the determined style, they can be asked to leave school. This can happen despite the fact that there's no data to support the contention that learning is disturbed when students wear boots or long hair.

It is not surprising that youth try to establish an identity, often through bizarre dress and hairdos. What is surprising is that adults have the effrontery to meddle in what is essentially someone's own private business. . . . *The real issue is:* Why do young people decide to express themselves in these ways? Why are there so few gratifications for poor youth in our society that they reject becoming part of the establishment? Whenever I see bizarre behavior in students, my initial reaction is to look to what the school is doing to *cause* the behavior.

School rules are differentially enforced. What is tolerably deviant and what is not depends on the child's background. In the case of middle-class boys, deviance will often be interpreted as a childish prank, a phase which the student will outgrow; in cases involving poor youth, deviant behavior is interpreted as a signal of emerging criminality which must be nipped in the buds.

It's important to insist on logical reasons for the rules of behavior in the schools. If education is to be rational, if it is to be a system which enables youth to learn to think clearly, to learn to work through problems, then a rule shouldn't be ad hoc. A rule shouldn't be made to conform to the personal prejudices of a school board or the personal whim of principals. School rules should be backed by empirical evidence that they are supportive or negative to the learning process; that they endanger health or safety of another person or school property.

Powerlessness.

The more deprived the background of the child, the less power he has in our educational system. To be totally powerless is to be placed in a terribly disquieting and uncomfortable position. Humans do not like to feel that they're nothing, that they have no control over their destiny. No one likes that feeling. . . . It's quite clear that there's a great difference between the poor and non-poor and their ability to defend themselves in the school system. A child of white middle-class parents has things going for him when he gets into trouble. He can talk the language of the system, and teachers and principals are much more likely to listen to him. But he can also turn to his parents. His parents also talk the language; they can negotiate for their child. The middle-class parent can do things for his child—he can hire a tutor, a psychologist, a lawyer; if worse comes to worse, he can take his child out of the system and put him in a private school. The poor have no escape, no voice. The whole system is a colonial imposition on them—made up by others, for others.

Meaningless Material.

For the poor, education is totally removed from their life experience. It cannot be related to their backgrounds or immediate circumstances. In middle-class families, parents can talk "algebra" with their child; the material he gets has some meaning in the context of his life. The material is presented in a familiar language, in an understandable style and at an acceptable pace. None of this is true for most disadvantaged youngsters.

Some social scientists have advocated replacing teachers with machines, insisting that machines can do everything teachers can do. There may be sense in this position because machines are more flexible (more human) than teachers. Machines, at least, can be made to change their pace. The child operates a learning machine and he operates it at the pace at which he is learning. Teachers cannot be so manipulated. They operate at one pace, at one track, and with one language style.

No linkage with a future.

Where do youth go with schooling? A middle-class child may find rules stupid, may bridle because of his powerlessness, may find most of the courses meaningless—but these are obstacles he is willing to suffer because he knows at the end there's a place for him.

What about the non-college-bound youth? What is that track leading to? What is he getting out of the educational experience? He's being told to stay in school to become an unemployed high school graduate. For the most part, a high school diploma leads to menial dead-end jobs. There is no meaningful linkage with the future for anyone who is not in a college-bound program in school. Vocational education is, to a large extent, antiquated. It's antiquated because the job may be disappearing. Or if the job is still viable, the youth does not have the informal credentials; e.g., many of the building trades offer preference in apprentice programs to union members' children. (We can't really reshuffle fathers as part of the vocational education program.) Much of the vocational education is delusional—a complex fabrication which disguises the reality of the world and perpetuates the inappropriate procedures which only ostensibly prepare youth for the world of work.

No gratifications.

Jobs aren't everything. Dignity and a sense of self-worth are also extremely important. And here the school's effect is the most devastating of all. We rarely allow students the opportunity to become a person in the school. We rarely allow students to have a sense of competence. . . . Schools permit some to obtain competence and these are the "brains" and the "athletes." But the largest number are subjected to a humiliating and degrading experience. The middle-class child gets the rewards bestowed by teachers who understand him because he dresses and behaves appropriately. The deprived youngster, for the most part, goes to school every day to be punished. He gets no reward from the system. Psychologists and social workers all treat his "deficiencies." But these are only more overlords reinforcing humiliation.

Not only do the poor fail to develop a sense of mastery, they are not permitted a sense of contribution. They are not allowed to be important to anyone else. These gratifications must be built into the school system if it's going to have real value to our children. If they have no conviction that they're mastering meaningful skills, that they're contributing to others, that they're a member of something, then it's hard to expect them to give very much to the school program. If they feel that the school is run by outsiders, with rules made by outsiders, in which they have little power to make decisions and no understanding of those that are made; if it leads nowhere and they're getting no "kicks" out of it—how do we expect them to put out very much?

HOW DO WE CONSTRUCT A
DIFFERENT KIND OF SCHOOL?

(a) *Test cherished beliefs.*

We "know" that if we reduce class size, education will be better. We "know" it's true that if we give teachers time to prepare for classes, they will do better. We "know" that if we improve pupil personnel services and pour in psychologists and social workers, we can overcome children's handicaps. And yet, there is *no* evidence to support this "knowledge." And if we researched it, I would predict that very few of these increments would pay off one iota over an extended period of time.

We had better begin to look at some of our most treasured, heartfelt assumptions and test them out. If education is to pay off, we have to recognize that it wasn't set up for the convenience of the teacher. We didn't really set up public education to keep middle-class adults off the streets. Schools were established to help the students, and we'd better test if it is working as intended.

Teachers have to accept the responsibility for teaching human beings to learn. One of the things I have tried to get across in my classes is that when I give a test it is not a test of my students. It is a test of me. I am testing whether or not I am a good teacher. If the students get poor grades, I interpret that as an indication that I failed to get the course material across. . . . After one of my tests, one of my students came up and patted me on the back and said: "Hate to break it to you, buddy, but you flunked." . . . And he was right. But this attitude is hard for teachers to accept. There is no other system in the world in which we flunk a product. We do a rotten job, and we flunk the student. We fail to teach, and the students are held accountable.

(b) *Employ the student as teacher.*

We have to build in the gratification which comes from having a sense of contribution—a sense of value to others. The student role as a passive sitter and absorber of knowledge is not particularly gratifying. The teaching role is. So one of the things to recognize is that it would be better if teachers did some learning and the learners did some teaching right from the very beginning. All students, particularly non-achieving students should be given the opportunity to help other students. Teachers should be prepared to give special assistance so that even the "worst" students can learn first what the "best" students will have to learn later. It doesn't take too much imagination to bring this kind of thing off. In one study in which school dropouts were trained as research aides and taught some complex statistical operation, the aides later acted as instructors to graduate students.[5]

(c) *Build quality control research into education.*

At the present time education is unmerciful because we know not what we do. We haven't the slightest inkling of what goes on in the classroom. It doesn't help to reduce class size if the teacher with fifteen students does exactly the same thing as the teacher with twenty-five students.

Schoolroom activities must be systematically monitored and the information fed back to teachers. Students, especially troublemaking students, should be interviewed and their impressions relayed to teachers. Teachers probably more than any others could heed Robert Burns' advice "to see ourselves as others see us" (many students feel that Burns had teachers in mind when he entitled the poem from which the line above was excerpted, "Ode to a Louse"). Amazing changes occur in teachers when they have an opportunity to review their performance and work out alternative strategies for the classroom. Each new effort of the teacher can also be monitored to determine if the projected approach was put into effect, and altered again if the desired impact was not achieved.

OPENING UP EDUCATION

At the present time many different functions are incorporated into the teacher role. If we analyze what a teacher does, we find many things that require little skill, training or experience; many things that require some skill; and some things that require all the professional expertise at his command.

An alternative route to the teaching credential should be established. We can begin with a *teacher aide* position. Teacher

---

[5] Pearl and Riessman, p. 181.

aides could operate audio-visual equipment, monitor hallways and lunch yards, perform clerical functions, read to children, and tutor students in need of special attention.

As they demonstrate ability, they should be given college credit for their on-the-job experience and be encouraged to enroll in essential college courses offered at a city college, university or extension division. These aides, with experience and some back-up courses, in two years can advance to the position of *teacher assistant*. The assistant can take on additional responsibility; can teach under the supervision of a professional and lead small group discussions. In another two or three years, having gained additional college credit for the increased work experience, and having taken some additional needed courses, the teaching assistant could become a *teaching associate*, performing much like a teacher does now. In another couple of years, the associate could become a *fully-certified teacher*. The role of the fully-certified teacher would necessarily be considerably different from his role today. The certified teacher would be a specialist, a consultant, a trainer, and a supervisor for those in training.

These various sub-professionals can liberate the teacher to truly reach every child in the classroom. Her assistants can lead small groups while the teacher can give individual attention to those who need special aid. Aides can help children with homework in the evenings; or they can communicate with the parents and pull them more closely into the educational experience.

Getting a teaching credential via the route of job-first, education later, could take eight to ten years. But throughout those years, a person is doing useful work. If motivation or ability are limited, he can remain at a landing and still make a contribution. If he wishes to go all the way, the system is open all the way to the credential. . . . This is not merely a proposal for aides in the schools. We have had aides in the schools for years. But aides to date have been limited to menial, dead-ended tasks, and a menial dead-ended job in the school is not much different from the menial, dead-ended job in any other field. . . . It's the opportunity to move up that is the essence of a "new careers" program.[6]

If we don't create this parallel road—this apprentice ap-

---

[6] For more detailed explanation, see Pearl and Riessman, *New Careers for the Poor.*

proach of on-the-job training, back-up college courses, and increasing responsibility which can ultimately lead to a professional status—we create two problems: (1) We'll continue to have alien schools—schools which belong to outsiders and never can attract and hold the students; and (2) we'll lock out the poor from the largest and fastest-growing industry in our country.

The teachers' aides should be recruited from the neighborhoods around the school. If this is done, a different atmosphere can be created in the school. School is then no longer a place where some people drop in from the suburbs at 8:00 A.M. and are sure they're on the way home by 3:30 P.M. Today, slum schools cannot be accurately described as neighborhood schools because the teachers never live in the neighborhood. One of the problems of the slum school is that it is difficult for a working parent to talk to a teacher because the teacher is miles away by the time the parent comes home from work. One way to create a neighborhood school is to have teaching resources in the neighborhood.

There are some who feel that this concept tends to further enclose the ghetto. However, if career development is institutionalized in the school system, and the indigenous poor are able to move in the system, they become eligible to move anywhere such jobs are available, thus facilitating a move out of the ghetto. At the present time, there's no way in the world to truly eliminate segregation because true integration requires economic liberation. Housing and school segregation will be reduced much faster when many more people have the credentials to work in higher paying jobs and have the financial resources to buy houses anywhere.

HOW CAN UNIVERSITIES RESPOND TO SOCIETY'S NEED FOR "NEW CAREERS"?

There are many who oppose any tinkering with higher education procedures, even though the great need to replenish the "vanishing professional" in all the expanding human services will not be met by the universities as they function today. It is somehow assumed that the model of higher education has stood the test of time and any effort to provide an alternative path in which "learning by doing" is heavily emphasized would be retrogressive.

Higher education needs to be critically evaluated. Universities have not achieved the ultimate. In fact, it may not be straining truth to suggest that higher education is the most atavistic of all systems—that it was made obsolete with the invention of the printing press. It made sense to go to the place where the book was when there was only one book. However, since books are both plentiful and relatively inexpensive, some of the palpable weaknesses of the system should be explored.

Higher education as currently constituted in the helping services provides very little truly simulated experience before a person is exposed to the pressure of the job. Practice teaching and field experience are trivial and only minimally relevant to job experience. A person may go to school for four years before he is exposed to a classroom situation and can then decide whether teaching is for him. Similar agonizing reappraisals are forced upon prospective candidates for careers in social work, medicine, law, etc. The problem of this "all or nothing" nature of training is further complicated because there are no intermediate landings in human service professions. A person can train for nearly a decade and become an almost-doctor (and probably then sell pharmaceutical supplies), go to school for seven years to become an almost-lawyer, -psychologist, -social worker, -teacher, etc. The lack of intermediate positions in the professions puts considerable pressure on credentialing agencies to pass unqualified candidates to professional status because the alternative of giving no reward for such investment of time, money and energy is unconscionable.

The new careers proposal, providing an alternative path to a credential, allows for much greater flexibility in the education process. A person unable to attain the terminal position can be offered an intermediate office commensurate with his ability and competencies. A person can utilize a number of combinations of training experiences to obtain a degree. Some might start off in on-the-job training and in a few years cross over to a university experience (at the equivalent grade); or a person may be at loose ends at the end of two years at a university and cross over to the learning-on-the-job alternative at an intermediate position (e.g., teacher-assistant). The existence of a number of career landings and the possibility of cross-over allows for much greater opportunity for persons to make meaningful contributions to society. While this increased flexibility would be of particular significance to the poor who are denied the conventional path to professional status, such a program would be valuable to affluent students who have difficulty negotiating the current route to a credential.

WHY WE MUST BEGIN TO MAKE CHANGES IN PUBLIC SCHOOLS

Pressure for educational change will continue to increase because of the "functional illiterates" that the schools are graduating or pushing out by the millions; because of the expanding need for more professionals; because of the millions who are locked out of the economic system for lack of a credential. There will be an increasing need to link up the population that needs jobs with the jobs that need doing.

Total change in the schools is not possible quickly. But demonstration projects can be set up which can be beachheads from which more extensive efforts can be launched. Demonstration projects can be started with "soft" money—funds from the Elementary and Secondary Education Act, the Anti-Poverty Act, the National Institute of Mental Health or the Ford Foundation. Small demonstrations can be expanded as effectiveness is demonstrated.

SUMMARY

It has been argued here that students do poorly in school primarily because the schools offer them little chance to do otherwise. Schooling for many youths is a degrading process and it is more likely to be degrading if the student is economically disadvantaged. Schools attack the dignity of youth through irrational rules, imposed powerlessness and senseless curriculum. The insistence on conformity is antagonistic to the goal of preparing citizens for democratic responsibility. There are alternatives to current practice. Opening up the school to the student will produce dramatic changes in attitude and behavior. Bringing the student into an active teacher role, making the classroom a cooperative venture and allowing the student to progress through negotiable steps to a certified educator (if he so desires) will be a welcome relief from the tedium of school as it now exists for rich and poor alike.

IT'S TIME

FOR A MOONSHOT IN EDUCATION

FRANK RIESSMAN

In the past several years, enormous interest has been expressed concerning the education of the disadvantaged, inner-city child. Programs being developed in various cities throughout the United States have met with varying success.

* The employment of the poor themselves as assistant teachers and parent education coordinators appears to be successful in Philadelphia and Pittsburgh.
* Assistant Superintendent of Schools, Samuel Sheppard, a Negro, has quickly brought youngsters up to grade level in St. Louis with special motivational appeals to parents and youngsters and a new "listening" approach to teachers.
* Homework helpers have been found to be effective at Mobilization for Youth in New York.
* Montessorian techniques have achieved results in Los Angeles and Mount Vernon.
* Imaginative, "hip" lessons combined with role playing have proved exciting in Syracuse.
* New readers have improved reading levels of educationally deprived youngsters in Detroit.
* New approaches used by the Army have overcome illiteracy in adults with surprising speed.
* Programed learning has had some marked effects on dropouts in New York and prisoners in Alabama whose level of intellectual functioning was quite low.
* In Flint, Michigan, disadvantaged sixth-grade youngsters with reading difficulties helped fourth-grade children who

had reading problems, and amazingly, the performance of both groups went up.

* Special teacher preparation developed at Hunter College in New York appears to aid teachers in "slum" areas.

These are just a few illustrations of promising approaches. Actually a great many other illustrations could be noted, such as team teaching, non-graded classes, multiple periods, the use of the Initial Teaching Alphabet, Warner's "organics" method, and Catherine Stern's reading improvement approach.

But despite these encouraging reports, the goals for the disadvantaged child still remain surprisingly low. In essence, most of the programs still talk about bringing the deprived child up to grade level as though this were some lofty, marvelous objective. Actually, a subtle pessimism runs through much of the discussion of the education of the poor. Perhaps it is time to consider not the piecemeal use of this technique here and that technique there, but a combination of a variety of approaches that seem to work both on a practical and theoretic basis. The present pessimism, whether unconscious or not, is really based upon the failure to produce consistent dramatic improvement in adolescents, dropouts, and adults on a large scale. Thus there has been a retreat from this potentially exciting objective and most of the effort, if not all, is going into pre-school education.

Whatever good results are achieved in improving performance, raising the I.Q., etc. in the pre-school program, will come to naught unless the schools themselves are changed to respond to the disadvantaged youngster. It is easy enough to get preschool improvement. Deutsch, Strodbeck, Grey, and others have all rather readily produced this improvement, and perhaps most dramatically, the Montessorians have done likewise. The problem is keeping this improvement—preventing fallback—as the child progresses through the grades. Martin Deutsch, an extremely honest and thoughtful advocate of preschool approaches, recently stated that these improvements drop away quite rapidly when the children are returned to the traditional school program. Similarly, in Ypsilanti, Michigan, Dr. David Weikart produced sharp rises in the average I.Q.'s of deprived children through special pre-school experimental programs. But when these children entered the traditional kindergarten, their scores declined.[1]

In light of Deutsch's and Weikart's findings with regard to the non-

Thus the pre-school panacea seems to be a distraction from the main arena, which must be the schools themselves. They must develop a rounded, intensive program combining what has been learned in many areas of the country, and aim for the moon; that is, aiming, not to bring a few selected children up to grade level, but for dramatic, powerful improvement in large numbers of disadvantaged children. The present period combines strong demands of the Civil Rights movement for quality integrated education with tremendous financial support from the Federal Government. In this climate it would seem that a revolutionary breakthrough in the education of the poor can now be planned. It is truly time to aim for the moon and not accept improvement only up to grade level.

What then should the ingredients be for our projected revolution in education? Should we combine all the various features that have worked in a kind of potpourri? Or should we rather selectively choose approaches based on a meaningful theoretic analysis which offers an explanation in a coherent fashion of why they have worked? The latter approach is preferred because it is not only more scientific and theoretically more meaningful, but probably is less expensive, too.

Also the new program could be placed within the framework of the developing educational parks or educational complexes which would allow for economic utilization of a great variety of new techniques and facilities (educational TV, programed learning, team teaching, etc.) under one roof. But it is not necessary or essential for our moonshot.

Let us look at the outlines of such a program.

---

lasting effects of pre-school stimulation in the traditional framework, the present hoopla over Operation Head Start and its supposed success is highly questionable. It has been said that improvements have been achieved through Operation Head Start and that the evaluation studies being conducted will show this. I do not doubt it; but it is far too early to determine how enduring these improvements will be. Much greater gains have been made in the programs mentioned above, but they do not appear to remain when the child is returned to the standard school curriculum. Head Start gains, which are probably far less than those achieved in other programs because Head Start is not as intensive, will undoubtedly diminish rapidly as the children "progress" through the school. As S. M. Miller states:

"Pre-school programs should not be used as a substitute for interventions at later stages of the school life-cycle. The best guess today is that interventions at the later stages can be effective without interventions at the early, but that interventions at the early stages without intervention at the later will have very limited payoff." (*Educational Strategies,* Syracuse University, 1965, unpublished ms.).

THE NEW MANPOWER

Perhaps the major complaint in the schools today is the large classes that each teacher must manage. The ratio of students to teachers is frequently greater than thirty to one. New manpower to assist the badly overworked teacher is the paramount need of the day. Where can it be found?

The utilization of large numbers of people drawn from the ranks of the poor themselves, so-called nonprofessionals, to serve as teacher assistants, teacher aides, parent-teacher coordinators and the like may be the answer.

Currently in the classroom there is but one designated role— teacher. Incorporated in that role are a great number of diverse functions—the teacher is an educator, but he is also a clerk, a custodian, an operator of audio-visual equipment, and an audio-version of a printed book. In many slum schools the impression gained is that the teacher is part lion tamer and part warehouseman. The latter roles must be eliminated and many of the others assumed by less qualified personnel.

The use of this new kind of nonprofessional manpower would serve a number of positive functions:

1) It would free teachers from the many nonprofessional tasks they now perform, e.g. taking attendance, helping children put on their boots, tying children's shoelaces, running moving-picture projectors, taking youngsters on trips, etc. The new teacher aides would take over many of these tasks, freeing teachers for their basic professional assignment, teaching—and teaching creatively.

2) The nonprofessionals (especially males), drawn from the ranks of the poor, would serve as excellent role models for the disadvantaged youngsters in the schools; the youngsters would see that it is possible for people like themselves, drawn from their own neighborhood, to "make it" in the system.

3) Communication between the trained nonprofessional and the disadvantaged youngster would probably be good since the nonprofessional drawn from the neighborhood speaks the language of the poor and understands his peers. Many of the advantages of peer learning or learning from people at the same level would be utilized.

4) The atmosphere of the school will be quite different, and many of the management problems that are anticipated in the urban, newly integrated schools might be dissipated.[2]

---

[2] The tremendous shortage of school personnel, predicted for the next

It goes without saying that the use of aides would not be imposed upon teachers. In fact, teachers' associations and unions should participate in the entire planning for the use of nonprofessionals, and guarantees should be introduced to ensure that no aide infringes on professional domain by engaging in actual teaching or other purely professional functions.

Probably the best way to introduce nonprofessionals into the system is to ask teachers to volunteer to accept an aide to assist them. The teachers who decide to use aides can then define the tasks on which they would like nonprofessional assistance. (They may also receive consultation on this from the planners.) It is quite likely that if the aides are really helpful, the program will spread and other teachers will request such assistance for their classrooms. In this way the idea can be institutionalized with the full cooperation of the professional staff and the new professional-nonprofessional team can be built on a solid foundation.

Teachers not only need new manpower to assist them in the classroom but they need a new approach as well. Too often nowadays, teachers are being asked to act like psychologists (understand the underlying emotional conflicts of the child); like sociologists (appreciate the environment and culture of the deprived); like prison guards (keep order and prevent violence); like parents (love the child); and, like ministers (impart the right values).

It is time that teachers concentrated on teaching, and develop and apply that art and science to the utmost. It is toward this objective that the following techniques are directed. But before turning to the techniques themselves, a word about basic classroom strategy.

BASIC CLASSROOM STRATEGY

Everything the teacher says and does in the classroom should be related to learning. He should repeat over and over and over again: "I am here to teach and you are here to learn." This

---

decade, might be drastically reduced through the employment of one million nonprofessionals in the schools. For a more detailed description of how nonprofessionals could serve the schools, see Arthur Pearl and Frank Riessman, *New Careers for the Poor* (Free Press of Glencoe, 1965), Chapter 4. *It is axiomatic that teachers would have to be trained and assisted in utilizing the nonprofessionals.*

should be expressed in the teacher's every action and should be related to every rule and value.

Thus all rules related to punctuality, aggression, etc. should be strictly oriented toward their usefulness in relation to learning. (E.g. "We can't conduct a class if children fight, come late, walk around, etc.") This is not a minister informing children about values—that fighting is "bad." It is, rather, a teacher conducting a class.

GOALS AND TECHNIQUES

The emphasis on teaching technology is very important in the entire effort. Teachers cannot be expected to become sociologists or psychologists and acquire an intensive understanding of the psychology and culture of the poor. Rather, they simply must come to understand something about how the techniques they are utilizing are related to the style and strength of the poor, but the emphasis must be on the techniques themselves. As teachers successfully utilize these techniques, their confidence will improve and their motivation will be enhanced. Our accent, therefore, is on giving the teachers what they want, namely know-how.

The techniques to be employed should be based fundamentally on the goals one is striving for with the disadvantaged. I do not have the goal of simply producing a carbon copy of the middle-class child.[3] To aim for this middle-class replica is not only inappropriate in principle, but actually not easily achievable in practice. The disadvantaged child will probably resist this objective and to the extent that he acquieces, will become a poor edition of the middle-class youngster—a very faded carbon copy. My objective, therefore, is to build on the strengths of the inner-city child, not to deny them or suppress them, but rather to utilize them as the key to developing, for example, language and interest in language. But my concern for building

_____

[3] The real question for those who want to "middle classize" the disadvantaged child, relates to which middle class and which middle-class goals and values—the professional upper middle class; the anti-intellectual lower middle class; the new hip class that has adopted much of the speech and some of the manners of various disadvantaged subcultures; the progressive student left, etc. Furthermore, isn't it possible that the disadvantaged youngster will selectively choose those middle-class characteristics that at least articulate some of his own traditions and feelings?

on the strengths of the disadvantaged child is not simply so
that he can be more efficiently brought into the mainstream of
American life; rather, I want also to have him bring into this
mainstream some of his characteristics: his style, his pep, his
vitality, his demand that the school not be boring and dull, his
rich feeling for metaphor and colorful language.

In another area one group of disadvantaged people in America, the Negro people, have made an enormous contribution to
the mainstream of American life through their articulate, non-
compromising demands for integration "now." These people
have brought a new morality to American life as a whole. To
the extent that we are beginning to move toward integration
through law and practice we are beginning to hold our heads
up high and feel again like democratic, ethical, human Americans. This is what one minority disadvantaged group has given
us in another area of life. In education, likewise, the mainstream of American life can profit from what the various
groups among the poor can bring to the school system, both in
terms of the demands made upon the system that it be peppier,
livelier, more vital, more down-to-earth, more real, and in the
style and interests brought to the school. This style will enable
the school to become far less bookish and will enable it to utilize a great variety of styles—an action style, a physical style, a
visual style—far more than the over-utilized and over-empha-
sized reading-lecture styles traditionally in vogue.

The techniques that I will discuss are uniquely related to
these goals and to the belief that there is a positive style in the
disadvantaged which can be utilized to the great benefit of all
classes. But if this goal is not accepted, the techniques can still
be utilized with varying degrees of effectiveness. Thus the
reader can go on even if he does not accept the overall objective.

THE DIALECT GAME

The best way to illustrate the relationship of the teaching
technology I am advocating and the goals being put forth is to
take a look at one very simple technique which I learned from
a teacher who evolved it out of her own practice. I call it the
dialect game.

One day a youngster said to this teacher, "Do you hear that
boid outside the window?" The teacher responded, "That's not

a boid, it's a bird." Following the old joke, the youngster replied, "He choips just like a boid." It is fairly clear that this way
of teaching the youngster the standard pronunciations of words
might not only be unsuccessful in its avowed objective, but
might, in addition, produce cognitive confusion about the object itself.

The teacher thereupon decided that it would be very easy to
teach youngsters the standard pronunciations if they would not
be required to reject their own dialects, their slang, their hip
language. So she decided to play a game taking any word at
random and asking the youngsters how it would be said in their
language and how it should be said in the standard language.
The youngsters, as well as the teacher, found this game very
exciting and both learned a great deal. They now were learning
the new words as they might learn a foreign language and they
were discovering that their own language was perfectly acceptable and merely had to be used in the proper circumstances—
in their discussions with friends, family, and on the street,
while for formal purposes, another language was appropriate
and was being taught in the school. But something else happened in this situation. The youngsters began to become very
much interested in language as such; e.g. in discussing the hip
word "cool," it was decided that words like "calm" and "collected" and the advanced word "nonchalant" were fairly appropriate synonyms. However, it was also noted that these words
were not perfect equivalents of "cool" and thus, indirectly, language nuances were taught. Youngsters began to understand
why we use certain foreign words that are not completely trans-
latable, e.g. "coup d'etat," because they have special connota-
tions or overtones in their original language which our language cannot duplicate.

They learned something else, too. They learned that their
own language was not something negative to be denied or sup-
pressed, but that actually many of their words had nuances and
meanings which had not been fully acquired in the standard
language and that therefore the slang and hip words had been
adopted by the larger culture. So today "jazz," "cooling it,"
"copping out" and many, many other rich, colorful words are in
accepted usage in the English language in conversation, etc.
This is building on their positives, not rejecting them, and
bringing their strengths and interests into the mainstream of
our life.

There are a number of other simple adaptations of this dialect game. Recently in tutoring a disadvantaged high school student in English, I employed a hiptionary in a completely systematic and formal fashion. The first and rather immediate result was that the student learned a great many new English word definitions for the "hip" words with which she was long familiar:

Hip Word [4]	Definition
"bug"	to disturb, bother, annoy
"cop out"	to avoid conflict by running away, not considered admirable or honorably accepted
"cool it"	to be quiet, peaceful, tranquil
"far out"	not comprehendable
"weak"	inadequate, inappropriate

Words such as "tranquil," "inappropriate," etc. were not known by this youngster, but through use of the hip word game she quickly became familiar with them and derived great pleasure from a new-found use of various "big" words.

Another interesting illustration is furnished by the problem of teaching English to Puerto Rican and Mexican children entering our school systems in New York, California and other parts of the country. The typical tendency is to force these youngsters not to speak any of their mother tongue, namely Spanish, but rather to insist that they speak only English, on the supposition that this would be the best way of their acquiring the English language. While this may be a perfectly acceptable way of teaching language to an adult in certain contexts, when it is associated in the child with rejection of his minority culture (something he experiences quite frequently), he is not likely to be an apt pupil in the new language. Furthermore, he is constantly in the inferior position of having to acquire this language while the remainder of the youngsters in the class already know it. The dialect game can be utilized beautifully to reverse the whole procedure. Instead of emphasizing the need for the Spanish children to learn English, the situation can be reversed for part of the day, and the Spanish children can be instructed to teach Spanish to the American children. In other words, both languages become important in the class. The English-speaking children have an opportunity

---

[4] The words in this list were taken from a hiptionary entitled, "The Other Language" developed by Anthony Romeo at Mobilization for Youth, January 1962, unpublished.

to learn a foreign language, presumably a positive benefit when that language is French or Latin, and the Spanish children can be placed temporarily in a position of some superiority through helping others. In addition, of course, in order for the Puerto Rican youngster to teach Spanish to the American child, the Puerto Rican child must be able to communicate to some extent in English, and in the very process of teaching the foreign language, he must acquire more English in order to communicate (unless *he* arbitrarily insists that only Spanish be spoken when he is instructing!).

Thus the dialect game, which can be utilized by anyone as a gimmick or an auxiliary technique in teaching, takes on considerable depth when seen in the context of two cultures, two languages functioning alongside each other, both being respected, both affecting each other with no condescension toward the minority culture.

THE HELPER PRINCIPLE:
LEARNING THROUGH TEACHING

Another fascinating approach to the expansion of classroom learning is to be found in Lippitt's intriguing "peer learning" experiments, which demonstrate that youngsters in the sixth grade can be helpful in teaching younger children—and can benefit themselves from playing the teacher role.

At the 1965 White House Conference on Education, Professor Jerrold Zaccharias proposed that we have students teach as a major avenue for improving their own learning. Montessorians have long utilized children to help other children learn in the classroom.

Mobilization For Youth has used homework helpers with a fair amount of success, in that the recipients of the help showed some measurable academic improvement. It may be that even more significant changes are taking place in the high school youngsters who are being used as tutors. Not only is it possible that their school performance is improving, but as a result of their new role these youngsters may begin to perceive the possibility of embarking on a teaching career.

A connected issue worthy of mention is that in the new situations in the schools, where (hopefully) integration will be taking place, youngsters coming from segregated backgrounds will need help in catching up, in terms of reading skills and the like. It is generally argued that the white middle-class children who do not need this extra assistance will suffer. Their parents want these youngsters to be in a class with advanced pupils and not to be "held back" by youngsters who are behind.

However, in terms of the helper principle, it may very well be that the more advanced youngsters can benefit in new ways from playing a teaching role. Not all fast, bright youngsters like to be in a class with similar children. We have been led to believe that if one is fast and bright he will want to be with others who are fast and bright and this will act as a stimulus to his growth. It does for some people, but for others it most certainly does not. Some people find they do better in a group in which there is a great range of ability, in which they can stand out more, and finally—and this is the point of the helper principle—in situations in which they can help other youngsters in the classroom. In other words, some children develop intellectually not by being challenged by someone ahead of them, but by helping somebody behind them, by being put into the tutor-helper role.

As any teacher can report, there is nothing like learning through teaching. By having to explain something to someone else, one's attention is focused more sharply.

The helper principle may be especially valuable for disadvantaged youngsters because in their informal out-of-school learning, they tend to learn much more from each other, from their brothers and sisters, than from their parents reading them a book or answering their questions. They are essentially peer learners by style and experience.

CAPTURING THE ACTION STYLE
THROUGH ROLE PLAYING

Role playing can be used, as Professor Senesch observes, to teach arithmetic and economics (by "playing" store); to teach history by acting out, for example, George Washington signing the Constitution; even language can be taught by acting out words (in fact, the game "In the Manner of the Adverb" consists of "doing" the adverb—e.g. walking *quickly,* writing *quickly,* etc.).

Role playing has long been popular with disadvantaged youngsters. This appears to be so because the technique is very congenial with the low-income person's style: physical (action-oriented, doing rather than only talking); down-to-earth, concrete, problem-directed; externally oriented rather than introspective; group-centered; game-like rather than test-oriented; easy, informal in tempo. In essence, disadvantaged youngsters tend to work out mental problems best when they can do things physically (whether it be through role playing, dance, taking a trip, etc.).

A Route to Verbalization. In role playing sessions it has been observed that the verbal performance of deprived children is markedly improved in the discussion period following the session. When talking about some action they have seen, deprived children are apparently able to verbalize much more fully. Typically, they do not verbalize well in response to words alone. They express themselves more readily when reacting to things they can see and do. Words as stimuli are not sufficient for them as a rule. Ask a youngster who comes from a disadvantaged background what he doesn't like about school or the teacher and you will get an abbreviated, inarticulate reply. But have a group of these youngsters act out a school scene in which someone plays the teacher and you will discover a stream of verbal consciousness that is almost impossible to shut off.[5]

We cannot detail here all the various techniques and approaches that might be utilized in our moon-directed program

---

[5] Role playing has been utilized to some extent in the schools, but there has been little awareness of its special potential for connecting with the style of the disadvantaged and as a crucial avenue for developing their verbalization. Its use may serve a very different function for middle-class children; it may force them to be more concrete and reduce some of their over-intellectualization tendencies. Teachers should be aware of these different potential uses of role playing.

of education for the poor. *Scope* magazine presents a great variety of games and approaches suited to the "action" style of these youngsters.

Any of the following might be important "extras" to be added, depending upon the *style, interests,* and *abilities* of the teachers involved in the program:

1. The "organics" approach of Sylvia Ashton Warner (*The Teacher*). This should be especially valuable in utilizing the interests and strengths of the youngsters, and guard against their being "acted upon" (the current trend in many of the "compensatory" programs designed for the disadvantaged, who are supposedly "deficit ridden").
2. A "modified" curriculum, developed by Gail Donovan in Boston, which stimulated vastly increased interest in literature among poor youngsters.
3. Use of the dance as a method for developing concepts and language as developed by Claire Schmais in Washington, D.C.
4. Jensen's techniques for developing "verbal mediators" (silent speech, so to speak) in problem solving.

BLUEPRINT FOR A REVOLUTION

Piecemeal approaches to the improvement of the education of the poor have provided many exciting experiments and some definite gains in learning. The time is now ripe for an all-out attack, integrating our best knowledge in an effort to produce truly large, enduring improvements in the learning of disadvantaged youngsters *at all ages.* This requires leadership, new techniques and new manpower.

In order to fly to the moon in educating the poor the following are proposed:

1. Nonprofessional teacher aides—recruited from among the poor themselves—to assist teachers so that they can more fully play their professional roles as teachers. This auxiliary manpower can also provide excellent male role models for educationally deprived youngsters.
2. Young teachers who would be trained in the use of teaching techniques (e.g. the dialect game, the helper principle, role playing, etc.), attuned to the styles and *strengths* of disadvantaged children. The positives must come first and around these positives we can begin to correct the limitations of the child in

relation to reading, school know-how, language skills, etc. If the teacher expects more, he will get more if his positive expectations are built on an understanding of why he is using the exciting new technologies.

3. In-service Teacher Institutes using trained Master Teachers to introduce knowledge and techniques related to immediate classroom problems. An attempt should be made to have teachers use techniques that fit not only the style of the children, but their own style and interests as well (style match).

   Full participation of the trainees should be intensively solicited with regard to encouraging them to formulate their needs, how they see their problems, and their suggestions for meeting these problems. Hence, small teacher meetings should be organized to discuss (and role-play practice) ways of meeting classroom difficulties. In this context, the trainers would offer for discussion, techniques that have evolved elsewhere. A group or team approach would be a central feature in the training with a strong emphasis on building esprit de corps.

4. New urban readers and other appropriate curriculum materials, especially the new teaching machines (programed learning). Readers that have been developed in Detroit by Follett Publishing Company and in New York by Bank Street College, and published by Macmillan should be included in the program. These readers incorporate disadvantaged people and themes in a more representative view of urban life and the research in Detroit indicates that *all youngsters read better with these readers*, not only disadvantaged children—that they laugh more and feel that the stories are more interesting and lively.

   The new literacy techniques, Words in Color published by the Encyclopedia Britannica and Woolman's Progressive Accelerated Technique are achieving dramatic rapid results with nonliterate adults and we would suggest that they become integrated in the proposed program.

5. New administrative arrangements such as team teaching, multiple periods, non-graded classes, educational parks, intensive extra school programs (during summers, weekends, and after school hours). These extra school programs can introduce specialists into the school, such as artists, dancers, and musicians to develop the artistic talents of the youngsters. Tutors could be brought in here also and special uses of programed learning and educational TV could be planned.

6. Special parent-teacher groups, led by nonprofessional parent-education coordinators, directed toward developing full, genuine *two-way communication* between the parents and the schools. Parents could be involved as important supportive elements in the program. They should be used to back up the role

of a school that really wants to teach the child and they should be listened to attentively by the school and by the nonprofessional parent-education coordinators who mediate between them and the school. They should not be asked, however, to read to the children or to do homework with them or any tasks which they find essentially uncongenial. They can function to check up on the homework as Sheppard has had them do in St. Louis and to work in a unified way with the school, encouraging the child to learn, to attend punctually, to do his homework, etc.

7. Finally, what is needed for our moonshot is an astronaut—an exciting, committed educational leader. Fortunately there are a number of such qualified individuals potentially available: George Brain, who did such a fine job in the Baltimore school system; Daniel Schreiber, whose charismatic leadership first brought Higher Horizons to national attention; Samuel Sheppard, whose experiment in St. Louis has been perhaps the most outstanding in the United States—just to name a few possibilities. This type of leader will "expect more" and he will get more. He must be flexible enough to permit and encourage the needed innovative classroom arrangements.

CONCLUSION

Large-scale improvements in the learning of disadvantaged youngsters have not been achieved in the past because most of the previous programs were unrelated to each other, accented deficits, and failed to focus on the teacher as the key to the revolution in education.

The moonshot we have presented is directed toward meeting the felt needs of teachers. Teachers want smaller classes, new materials and methods to aid them in teaching, a voice in decisions that affect them, a reduction of discipline problems, a greater feeling of importance and respect.

The program is intended to meet these objectives to varying degrees. It attempts to provide nonprofessional assistance for teachers in the classroom; it introduces new methods for teaching the children; it encourages the participation of teachers with regard to the use of the new manpower and the new techniques; it does not impose new methods on the teachers, but rather stimulates them to select and develop methods appropriate to their styles and interests; it leaves entirely to the individual teachers the decision whether they will select nonprofessional aides to be used in their own classes; it endeavors, through the use of added personnel, to meet the discipline problems within the classroom, in the lunch period, and in the corridors; it brings new importance to the teacher by centering on him as the significant agent of change. And it also places somebody below the teacher in the school hierarchy.

The program endeavors to help the student by building on his positives and expanding them. It aims to do this by assisting the teachers to develop and utilize approaches especially suited to the styles and strengths of disadvantaged youngsters, but *applicable to all youngsters*. The program, in essence, endeavors to overcome the difficulties in the student's learning by concentrating on his positives. It hopes to build bridges from his strengths that will enable him to overcome deficits.

The approach is directed toward convincing the disadvantaged student that he can learn and become educated without necessarily becoming a middle-class stereotype—that he can retain his own identity. The keynote is the following quotation from Ralph Ellison:

> "If you can show me how I can cling to that which is real to me, while teaching me a way into a larger society, then I will drop my defenses and my hostility, but I will sing your praises and I will help you to make the desert bear fruit."

Part
Six

GUIDANCE

@@@@@@@@@@@@@@@@@@@@@@@@@@@@@@@@@

INTRODUCTION

@@@@@@@@@@@@@@@@@@@@@@@@@@@@@@@@

Guidance, more and more guidance, is seen by many individuals, especially legislators and lay persons, as the surest and simplest way to resolve the dropout problem. Guidance before dropping out, guidance at the time of dropping out (the exit interview), guidance after dropping out (to get the dropout to return to school)—all are being tried out. And as the number of guidance counselors increases and the ratio of counselors to students decreases, the incidence of dropping out decreases too. The rate of decrease is small but it is in the right direction. Furthermore, it is believed that because at the time of dropping out, the dropout is less capable, less competent, and less organized than the student who remains, the guidance counselor is the one member of the school staff who can help the dropout appreciate and understand his own strengths and weaknesses as he tries to enter the adult world. Also, several studies of dropouts have revealed that a large proportion of school dropouts wish they had had more guidance and also greater opportunity to discuss their decisions with counselors.

Underlying this faith in the efficacy of counseling is a strong belief that a one-to-one encounter between the counselor and student will enable the student to gain a better understanding of himself and his situation. He then will remain in school through graduation. It ignores, or it believes it can overcome, the long history of school failure—failure piled on failure until the burden becomes too great for the student and he flees by dropping out. Yet the attempt to keep youths in school is praiseworthy because even a bad school situation is less damaging to youths than the demoralizing effect of loafing in bed or loitering on streets. School programs which have employed counselors to visit dropouts in their homes to persuade them to renounce their decision and return to school have received both acclaim and severe criticism. They have been criticized because after the dropout has returned to school, quite often the school makes no provision for changing the curriculum or adjusting its program to insure that the dropout-returnee will succeed. Edmund Gordon believes that once the process of social maladjustment, including school failure, has begun, the school's successes are the exception rather than the rule.

Although the authors in this section are not in agreement about the role and function of the counselor in helping the actual or potential dropout, all agree that because he has been a constant failure, the school makes it extremely difficult for the dropout to retain his self-respect. C. Gilbert Wrenn sees the elementary and secondary guidance counselor performing different roles. In the elementary school, the counselor's chief task is to help the teacher better understand his pupils, while in the secondary school, the counselor's major objective is to help the student understand himself.

Because failure begins early for the dropout and becomes clearly evident by the third grade, John H. Niemeyer believes that the greatest contribution the elementary school can make to a solution of the dropout problem is to find better ways of helping children to learn. Obviously this is of importance for all children but it is particularly relevant for those children who must depend mainly on the school for their successes rather than on the socioeconomic status of their families. Not only must the school help the child realize a sense of achievement but it must reenforce this habit by helping the parents to help their children. The counselor's role shifts from one of working with children and teachers, to engaging the parents in an active and ongoing educational program.

In addition to working with the parents, the counselor's role then is one of convincing school authorities to take on additional activities, possibly some belonging to other agencies which have as of now defaulted in their responsibilities.

Unlike Wrenn who believes that the counselor's function is to increase self-perceptions so the dropout may relate better to himself and to others, Gordon is convinced that unless the environment in which the dropout finds himself can be altered, a change in the dropout's attitude toward himself and others is of little consequence. He believes that our goals have been misdirected and are inherently dangerous because they are geared to helping the individual adjust to his environment even when the environment contains many elements destructive to his best interests. Must the counselor leave his desk and the four walls of his office and fight for change in the greater society so that his students will be able to achieve meaningful success? Or should the counselor accept Wrenn's dictum that the counselor's action vis-à-vis society should be indirect and hence the responsibility for initiating change is not his.

Whether the role of the counselor is primarily to minister to the student's resourceful inner self or to intervene and bring about changes in the environment is debatable. But there is no debate that the counselor has an important and significant role to play in reducing the dropout rate.

෯෯෯෯෯ ෯෯෯෯෯෯෯෯෯෯෯෯෯෯෯෯෯෯෯෯෯෯෯ ෯෯

HOME-SCHOOL INTERACTION

In Relation to Learning
in the Elementary School

෯෯෯෯෯෯෯෯෯෯෯෯෯෯෯෯෯෯෯෯෯෯෯෯෯෯෯෯ ෯෯

JOHN H. NIEMEYER

The psychological and social causes of boys' and girls' dropping out of school are many and complex. Solutions to some do not lie with the school. I am concerned here with a factor that the elementary school can do something about: the fact that by the end of elementary school—particularly in those schools contributing most to the ranks of dropouts—many children have known only failure in school: not only because they have failed to master basic academic skills but because the school has not been able to give them the social skills, attitudes of self-respect and social sensitivity, and quickening of mind for continuing learning which are the other necessary cognitive and affective elements of a healthy, productive personality. In this respect, the dropouts are perhaps no greater tragedy than the stay-ins who emotionally and intellectually dropped out years before.

EMPHASIS LAID ON BACKGROUND

The great contribution of the elementary school, therefore, to the solution of the school dropout problem is to find ways of helping children achieve learning—as defined in the cognitive and affective terms suggested above. This of course should be the goal for all schools, but I direct my attention here particularly to those schools which enroll children who must depend upon the school rather than the socioeconomic status of the family to help them open doors of opportunities in society. Everyone agrees on this goal but there is no agreement as to how, or even if, these schools can accomplish it. The first reason why the question of home-school relationships is so important is that too many of our elementary schools, and too many educators in general, believe that it is precisely because of home background that the school cannot help these children achieve a desirable level of learning. This point of view is dramatically presented in Dr. Conant's recent book, but it pervades the attitudes of teachers and administrators who state that the school cannot really teach these children because of the type of verbal skills, knowledge, discipline, and attitudes which they have developed in the home and neighborhood even prior to school entry. Hence, the argument goes, we must change the homes, or at least compensate for the home-neighborhood background, before genuine learning can take place in school.

For many years we at Bank Street have been working cooperatively with public schools in New York City, mostly in so-called deprived neighborhoods. Since 1957 we have devoted a great deal of attention to schools facing problems of integration and resegregation, the "special services" schools in deprived neighborhoods. Some of our involvement in these schools has been through carefully designed research studies; much has been in working cooperatively to try to effect change in the school and at the same time to study the process of change. I mention these facts only because I want to establish that the point of view which we have developed about the problem under discussion has evolved from first-hand experience with the real school world.

Low Expectations on Part of Schools

Although each piece of our work is usually concerned with a particular aspect of the problem, we have had before us one overriding question: Why in these schools is there so little positive learning? And the answer—still a hypothesis, but one from which we are increasingly unable to escape—seems to us to be that the chief cause for the low achievement by children in these schools is the low expectation as to their learning capacity held by the professional staff and a general unwillingness or inability on the part of the school to make the adaptations of curriculum[1] and school organization necessary for the children in these schools to learn. We firmly believe, that regardless of family and neighborhood background, the elementary schools can, if they will, create a program in which the majority of the present nonlearners will learn. To accomplish this is not easy, because no one knows precisely what modifications of curriculum and organization are necessary. But if the educational world will only spend as much effort in trying to find this out as it now spends on blaming "home-background," "low IQ," "non-future orientation," "nonverbal ability," and so forth, the task will be moved toward reasonable accomplishment.

High Expectations on Part of Students and Parents

One fact, with many implications for curriculum, is startlingly clear. These children do know how to learn, and their parents—even many of those who live in degradation—want their children to gain something valuable from the school. For five or six years before entering school, these children have been developing learning patterns of their own. They may not

---

[1] The word "curriculum" is used here to mean all learning experiences organized by the school for children.

know very much about how the school can help them or very much of what the school would wish that they had learned, but they do want to grow up with an effective mastery over the culture in which they live. The parents may be naïve, but they have deep hope that through the school their children will achieve a better life than they, their parents, have had—even though they may not know how to give the support which is the logical concomitant of this attitude. They see no other agency through which this hope can be fulfilled. In terms of the fundamental motivations which can serve as the well-springs of learning, what more can the school ask?

Home-School Cooperation

This leads me to the important connection between home-school relationships and the school's responsibility for fostering learning. I assume that no influence upon the child's early years is as powerful as that of the home. With such an assumption, it is obvious that the school has a responsibility for doing whatever it can *to help the home help the child learn effectively in school.* By and large, the schools we are talking about do not do this, although most of them will point out that they try. The problem, they say, is lack of cooperation. The questions which ought to be pursued are: In what ways do they try? In what new ways should they try? Why don't they get cooperation? The truth is, I fear, that in spite of all the talk about the importance of the home and in spite of existing programs involving parents (PTA, PEA, etc.), we in the schools have actually not developed a sound rationale for the importance of working with parents. We have not decided upon what ought to be done, nor have we set up machinery for accomplishing it.

In the usual middle-class community parents will seek out, or at least not be frightened by, contacts with their children's teachers. Teachers and parents "talk the same language." In many of these elementary schools the teachers and the parents have a sense of warm partnership. In these schools an organization of parents holds meetings to hear educational lectures, raises funds in support of school activities, and organizes groups of mothers to assist the teachers. Occasionally the principal of such a school gives the kind of leadership which induces parents to probe their thinking, and the school's assumptions, about education and child rearing. Even when the activities remain on a superficial level, at least the organization serves as an escape valve for the feelings of parents who believe that they ought to be doing something about their children's education! One must conclude that, for the average middle class group, the organization is its own *raison d'être*.

Parent Aggressiveness

But the schools we are concerned with are not located in this type of neighborhood and are not dealing with parents who have these patterns of social behavior. Our neighborhoods are characterized by poverty, poor and crowded housing, high incidence of threat to health and safety, and often a rapid turnover in population. The parents, even though they may have blind hope in the school, often are suspicious of schools and teachers and frequently are fearful, if not hostile, toward both. Such a set of attitudes would normally be expected in lower social class life, but today it is heightened and given a dynamic by the world-wide rising tide of integration. The result is that many of these schools face not only the apparent resistance or lack of interest which comes from a feeling of fear or suspicion but the fact that many of the parents are becoming actively aggressive toward the school.

In a recent meeting bringing together 30 elementary school principals from neighborhoods of this kind, I found that almost without exception these men and women were concerned with how to meet this new aggressiveness. One man pointed out, "First we couldn't get them to come to school. Then they began to tell us how to run the school. Now they march in and sit down and say, 'If you don't do what we ask, we'll sit here until you do.'" I am not sure how persuasive was my comment to the effect that this behavior, however unreasonable it may seem, can still be viewed as the priceless ingredient which every teacher should seek: namely, a deep motivation for learning. We cannot evade the fact that all these parents are, in one way or another, asking the basic question: Why are our children not learning in school? I usually would not agree with their definition of the content of learning nor with their proposed solutions to the problem. But the fact remains that they are probing embarrassingly close to a central issue which all educators will soon be unable to ignore.

PARENT-TEACHER CONFERENCES

Let us look at the problems involved in holding conferences (widely accepted in middle-class schools) between individual teachers and parents in any of these schools. In the pilot phase of one of Bank Street's projects,[2] a team consisting of a sociologist, a social psychologist, and an educator worked with the kindergarten and first- and second-grade teachers of a school on the difficulties they were facing in trying to carry out the policy of holding individual conferences in grades K-2. The teachers were baffled by the fact that they often failed to get parents to come to the conferences, and that when the parents did come, little true communication occurred. A study of these questions led to some interesting understandings.

The Note

Consider the apparently simple problem of setting up an appointment. A note carried by a child was often lost. If it was mailed, chances are that it was sent to an apartment house without locked mail boxes and in which mail accumulates on a table in a dark hall. Furthermore, the residents ordinarily do not expect mail or may have recently moved and left no forwarding address. But let us say that the note was received by the parent. It made, in the eyes of the middle-class teacher, a perfectly normal request—and it was probably written both in English and Spanish:

> Dear Mrs. _____,
> I should like to talk with you soon about _____'s progress in school. Please come to see me at 2 P.M. on November 8 or write below alternate dates and times.
> Thank you.
> *Signed*

However, the home in which this very nice note was received probably did not contain a calendar. Also, the concept of planning a date in advance was totally foreign. In our records of

---

[2] Teacher-Parent Communication Project, financed by a grant from the Field Foundation, Inc. The preparation of a report is in progress.

interviews with parents who were part of this project occur over and over such expressions as "God willing . . ." or "If I am alive . . ." or "If we are still here . . ." relative to the possibility of doing anything tomorrow, next week, next month.

Parent's Reaction

The mothers' uncertainty about the future had to be coupled with their fears of the school, even when the fear sprang mainly from a sense of dressing and speaking inappropriately. (We have in our records the amazing story by a social worker who got a mother—a prostitute—to come to school to talk about her son who was in trouble. The social worker succeeded by taking the mother to a store and buying her a simple, attractive dress for the occasion. The dress was saved for other school visits. The last note we have tells how the social worker one day found the woman furious because "that blankety blank school wasn't giving the homework it promised.") Another difficulty was that many mothers had irregular employment. Also, nearly all of them knew that they would have to take at least one younger child along if they were to go to school at the time appointed.

School's Atmosphere

Consideration of the problem of getting fearful and insecure parents to come to the school led also to an evaluation of the face which the school presents to them. Too often the visiting parent enters a building in which she first sees a sign, "All visitors report to the main office." She follows arrows to the office, enters, and sees before her a long dull-metal counter behind which busy clerks are working. There is no receptionist. There are no names in evidence. The parent stands and waits until someone finally comes and asks, "What is it you want?" Such a school needs to question very seriously whether or not it is truly making an effort to involve parents. In some of our schools, also, we discovered that many parents come to the building each morning and afternoon to deliver or pick up the younger children. Even in cold weather, however, there is no place inside the building where the parents can wait in comfort. Yet in these very schools the teachers are asking, "But how can we reach the parents?" Are they overlooking some of the simplest answers?

PARENT-TEACHER COMMUNICATION

Individual Parent-Teacher Level

When we turn to the problem of communication between teacher and parent once a conference has occurred, we come to still other baffling problems. When the teacher has to try to communicate to a non-English-speaking mother through a neighborhood child acting as an interpreter, or when she has to carry on a conversation with a mother holding a crying baby, or when she fails to convey ideas because she has never learned how to talk professionally without using educational jargon, she faces serious difficulties. These, however, are apparent and are relatively easily solved by any school or school system which takes the need for home-school communication seriously. There is a more subtle and not so apparent difficulty in trying to achieve communication between a teacher and a mother who come from substantially different worlds. The teacher most likely looks at children developmentally. She does not believe in the constant use of physical punishment. She is likely to think of the present as a stage in preparation for a future. She may even want children to ask many questions and be reasonably free in self-expression. Although this value system may not be professionally internalized so that an observer of the teacher's classroom would recognize it from her behavior, it is likely to be present on a verbal level.

In contrast, the parent is not likely to have a concept of the phases, the psychological tasks, of children's development. Children are children. The parent probably wishes, and states that she wishes, that the teacher would use physical punishment to make the child behave and learn. Also, she would feel threatened if her child asked many questions, and very possibly the entire family structure would resist the kind of freedom of expression and inquiry which the teacher holds as an ideal. Also, the mother wants the child to read and be able to do arithmetic right now. Everything else is unnecessary—certainly such activities as block-building, painting, or even the taking of trips are strange frills in the strange world of teachers and schools. Finally, she probably has no understanding of the vari-

ous stages of schooling as a road to the future. Both these portraits may seem extreme. Yet our interviews with many lower
social class Puerto Rican and Negro parents and with the
teachers of their children would indicate that these portraits
may serve as useful backdrops against which to think of the
individual teacher and parent as they try to communicate in
the interest of helping a child realize his full learning potential
in school. Little wonder that many teachers cease to try.

But if parent education in these schools faces grave difficulties at the individual teacher-parent level, so does it at the
whole-school or parent-group level.

Whole-School or Parent-Group Level

The typical program is organized according to the pattern
which obtains in most middle-class schools. There are the annual Open School Week and a number of special assemblies and
events to which parents are invited, but the majority of the
activities center around an organization which is either a
parent-teacher association or a parents association. These organizations tend to assume functions similar to those of organizations in middle-class schools. Increasingly in the big cities
these organizations have a deliberate policy of bringing pressure to bear upon the school and the school system. Whether
they do this or not, they serve as one of the channels to the
principal for grievances and often alert the principal to parts of
his program needing assistance. The weaknesses in these associations pointed out by most school people are that only a very
small number of parents ever attend the meetings or participate in the activities, and that the leadership tends to become
established in the hands of a clique. When the small group of
middle-class Caucasian families who are often enrolled in a deprived school are in control, the minority groups stay away.
When Negroes hold the offices, whites and Puerto Ricans do
not participate, etc. At best, therefore, such an association is a
weak instrument for communication between the total school
and the parents; it is entirely inadequate for educating parents
so that they know how to support their children's school
achievement.

Dilemmas of Principals

The problem of strengthening this particular instrument is complicated by two dilemmas which have long plagued school leaders even in stable communities. The first of these confronts a principal who, on the one hand, wants to bring parents closer to the life of the school, and on the other hand, fears that he may not be able to maintain the boundary between what is appropriate involvement and what is meddling in the professional work of the school. The second dilemma is that between the principal's desire to encourage greater interest on the part of parents and his feeling of obligation to defend his teachers and the school system against criticism and attack. This time-honored problem is, of course, inherent in a democratic society in which every citizen, by being a voter and even a potential school board member, has a voice in the running of the schools.

The differentiation needed to distinguish between over-all community policy and professional enactment of policy is a highly sophisticated one. In the conference with the 30 school principals referred to above, the question was asked whether or not a principal ought ever to admit to parents that in his judgment the school system is in error. In the discussion it was clear that all but a few members of the group felt that loyalty to the school system was pre-eminent. The truth is, that faced with these two dilemmas, the average principal even in stable communities is strongly tempted to give no more leadership to parent education than is necessary for keeping his parents "feeling good" about their school. When affecting middle-class schools, this fact has little impact upon the dropout problem. When it applies to the schools I am discussing, its results are tragic.

INNOVATIONS IN SPECIAL-SERVICES SCHOOLS

Introduction of the S.A.T.

Many of the special-services schools in New York City have attempted to introduce innovations in their work with their parent associations. The continued ineffectiveness of this machinery for parent education results, in my judgment, from the absence of adequate organization within the individual school and the school system to provide for continual evaluation of all innovations, which would take place within a framework of serious study of the total problem of home-school interaction. For example, the introduction of the S.A.T. (Substitute Auxiliary Teacher), a Spanish-speaking teacher who acts as a liaison between the school and the Spanish-speaking parents, was a bold and important effort on the part of the school system to bring about improvement. However, our observations suggest that full value from this effort will be received only if the evaluation suggested above is built into the school organization. We note, for example, that in some schools the work of the S.A.T. seems to have the effect of setting the Spanish parents off as a specialized group, in contrast, especially, to the group of native-born Negro parents. Also, we see little evidence that the schools are taking advantage of the knowledge of the S.A.T.'s for educating the classroom teachers about the attitudes and lifeways of Spanish-speaking families. Surely the S.A.T. is a rich source of this knowledge. Yet, although they occasionally confer about individual children, teachers and S.A.T.'s seem to operate too often in separate worlds.

Introduction of Orientation Program for New Parents

A second important innovation in some of our special-services schools is the introduction of an orientation program for new parents. The "spring roundup" in many middle-class neighborhoods has been successful for many years, and the orientation periods in the big city schools are a worthwhile adaptation of this practice. However, we find that in general a basic mistake is made: that is, the school has its orientation program early in the fall and ignores the fact that there is a rapid turnover of population in the neighborhood. By Christmas and certainly by midwinter, in many of these schools, half of the families in the school had not been there the previous fall. In such schools there is a continuous need for orientation. Again the problem points to the lack of machinery for continual evaluation.

Meeting of Principal and Staff
with Small Groups of Parents

Another type of innovation we have found in some schools is the plan whereby the principal and some of his staff meet on a regular basis with small groups of parents. In two schools in which we are working the principals meet with executive committees set up by the parent associations. In some of the Higher Horizons schools special staff members meet with groups of mothers who actually constitute study groups. I remember being greatly impressed by such a group in the school of which Daniel Schreiber was principal. In this group on the day I visited, mothers were reporting on pamphlets and books which they had read on a given subject, just as if they were members of the typical study group in a well-to-do suburb.

Our Bank Street experience convinces us that this kind of work needs to be extended, and can be extended if only the schools and school systems will consider that it is important. We have found the most "ignorant" of parents eager to come to school to hear an explanation of how their children are being taught reading, or to learn how to read a book to a child, or to learn how to conduct a meeting in preparation for a visit to the superintendent. We have found that the participation of diffident Negro and Puerto Rican parents has been facilitated by their wearing name tags at meetings. We have found that teachers who could not get individual parents to come for conferences could get a majority of their parents together for a "party," during which they could explain why conferences were to be held. We have found that in one extremely low economic neighborhood nearly 100 percent of the families, including fathers and grandparents, overflow the large auditorium on the occasion of the graduation exercises for the sixth grade. Also, all of the children are in bright new frocks and suits, even though the proportion of parents on relief is high.

We have also found that the interest of parents in participating in all the activities designed for them is a function of the confidence they feel that the personnel of the school are truly concerned with the welfare of the particular community.

Placement of Field Worker in Neighborhood

The final point I wish to make relates to this question of confidence and is suggested to me by Bank Street's experience in another project. In this project, dealing with a cluster of three elementary schools facing various problems of integration and resegregation, we placed a field worker in the neighborhood to explore the attitudes of parents toward the schools. For months he failed to get very much information or to understand the dynamics of the parent community. Then, finally, he became involved in a problem over housing and was of assistance to the social worker in the nearby public housing project. The news of his participation spread like wildfire, and suddenly he was being invited into homes to sit down at kitchen tables and drink coffee. The barriers to communication had disappeared.

With this experience began the growth of our conviction that if the schools under discussion are to develop effective parent education programs, the schools must be concerned with the development of a true community of parents. The question can be raised: Should the school be a social agency? The answer seems to me to be clear: If the school is to do its best job for children, the community must be organized to support a better community life for children. If other agencies take the initiative, splendid. If no other agency will take the initiative, then the school must assume this role.

SCHOOL-COMMUNITY RESPONSIBILITIES

In assuming the role of social agency, by the way, the schools will come to grips with another problem affecting school achievement and the school dropout problem which I want to mention, even though I cannot treat it in full detail. I refer to the problem that neither the school nor the home exercises adequate control over many of the children in these neighborhoods as these children reach the upper grades in school. This is ironical, because the schools, in general, place major emphasis at the kindergarten and the first- and second-grade levels upon the children being obedient, quiet, and conforming. Then, after three years of such training, the children are reported to us by most of the third-grade teachers with whom we work as unmanageable and lacking in any understanding of why they are in school. The school's procedures have not offset the other influences in the children's lives and have been psychologically unsound even in terms of behavior within the school.

When the community of parents is organized in support of children, there are many things that can be done. In two of the schools in which we are working the parents associations have been concerned with the following. They have had two streets set aside as "play streets." They help in the enforcement of observation of the play street signs by reporting to the police the license numbers of any cars which violate the restriction. They have put pressure upon the city government to provide an adequate playground, the place for which exists. They evaluate and work through various channels to receive adequate police protection. A committee of the mothers actually guards the outside doors and the washrooms in one of the schools to be sure that children are not molested by older youths and adults who often hang around the school. They have had many discussions on the problem of control of narcotics in the neighborhood. The involvement of the underworld in this problem constitutes a hidden, but pervasive, terror; and yet the parents feel that by their alerting all the agencies and through their persistent pressure for adequate police protection, they have reduced this threat to their children considerably.

These are only examples of some of the more dramatic things which parents can do, and in certain neighborhoods, are doing. I think also of Dr. Samuel Shepard's account of the way in which, in the Banneker school district in St. Louis, he mobilized all of the proprietors of the corner stores, in which the older children would spend many hours each week, to understand and give their support to the "higher expectations" program of the schools of that district.

IN SUMMARY

The observations and opinions given above open up only some of the multifarious aspects of the ways in which the elementary schools, which now contribute so heavily to the dropout problem, can, and should, use a process of interaction between home and school for raising the level of school achievement. These observations and opinions will, I hope, not only open up the whole topic for discussion but also define the position which I shall take at the beginning of the Washington Conference. I should perhaps restate the position explicitly:

1. The fundamental contribution which elementary schools for the educationally disadvantaged can make to the solution of the dropout problem is to increase the learning of the children in these schools.

2. These schools can do more than they are now doing to raise the level of meaningful school achievement without doing anything whatever to improve the home and neighborhood situation.

3. But, to do the job with full effectiveness, the school must mobilize support of parents for their children's learning in school. (And this, completely apart from the important need for public support at the polls.)

4. To accomplish this mobilization of support, the school must devise new procedures for educating and for gaining the cooperation of parents. It cannot rely upon the pattern of home-school relationships which has been reasonably—but only reasonably—effective in middle-class communities. The fact that schools for the educationally disadvantaged require more, not only the same parent support than middle-class schools, should be obvious.

5. To develop new and effective procedures, the school needs to do two things: (a) recognize the true importance of positive parent education and (b) organize machinery within the institution for accomplishing its task with at least the seriousness with which it now sets up machinery to convey instructions from headquarters to teachers or to run staff retirement parties. Such machinery would put analysis of the problem, proposals for solutions, and evaluation of existing procedures as regular and persistent items on the school's agenda. The machinery would operate in cooperation with the machinery of the total school system but would recognize the fact that almost every neighborhood will have characteristics which are idiosyncratic. The scrutiny of the problem would reach out to every detail in the school, from report cards to the public stance of the total institution. The machinery will also develop out of recognition that—

(a) The principal needs help—

He cannot do the job alone. Whether he should have assistants who carry the brunt of the educational work with parents, or whether he should carry the heaviest load and be relieved of other duties, cannot be decided in the abstract. Certainly he must carry the top responsibility for this program, and all assistants must report directly to him. Regardless of the proportion of his time given to this area of responsibility, he must have time to study the problem both with his own teachers and with other principals in the school system.

(b) The teachers need help—

In understanding and respecting culture patterns, so as to know what modifications can be reasonably expected in these patterns and their implications for school procedures; in being able to reach individual parents; in writing meaningful reports; in improving their skills and interpreting the school and the needs of children to parents.

6. The school system can help by—

(a) Giving as much autonomy as the leadership of each school can and will use.

(b) Providing consultants and special personnel to support the machinery set up in each school.

(c) Establishing in-service study opportunities for teachers and principals.

(d) Developing or causing to be developed new materials and techniques for educating the educationally disadvantaged parents, particularly in the following three areas: child development, the learning process, and "the road of the school."

7. Teacher education institutions can clearly help by providing consultation and other leadership services to school systems and individual schools and by thoroughly overhauling their own curriculums in the light of the needs of the educationally disadvantaged.

8. Foundations and state and federal governments can help by bringing together, or providing the money so that other agencies can bring together, experts from the fields of the behavioral sciences and the communication arts—always in-

cluding persons from the practical world of the school—to develop the new and imaginative teaching materials and procedures needed in such a parent education program.

❧❧❧❧❧❧❧❧❧❧❧❧❧❧❧❧❧❧❧❧❧❧❧❧❧❧❧❧❧❧❧ ❧❧

THE DROPOUT
AND THE SCHOOL COUNSELOR

❧❧❧❧❧❧❧❧❧❧❧❧❧❧❧❧❧❧❧❧❧❧❧❧❧❧❧❧❧❧❧ ❧❧

C. GILBERT WRENN

The sequence of the papers in this volume reveals a particular rationale. The papers examine, successively, the major political, economic, and social conditions that influence the prospective dropout, then the school environment, and then the school process itself. This procedure might be described as a series of concentric circles—the outermost and most encompassing representing the economic and social dimensions of the society of which the dropout is a part. These dimensions and structures are most crucial to the problem under consideration and most difficult to change. The second circle would represent the structure and organization of the school—the total school environment in which the student lives. Changes here would affect objectives, curriculum, regulations, relations to the home—the total school atmosphere. The third circle encompasses the influence of teacher, counselor, and parent upon the dropout, potential or actual. This is, strictly speaking, neither a social nor an educational environment, but a psychological environment, personal in its impact. The counselor is influential in this third circle and may have some impact upon the second.

From a perspective of 30 years of close association with the so-called school guidance movement, I find it somewhat difficult to relate "the counselor" to the needs of the actual or the potential dropout. In a recent report, *The Counselor in a Changing World*,[1] the Commission on Guidance in American Schools and I discuss the continuing usefulness of "guidance," as a term. It was an important missionary term, whose significance has diminished as its functional point of view has increasingly become part of the working philosophy of the total school program. I proposed in this report that "guidance" is a point of view appropriate to all educational workers—teachers and administrators included. Greatly responsible—but not exclusively so, by any means—for translating this point of view into action is a team of pupil personnel specialists consisting of school counselor, school psychologist, school social worker or visiting counselor, and school health specialist. The pupil personnel program of a school consists of the work done by as many members of the team as exist in that school or school system. In this paper I will concentrate on the work of the school counselor as the most broadly concerned member of this group.

What can be done for the school dropout by the school counselor might be broadly categorized into three areas: (a) influencing others to provide a more meaningful environment, both school and nonschool; (b) modifying others' perceptions of the dropout in the direction of better identification and understanding; and (c) modifying the self-perception of the dropout so that he may be able to relate better to others and also to know how to make more adequate use of whatever environmental resources are available to him.

These are, of course, interacting dimensions of activity. One is almost tempted to suggest that modifying any one of these areas would modify the others. School curricular and work experience opportunities, however, might be enlarged, but for reasons inappropriate to the dropout—or with poor communication to those most concerned. As a consequence, there might be little change in how the dropout perceived himself, or in how others saw him, and little use by him of the enlarged opportunities.

---

[1] C. Gilbert Wrenn, *The Counselor in a Changing World* (Washington, D. C.: American Personnel and Guidance Association, 1962), pp. 139-142.

THE COUNSELOR AND A MORE
MEANINGFUL ENVIRONMENT

There is much that a counselor can do in this area, most of it indirect in nature. He can systematically supply information on the total school population, or on important segments of it, to those responsible for curricular provisions and the maintenance of school regulations. There is enough known about the potential dropout to identify him with reasonable assurance for some years before the break. To assist the teacher in identifying the potential dropout, to indicate his probable course of development, to describe the school conditions that apparently contribute to the academic demise of the dropout—these are useful functions. The counselor may have ideas about what needs to be done in the school environment and in the out-of-school environment to make life more livable and productive for the potential dropout.

Much is said in the papers of this volume and elsewhere about essential changes in the school curriculum, about school board policies, about compulsory school attendance, about the values of a "part-time work, part-time study" program. To these the counselor may contribute information regarding present and past pupil characteristics and the needs to be inferred from them; but the responsibility for change is not his. Too often the counselor has been encouraged to "get something done," when, in fact, to do these things would be usurping the responsibilities of others and incurring resentment. More important, to "do something" directly in this area is to distract his attention from areas (b) and (c) where he has more direct responsibilities.

I should hope, of course, that the counselor might express strong convictions on many points. For example, he may well emphasize the importance of the guidance point of view and the counseling job in the junior high school. This unit has two major and superficially opposed functions: that of focusing on the needs of those who may drop out of school at age sixteen, and that of providing an intellectual development bridge between elementary school and high school. He might express himself on the impact of mass testing or of a "tracking system" on the already psychologically bloodied underachiever and potential dropout; on school discipline regulations that do not provide for an adjustment between middle-class and lower-class mores; on the need for a vocational investigation and employment skills course in even the "best" curriculum; on the need for counseling help to be made available to out-of-school youth who are still in the community.

The counselor might even request permission to counsel with out-of-school youth, on school time or off, *provided* he thinks that the relationship established between the dropout and the school is one which would permit the dropout to return to a school setting or to a school counselor. John Gardner in his Carnegie Corporation *Annual Report* suggests that communities should prepare to provide this kind of service for all their youth, whether in school or not, up to age twenty-one. But I think that Gardner failed to appreciate how difficult the school has made it for the dropout to retain his self-respect in returning to school for help. These young people seldom leave school with any feeling that the school would be glad to see them again—or they the school.

Focusing on the "Alienated"

It has been proposed elsewhere that one of the four major tasks of the school counselor is to "study the changing facts about the school population and interpret what is found to school communities and administrators." [2] This is a broad task, cutting across the total school population and pointing up the existence of various groups of students and their needs. More specifically the counselor should be familiar with the various minority groups which contribute disproportionate numbers of potential dropouts. Sometimes broadly called "the alienated," they embody economic, cultural, and racial alienations. They may be the newcomers of a school, they may be members of migrant families. Their sense of isolation is often so crippling as to breed resentment and hostility. At best it reduces the likelihood that they will easily respond to school opportunities.

Several papers of this volume focus special attention on problems of minority group children. Quite significantly, they have identified some of the *positive* values of a nonmiddle-class

---

2 *Ibid.*, pp. 137, 141, in Chapter 6, "The Changing Guidance Program and the Counselor." The other three functions are counseling with students, consulting with staff and parents, and coordinating counseling resources in school and community.

sub-culture. It is important that the counselor understand some of the values and strengths of a culture that is different from his own, that he study the family and community mores of different groups for what he can learn *from* them, not only for what he can do *for* them. As he learns, he can transmit his knowledge to teachers and staff, little by little. He can, together with other pupil personnel specialists, examine the school's program and services to see what could be done that is not now being done for the discouraged and the disenchanted. Most of all he can examine squarely whether he thinks he is focusing adequately on the disadvantaged groups in the face of the pressure on him to spend most of his time with students who plan on college. This sort of pressure is very real, and there is seldom any balancing pressure in the interests of the potential dropout.

Elementary School as a Starting Point

In general, the environment of the elementary school is more favorable for treatment of symptoms of dropout than is that of the high school. The structure is looser, there is more ungraded instruction, more focus on the individual pupil, more time per day with one or two teachers, more informed concern of the teacher with the pupil. The elementary school teacher is generally better equipped professionally to deal with the developmental and adjustment needs of pupils than is the high school teacher. Whereas high school counselors developed in order to help *students* with needs that were not seen or met by high school teachers, school psychologists and counselors in the elementary schools focus on helping *teachers* who saw pupil needs and wanted to do more about them. Elementary school counselors work more with teachers than with pupils.

If high school dropout behavior patterns have their origins in the elementary school, and they do, there is much good will and intelligence there to sense the problem and grapple with it. More manpower is needed in the elementary school,[3] as well as someone to vitalize the attack upon a stubborn and resistant problem. Perhaps the counselor can provide this spark, can be encouraged to consider this a major part of his task.

---

[3] In one very large metropolitan center on the West Coast, I discovered —in the year of our Lord 1963—a ratio of 1 elementary school counselor to each 6,000 pupils!

MODIFYING OTHERS'[4] PERCEPTIONS
OF THE DROPOUT

The first assumption here is that the counselor has in actuality a more realistic understanding of and acceptant attitude toward the potential withdrawal student than do most of the other adults in the life of the student. Such an understanding is not easy to come by. The counselor must "live a little" with the dropout, his family, and his community before he can modify his own academically proper and safely middle-class attitudes. Some of this may come through study; some through active follow-up of the careers of dropouts of preceding years; some, I am sure, must come out of a direct and relaxed contact with the psychological world of the dropout. Unless this is done, understanding will not be coupled with compassion.

To comment in condensed fashion, it is proposed that the counselor explore and then interpret to school personnel and parents what is known regarding certain general "characteristics" of dropouts, e.g.:

1. That the poor academic achievement found in secondary schools is part of a continuing pattern that may go back to the fourth and fifth grades. That if hostility toward school and adults is evidenced in high school, this is not necessarily directed specifically toward the high school teacher. (Because underachievement is often the result of a basic psychological pattern, it is a great waste of time to channel all underachievers routinely to a counselor for brief interviews in the vain hope that the counselor can do something with them. This generally is understood to mean that the counselor can successfully admonish them to become better students—and when this doesn't succeed the student is said to be uncooperative!)

2. That potential dropouts represent a wide range of academic aptitude. It is true that over-all estimates suggest that something in excess of one-third of the dropouts have academic

---

[4] "Others," of course, refer particularly to school personnel and to parents. There is frequently a particular "significant other" adult in the life of a youth who means more to him than teachers and parents. What the counselor may do here, in terms of his relationship to the students, may be particularly delicate but of overwhelming importance to the youth.

aptitudes below the so-called average range. It is *also* true that from one-half to two-thirds are in the normal range and that a respectable percentage have ability levels equal to those of students who enter college. It is true that in urban areas more than the normal percentage of dropouts come from low status sections of the city. But again many come from "good" sections and families.[5]

These are familiar data, and more could be given. They are presented only to indicate that the counselor has tasks to do in breaking down the tendency of adults to type students. The pernicious influence of such stereotyping is at its worst when applied to students who fail to conform to the school's expectations of them. Some stereotypes, serving defensive purposes, directly contradict the facts. Who in Vermont or Massachusetts, ignorant of the facts, would believe that there is a higher dropout rate in these states than in Wisconsin or in Minnesota? [6]

Need for Male Models

I would feel remiss in my task did I not mention two less well accepted conceptions. Boys have much more difficulty than do girls in finding an adult model with whom to identify. The girl sees her mother often in adult roles in the home, work roles in which the boy seldom sees his father. This statement calls for development, but I will make only one comment: A significant task for the counselor is to interpret this need for male models to the men teachers in the school so that they might respond more wisely to any fumbling overtures on the part of a boy.

---

[5] Studies by sociologist Allen Wilson recently revealed that peer influences in the high school—the "climate" of the school—were sufficient to override the tendency for boys from the "right" families to attend college in larger than normal proportions.

[6] "East and West," (editorial) *Saturday Review*, Vol. 45 (July 21, 1962), 37-38. Data taken from the following: National Education Association, Research Division. *Rankings of the States*. Research Report 1962 —R1 (Washington, D. C.: the Association, 1962).

Parents' Indifference

It is well known too that the parents of many potential drop-out students are not much interested in their children or in their children's progress in school. Direct work with such parents seems hopeless, but again generalizations are unwarranted. The parents are interested in *themselves,* often are buried in their own sense of worthlessness and guilt. A counselor might open up communication channels (a) if he informed the parent about positive attributes possessed by the child in such a manner that the parent's own, perhaps small, contribution to the attribute is recognized, and (b) if he became interested in the parent's troubles and listened. The counselor need not grope each time for a solution because the parent may, most of all, simply need someone who at least briefly tries to understand. This provides one positive association with the school and some of this gain may rub off on the child.

MODIFYING THE DROPOUT'S PERCEPTION OF HIMSELF

This is without doubt the counselor's most unique role with the dropout. I did not say the most important, for I do not know how to weigh these three areas of contribution. The counselor is in the best position of all school personnel to see the world from the dropout's point of view, i.e., he is concerned with the over-all life of the student, not his English only or his school life only; he is interested in the student's future as well as his present; he has contact with many kinds of deviant student behaviors so that he is not easily shocked; he, by virtue of certain emphases in his professional education, is moderately capable of understanding the psychological dynamics of the academically or socially deviant student. (Need I comment here that I refer to the *best* counselors in our schools, the upper one-half to one-third?)

Acceptance

This business of the counselor's "understanding and accept-ing" the dropout (or any other student who is not in the groove) may sound wispy and gossamer-like to some, but not to the practicing counselor. He knows that he can do little di-rectly with a hostile and uncooperative student until lines of communication can be established. This means that the student must accept the counselor as an interested and nonthreatening person—and this will not happen until the counselor has proved *his* acceptance of the student as he is—acceptance, hopefully, with some understanding. The dropout is not always a lovable person—he may be aggressive or sullen and with-drawn; he sees little sense in school, and has little respect for himself or most others. He is different; he has had his difference criticized; and he may therefore cherish his difference as the only weapon he has with which to fight back. He is certain that the school is against him—there is some evidence for this in that the dropout is likely to have been "failed" in one or two grades, and in that teachers have been critical of him over the years.

Understanding

The counselor must somehow convince the student that he, the counselor, does not react to the student as he, the student, thinks everyone else has reacted to him. In many ways the counselor must react in the same fashion that he does to a crea-tive or intellectually nonconforming student. For the creative student too is uncomfortable to live with, is often thwarted by adults and peers alike. He has been pushed around intellec-tually as the potential dropout has been pushed around aca-demically and socially. The talented student may be "getting by" academically and adjusting to social requirements, but his creative potential will die on the vine unless someone helps him to appreciate it and fight to retain it. The dropout is not getting by academically and is often rebelling socially. Both have lost faith in themselves and in their right to be different. The tal-ented does have a brain to fall back upon, but all too often the dropout's brain is of only average caliber or less. All he can fall back upon is rebellion.

Concern

The counselor then must help the dropout to restore a little of his confidence in himself before a rational examination can be made of the alternatives open to him. The counselor must respect the potential dropout as a person, even though he may be unlovely and in a state of academic rebellion. He must show an earnest concern in him. He will need to "look up" this person and ask him in, for the potential dropout may never come voluntarily until it is too late. There are many ways for the counselor to communicate that he is interested in the student, but it may take time for the student to believe him.

PERSONAL VERSUS LEGAL INTEREST

A major conflict in school functioning is between the attendance officer's administrative interest in a student's absence from school and the counselor's interest growing out of a desire to be helpful to the student. Often the only interest evident to both student and parent is the official and legal interest. Some cities have changed the attendance officer to field counselor or visiting counselor. Recently I learned that in Vancouver (Washington) Junior High School, counselors are informed of a child's absence early in the school day and call at once to see if they can be helpful. If the child is playing truant it is better that the counselor, who has an interest in the child, learns of it, rather than an officer whose primary interest is apparently in school regulations. If the child is home ill, the counselor offers to tell the teachers, check on assignments, etc. Following this, he turns the name over to the attendance office, thus transferring to someone else the official concern for the absence. The counselor's concern for the student who is frequently absent (a common symptom of the potential dropout) can be then expressed in a manner which suggests that someone really cares whether the student is present or absent.

The counselor, of course, wishes to help the student to plan realistically for vocational entry—hopefully, for vocational preparation prior to entry. A recent report from the Amarillo,

Texas, vocational adjustment classes for the slow learner indicates that a *general* approach to vocational entry can be organized. Vocational help can be limited and practical as well as focusing upon counseling toward a considered choice.

THE CONCEPT OF WORK

There is a fundamental consideration of the nature of work, however, that must be weighed by the counselor of the slow learner or potential dropout. In a chapter entitled "The Place of Work in American Life," just recently completed for the anniversary volume of the National Vocational Guidance Association,[7] I wrote that "Harvey Swados in the *Saturday Review*[8] and Paul Goodman in *Commentary*[9] speak almost angrily of the meaningless and degrading nature of work done by millions of Americans." The average middle-class-oriented American, and this includes most counselors, still believes that work is virtuous and an occupation a channel to self-realization and a sense of personal significance. These aphorisms are time-bound; they are no longer true for a large portion of the American population. Work for them no longer provides a sense of achievement, and an occupation (a job or succession of jobs) may not contribute greatly to one's self-realization.

No one feels these limitations more keenly than the potential dropout. For some, this results from seeing what work and occupation mean and do not mean to their family. For others, it is an adoption of a superficial but general mode of thinking in America regarding the importance of "getting by" with as little work as possible and selecting an occupation for personal gain and status. For many, it is a *reality* as we move from the Organization Age into the Automation Age. I will not suggest here what might be developed as an answer to this disenthronement of former values. All that is needed here is to point up that the counselor must not assume that the value structure of the student is the same as his own. Conventional vocational guidance will not work well here. The counseling done must be based

---

[7] Henry Borow, ed., *Man in a World at Work* (Boston: Houghton Mifflin Co., 1963).

[8] Harvey Swados, "Work as a Public Issue," *Saturday Review*, Vol. 42 (December 12, 1959), 13-15; 45.

[9] Paul Goodman, "Youth in the Organized Society," *Commentary*, Vol. 29 (February 1960), 95-107.

upon work and occupational concepts which *start* from the potential dropout's frame of reference about work.

PERSONAL COUNSELING

It occurs to me that some reader might see the title of this paper and say, "Now there's something—let's have the counselor work on him!" And, of course, that is just the trouble. Everyone has worked on him. If the counselor isn't different from the other adults in this student's life, the results will be just what the results have been when other adults worked on him! He has been worked on until he is thoroughly calloused in all of the vulnerable spots.

Dean L. Hummel has reported informally upon a study of high school students in Ohio. Only 10 percent of them said that they had had an opportunity to talk with *anyone* about concerns which were personal and deeply meaningful. Educational planning, school failure rates, vocational choices—but not about troubling personal problems and anxieties. Most of them reported that they would like to talk about the latter with someone. There were counselors in most of the schools surveyed, but counseling in a meaningful way on things that really matter takes time—relaxed time—time that it is *expected* that the counselor should spend in this way. Counselors can be too efficient, too busy, too ready with answers, too quick to labor the obvious. This is not what the troubled and uncertain student is seeking.

Above all else, a plea must be made for the counselor's having a nonevaluative relationship with the student. The teacher must evaluate, particularly in high school and college. He tries to counsel, and he may counsel well, but the student is often confused by the seemingly opposed roles of counselor and manager-evaluator. This confusion must not cloud the student's image of the counselor. The counselor may inform, he may help analyze—but he is also sensitive to the unspoken and he does not judge on goodness or badness.

Let me illustrate—I will use the second person to identify the counselor. Joe comes in for an appointment and it is apparent that he wants to talk about the courses he is to take next semester. He raises a question, a good one. You give him plenty of time—you listen well. Then you come back with a thoughtful answer and ask for Joe's reaction. The discussion flows along fairly easily. The appointment time is about up and Joe moves toward the door. You wait. You refrain from busying yourself about your desk, you just wait. Because the chances are good that Joe may turn around and say "Oh, yes—I kinda wanted to talk to you about. . . ." He's been testing you out, seeing whether you can listen without telling him everything, without advising him, seeing if you have time for him. Perhaps there's some self-testing here too, for Joe had to stall for time to get up the courage to bring out his real concerns. So the counselor must be sensitive and relaxed. He must be sensitive also to the hostility that may be in the student who is *sent* to the counselor's office. This student's anger toward self or parents may have been displaced on the teacher—now it can focus on the counselor. He can take it better than the teacher— he does not have a group situation to protect. So the counselor expects and is prepared for this sullenness, anger, bitterness; and he waits again while the student tests him out.

The counselor must be competent, or we might as well save his time and the taxpayer's money. He must first know the unique world of the young in general, of the young who accept change and the pace of life more readily than we do. Then he must understand a little of how the world must appear to a slow learner, a boy or girl who has lacked academic approval for years, and often parental approval as well. This is a boy or girl who *knows* that he doesn't have the same learning tools that other students have—and, often, a boy or girl who hasn't much faith in himself. To restore a little of the dignity of life is the task here, perhaps helping him to see that life is not lost because he is failing academically. Life is more inclusive than either school or a job, although we often lead students to believe that we think otherwise.

NEED FOR CHANGE

Along with the monumental changes needed in society and the school—changes in the attitudes of teachers and parents, in adjustment to a work world which has a disappearing fringe of jobs for the typical dropout—can the counselor help the student believe a little more in himself as a person? Paul Goodman believes that the youth is trapped in our organized society —that he needs more room "to bang around in," space that is not always somebody's property. Friedenberg feels that, unless the school in general and teachers in particular accept the lower-class order of life as a reality and see normal children normally coming out of it, there isn't much chance for the dropout. And he doesn't believe there is much chance. Nor apparently does Goodman. Both of these men write beautifully, but hope is not in them. On the other hand, we cannot afford the luxury of pessimism. To believe that something can be done, even though with only fractional success, is the way we move ahead.

Society must be changed, schools must be changed. But while this is being done over a period of years, the counselor must focus on helping the potential dropout to accept unpleasant reality and to live within it, as well as on helping to change the school and the attitudes of parents and teachers. This is a one-by-one job—a batting average of .200 is worthy—but some boys and girls will profit from it. That is why a counselor's work is so unglamorous—and is so vital for the person who is affected by it.

SOCIAL STATUS DIFFERENCES

Counseling and Guidance for Disadvantaged Youth

EDMUND W. GORDON

INTRODUCTION

A problem of increasing proportion in education and social planning is that of providing educational opportunities appropriate to the characteristics and needs of large numbers of children who live in communities where income level and social status are low; where general intellectual stimulation is inappropriate to a high level of academic achievement; and where patterns of social organization, cultural characteristics, and cultural values differ markedly from those which are dominant in middle-class society.

Several studies of children attending school in many of our disadvantaged communities have pointed to atypicalities in development, in attitudes toward academics, and in school achievement. Children living under varying conditions of deprivation and social-cultural atypicality are also reported to show disproportionately high rates of social maladjustment, behavioral disturbance, physical disability, and mental subnormality. The fact of academic deficiency among a high percentage of this population is also well documented. The specific nature of these deficiencies is not so clearly documented; but in the few attempts at specifying the characteristics of these learners, several conditions are generally accepted. Among these are:

1. Contradictory attitudes toward self and others with low self-concept and the resultant exaggerated positive and negative attitudes toward others prevalent

2. Utilitarian and materialistic attitudes, not unlike those which dominate in our society, but which in the light of limited horizons and opportunities function as depressants on motivation, aspiration, and achievement

3. Low-level aspiration and motivation concerning academics and academic products, as well as in relation to some social norms

4. Low-level academic task orientation and variable levels of general test involvement

5. Styles and modes of perceptual habituation which do not complement the emphases which are important to traditional academic efficiency

6. Weaknesses in the utilization of abstract symbols and complex language forms to interpret and communicate

7. Weaknesses in the utilization of abstract cognitive processes with marked tendency to favor concrete, stimulus-bound cognitive processes

8. Marked social-cultural patterns in their conditions of life which tend to be noncomplementary to traditional standards of academic achievement and social stability; these include hy-

permobility, family instability, distorted model relationships, economic insufficiency, housing inadequacy, repeated subjection to discriminatory treatment, as well as forced separation from many of the main channels of our society.

Even fewer attempts have been made at identifying the *positive* characteristics of socially disadvantaged children. However, among these may be listed the following:

1. Selective motivation, creativity, and proficiency
2. Complex symbolization in in-group language forms and ritual behavior
3. Functional computational skills
4. Accuracy of perception and generalization around some social, psychological, and physical phenomena
5. Selective recall, association, and generalization
6. Capacity for meaningful and loyal personal relationships
7. Capacity for meaningful and sustained selective task involvement
8. Ingeniousness and resourcefulness in the pursuit of self-selected goals and in coping with the difficult conditions of life peculiar to states of economic insufficiency and poverty, low social class status, and low racial-caste status.

WHAT KIND OF GUIDANCE FOR THE DISADVANTAGED?

The high incidence of norm variance with respect to school adjustment and persistence of school attendance in some of our minority groups is well established. Recognizing, as all of us do, that there are many minority group children who require no more or less in counseling than do majority group children, I shall attempt in this paper to wrestle with some of the special problems that may require attention in the counseling of youth who are *handicapped* by social status differences.

My topic suggests that there are some special considerations, some unique problems, and some specific approaches to counseling which must be taken into account when we apply this process of guided behavioral development and guided behavioral change to youth so handicapped. I will deal with some of these in this paper. However, I seriously doubt that there are any such factors which are fundamental to counseling or guided behavioral development and change. Still, our focus on a handicapped group and some of the special problems and considerations involved may lead us to the identification or support of concepts and theoretical positions that are fundamental to counseling. In medicine, when concerted attention has been given to the epidemicity and control of pathological syndromes, we have often gained insight into and understanding of some of the basic postulates in medicine. It also may be that as we look more closely at the guided development of children who are handicapped by differences in social status, we may gain a better understanding of some of the postulates basic to the process of guided behavioral development and change in general, and counseling in particular.

I have the feeling that readers of this paper will be looking for something very practical regarding counseling minority group children. However, if I am asked how to counsel minority group children, I must say that I don't know, since I am not at all certain that we know how best to counsel or that counseling is our most effective tool of guided behavioral development and change. I am not at all sure that what we do in the counseling relationship is meaningfully significant in the life of a child whose conditions of life deny at crucial points the validity of democracy's promises and humanity's hopes. I am sure that we can make him feel better. If we are lucky, he may see in us a spark of humanity with which he may identify and which he may use as a model. Or we may be able to help him gain insight into the ways his own behavior helps to defeat his purposes. But those of us who have worked with these children know that once the process of social maladaptation has begun, our successes are the exception rather than the rule. These successes occur, it seems to me, when changes in the conditions of the pupil's life are experienced by accident or through significant positive intervention.

If I am asked in what direction we should move to achieve behavioral change and growth in minority group children, in socially disadvantaged children, and probably in all children, I can only suggest that the experiencing of self in interaction with objective and subjective reality is the only way in which consciousness and behavior develop and the only way in which they change. In my frame of reference, it is not so much in the isolated and insulated counseling relationship but in the main stream of life experience that these interactions are maximally operative. Consequently, the focus in our efforts at behavioral growth and change should be on the guided interaction of self with environment. Counselors, therefore, should focus more on the design and provision of environmental encounters calculated to best complement individual human potential and need.

In recent years, counseling and guidance have emphasized concepts from psychotherapy, frequently analytically oriented, generally passive and permissive, sometimes manipulative and directive. This emphasis on concepts from psychotherapy and the role of the therapist has been reflected in counselor training programs, is prominent in counseling theory, and tends to dominate in professional aspiration and professional practice. Unfortunately, this emphasis has led away from concern with broad problems of public mental health and away from a focus on the realities of the current life situation. We have tended to level our sights on the psychic factors, conscious or unconscious, within the individual. Our goals have been geared to the adjustment of the individual to his environment even when that environment contains many elements which are destructive to the best interest of the counselee himself. We have not given adequate consideration to the concrete realities in the lives of many of our children which retard their development. In seeking to meet the mental health needs of underprivileged minority group children, an approach which does not take into consideration their special conditions of life and which does not concern itself with modifying these is unrealistic and limited in its effectiveness. The great importance in psychotherapeutic work of changes external to the individual has been discussed by such workers in the field as Allen,[1] Alexander and French,[2] Janet,[3] Kardiner and Ovesey,[4] Plant,[5] and Wortis.[6] Our concern with a more meaningful approach to counseling and guidance for underprivileged minority group children might well begin with a review and recast of our present concept of psychotherapy.

GUIDANCE IS A PROCESS, NOT AN ART

Therapy has been defined as the treatment of disease by various methods. The term has its origin in two words from the Greek: *therapeutikos,* meaning attendant or servant, and *therapeutia,* meaning healing or medical treatment. The word has long carried the connotation "curative" and has been concerned with remedies for disease. Psychotherapy has been defined as treatment of disease by suggestion, treatment of mental disorders, and the mental treatment of illness, especially nervous diseases and maladjustments. *Psycho* in the word *psychotherapy* has its origin in the Greek word *psyche* which is translated "soul" or "mind." Psychotherapy carries the connotation of a "mental curative" and is concerned with remedies for mental diseases or maladjustments. The emphasis in the definitions of these words has reflected their usage as pertaining to the healing arts.

The concept of therapy and psychotherapy to be presented here is somewhat different from the concepts presented above. The position held is that therapy has to do with the process of healing rather than the art of healing. Healing is not an act or accomplishment of the therapist. Healing is an act or accomplishment of the infirmed or maladjusted organism or personality as it attempts to recover and grow into wholesomeness. This connotation can also be traced to the Greek. The word *therapeutikos* from the Greek is translated "attendant or servant." The therapeutist or therapist, then, is the servant or attendant of the infirmed or maladjusted—serving his needs, helping him, creating the conditions and circumstances whereby the healing or curative process, the process of recovery, or the process of growth can be accomplished by the person attended or served. The therapist has no bag of tricks out of which he pulls a cure for a specific illness. Indeed, it is his job to study the counselee, the environment, the circumstances, the history, the etiology, and the symptoms, and then to help create the conditions—the psychological climate—whereby the process of healing or adjustment can take place.

Some of us, who have regarded medical science as a healing art and the physician as a near miracle man, along with those of us who may have regarded the psychiatrist as a supermiracle man, may find this viewpoint hard to accept. In the past few years, many rather dramatic results have been reported in the medical literature following the use of the so-called "miracle drugs." At a glance, it would seem that the medicine man of old with his magic was again on the scene, only with far greater skills and far less fanciful equipment. But a close analysis of what happens when ACTH, streptomycin, aureomycin, penicillin, cortisone, and the other drugs are used suggests that these drugs serve only to create conditions under which the body can heal itself or return to normalcy. It is true of the sedatives, the tranquilizers, the anesthetics, the vitamin and hormone supplements, and it is true of the stimulants. When the surgeon is observed with less rose-colored glasses, he is seen removing or altering tissue or organs that interfere with the normal growth or functioning of the body. After the tissue is removed, the body then sets about to heal itself, to make a more wholesome adjustment, to return to normalcy. The medical therapist is an enabler rather than a healer.

Psychotherapy then pertains to the healing process rather than the healing art. It seems hardly necessary to repeat that the psychotherapist, like other therapists, is an enabler rather than a healer, an attendant rather than a magician, the provider of the catalytic agent. Just as the medical therapist helps to create a structural or physiological condition which is conducive to growth, recovery, and healing, the psychotherapist helps to create such a psychological condition or climate.

GUIDANCE AS A MODIFICATION OF ENVIRONMENT

If we grant, then, that psychotherapy is a process whereby the psychological environment is so structured as to permit and encourage growth toward wholesomeness and normalcy on the part of the counselee, the question which now presents itself is one of methodology. This psychological climate or environment is not simply permissive. Its essential characteristic is not that it allows positive change. Its integral factor is its nourishing quality, its stimulation of growth. Healing, growth, and development are not solely dependent upon the capacity of the organism or personality to change; neither are they just dependent upon prevailing conditions conducive to growth. The quality of development depends, in large measure, on the nature of the stimulation provided and the resultant interaction. How, then, is such stimulation insured? What is the role of the counseling and guidance service in the creation and maintenance of such a climate?

Within certain broad limits set by the laws of universe, man has within himself the capacity to develop the kind of environment, the kind of society he chooses. The history of the development of mankind is but a record of the efforts of individuals and groups to do just that. It remains, then, for men, institutions, and governments working cooperatively to create the kinds of environments and the kinds of stimulation that make for wholesome growth and adequate development. The counseling situation, the guidance program, the school alone cannot meet this need. Joseph K. Hart has said:

> The democratic problem in education is not primarily a problem of training children; it is a problem of making a community in which children cannot help growing up to be democratic, intelligent, disciplined to freedom, reverent to the goods of life—eager to share in the tasks of the age. A school cannot produce this result; nothing but a community can do so.[7]

Counseling and guidance are among the community's instruments through which total growth needs are met and by which life experiences are designed and molded. Many functions must be served through the counseling and guidance processes. The traditional concern with diagnosis, evaluation, and interview-focused counseling must be continued. Those services designed to provide support, interpretation, remotivation, rehabilitation, and ego strengthening are essential. The involvement of family, school, church, labor union, and other community agencies will require enhancement and integration. The insights of the guidance specialist will need to be interpreted to others who contact and influence the children served. The relative emphasis on intensive, individual interview-type therapy will need to be reduced and shifted to an emphasis on interpreting and restructuring the life experience of the child. Where reality problems are severe, concentrated effort will need to be placed on the relief of such conditions. The staff of the counseling service will need to dislodge itself from the desk and playroom and become actively involved in the actual experiences of the child and with the persons who influence and determine those experiences. The counseling and guidance program must have its influence on the political and economic developments in the community. It must command the respect and cooperation of the religious and social institutions. At all points where the child's development may be influenced, the counseling and guidance service must stand ready to bring its insight to bear.

Witmer[8] has described four points of focus in child guidance. She reports that some agencies place emphasis on attempts at making the environment an easier and pleasanter place for the patient to live. Other agencies place their emphasis on attempts at finding new outlets for the patient's energies and capacities. A third approach places emphasis on remedying the patient's specific disabilities, while the fourth is primarily concerned with dealing directly with the patient's psychic problems. While she concedes that most clinics use a combination of these four approaches, she sees a fundamental difference between those who emphasize the adjustment of the environment to the individual and those who feel that the individual can make his own adjustment if he is helped to overcome his anxieties and fears. Counseling which seeks to meet the mental health needs of underprivileged minority group children should use a combination of the four approaches. It is the responsibility of the counselor to guide the modification and utilization of the environment as well as the utilization and modification of the capacity for change in the individual.

Such a comprehensive approach has many implications for practice. I think in the first place that a far more meaningful approach to counseling and guidance is required than that provided by the concepts which have guided us in the past. It may be that we need to look at some of our concepts with a view to reformulation, at others with a view to re-emphasis, and probably at still others with a view to discarding them and replacing them with more valid and appropriate theories.

Greater Emphasis on Qualitative Appraisal Needed

I have suggested that our concern with the problems of underprivileged children, socially disadvantaged children, children who are culturally different, leads us to some ideas that may have real meaning not only for the disadvantaged child but for all children. Among these ideas may be the need or requirement that we pay more than tangential respect to the systematic and continuous qualitative appraisal of children for whom we provide guidance services. Certainly most of our guidance practices have been concerned with the utilization of many approaches to the observation and classification of behavior from which we make estimates with respect to intellectual potential, academic achievement, and social adjustment. Evaluation and appraisal are not foreign concepts to us. However, I submit that we have been far less concerned with the qualitative aspects of appraisal and evaluation than the needs and characteristics of the population with whom we are dealing require.

I like to think of pupil appraisal and evaluation as "typographical" and "topological" studies of children. I use these terms to refer to the detailed qualitative analysis of the specific character of the learner and of the specific nature of the learner's experience. This kind of analysis is produced by qualitative as opposed to quantitative appraisal, descriptive as opposed to impressionistic reports, and leads not simply to diagnosis and classification but to prescription and treatment. Just as we study geographic areas to determine the nature of the terrain, the kind of soil, the depth of ground water, the kinds of rock formation, etc., when we look at each child in a qualitative appraisal we need to study all factors that enable us to understand the specific character of the individual. In the topological study we are concerned with the way in which the child has developed, what the important events and circumstances have been, and what the conditions and the total life experiences of this child are that have created the current condition. So as a first concept I would suggest (and this is possibly not new in guidance but probably reformulated and re-emphasized) the need to pay much more attention to appraisal, not just quantitative appraisal, not just diagnosis and classification but qualitative appraisal.

Designing More Optimal Learning Experiences

A second idea has to do with the use of these qualitative appraisal data as a basis for a detailed prescription of positive and meaningful learning experiences. Following the position set forth by Hunt,[9] it is very likely that the way in which the individual moves ahead intellectually, that is, the way in which he learns, is greatly influenced by the nature of the individual and by the nature of the encounter—the experience—to which he is exposed. Putting it another way, it simply means that the content, the sequence, and the pattern of the learning experience must be so organized, so designed that these facilitate and to some extent determine what is developed. This concern with the design of learning experiences may appear to be contrary to the traditional concerns of counseling. I would like to think of guidance as the field that is concerned with educational architecture, the design of learning experiences in the light of the kind of insights, the kind of knowledge, the kind of understanding that has been arrived at from our qualitative appraisal. As we move into a period when the knowledge required for effective and adequate preparation of teachers is increasing, at a time when the requirements of certification of teachers are being moved in the direction of greater concentration upon academic content, it may very well be that the functions of the guidance *person* will have to focus on the individualized design of learning experience and the facilitation of this design as an adjunct and parallel service to the teacher's primary concern—the content of the learning experience.

De-emphasis of Counseling

A third general concept is one which I think is most crucial in our concern with counseling and guidance for this population. The needs of the socially disadvantaged children require that we remove the interview and counseling from their central and dominating position in guidance. If we look at state certification requirements, our textbooks in guidance, or at much of our current practice, we see that they all reflect an emphasis on the interview or the counseling relationship as essential, as probably the most important function of the guidance person. One tool which we insist the guidance person have is competence in counseling. Testing we may leave to the psychologist, but under no circumstances may we delegate counseling. Nonetheless, in working with socially disadvantaged children, guidance as a person-to-person process—through which information is provided, through which catharsis may be experienced, through which insight is achieved or support is provided—appears to me to be an insufficient, if at all an appropriate, emphasis. I suspect that under the influence of our exaggerated respect for the many forms of psychotherapy and psychoanalysis, we have come to view the counseling relationship, this person-to-person aspect of guidance, as a tool of far greater significance than it merits. I feel that guidance must be chiefly concerned with the motivation and facilitation of development and learning. I am not at all sure that this objective is best accomplished through the person-to-person interview of the counseling relationship. Using qualitative appraisal and uniquely detailed prescriptions for learning, I think that a more productive approach involves the identification and correction of factors in the physical and social environment which predispose inadequate function. It is far more important in the development, or redevelopment, of children who are greatly handicapped by poverty, by prejudicial attitudes directed toward them, by limited opportunities, and by limited experiences, that we attempt to make significant changes in their conditions of life, modifying and removing the things that are standing in their way, rather than emphasizing a change in the individual's attitude toward these obstructions. Certainly, in a society where nothing can be done about poverty it may be advisable to counsel for accepting it and adjusting to it. However, in our society I consider that the *least* we can do is to tell the person who is poor not to feel badly. A far more productive approach to rehabilitation involves the development of meaningful learning and postschool opportunities for upward mobility as well as involvement of these individuals, their families, their communities, and their schools in the process of changing those physical conditions of life, the social condition of life, those conditions in family relationships and in the teacher-pupil relationship which make for maladjustment and under-productivity, rather than placing emphasis on a change in the attitude of the individual toward the competing forces. This is particularly true in view of the fact that very often the attitudes that we seek to change are attitudes of rejection and rebellion against unwholesome forces. I think that this de-emphasis of counseling could very well lead guidance workers into giving greater attention on the one hand to providing the assistance the school and the school personnel may need and on the other hand to the development of reciprocation, communication, and cooperation between home, community, and school, to the end that maximal opportunities for counselee development are achieved.

Better Use of Data About Pupil Backgrounds

Some attention has been given to the kinds of interpretations schools might provide for parents, with respect to their children's school adjustment, so that parents could be somewhat more helpful to both the school and to their children. However, little attention has been given to communication in the opposite direction; that is, helping the school to use some of the insights, some of the contributions from home and community in facilitating the child's development and learning. A process of reciprocal communication flowing between the home, the community, and the school is greatly needed and must draw much more heavily on that which the home and community can contribute. This requires a more appropriate utilization of the content and material that is referable to the life and environment of the child. Some of us have become concerned with the way in which our textbook materials and other materials reflect this life and environment, and of even greater importance, the way in which the experiences and values of some of these children are not adequately reflected in our teaching materials. The counselor can do much to help teachers become more aware of and more sensitive to the meaning of the life experiences of their pupils. Certainly in those areas where we already have some primary responsibility, as in the preparation and use of guidance materials, we can do a far better job of relating them to the realities of the worlds in which these children live.

Probably at no point have we given adequate attention to the contributions which can be made to pupil growth through identification with the struggles of disadvantaged children and their families. It has been suggested that the current civil rights crisis and the struggle for equal rights, particularly in the Negro community, may provide a level of immense usefulness in reaching minority group children. The teacher or the guidance worker who can creatively use material derived from that source may rapidly increase interest, involvement, and motivation. Those of us who are or can be identified as sympathetic to or involved in the support of this struggle may find new and more meaningful bases for pupil-teacher or counselor-counselee identification. Similarly, some of the messages that have been developed in this struggle have pertinence. The appeal of the Negro nationalist groups is in no small measure due to the concepts of self-respect, race value, race pride, and race expectation that their leaders preach. In many instances this message has found sympathetic reception among some of the most disorganized and hopeless elements in the Negro community. I don't know whether it can be used in other contexts or by non-Negro authority figures, but it deserves attention. The possibility that children can be more greatly motivated by material relating to the problems that are immediate to their experience and concern is certainly not a new concept, but it is one that we cannot ignore.

The Role of Counseling

The last point I will make, again in the context of a reduced emphasis on the counseling relationships and a greater emphasis on other aspects of guidance behavior in influencing the development of the child, is that we should not throw out counseling altogether. I think that it would be somewhat idealistic and probably impractical to anticipate that in the immediate future the many things that stand in the way of the fuller development of all children in our society will suddenly be changed. These children need support, interpretation, and opportunities for ventilation. One of our important counseling functions is to support and strengthen the child's ability to cope with destructive forces as long as they are operative. But this does not mean an acceptance of the implication that things will always remain as they are or should remain that way or that one has no responsibility for changing them. There used to be a chap who wrote in one of the tabloid newspapers in New York City on mental health, and one of the more appropriate suggestions he made had to do with the value of resistance in mental health. He wrote of the extent to which a person is defeated simply by the feeling that there is nothing he can do about adversity. What we are suggesting here is that a part of our function in counseling is to strengthen children, to help them deal more effectively with destructive forces than by simply accepting them, and to help these children understand how they can resist, how they can fight back, how they can more appropriately equip and acquit themselves in the major struggles for survival and advancement.

Another aspect of our function in counseling is to identify and nurture those attitudes, aspirations, and motivations which may be used productively in the maximal achievement of appropriate goals in education and socialization. We can do a great deal about creating consciousness of potential, consciousness of what can be done, and recognition of those levers that can be used to move ahead, those levers that can be used for salvaging unrecognized talents, unrecognized aspirations, and for developing fuller lives. We can do this through family counseling, through individual counseling, and even more so through guided group interaction.

SUMMARY

Much of our efforts that identify interests, aptitudes, and potentials in children stop at the point of classifying that which is presently observable. I am suggesting that we de-emphasize our concern with counseling and adjustment and turn our focus instead to the broader areas of environmental encounters. This will make possible the design of more meaningful learning experiences and the creation of conditions of life and psychological climates more appropriate to man's hopes. We may then move into the areas of the development of skills, the development of intelligence, the development of interest, the development of aspiration, and the development of competence.

The environmental encounters and interactions are the crucial determinants, and it may well be that our preoccupation with the interpersonal relationship we call counseling and interviewing is entirely inappropriate. Both our theory and the needs of our children may force us to adopt new models and new techniques of guided human development and behavioral change. It may be that we depend too heavily on vicarious experience when the situation requires real life experience in healthy situations, under growth-stimulating circumstances, with appropriate resources, supports, and direction. Nonradical modifications could be made through group guidance, guided group interaction, interfamily consultation, or sheltered work study or social functions. More radical moves will take the counselor into social service, into community organization, into politics, into the manifold jobs of developmental facilitation, i.e., facilitating development through the management of environmental encounters at school (curricular and extracurricular), home (family relations), and community (economic growth, jobs, equality of opportunity, and democratic living).

If we recognize that much of what is wrapped up in what we call behavior is the product of that which has occurred in the pupil's past—the interaction between that which is and that which has been—it is possible that the potential for pupil development is greater than what we presently believe. By positive intervention, to manipulate and modify that which is (the present experience), we may come close to the creation and achievement of much that we know to be possible for modern man.

REFERENCES

1. ALLEN, FREDERICK H. *Psychotherapy with Children* (New York: W. W. Norton & Co., 1942).
2. ALEXANDER, FRANZ, and FRENCH, THOMAS M. *Psychoanalytic Therapy* (New York: Ronald Press Co., 1946).
3. JANET, PIERRE. *Psychological Healing*. Vols. I and II (New York: Macmillan Co., 1925).
4. KARDINER, ABRAM, and OVESEY, LIONEL. *The Mark of Oppression: A Psychological Study of the American Negro* (New York: W. W. Norton & Co., 1951).
5. PLANT, JAMES S. *Personality and the Cultural Pattern* (New York: The Commonwealth Fund, 1937).
6. WORTIS, JOSEPH. *Basic Problems in Psychiatry* (New York: Grune & Stratton, 1953).
7. DELLA-DORA, DELMO. "The Culturally Disadvantaged: Educational Implications of Certain Socio-Cultural Phenomena," *Exceptional Children*, Vol. 28 (May 1962), 467-471.
8. WITMER, HELEN, and KOTINSKY, RUTH. *Personality in the Making* (New York: Harper & Brothers, 1952).
9. HUNT, J. McV. *Intelligence and Experience* (New York: Ronald Press Co., 1961).

ABOUT THE EDITOR

DANIEL SCHREIBER has been for twenty-five years, teacher, principal, and superintendent in the Harlem schools, where he initiated the nationally acclaimed Higher Horizons Programs for the deprived child. At present he is an Assistant Superintendent of Schools in the New York City school system, in charge of education of the disadvantaged. He has also directed the National Education Association's Project: School Dropout.

Mr. Schreiber received his B.A. from New York University, his M.A. from City College, and has done advanced graduate work at Teachers College of Columbia University, and at New York University. He holds a law degree from Brooklyn Law School. In addition, he has written numerous books on the problem of education for the disadvantaged, among them *The School Dropout, Guidance and the School Dropout, Holding Power/Large City School Systems,* and *Dropout Studies, Design and Content.* His articles have appeared in many education journals and popular magazines.

He lives in New York City with his wife and three children.